Contemporary Muslim and Christian Responses to Religious Plurality

Contemporary Muslim and Christian Responses to Religious Plurality

Wolfhart Pannenberg in Dialogue with Abdulaziz Sachedina

∼

LEWIS E. WINKLER

◆PICKWICK *Publications* • Eugene, Oregon

CONTEMPORARY MUSLIM AND CHRISTIAN RESPONSES TO RELIGIOUS PLURALITY
Wolfhart Pannenberg in Dialogue with Abdulaziz Sachedina

Copyright © 2011 Lewis E. Winkler. All rights reserved. Except for brief quotations in critical publications or reviews, no part of this book may be reproduced in any manner without prior written permission from the publisher. Write: Permissions, Wipf and Stock Publishers, 199 W. 8th Ave., Suite 3, Eugene, OR 97401.

Pickwick Publications
An Imprint of Wipf and Stock Publishers
199 W. 8th Ave., Suite 3
Eugene, OR 97401

www.wipfandstock.com

ISBN 13: 978-1-60899-742-8

Cataloging-in-Publication data:

Winkler, Lewis E.

    Contemporary Muslim and Christian responses to religious plurality : Wolfhart Pannenberg in dialogue with Abdulaziz Sachedina / Lewis E. Winkler.

    xii + 338 p. ; 23 cm. Includes bibliographical references and indexes.

    ISBN 13: 978-1-60899-742-8

    1. Pannenberg, Wolfhart, 1928–. 2. Sachedina, Abdulaziz. 3. Religious pluralism—Christianity. 4. Religious pluralism—Islam. I. Title.

BR127 W49 2011

Manufactured in the U.S.A.

For Barbara, my life dialogue partner for life

Contents

Foreword by Veli-Matti Kärkkäinen ix

Acknowledgments xi

Introduction 1

1 Contemporary Muslim and Christian Responses to Religious Plurality 14

2 Contemporary Christian-Muslim Relations: A Brief Historical and Thematic Survey 43

3 God, History, the Future, and Religious Contestation: Wolfhart Pannenberg's Theology of Religions 87

4 Islam, Tolerance, and Democracy: Abdulaziz Sachedina's Ethically Inclusive Response to Religious Plurality 125

5 Pannenberg and Sachedina in Critical Conversation: Conflict, Cooperation, and Convergence 175

6 Problems and Possibilities of Religious Plurality Revisited: A Contemporary Vision for the Pluralistic Now and Not-Yet 214

7 Applying Principles of Interfaith Dialogue: Father, Son, and Holy Spirit—A Trinitarian Look at Potential Problems and Possibilities 268

8 Hope against Hope: Potential Progress in the Face of (Seemingly) Intransigent Ideologies 298

Bibliography 315

Index 325

Foreword

This book is innovative and groundbreaking in more than one way, not least in its choice of topic. Even though a number of studies are available on various aspects of Christian-Muslim dialogue and mutual encounters, very little has been written on how each religion, particularly the Muslim religion, approaches the challenge of religious plurality. Much has been written on the various Christian "theologies of religions"; finally, an analysis of Islamic views of how to relate to other religions is available for us. Moreover, this is not just at a general and abstract level but analyzed in the context of a particular significant contemporary Muslim thinker.

What makes this monograph also innovative is the fact that the book puts two leading religious thinkers of contemporary times in mutual dialogue, neither one of whom has himself developed a theology of religions—even though the thinking of each naturally contains the basic ingredients of such an enterprise. In fact, what Dr. Lewis Winkler is doing means nothing less than picking up from where his two dialogue partners left off, that is, to boldly construct contemporary Christian and Muslim visions of the role of religion in human life and society as well as of the way religious plurality should be embraced and appropriated.

The two dialogue partners make an unexpected and courageous combination. Who would have thought that the renowned German Lutheran systematic theologian Wolfhart Pannenberg and the cosmopolitan Muslim ethicist and religious scholar Abdulaziz Sachedina have much to do with each other! Pannenberg is well known among theologians; Sachedina, a revisionist practicing U.S.-based clergyman and university professor, much less so. What makes Sachedina so important to this dialogue is his creative and untiring effort to argue for an authentic democratic pluralism based on Quranic and other Islamic religious and spiritual resources. This is boldly and persuasively argued in *The Islamic Roots of Democratic Pluralism*.

What makes this dialogue so fruitful and rich is that both protagonists are simultaneously revisionists and traditionalists. Pannenberg's broad theological vision honors and engages the best of classical Christian tradition. Similarly Sachedina's effort to produce a contemporary social ethic and religious vision drinks from the deepest Muslim wells of tradition. Neither thinker, however, suffices to only repeat tradition. At every juncture of argumentation they also listen carefully to contemporary voices and are acutely aware of the radically transformed intellectual, philosophical, social, political, cultural, and religious situation of our times.

Religion matters to both thinkers. In their own respective ways, they argue for the essential religious nature of the human being and thus the inalienable right for religion of all men and women in a religiously plural society. Neither one of them is a pluralist in the typical sense of the word. Pannenberg is a committed Christian. Sachedina is a committed Muslim. Yet their philosophical and religious visions reach beyond their own ghettos and attempt a vision of a free society in which men and women could freely and respectfully argue for the truthfulness of their deepest convictions in a way that does not subsume the other under one's own world of explanation. Commitment and openness, particularity and universality go hand in hand in such a bold vision. Religion and politics have everything to do with each other, but neither one can be reduced to the other.

Dr. Winkler's firm grasp of not only his own Christian tradition but of the key ideas of Muslim religion is a wonderful example of the direction of not only Christian theology of religions but also of comparative theology. Many wonder if that is *the* task for Christian theology for the third millennium. Hopefully our Muslim colleagues will similarly labor in their own tradition to pursue a similar task.

Veli-Matti Kärkkäinen
Temple City, California

Acknowledgments

In seeking to acknowledge all who contributed in major and minor ways to the completion of this formidable project, I fear some will be wrongly left unmentioned. To these, I apologize in advance and simply say that God sees what you have done, and you will be duly rewarded in heaven. For the rest who *do* get mentioned, you, perhaps, have your reward in full, but I seriously doubt it. There are too many hidden and unspoken praises that only He can render for a job well done and a life well lived.

    I would like to thank Dr. Dudley Woodberry, a man of great wisdom and humility, who agreed to take on this project at a time in his life when he was already inundated with other worthwhile endeavors. His meticulous care, graciousness, and encouraging input for this project have not been in vain, especially when he had to read one of the final drafts in the hospital while recovering from acute appendicitis!

    Gratitude is also due Dr. David L. Johnston, who helped put the finishing touches on this work and added a wealth of encouragement, insight, and aid—especially concerning contemporary trends in Islam—to make what I had written even better.

    Rich and enduring gratitude goes to my mentor and guide, Dr. Veli-Matti Kärkkäinen, who always believed in me, even when I did not believe in myself. His constant prayers, ideas, and teaching opportunities gave me the structure, wisdom, and spiritual capacity to continue to grow in the grace and knowledge of our Lord Jesus Christ.

    Special kudos and thanks go to Dr. Mark Linder, who encouraged and exhorted me when the path appeared too protracted to traverse. All those trips to the coffee shop for prayer and conversation gave me hope

Acknowledgments

and fortitude when I thought I could not continue. Thanks too, to Dr. Dale Fisher, who always made me feel smarter than I am and spurred me on to finish what I had started with his exhortation, "Go, Lewis, go!" My long-time friend and mentor, Jon Rittenhouse, must also be noted. Thanks, Jon, for helping to set me on my path into a full-time teaching ministry over twenty years ago, and for proleptically calling me "Dr. Winkler" long before that designation was actually bestowed.

The faculty and staff of Singapore's East Asia School of Theology deserve special mention for their fervent prayers, enduring patience, extravagant grace, and unending encouragement through the closing stages of this process. Without two entire quarters of teaching sabbatical and their picking up the slack for me, I would never have finished. Thank you, thank you, thank you!

Mention must be made of supporters, friends, and family who stayed with and prayed with and for me and my family, not only through the joys and victories, but also through the dark nights of the soul. I am forever in your debt. I am especially grateful to my parents, George and Sally Winkler, for their prayers and special patience through the times when I thought I was just too busy to write, call, or Skype. Thanks, Dad, for "backing me up" and serving joyfully and generously in my many moments of need!

Of course, I would also like to thank my precious children, Bethany, Joshua, and Christine, for being so wonderful, patient, and encouraging to me through this perilous and plodding journey. You have sacrificed and suffered much to enable me to produce this book. When I started you were all small children, and now you are young women and a young man. I am so blessed to be your father and am so very proud of each one of you!

Deepest praise, thanks, and admiration must be offered for my godly, beautiful, and wonderful wife, Barbara. Without her prayerful patience, love, wisdom, encouragement, and exceptional editorial work all along the arduous pathway to completion, I (better, *we*) would never have come to this place. I love you, my sweet. You are the wife of my youth and my lily among the thorns.

Most importantly of all, I would like to fall down before my magnificent Creator in deep gratitude for loving me, forgiving me, and making Himself known to me in such a way that I might know that my Redeemer lives.

Introduction

Growing Globalization and the Challenges of Religious Plurality

In many ways, globalization has become one of the distinctive characteristics of the early twenty-first century. "The astonishing technological developments of the twentieth century, especially in transportation and communication, heightened our sense of the world as 'one place,' smaller and more intimately interrelated than before."[1] Talk about our "shrinking planet" has become the focus of numerous recent books and articles.[2] Increasing mobility and instant access to worldwide information have enabled more and more people from a myriad of cultures and worldviews to be confronted with the prospect of learning to live, work, and play alongside one another.[3]

---

1. Netland, *Encountering*, 80.

2. A good place to start looking at some of the aspects of globalization is Held et al., *Global Transformations*. Granted, the term itself is quite contested and controversial, but it does capture the growing awareness that human beings and societies are increasingly interdependent in a variety of ways. For a broader look at some of the religious aspects of globalization, see Vasquez and Marquardt, *Globalizing the Sacred*. While concerned primarily with case studies in the Americas, its principles and themes have good transferability to other cultural and religious contexts.

3. The issue of globalization is complex and multifaceted, encompassing not merely technological aspects of human life, but economic, political, social, cultural, ethical, biological, ecological, educational, religious, and a host of other aspects each deserving a thorough analysis in the light of numerous rapid changes taking place in our world today. The focus here is primarily on the ramifications of this globalization with respect to its religious aspects, particularly aspects of Christian-Muslim dialogue.

These challenges have produced a growing consciousness of the sociological reality of religious plurality. In Wilfred Cantwell Smith's words,

> The religious life of mankind from now on, if it is to be lived at all, will be lived in a context of religious pluralism.
>
> This is true for all of us: not only for 'mankind' in general on an abstract level, but for you and me as individual persons. No longer are people of other persuasions peripheral or distant, the idle curiosities of travelers' tales. The more alert we are, and the more involved in life, the more we are finding that they are our neighbors, our colleagues, our competitors, our fellows. Confucians and Hindus, Buddhists and Muslims, are with us not only in the United Nations, but down the street.[4]

In short, religious plurality can no longer be reasonably ignored in today's increasingly global society.

Current Challenges in Islam

Recent international events, especially those surrounding September 11, 2001, have catapulted Islam and the importance and nature of interfaith relations into the intercontinental spotlight.[5] Significant concerns have arisen over the nature of Islam, not only as a religion of peace, but also as an important resource in the growing worldwide need for societies that are religiously plural, free, and just.

Beyond the theoretical challenges are the practical trials of immigration. The cultural push for Islamic foreigners to assimilate into new and different ways of living often results in a crisis of faith and/or identity. Because the relationship between cultural identity and religious faith in Islam is extremely intimate and complex, there is a significant debate over the relationship culture and religious faith have with one another, as well as how much identity is linked with cultural

---

4. Smith, *Faiths*, 11.

5. In addition to the more recent events surrounding 9/11, including the wars in Iraq and Afghanistan, Noor ("Victory," 320) notes that "[other recent] events such as the Satanic Verses controversy, the Gulf War of 1990–1, the military coup in Algeria after the elections of 1992, and the Bosnian crisis . . ." have also been vitally formative, not only for Muslim identity and attitudes, but also for non-Muslim perceptions of Islam as well.

and religious forms.⁶ In the real world, the connections and distinctions between faith and culture are frequently unclear, and not always overtly recognized, appreciated, or agreed upon in the process of "enculturation."

In contemporary Islam this question is especially acute since many Muslims believe that authentic Islamic faith must be overtly coupled with Islamic law (*Sharī'ah*) enforced within an Islamic state.⁷ *Sharī'ah* tends to be quite detailed and closely related to the cultural forms in which it is codified and enforced. For example, the call for feminine modesty is variously expressed in different Islamic societies and cultures. In Singapore (where I live and teach), devout Malaysian Muslim women cover their heads in public, but can show their faces. In addition, these head-coverings come in a beautiful array of colors that reveal tremendous creativity and variety. In contrast, the pre-9/11 Taliban in Afghanistan required women to wear all-black *burqas* showing only the eyes. The point here is not to question such practices, but only to highlight the fact that the link between the principle of modesty and its particular expressions is too often confused.⁸ Thus, historically conditioned cultural forms of expressing modesty can become absolutized into universal, timeless, and cross-cultural standards of righteousness and godliness. Thus, according to Tariq Ramadan, "it is assumed that Muslims are by definition 'not capable of integration' into secularized societies because their religion prevents them from accepting modern demarcations between the categories [of sacred and secular] we have mentioned."⁹ But *Sharī'ah* is still "the work of human intellect."¹⁰ While the texts do contain certain timeless religious absolutes, "In the wider area of human and social affairs . . . everything is permitted except that

---

6. For a helpful survey on some of these debates, as well as a postmodern view of culture as it relates to religion in general and Christianity in particular, see Tanner, *Theories*. I do not agree with much of what she says, but she does an excellent job of pointing out the numerous challenges of strictly separating religion and culture. Also helpful in this regard from an evangelical perspective is Dyrness, *Earth Is God's*.

7. When pertinent, I will refer to Arabic terms throughout. For a helpful glossary of important Arabic terms see Anderson, *Islam*, 259–70.

8. This is not strictly a Muslim problem, of course. Not far from where I grew up in Chicago, Christian Bill Gotthard was holding seminars suggesting women could only be godly if they wore dresses or skirts below the knee.

9. Ramadan, *Western Muslims*, 34.

10. Ibid.

which is explicitly forbidden by a text. . . . Thus, the scope for the exercise of reason and creativity is huge, . . . and people have complete discretion to experiment, progress, and reform as long as they avoid what is forbidden."[11] The temporal practice of these principles is necessarily relative to the concrete contexts in which they are lived out. But this is often forgotten in the cultural conversations taking place today.

To illustrate, at a joint Muslim-Christian conference discussing the issue of Islamic law in 1993, the difficulties faced by transplanted Muslims was highlighted by Jørgen Nielsen. He noted, "participation in a highly structured system [like that of Western Europe] which has been developed over centuries tends to be difficult for those who come in late with a different experience."[12] In short, the myriad of cultural adjustments that all foreigners face when moving into a very different society also thrusts Muslim immigrants into those challenges related to cross-cultural assimilation and adjustment. But there is more to this problem than mere enculturation. Nielsen also points out that the inevitable discomfort and clash of traditions, religious and cultural, "tends to centre on *Sharī'ah*. In Western eyes, the Islamic state is one which implements barbaric punishments, persecutes non-Muslim minorities and suppresses women. In Muslim eyes, the West is atheistic, promiscuous, corrupt and—worst of all—anti-Islamic."[13] Thus, many Muslims see the pluralistic West as not merely different, but hostile to religion in general and Islam in particular. This has resulted in a popular perception among many Muslims that Western plurality inevitably compromises the traditional Islamic ideal of living under governmentally (i.e., *publicly*) imposed and enforced *Sharī'ah* law. Due to the perceived comprehensive and uncompromising nature of Islamic faith, it is difficult for many to envision plurality where other religious and legal systems might be significantly compatible with a more conservative, authentic, and explicitly public expression of Islam. Thus, especially concerning second-generation Muslim youth in non-Islamic contexts, Marcia Hermansen observes, "we are passing through a transitional and critical period in the history of the Muslim community" with re-

---

11. Ibid., 35. This is akin to what Kurzman ("Liberal Islam," 14) calls the "silent mode" of understanding *Sharī'ah*'s applications in variable contexts.

12. Cited in Sperber, *Christians and Muslims*, 203.

13. Ibid.

spect to their long-term identity.¹⁴ Ramadan succinctly summarizes the issues by stating that for Muslims living in the pluralistic context, "three questions are fundamental and urgently demand precise answers if we are to build a future for ourselves . . . : *Where are we? Who are we?* and finally, *In what way do we want to belong?*"¹⁵ I might add to this list a fourth concern: *How do we want to relate and respond to those who are different from and disagree with us?*

Global Trends of Growing Secularization

Islam is being used here to illustrate the challenge *every* religious person and community faces when encountering foreign cultures and religions. In our pluralistic world, the question of how people of different religious views can and should respond and relate to each other is not easily answered. Fortunately, many within these religious communities are seeking to build deeper understandings of the other and find ways to engender more significant cooperation. This is especially important in light of two disturbing and interrelated trends.

The first is the increasing "secularization" of nations and cultures in both the East and West. Muslim scholar Abdulaziz Sachedina describes it this way: "The secular culture tends toward a negative characterization of anything religious as soon as it crosses the boundary from the private to the public sphere."¹⁶ Thus, religion's influence has been increasingly marginalized. Sachedina calls this secularist push to exile religious impact to the margins of public life "the 'disestablishment' proposition," which "privatizes religion, banishing it from a secularized public arena . . ."¹⁷

This leads to a second trend, where some religious communities, feeling the need to assert the universal character of their belief system, are attracted to reactionary responses that move them "toward militan-

---

14. Hermansen, "'Identity' Islam," 318.

15. Ramadan, *Western Muslims*, 63. Granted, Ramadan is primarily concerned here with Muslims attempting to be authentically Muslim and *Western* (especially in Europe), but the principles he lays out are useful for people of other religions to consider and apply as they seek to make sense of the relationship between their religious faith and cultural identity.

16. Sachedina, *Islamic Roots*, 3.

17. Ibid.

cy, aggression, and separatism."[18] Secularists use such responses to bolster their claims that religion is dangerous and should remain a purely private affair. Ironically, the vast majority of religious people agree such radical zeal is morally misguided and corrupts the true nature of religious belief. In fact, religious values, when appropriately inculcated and practiced, serve as rich repositories for societal stability and harmony between peoples of highly diverse cultural and religious backgrounds. That is to say, "The religious culture, on the contrary, holds that religious values are a valuable resource in combating social and political injustices."[19]

In light of these disturbing trends, Christians and Muslims have sensed a profound urgency to pursue mutual dialogue to provide immediate and long-term solutions to the growing problem of violence against others in the name of organized religion. Instrumental in this process has been the World Council of Churches' attempt to engage Islamic thinkers in a process of respectful ongoing dialogue. In addition, there have been many local attempts (formal and informal) to participate in interreligious interaction.

Two Important Responses to Religious Plurality

To provide more focused attention to this vitally needed conversation in our religiously plural world, we will look closely at two of the more recent and important contributors to this ongoing engagement. They are Christian systematic theologian Wolfhart Pannenberg, and Muslim ethicist and religious scholar Abdulaziz Sachedina. To understand their significance and qualifications with respect to the task of addressing Christian and Muslim responses to religious plurality, a brief profile of both thinkers is provided below.

Wolfhart Pannenberg

German Lutheran theologian Wolfhart Pannenberg has authored numerous books and articles spanning an impressive forty-year academic

---

18. Ibid.
19. Ibid.

career that included posts in Europe and the US. In particular, what many have called the magnum opus of his career, his three-volume *Systematic Theology*, is having an increasingly significant influence on the Christian community worldwide. Its comprehensive scope, creative and insightful interaction with biblical and extra-biblical resources, coupled with its coherence and tight integration have compelled some of the greatest theological minds of our day to mine (and sometimes malign) its depth of riches. Pannenberg's ongoing passionate interest in the nature and importance of other religions has caused him to write on many aspects of religious plurality and its impact on the church and our future world. Concerning this he states, "Catholic theology is today trying to do justice to the fact that the Christian religion exists as one religion among many. . . . If Protestant theology also does not once again face this fact openly and without dogmatic restrictions, then general critiques of the phenomenon of religion will inevitably further undermine the credibility of the Christian message as well."[20] Thus, for Pannenberg, a concern for a theology of religions is inherent to the credibility and truth of Christianity as one faith among many others.

Closely related to Pannenberg's notion of truth and its comprehensive nature, he sees the unfolding history of all religions as the means by which God reveals himself and his purposes for all creation. Thus, interfaith dialogue is not merely *missional*, it is *theologically essential* for a truer and more comprehensive understanding of God's character and plans. Pannenberg is particularly suited to participate in interfaith dialogue since he desires to see the other as truly other rather than trying to make the other into an inclusive subset of his own religion. In addition, because he sees truth as public, comprehensive, and coherent, his views closely mirror certain Islamic notions of truth and religion, making him an ideal discussion partner on important topics like the nature of God, humanity, divine revelation, other religions, and free and just societies.

Ironically, despite his overt recognition of its importance, Pannenberg never fully provides a separate systematic treatment of a theology of religions. I will initiate that project, bringing together a variety of Pannenbergian resources to give a more systematic look at such

---

20. Pannenberg, "History of Religions," 67.

a theology. I will then utilize those Christian resources to interactively converse with Muslim scholar Abdulaziz Sachedina.

Abdulaziz Sachedina

Abdulaziz Sachedina obtained his academic degrees in India (BA in Muslim Studies, Aligarh Muslim University), Iran (BA in Persian Language and Literature, Ferdowsi University) and Canada (MA and PhD in Islamic and Middle Eastern Studies, University of Toronto). Fluent in seven different languages,[21] he has taught at numerous institutions throughout his academic career and is currently a professor of ethics and religious studies at the University of Virginia. He has also produced an impressive array of books and publications on many topics pertinent to Muslims, especially concerning Islamic jurisprudence, ethics, and social justice. Sachedina is important to this dialogue because he is one of the few Muslim scholars writing in any comprehensive way about religious plurality and the possibility for Muslims, on the basis of their own internal spiritual resources, to create democratic, pluralistic, and tolerant societies.

In his recent landmark book, *The Islamic Roots of Democratic Pluralism*, Sachedina makes the controversial claim that authoritative Muslim resources actually provide the basis for a free democratic society that is not free from religion (as in secularism), but freely religious (as in religious plurality). He claims human beings are created with a universal primordial nature (*fitra*) that enables them to understand and pursue upright moral goals and ideals. Thus, the best way to create tolerant and moral societies is to pursue an ongoing dialogue and exchange of rational and ethical ideas with all people. Suppression of alternative viewpoints leads not to righteousness, but an impoverished and narrow understanding of the universal scope and purposes of God for all mankind. Because it is pre-revelatory, the *fitra* is not dependent on overt knowledge of or adherence to the Qur'an. The Qur'an is supplemental and helpful in the process, but all human beings have an innate moral sensibility enabling them to structure a universal society

---

21. These include Gujarati (his native tongue), Swahili, Persian, Arabic, Urdu, Hindi, and English.

built around godly ideals and purposes without the need for special divine revelation.

For Sachedina, Islam as an institutional religion and the human need to be in submission to God through morally upright living must also be clarified. Islam became an institutional religion over time, but the principle need for humanity remains: to submit to God's perfect will and do what is right. Thus, one is islamic (lowercase *i*) not on the basis of affiliation with institutional Islam (capital *I*). Rather, one is islamic by virtue of living a life that demonstrates the exercise of one's innate moral freedom to *submit oneself* to the plan and purpose of the one true God. A holy life is characterized by serving God, no matter what religion one is formally affiliated with. In this way, Sachedina redefines crucial terms to point toward more inclusive Islamic meanings obscured by time and convention.

In the end, Sachedina makes the potentially surprising claim that, rightly understood within its historical context, the Qur'an actually affirms a religiously diverse and publicly moral society wherein God ordains the presence of competing alternative perspectives.

Sachedina has written courageously on these topics, and currently stands under the shadow of critiques from more traditionally-oriented Muslim leaders for his claim that universal, conservative, and Qur'anic Islam brings many resources for the creation of peaceful, plural, and moral societies.[22]

Purpose and Preview

This book aims to bring these two religious representatives into a more direct and systematic conversation with one another. Through such a dialogue, resources within Christianity and Islam for a truly plural society will be discovered and implemented. This will be a society where the goal is not mere toleration, but something more important—genu-

---

22. Placed under a fatwa in 1998 by Ayatollah Ali Sistani of Najaf, Iraq, which was intended to prevent him from teaching or lecturing on the subject of Islam, it is significant when he notes (in *Role of Islam*, 9n3), "It is not an easy task for any conscientious Muslim intellectual in the Muslim world or in the West to undertake this critical task [of reassessing the foundations of traditional Islamic beliefs and practices] without endangering his/her life."

ine mutual engagement. As Omid Safi reminds us, there is a higher hope and goal:

> [T]he root of the term "tolerance" comes from medieval toxicology and pharmacology, marking how much poison a body could "tolerate" before it would succumb to death. Is this the best that we can do? Is our task to figure out how many "others" ... we can *tolerate* before it really kills us? Is this the most sublime height of pluralism that we can aspire to? I don't want to "tolerate" my fellow human beings, but rather to engage them at the deepest level of what makes us human, through both our phenomenal commonality and our dazzling cultural differences.[23]

Because of my own religious background and loyalties, this will be pursued with distinctively Christian emphases and concerns. Hopefully an expanded and truer vision of Christianity will emerge through a fair and sincere dialogue with the Islamic other. This will be achieved through an analysis and comparison of relevant scholarly works. Chapter 1 will briefly survey and categorize Christian and Muslim reactions to religious plurality before looking more closely at the current state of Christian-Muslim dialogue in chapter 2. Chapters 3 and 4 will then lay out the respective theologies of religions of Pannenberg and Sachedina. In chapter 5 a critical interaction with these views from an evangelical perspective will be provided along with an interactive "conversation" of comparison and contrast. In chapter 6 I offer perspectives on how and where Christian-Muslim dialogue might move forward. Special attention will be paid to the importance of allowing dialogue to proceed without any undue prior ideological demands on participants, and conditions that will help make Christian-Muslim dialogue more fruitful will be explored. After this, political aspects of dialogue and societal formation will be examined to encourage more democratically free, morally just, and religiously plural human communities. Chapter 7 will explore some of the distinctly Christian and trinitarian aspects of God and his nature, along with the significant potential these have for creating fruitful interactive dialogues with Muslims.[24] Chapter 8

---

23. Safi, "Introduction," 24.

24. Given the centrality of the Islamic doctrine of God's absolute oneness (*tawhīd*), this claim may initially seem strange. How such a concept will be laid out as both an invitation and a challenge to past, present, and future Christian and Islamic theology will be further explained in chapter 7.

Introduction

will wrap up by giving additional recommendations for how Christian-Muslim dialogue might continue. It will also lay out important areas still requiring significant interfaith interactions between Christians and Muslims.

Defining Key Concepts

Before going any further, key terms need advanced explanation and clarification. These are "theology of religion," "theology of religions," "religious pluralism(s)," and "religious plurality."

Confusion over the difference between a theology of religion and a theology of religion*s* is common. "Theology of religion" refers to the broader and more abstract concept of religion in general.[25] From a Christian perspective, it is a broadly descriptive and explicatory project sociologists and anthropologists have carried out that understands religion as a universal, cross-cultural, and trans-temporal phenomenon. In the words of Jacques Dupuis, "The [Christian] theology of religion asks what religion is and seeks, in the light of Christian faith, to interpret the universal religious experience of humankind; it further studies the relationship between revelation and faith, faith and religion, and faith and salvation."[26]

As beneficial as this pursuit is, the primary concern here is with a related but different project, namely the concern to look at a theology of religions—in the plural. Theology of religions focuses upon particular religions as they actually exist and are practiced in our world today rather than a general concept of religion. As Veli-Matti Kärkkäinen states, "Theology of religions is that discipline of theological studies which attempts to account theologically for the meaning and value of other religions. Christian theology of religions attempts to think theologically about what it means for Christians to live with people of other faiths and about the relationship of Christianity to other religions."[27] Thus, particular religions and even regions (e.g., Asian or African the-

---

25. In many ways, this is a continuation of the project initiated by Friedrich Schleiermacher. In his attempt to describe religion in general rather than a particular religion, he claimed (in *On Religion*, 106) that "the essence of the religious emotions consists in the feeling of an absolute dependence."

26. Dupuis, *Theology of Pluralism*, 7.

27. Kärkkäinen, *Introduction*, 20.

ologies of religions) can become the concern of a Christian theology of religions. But as Kärkkäinen goes on to point out, what theology of religions is concerned about need not be—perhaps even should not be—limited to Christianity alone. Thus, "In principle—even though not much work has yet been done—there could be theology of religions from the perspective of other religions, such as a Buddhist or Hindu theology of religions. The goal of these theologies would be to reflect on the meaning of other religions in relation to its own convictions and underlying foundations."[28] Accordingly, the hope here is to follow this principle by describing, developing, and synthesizing Pannenberg's Christian theology of religions alongside Sachedina's Islamic theology of religions.

In literature on theology of religion and theology of religions, it has been customary to call the sociological reality of having many religious adherents living in close proximity to one another "religious pluralism." More recently, theology of religions has associated the term "religious pluralism" with the ideology of John Hick and others like him, who claim that that religious differences observed in our world today are merely variable phenomenal human expressions of responses to the one noumenal God (or more recently in his thought, the *Real*). As Bernard Adeney observes, "*Pluralism* used to refer to the fact that one society contains multiple religions. Recently it has come to be used as a normative term for a particular theology of religions,"[29] namely, the pluralist perspective. Here, all major world religions are roughly equal in their salvific ability to move a believer from more self-centered ways of living toward more other-centered or God/Reality-centered forms.[30] Since Hick's view has been popularized, there has been a tremendous proliferation of these types of perspectives that are quite distinct. Consequently, those who promote them are often referred to as "religious pluralists." Due to this proliferation, it is now more helpful to speak of "religious pluralism*s*" rather than the more general term "religious pluralism." To avoid any confusion with Hick and other pluralists, the term "religious plurality" is used to refer to the sociological reality of the presence of many major religious views (usually in close proxim-

---

28. Ibid., 21.
29. Adeney, *Strange Virtues*, 178.
30. Hick's views will be looked at more closely in chapter 1.

Introduction

ity) without necessarily evaluating this situation in any theological or philosophical manner.

With a few of these basic terms defined and clarified, we can now survey ways Christians and Muslims have recently responded to religious plurality beginning in chapter 1.

1

Contemporary Muslim and Christian Responses to Religious Plurality

Religious Plurality and the New Global Climate: Present Problems and Possibilities

Religious plurality is nothing new to Islam or Christianity. Both were forged in the fires of multiply religious cultural settings. As Harold Netland observes of first-century Christianity,

> It is tempting to assume that the perplexing problems of religious pluralism we face today are unprecedented, but nothing could be further from the truth. The world of the New Testament was characterized by social, intellectual and religious ferment. Traditional Jewish religious values and beliefs were being challenged by powerful competing forces within the Hellenistic-Roman world. Even within Palestine itself, Jews were confronted with alien beliefs and practices. . . . Not only did they face the formidable challenge presented by Greek philosophy and literature but also they had to contend with the many popular religious movements of the day—the cults of Asclepius and Artemis-Diana, the "mystery religions" of Osiris and Isis, Mithras, Adonis and Eleusis, the ubiquitous cult of the Roman emperor and the many popularized versions of Stoicism, Cynicism, and Epicureanism.[1]

---

1. Netland, *Encountering*, 25.

Contemporary Muslim and Christian Responses to Religious Plurality

Islam was also born in the cradle of Arabia where pagan polytheism, widespread idol worship, tribal sectarian and cultic religiosity, as well as Jewish and Christian monotheisms were all present and vying for personal and communal adherence.[2] The presence and influence of Christianity upon Islam in its formative years reminds us that Muslims and Christians have been dialogically engaging one another for fourteen centuries.[3] At best, this has been a checkered history with mixed results. One need only reflect upon the Christian Crusades, for example, to recall some of the deplorable decisions made by Christians to try and deal with Islamic successes and Christian losses.[4] So, Christian and Muslim encounters are nothing new. Nevertheless, as Yvonne and Wadi Haddad point out, "The fourteen-century history of the encounter between Christianity and Islam has taken many forms of conflict and cooperation, diatribe and dialogue, hatred and tolerance, community hostility and personal friendships. . . . At this moment . . . , we find ourselves in a distinctively different situation. The reality of mass communication alone has changed circumstances radically. . . . [W]e can have information at the touch of a . . . button. . . . We are, in effect, instantly accountable to one another."[5]

This accountability presses us to live with one another in more tolerant and peaceful ways. This is especially true as we witness the growing moral challenges of our global society, coupled with a creeping secularization that seeks to privatize and marginalize all religion. Admittedly, this secular attitude is especially prominent in the West, but the new world climate has forced other regions and nations to grapple with the "disestablishment" of religious influence in the public

---

2. For a very brief but excellent summary of the historical milieu during Muhammad's time, see Tennent, *Religious Roundtable*, 142–44.

3. These interactions have been variously divided into eras where much interfaith encounter was followed by long periods characterized predominantly by isolation. For an interesting look at the first two hundred years of interaction between Christians and Muslims, see Goddard, *History*, ch. 3. The degree of Christianity's influence on Islam in the early years is debated. Initially Judaism had a far more direct impact than Christianity, but the Qur'an makes it clear that early on some form of Christianity was known about and responded to by Muhammad and his followers.

4. The history of the Christian Crusades is complex and voluminous and cannot be unpacked here. For a brief examination and evaluative summary of the Crusades, see Cairns, *Christianity*, 212–25.

5. Haddad and Haddad, *Encounters*, 1.

arena. Is there a legitimate place for religion in public discourse? Is this possible without amalgamating religious adherence and political governance? Can a Muslim, for example, live righteously and publicly before others without pressing for an Islamically governed state and nation?[6] Must Christians pursue reconstructionistic legal policy to be true to their religious faith?[7] Or is it possible for people of all faiths to pursue publicly their religious ends in a democratically free and moral society? If so, how, and what resources might Christianity and Islam provide?

These are complicated questions, and the proper relationships between religious faiths as well as other aspects of public society are not perfectly clear. Nor are they likely to be clarified fully by any one person or group of persons in the near future. One thing is clear: historically, Islam and Christianity, to varying degrees, have always been publicly practiced. In addition, most contend this religious publicity cannot be completely compromised. The degree to which their faith can be openly practiced alongside the faiths and ideologies of others is hotly debated. But some level of publicity is inherent in their respective views of God as sovereign Master of all, since "The Lord has made everything for His own purpose, even the wicked for the day of evil" (Prov 16:14).

Ultimately, answers to these problems go beyond the scope of this chapter. For now, recognition of the public nature of these two great faiths, along with the claim that they offer tremendous resources for the creation of democratically and religiously free and moral societies, will have to suffice.

We will begin by surveying how Christianity and Islam have recently responded to religious plurality. The responses concerned will be primarily *intra-religious*, noting how these faiths have tried to make sense of themselves among other faiths. We will look first at various Christian rejoinders before examining Muslim reactions. Sometimes such reactions mix political and secular concerns into the category of plurality, making them more fluid and less strictly related to religious plurality. In chapter 2 we will explore in more detail how various

---

6. Many conservative Muslims simply answer no to this question.

7. Christian reconstructionists, also known as "theonomists" and "dominion theologians," claim Christians should seek to implement Old Testament law worldwide, since this is the only viable and God-honoring way to create a truly moral and just society. For a look at their views, see Rushdoony, *Biblical Law* and *Law and Society*. For a fair but devastating critique of this movement, see House and Ice, *Dominion Theology*.

Contemporary Muslim and Christian Responses to Religious Plurality

Muslims and Christians have responded to each other through deliberate interfaith dialogue. Reviewing and categorizing the resulting themes and impasses will open the way to consider how Pannenberg (chapter 3) and Sachedina (chapter 4) might be utilized to help move the conversation forward in new and promising directions.

Taxonomical Problems of Classifying Christian Responses to Religious Plurality

Before turning to some Christian responses to religious plurality, taxonomical questions must be addressed. How can various Christian reactions to religious plurality best be classified? One of the problems here is that it is difficult to find a universal system of taxonomy. Many of the responses are generated by the way religious persons or groups see the world and others in it. Because theology of religions is more developed in Christianity than other world religions, several classification systems have been offered for arranging Christian responses to religious plurality.

The origin of the initial classification system for Christian responses is unclear. However, it is generally agreed that Alan Race was the first to put in print the widely used tripartite system of exclusivism, inclusivism, and pluralism.[8] Because early work in this area was done by those like John Hick, who tended to be more pluralistically minded, the term "exclusivism" was given to Christians who held more restrictive views of salvation and religious value in other religions. The term, assigned by those who disagreed, can admittedly be understood derogatorily. As Netland observes,

> It seems that the term *exclusivism* was introduced into the discussion not by adherents of [what Netland calls] the traditional perspective but rather by those who rejected this view and wished to cast it in a negative light. It is a rather pejorative term with unflattering connotations: exclusivists are typically branded as dogmatic, narrow-minded, intolerant, ignorant, arrogant, and so on, and those rejecting exclusivism for more

---

8. See Race, *Religious Pluralism*.

accommodating perspectives are regarded as exemplifying the virtues believed deficient in exclusivists.[9]

To avoid this connotation, Netland substitutes "*particularism*" for "exclusivism," a more recent term offered by Okholm and Phillips.[10] Yet he chooses to retain the other two more commonly used categories of inclusivism and pluralism.[11] Despite this, the term "exclusivism" (along with the other two) is still customarily used to describe more conservative Christian responses to religious plurality. And since exclusivism has gradually become more widely and fairly explained by its own adherents and better understood by others, the pejorative connotations are not nearly as forceful as they once were. Thus, the use of the term is still acceptable to describe what are considered more traditional points of view concerning this subject. However, with the rise of significant variation among alternative Christian views, more accurately descriptive typologies have now been proposed.

One of these, utilized by Paul Knitter, employs this terminology: "Total Replacement," "Partial Replacement," "Fulfillment," "Mutuality," and "Acceptance."[12] In Total Replacement, Christianity is called to replace completely other world religions since they are largely, if not completely, false and demonically motivated. A second and closely related position is that Christianity should *partially replace* and *complete* those areas of other religions where the truth of God has been corrupted or missed. While salvation is not possible apart from Christianity, it is likely God is currently at work revealing himself in other religions. Dialogue becomes an opportunity for gathering truth and for witness. As Knitter puts it, those who hold to a Partial Replacement model are concerned that "the Total Replacement Model . . . misses the very real presence of God within the world of other religions."[13]

The third option, the Fulfillment model, affirms that "other religions are of value, that God is to be found in them, that Christians need

---

9. Netland, *Encountering*, 46.

10. Okholm and Phillips, "Introduction," 16.

11. In *Encountering*, 50, Netland goes on to distinguish particularism from the more specialized restrictivism that claims only those who have explicitly heard the gospel of Christ and embraced its truth can be saved.

12. Knitter, *Introducing*.

13. Ibid., 33.

to dialogue with them and not just preach to them."[14] Thus, Christianity is the *fulfillment* of what God wants from religion, but not the exclusive possessor of religious truth. Still, advocates wish to retain the centrality of Jesus, not only to Christianity, but to every person and religion. They do this by claiming (with Karl Rahner and others like him) that while other religions demonstrate and possess God's grace, this grace is still mediated through *Christ alone*. Consequently, salvation is available to those outside Christianity and the institutional church, but it is still based upon the person and work of Jesus Christ, whether or not religious others overtly believe or embrace this fact.[15] Thus, in Jesus, Christianity represents the fulfillment of all the good other religions long for and possess.

Fourth is the Mutuality model. Here, Knitter notes three important bridges that have moved Christians into more pluralistic territory.[16] They are the "philosophical-historical" bridge (Hick), the "religious-mystical" bridge (Panikkar), and the "ethical-practical" bridge (Knitter—although he never names himself here). Each challenges Christianity's uniqueness and particularity in slightly different ways, but they all emphasize the many similarities all great world religions exhibit. Thus, they claim the great world religions stand roughly as equals, pursuing similar goals in different and contextually situated ways. As such, they all need one another for mutual discovery, encouragement, enrichment, and cooperative moral action.

The fifth and final view is the Acceptance model. Nurtured in the context of postmodern relativism, this view suggests religions may well express incompatible notions of God, truth, goodness, and reality, but the best way to live with plurality is to embrace it without smoothing over differences (mutuality), incorporating other views into one's own (fulfillment), or refuting everyone else's truth claims on the basis of one's own (replacement). Not surprisingly, the ways and degrees in which this embrace and acceptance is accomplished varies greatly among its adherents. As Knitter puts it, "the motto of the Acceptance Model might well be, 'Vive la difference!'—let the differences thrive! If that be so, we should expect to find diversity within the model itself.

14. Ibid., 63.

15. While it has now been extensively critiqued, Rahner was the one who first developed the concept of the "anonymous Christian."

16. Knitter, *Introducing*, 112–13.

And we do."[17] What matters most is not to misrepresent other views, but *let them stand as they really are*. Because we all have our own points of view, we are never fully able to see the world of others as they do, but in dialogue we can begin to expand our vision.

I have explained this latter classification system for two reasons. First, it highlights the diversity of responses to other religions within Christianity. Second, the categories are more accurately descriptive, allowing greater room for the genuine diversity present in Christian theologies of religions. Still, I am not fully satisfied with the system since it subtly tips the scale in favor of pluralistic responses to other religions. However, I will not use it primarily because there is a more *distinctively Christian* typology that more clearly describes ways Christians are responding to religious plurality. This is called the "centrist typology."[18]

Survey of Christian Responses to Religious Plurality: A Diversity of "Centrisms"

This system is called the "centrist typology" because each category describes the aspect of Christian theology it centers its understanding of other religions around.[19] Thus, it represents a truly *Christian* theology of religions. Furthermore, it is more descriptive of each view so the categories are not only more accurate but more informative. This does not mean the system is perfect, of course. Every typology suffers from its own attempt to generalize at the expense of being fair to the particulars of any given view. Still, without categories, understanding and analysis diminishes, so we must embrace such a system—cautiously and humbly, but unapologetically nonetheless.

The centrist categories are: 1) ecclesiocentrism,[20] 2) christocentrism, 3) theocentrism, 4) ethicocentrism, and 5) eschatocentrism.[21]

17. Ibid., 202–3.

18. Incidentally, I am not intentionally using terminology that could be attributed to Islam by using the word "centric." Its use here bears no relation to the call in Q. 2:143 for Muslims to be a community of the "middle way."

19. This system comes from Kärkkäinen (*Introduction*, 25) via Dupuis' system in *Theology of Pluralism*. I have modified it by adding two more categories I believe deserve separate treatments.

20. This term is derived from the Greek word *ecclesia*, meaning "church."

21. This term is derived from the Greek word *eschatos*, meaning "end."

Contemporary Muslim and Christian Responses to Religious Plurality

These will all be explained more fully as each is developed and illustrated. Ethicocentrism, following Paul Knitter and others like him, centers on the ethical aspects of the kingdom of God, especially justice for the poor and living righteously in peace with others.[22] Eschatocentrism arises from S. Mark Heim's creative proposal for a religiously plural world. It concentrates on the various religious ends after which each world religion strives and consequently, he argues, *ontologically creates for itself*.

Outside of a general critique of pluralism and inclusivism in chapter 6, I will not significantly evaluate the following responses since that has been ably done by others and ultimately goes beyond our current concerns.[23] These perspectives are offered to give a better context and understanding for Pannenberg and Sachedina's views. We begin by looking at the ecclesiocentric view of other religions.

Ecclesiocentrism

Ecclesiocentrism is sometimes called "particularism" or even "christocentric exclusivism." According to Kärkkäinen, there are two major forms, an older one associated with Karl Barth and Hendrik Kraemer, and a newer one identified with evangelicals like Millard Erickson, Harold Netland, and Vinoth Ramachandra.[24] For the sake of focus, only contemporary ecclesiocentrisms will be considered.

In ecclesiocentrism, concern about salvation and the status of other world religions centers around the ministry of the church. Therefore, "salvation in Christ is to be found in the church and in a faith response to the Christian gospel."[25] Typically, ecclesiocentric views fo-

---

22. Admittedly, Knitter does not use this term for his own view. Rather, in his article "Liberation Theology" (187), he calls his view "soteriocentric," from the Greek word *soteria*, meaning "salvation." I think this automatically skews his viewpoint in a confusing way since many Christians would not entertain the possibility of salvation for those who remain outside of Christianity. Thus, "ethicocentric" is more accurately descriptive of Knitter's views and less confusing.

23. For two good critiques of major pluralisms, see Heim, *Salvations*, esp. chs. 1–4; and Knitter, *Introducing*.

24. Kärkkäinen, covers the earlier forms in *Introduction*, chs. 18–20, and the contemporary forms in chs. 36–38.

25. Ibid., 319.

cus on questions about those outside the church and their relationship to God through Jesus Christ. This is especially the case with Erickson, who seeks to answer questions like "How much does one need to know to be saved?", and "How many will be saved?" In the end, the Bible seems clear that "general revelation is insufficient to bring persons to salvation."[26] As hard as this truth is to hear, Erickson is unequivocal: "without hearing the gospel explicitly, people are eternally lost."[27]

A similar but more open view is that of Harold Netland. In *Encountering Religious Pluralism*, Netland evaluates the inheritance of modernity[28] and then argues against what he sees as Hick's reductionistic claim that all religions are merely phenomenal, contextualized expressions of noumenal reality-in-itself.[29] Instead, Netland argues, "Religious traditions do make distinctive claims about reality, and these claims do at times conflict. . . . Moreover . . . , the problem of conflicting truth claims presents a formidable obstacle to any genuinely pluralistic model of the religions."[30]

At the heart of his view is the affirmation that "where the central claims of Christian faith are incompatible with those of other traditions, the latter are to be rejected as false."[31] He then provides two criteria that enable Christians to evaluate competing religious truth claims: "logical consistency" and "the moral criterion."[32] The biblical testimony provides the source of authority to assess the claims of all religions as they stand, rather than demanding they conform to a preconceived grid of meaning.

Similarly, Vinoth Ramachandra emphasizes the importance of the authoritative texts of Christianity, concluding Jesus is the unique and only Savior. Yet Jesus' particularity is not restrictive but expansive, as it seeks universality in missionary outreach. Thus, "The normativeness and ultimacy of Jesus Christ in God's salvific dealings with his world

26. Erickson, *How Shall They Be Saved?*, 158.
27. Ibid., 268.
28. Netland, *Encountering*, chs. 1–4.
29. Ibid., 231ff.
30. Ibid., 188.
31. Ibid.
32. Ibid., 293–300. In his earlier book, *Dissonant Voices* (180–95), he gives six, although in *Encountering*, under critical pressure, he appears to have relented down to only two cross-cultural criteria.

..., far from being an arbitrary and repressive doctrine, is *intrinsic to Christian praxis and self-understanding*, then and now."[33] Otherwise, our call to share the gospel with the world makes little sense.

Christocentrism

It could be argued that "christocentrism" is something of a misnomer since most Christians claim the centrality of Jesus Christ for faith and life. However, the christological focus of this view, especially with respect to the soteriological status of people from other religions, warrants the title. What, then, is the christocentric view of other religions? Knitter claims this view "embodies the majority opinion of present-day Christianity."[34] Thus, there are numerous possible advocates who could be used to illustrate it.[35] From our survey of Knitter's categories, we saw one of the most influential promoters of this view is Karl Rahner with his concept of the "anonymous Christian." While this view has been extensively criticized, its basic ideas still aptly illustrate the christocentric view. Thus, we will use Rahner's thesis to explain it.

At the core of this view stands the assertion that, through the communicating action of God's Spirit, divine grace extends to every person, regardless of religious affiliation. A universal transcendence draws us into the mystery of God and toward the infinite as we are in relationship with one another. However, this communication of the Spirit never remains abstract but is always manifest in the concrete aspects of real-time history. In Rahner's words, "This Spirit is always, everywhere, and from the outset, . . . the determining principle, of the history of revelation and salvation; and its communication and acceptance, by its very nature, never takes place in a merely abstract transcendental form. It always comes about through the mediation of history."[36]

Because the Spirit is self-communicating to all humanity, other religions, to varying degrees, exhibit manifestations of this same Spirit,

---

33. Ramachandra, *Recovery of Mission*, 216.

34. Knitter, *Introducing*, 63.

35. This breadth is illustrated by Kärkkäinen in *Introduction*. He explicates the christocentric views of four Catholics, four mainline Protestants, and three evangelicals, for a total of eleven!

36. Rahner, "Jesus Christ," 46.

creating historically conditioned revelation that is real but tainted and dimmed by the depravity of sin. In contrast, nowhere has that communication been clearer and brighter than in the person and work of the incarnate Christ. Again, Rahner claims,

> Until the moment when the gospel really enters into the historical situation of an individual, a non-Christian religion . . . does not merely contain elements of a natural knowledge of God, elements, moreover mixed up with human depravity which is the result of original sin and later aberrations. It contains also supernatural elements arising out of grace which is given to men as a gratuitous gift on account of Christ. For this reason, a non-Christian religion can be recognized as a lawful religion (although only in different degrees) without thereby denying the error and depravity contained in it.[37]

Because these Spirit-mediated communications are genuine revelations from God, tainted as they are, other religions are not merely *prepared* by them to receive the gospel of Christ. They *already possess*, in varying degrees, the actual grace and love of God through Christ. In the final analysis, if a person responds positively to these transcendent workings of God's Spirit, they are, in fact, open to the saving grace of God in Christ and can be described as "anonymous Christians" since this grace is finally and fully mediated through Jesus Christ.

This view is ultimately christocentric because the grace of God is still centered within the Lord Jesus Christ and his saving work on behalf of all humanity. Whether or not that grace is recognized as explicitly grounded in Jesus, it is nevertheless present in all religions and persons to greater or lesser degrees. Thus, Jesus Christ is still the *norm and standard of salvation*, but an overt affirmation and confession of this reality is no longer required for salvific grace to be received and enjoyed by those who are not visible members of the institutional Christian church.

The christocentric idea that God's grace is transcendently given to all through revelatory communications of the Spirit and mediated by Christ is, for many theologians, a relatively short stopover on a journey into pluralism. The move from a christological mediation to a more general *theological* mediation is a fairly small step if saving grace is given to other non-Christian religious peoples. Thus, all grace is God's grace, but its concrete contextual manifestations account for the mani-

37. Rahner, "Christianity," 121.

fold differences apparent in any interreligious survey of practices and beliefs. Thus, *Christ* is no longer the focus and source of grace; *God* is—and so we move into full-blown *theocentrism*.

Theocentrism

Perhaps the most famous and articulate advocate of theocentrism in its early forms is John Hick.[38] As he wrestled with religious plurality and what he saw as the intractable problems of an exclusive and ecclesiocentric theology of religions, Hick decided there must be another way to understand the universe of faiths. Consequently, he developed a Kantian view of religion where all religious claims and experiences are nothing more than phenomenal manifestations of an experience of and response to the revealing presence of the one true noumenal God. Using the Copernican model of astronomy from the Middle Ages as an analogy, Hick claimed the world's many religions are similar to planets revolving around the sun. They are all different, yet they circle around the one and only God of the universe. Therefore, all religions, Christianity included, must be reinterpreted to emphasize their common source and destiny and to deemphasize the many differences that arose in the concrete contexts of space and time. Kärkkäinen summarizes this early Hickan view this way: "[Hick] came to the conclusion that religion is a human interpretation of reality, not absolute fact statements, and that consequently all religions are in contact with and describe the same reality."[39]

To maintain this view, Hick reinterpreted the way Christian language speaks about God and other theological claims, and significantly modified traditional concepts of Christology to reflect more pluralistic notions of both. By claiming religious truth claims were actually attempts to describe the divine mythically, he believed many of the apparent contradictions could ultimately be resolved or attributed to concretions of historicity. In addition, claims about God's nature could be seen as complementary rather than contradictory, especially since they attempt to describe the One who is ultimately indescribable. As

---

38. Some of Hick's earlier works include: *Universe of Faiths, Truth and Dialogue, Myth of God Incarnate,* and *Myth of Christian Uniqueness.*

39. Kärkkäinen, *Introduction,* 283.

Kärkkäinen puts it, "even though various religions seem to have dramatic differences at the surface level, deep down they share a common foundation."[40]

Christologically, in light of his pluralist thesis, Hick only sees Jesus as a holy man, rather than the *ontologically unique* Son of God. Consequently, Hick speaks of incarnation this way:

> Incarnation, in the sense of the embodiment of ideas, values, insights in human living, is a basic metaphor.... Now we want to say of Jesus that he was so vividly conscious of God as the loving heavenly Father, and so startlingly open to God and so fully his servant and instrument, that the divine love was expressed, and in this sense incarnated, in his life.... He was wholly human; but whenever self-giving love in response to the love of God is lived out in a human life, to that extent the divine love has become incarnate on earth.[41]

Sometimes called "degree Christology," the idea here is that Jesus was different than most others, but only by *degree*. His openness and passion for God was greater than perhaps every other person who ever lived. But this difference was not *qualitative*. Perhaps if Jesus had been born in another time and another place, "he would have been identified as a Bodhissattva who, like Gotama some four centuries earlier, had attained to Buddhahood or perfect relationship to reality..."[42] In short, "Christ's 'divinity' means that he had a specific God-consciousness, but that does not mean that other religious leaders could not share the same consciousness."[43]

In the final analysis, all religions have strikingly similar concepts of what Hick calls the "Ultimate Divine" or "the *Real.*"[44] In addition, they all represent legitimate means by which adherents are moved from self-centeredness toward God-centeredness, or perhaps even better, *Reality*-centeredness. Thus, to be more inclusive of Buddhistic ways of looking at religion, Hick has moved toward a "reality-centric" approach to world religions.

40. Ibid., 288.
41. Hick, *Many Names*, 58–59.
42. Hick, *Universe of Faiths*, 117.
43. Kärkkäinen, *Introduction*, 291. For Hick's mature Christology, see *Metaphor of God*.
44. Hick traces some of these similarities in *Rainbow of Faiths*, 69.

Ethicocentrism

The next category of responses I have chosen to call "ethicocentrism." It is debatable whether this category warrants a separate treatment, since its major proponent is Paul Knitter, a theologian many consider to be a thoroughgoing pluralist in the vein of John Hick and others like him. However, I have created it because of Knitter's emphasis on social justice and global moral concern. Thus, the focus of this reaction to other world religions is not upon God per se, but upon the *ethical aspects* of God's kingdom on earth. Consequently, some, including Knitter himself, have categorized this view as "Kingdom-centered."[45]

In this view, what matters most are the moral concerns and actions we take in light of our increasingly global context. Influenced by liberation theology, Knitter first hinted at an ethicocentric approach to other world religions in his 1987 essay "Toward a Liberation Theology of Religions."[46] Here, Knitter calls for a new way of approaching the ethical challenges of our modern world:

> For Christians, what constitutes the basis and the goal for interreligious dialogue, that which makes mutual understanding and cooperation between the religions possible . . . , which unites the religions in common discourse and praxis, is *not* how they are related to the church (invisibly through "baptism of desire"), or how they are related to Christ (anonymously or normatively), nor even how they respond to and conceive of God, but rather, to what extent they are promoting *Soteria* (in Christian images, the *basileia*)—to what extent they are engaged in promoting human welfare and bringing about liberation with and for the poor and nonpersons.[47]

More recently, Knitter has stated that what arises from this commitment is a "global responsibility" that seeks "not just social justice but eco-human justice and well-being." But it "must be an effort by the entire globe and all its nations and religions."[48] The content of such

---

45. Knitter, *Introducing*, 145.

46. Found in Hick, *Myth of Christian Uniqueness*.

47. Knitter, "Liberation Theology," 187. Here he takes issue with all three of the aforementioned categories, ecclesiocentrism, christocentrism, and theocentrism. *Basileia* is Greek for "kingdom."

48. Knitter, *Many Religions*, 15.

ethical concerns must be worked out together in interreligious dialogue and active service of humanity. Only then can we live under the ethical kingdom-reign of God and solve the global problems plaguing our world today.

Eschatocentrism

The final responsive category I have chosen to highlight is something I call "eschatocentrism." It is based on one of the most creative recent suggestions for a more pluralistic Christian theology of religions, from S. Mark Heim.[49] His proposal is difficult to categorize in the universe of centrisms because it does not easily conform to any of the previous categories. On the basis of a brilliant critique of other pluralisms, he demonstrates that all collapse into inclusivistic views. Thus, Heim willingly admits that his view is also ultimately inclusivistic and not strictly pluralistic. Nevertheless, he argues that his inclusive view of the world religions is, of all recent proposals, the most pluralistic. In his own words, "I argue on behalf of a certain type of [inclusive] perspective . . . which I believe goes a step beyond inclusivism . . . maximizing the credibility and significance of the various religions' self-descriptions. It does so by offering a 'more pluralistic hypothesis': the contention that there can be a variety of actual but different religious fulfillments."[50]

In *The Depth of Riches*, Heim gives a fuller explanation of what he considers a Christian, yet genuinely pluralistic, view of multiple religious ends. Utilizing the idea of plentitude as a conceptual resource, he asserts that inherent within the relational and trinitarian God is *plurality*. Consequently, he argues that all religious persons, while not necessarily "saved" in a *Christian* sense, nevertheless can be related to one or more dimensions of the trinitarian Godhead. Thus, for example, while Buddhists may not seek salvation as Christians would, they are still directly (although not fully) related to the *impersonal* aspect of God's intertrinitarian life. What this means is that all religious people, while they may not experience *Christian* salvation as full and personal communion with God (the highest goal in Heim's view), they are still

---

49. First hinted at in part 2 of his book *Salvations*, this view is more thoroughly developed in his *Depth of Riches*.

50. Heim, *Salvations*, 131.

truly related to God through his triune plenary dimensional fullness. Thus, a Muslim may be related more closely with God as personal, but he misses much of the plural aspect of God and so only reaches his own *tawhīd*-bound religious end.[51]

Thus, according to Heim's revised vision of Dante's *Divine Comedy*, religious ends are truly plural and simultaneously multiple rather than unified and monolithic, *even into the eschaton of God*. While those who are not Christians will not achieve the highest goal of communion with God (that is, *Christian* salvation), they will receive, through the plenary, trinitarian, multi-dimensional divine life, the religious end they seek. For them, it will be fulfillment, even though it will not appear that way to Christians. Thus, all religious ends are grounded in Christianity's God, but are constituted by religious choices and the desired ends people seek after. This is not a bad thing, but a blessing from God who respects the autonomous freedom of human beings made in his image. Ultimately, all religions are included in the triune God whether or not they recognize or accept it—even throughout the course of their respective, self-created, and eternal destinies! Heim summarizes his thesis this way:

> I distinguish salvation, communion with the triune God in Christ, from other religious ends, as well as from any natural [i.e., non-religious] end. But I distinguish religious ends from the so-called natural end also. These religious fulfillments are beyond attainment by purely natural human capacities. Alternative religious ends define God essentially in terms of one dimension (other than communion) of the triune life. That is, they are rooted in authentic revelation *of* the triune God, but not revelation of God *as* triune.[52]

In short, Christians enjoy the full revelation of God in Christ and will consequently experience the fullness of fellowship with him for all eternity. Other religions will also enjoy the trinitarian life of God as they eternally experience their own religious ends, but in fewer dimensions and with less fullness. By putting forth such a thesis, Heim believes he allows all religions to stand as they actually are—even into eternity.

---

51. The Muslim doctrine of *tawhīd* affirms the absolute oneness of God, who in the Qur'an's language "has no partners" and so cannot be triune.

52. Heim, *Depth of Riches*, 275.

On this view, the implications for interfaith dialogue are many. Unfortunately, they cannot be explored here. However, if his perspective is true, Heim admits that it creates an interesting result for Christians seeking to persuade the followers of other religions to convert to Christianity. He states:

> If, as I have maintained, valid religious ends in fact embody a relation with God in some dimension of the divine life, then Christian witness as a flat contradiction of the other's faith is not only likely to be ineffective but is wrong. Though Christians can witness to distinctive features of their faith and of salvation, they will have to witness in some way through affirmation of the other tradition.[53]

As with other views laid out here, to limit the scope of this study I leave the task of evaluation to others.[54] For now, we must take stock of where we are before moving forward by looking more closely at recent Islamic responses to religious plurality.

It must be admitted that, due to the highly developed and developing nature of Christian theologies of religions, the space devoted to the topic is frustratingly small. However, it was never intended to provide an extensive survey and critique of this field. It is only introduced here to provide a snapshot of the current scene with a view to examining Pannenberg's and Sachedina's unique theologies of religions in context. Thus, to help place Sachedina into his Islamic context, we will now briefly look at some corresponding Muslim responses to religious plurality, considering ways they are alike and different from Christian reactions to religious plurality.

Muslim Responses to Religious Plurality

By way of introduction, recall that when religion, a centrally important aspect of life for huge numbers of people, is pushed out of the public arena, some respond with exceptional—even violent—frustration. This type of response (especially by certain Muslim groups) has, in recent years, been frequently and internationally displayed by mainstream

---

53. Ibid., 294.

54. For two excellent critiques of Heim, see Knitter, *Introducing*, 229–37; and esp. Kärkkäinen, *Trinity and Religious Pluralism*, 145–51.

media.⁵⁵ Unfortunately, some scholars, while not wholly excusing such responses, have shifted blame for them away from Islamic terrorist groups toward the abstract concept often deemed "Western culture."⁵⁶ For example, Abid Ullah Jan, responding to an article by Khaled Abou El Fadl,⁵⁷ rants that, "When he seeks to assign responsibility for intolerance, Abou El Fadl should look no further than the Western quest for dominance."⁵⁸ In fact, in Jan's thinking, the world is "now witnessing the second phase of an organized attempt to eliminate Islam" by the West.⁵⁹ Citing Q. 4:135, Jan goes on to say, "the frustration of Muslims around the world is not a consequence of faulty interpretations of Islam but of an inability to tolerate continued Western double standards and the treatment of Muslims as second-class citizens of the planet."⁶⁰ Thus, "The supposed problem of Islamic 'intolerance' is in fact principled resistance demonstrated by the Muslims who stand up for justice even against their own self-interests."⁶¹ Consequently, such militant responses can be classified as selfless and courageous stances for Islamic justice and long-term survival.

Fortunately, a growing number of increasingly vocal Muslims are more thoughtfully and sensitively responding to the challenges of

---

55. This has not been without reason. Islamic terrorist attacks warrant widespread media attention, international concern, and condemnation. What are covered far less frequently are the activities and writings of those responding thoughtfully and sensitively to these heartbreaking problems.

56. Vilifying an abstract, unspecified entity is a classic tactic for those who shy away from actually dealing with living individuals and people groups. By depersonalizing the enemy and abstracting them into something that can't quite be pinned down or defined, such thinkers are able to create a target for hatred and action that is sufficiently pliable to describe almost anyone or anything that lies outside the views of the one (or ones) who incite such radical responses.

57. Abou El Fadl, *Place of Tolerance*, 3–23.

58. Jan, "Limits," 43.

59. Ibid., 44. By way of explanation, Jan later claims, "The first phase was launched in the early and mid-twentieth century, and the present state of virtual anarchy in the Muslim world is the direct result of that colonial aggression."

60. Ibid., 45.

61. Ibid. It is not the purpose of this paper to present and examine Jan's claims fully. Certainly, some culpability must be assigned to US (and other so-called Western) foreign policies for stirring resentment and frustration in various (not merely Muslim) religious and cultural communities around the world. But analysis of this Western colonial history goes beyond the scope of this book.

secularization, modernization, globalization, and religious plurality. For them, it is more important for Islam to be continually self-critical and constructive while seeking to solve these problems. For example, Malaysian Islamic activist Farish Noor does not ignore the ways Islam has been vilified and misrepresented by Western media, but he also admits "this mess is partly of our own making, [and] the question remains: how do we extricate ourselves from this impasse while maintaining our identity and right to speak about matters that are of pivotal concern for the Muslim community?"[62] For him, one of the solutions is to reject Marxist dialectic attitudes that demonize and depersonalize the other and gain energy and momentum through a process of defining the self against the enemy outside the gate. Only by first seeing and defining themselves *internally* can Muslims embrace the multiplicity within Islam. Thus, "Recognizing the multiplicity within [Islam] opens the way for [Muslims] to recognize the multiplicity of others as well."[63] Then Muslims can "step beyond the narrow communitarian concerns of [their] faith community and work with others to tackle these problems that affect humanity and its destiny."[64]

Taxonomical Problems of Classifying Muslim Responses to Religious Plurality

As in Christianity, categorizing fairly the many Islamic reactions to religious plurality is difficult. Presently, there is no agreed upon taxonomy among Muslims for classifying these Islamic responses.[65] For

---

62. Noor, "Victory," 322.

63. Ibid., 327.

64. Ibid., 331.

65. Many ways have been proposed, but not nearly as many that are specifically applied to Muslims and religious plurality. For a summary of the struggle to classify some of Islam's response to modernity and postmodernity, see Kurzman, "Liberal Islam," esp. 5ff, where he notes how such terms as "customary," "revivalist," and "liberal" have been variously applied to Islam's reactions to modernity. Kurzman chooses the term "liberal" for the Muslims he showcases in his book. Still, he admits this concept is too broad to demonstrate the breadth of differences among modern Muslims. Nor is it very specific with respect to the time frames involved, since some of the Muslims who are considered "liberal" date back to as early as the eighteenth century! In his own taxonomy (see ibid., 13–14) he breaks down liberal Islam into three major branches (what he calls "modes") of thought: "liberal," "silent," and "interpreted." The scope of

example, Omid Safi muses that the decision to adopt the term "progressive Muslims" for his book of compiled essays on justice, gender equality, and pluralism was difficult since "none of the alternatives was totally problem-free."[66] Terms such as "liberal" and "critical" were also considered and rejected. What compounds the taxonomical problem is that while much work has been done in Islam concerning their response to modernity,[67] not nearly as much work is devoted to the narrower arena of a theology of religions. Consequently, few have carefully thought through a distinctly Islamic classification of Muslim responses to religious plurality. Nevertheless, for clarity's sake, some system must be adopted to help sort through these various responses.

With many reservations and great reluctance, one of the previously discussed systems of classification in Christian theology will be broadly applied to three of these Islamic reactions under the headings of exclusivism, inclusivism, and pluralism.[68] A fourth category, the *sociopolitical response*, is more closely associated with secular and political concerns than religious ones. While Muslims in the previous three categories also care deeply about such issues, they tend to see religious aspects as more important than this fourth group. Due to the volume of materials produced by Muslims in this fourth category, it must be included, and will be examined first followed by the other three.

---

our current work prevents any real analysis of this taxonomical structure, but it bears mentioning to illustrate the complex nature of Islam's responses to the contemporary context and a growing awareness of religious and cultural diversity across the globe.

66. Safi, "Introduction," 17.

67. As Bennett (*Muslims and Modernity*, xv) points out, there is an "almost daily rate of publication of books and articles relevant to this enquiry" of Muslim responses to modernity.

68. This tripartite system is also used for Muslim responses to religious plurality by Goddard (*History*, 158–68). These were chosen because they do seem to apply broadly to the majority of Islamic responses. It can be argued that using categories originating in Christian theology is somewhat disingenuous to Islam. Yet, as I am using them, they are not strictly Christian in nature. I am also aware that many of the Muslim scholars mentioned below would consider themselves to be "pluralistic" since they are, to varying degrees, accepting of other religious views and practices. Still, as will become clearer below, according to these categories, *taxonomically and technically speaking*, being pluralistic in a broader sense does not mean one is a "pluralist." I offer this system not as a standard but as a proposal to be rigorously critiqued and modified by Muslims and others who wish more accurately to represent and describe the views that follow.

Sociopolitical

Since Islam often tightly integrates its faith with political concerns, it is perhaps artificial and somewhat unfair to place these Muslim thinkers into a separate and somewhat pseudo-secular category. However, in terms of emphasis and reliance upon solutions to plurality in general and religious plurality in particular, those I am calling "sociopolitical respondents" are clearly more concerned with sociological and political answers to these problems. For example, when discussing Khaled Abou El Fadl's treatment of tolerance in the Qur'an, Tariq Ali calls such activities "theological distractions" from the real issues involved. Ali openly states he "fundamentally disagree[s] with [Abou El Fadl's] emphasis on theological issues to explain the actions of people and societies."[69] Instead, he believes emphasis should be put upon political and sociological contexts that motivated Osama bin Laden and others to carry out (supposedly) religiously motivated attacks upon the US citizenry. As he puts it,

> The answer has very little to do with religion but a great deal to do with history and politics. Because the causes are political, not religious, the solution has to be political. We need to move beyond discussing whether or not the Qur'an promotes tolerance and grapple with the urgent social and political problems that affect the Muslim world.... The situation demands political solutions.... Theology in this regard is useless.[70]

Similarly, Akeel Bilgrami recognizes the need for elucidating Qur'anic notions of tolerance, but remarks that "the real issue [concerning Muslim militancy] is only secondarily about a doctrine and a book, and primarily about Muslims as a people and their political life..."[71] And Mashhood Rizvi adds that Abou El Fadl's project "diverts attention from the real issues," contending instead that "[t]he events of Islam had little to do with Islam."[72] For him, the real issues revolve around "international systems of oppression and injustice,"[73] rather than Islamic

---

69. Ali, "Distractions," 37.
70. Ibid., 38, 41.
71. Bilgrami, "Democracy," 65.
72. Rizvi, "Intolerable Injustices," 67.
73. Ibid., 69.

religious ideologies promoting intolerance of non-Muslims. As such, these Muslims are convinced the only viable solution is a sociopolitical one, and religious and theological concerns play only minor roles (if any) in the process of quelling Islamic militancy and intolerance towards non-Muslims.

Of course, international, national, and local politics and sociological movements certainly *do* influence theological interpretations of religious texts and traditions. As Sinasi Gündüz persuasively argues in "Hegemonic Power Versus *Tawhid*: A Decisive Concept of Islam on Interfaith Relations," often the sociopolitical climate of the culture has an enormous impact on religious movements and agendas.[74] And Abou El Fadl also admits, "In many ways, [Muslims such as the Taliban] are not the outgrowth of a religious process, as much as a reaction to external secular forces, such as colonialism or corporate capitalism."[75] However, because they claim "Islamic authenticity and legitimacy . . . , [one] reason for engaging in theological thinking is to deny such groups their Islamic banner and to challenge their claim to authenticity."[76] But even beyond this, "a just and good life is not possible without acknowledging the company and participation of God. Millions of human beings, justifiably in my opinion, acknowledge God as part of their moral and material universe. That is why theology matters."[77] Thus, there is a reciprocal relation between religion and politics, especially in more universally minded religions like Islam, where the two are often intimately associated with one another. The influence is not solely unidirectional, but the emphasis here is more upon the material and sociological side of human existence. In contrast, the following three responses to religious plurality emphasize the specifically religious aspects of Islamic viewpoints. The first response is the exclusivistic one.

Exclusivism

Here "exclusivism" pertains to those Muslims who refuse to grant salvific or epistemic legitimacy to other world religions. Virtually all

74. Gündüz, "Hegemonic Power," 123–34.
75. Abou El Fadl, "Reply," 104.
76. Ibid.
77. Ibid.

conservative and fundamentalist Muslims fall into this category. It is frequently on these bases that Muslim aggression is justified by militant groups such as al-Qaeda, Hamas, and the Taliban. Mansoor Moaddel and Kamran Talatoff have compiled an anthology of fundamentalist Muslim thinkers who are both intelligent and articulate in espousing their views concerning Islam and its relationship to other world religions.[78] Muslim Sayyid Qutb, for example, speaking about justification of *jihād*, says this:

> Islam is not the inheritance of any single nation or country. It is the religion of God and is for the whole world. It must have the right to shatter all those impediments that are found in the form of traditions and systems, and that fetter the freedom of choice of human beings. . . . As such it becomes obligatory for Islam to put an end to all such systems that serve as obstacles in the way of complete freedom of mankind. Religion can be established for God in all its fullness only in this way.[79]

Thus, for Qutb, *jihād* is not merely justified against immoral, non-Islamic systems of governance and belief, but is an "obligatory" aspect of being a true Muslim.[80]

Of course, such fundamentalist views are only one small portion of the Muslim community that falls into this broader exclusivistic category. In fact, the vast majority of Muslims are "not fundamentalists and do not have a dogmatic or uncontextualized and literal reading of their book."[81] Yet most Muslims would still consider Islam the one and only true religion for all, even if they would not advocate military means for removing all "impediments" and "obstacles" to the worldwide establishment of Islam.

---

78. Moaddel and Talatoff, *Contemporary Debates*.

79. Qutb, "Islamic Jihad," 244–45.

80. Qutb (ibid., 231) does state that once under an Islamic system, "there is the possibility of many . . . habitations, which may be loyal to the country's Islamic laws but . . . have not accepted Islam." But what is far less clear, especially when one surveys the past and present treatment of such protected religious minorities, is how that unconverted minority (or majority) will actually be treated as religious others by fundamentalist Muslim regimes. In fact, as will be seen in chapter 2 below, this has been a major point of discussion (and contention) throughout the interreligious dialogues of Muslims and Christians.

81. Bilgrami, "Democracy," 65.

Contemporary Muslim and Christian Responses to Religious Plurality

Perhaps a more moderate advocate of this viewpoint is Sinasi Gündüz. When addressing the question of absolute truth in religion and its relationship to inter-religious dialogue, he asks:

> Is the absolute truth claim of religions an obstacle for sound inter-religious relations based upon mutual trust and understanding? The pluralist approach thinks it is, but I disagree.... First of all, an absolute truth or salvation claim of a religion does not require one to see the other(s) as an enemy or to be disrespectful of the other(s).... [S]alvation or truth in a religious sense, is a relation between man and deity.... Religion, in other words, only shows what the way of salvation and reality is and how to achieve it, but the judgment and decision [concerning truth and salvation] belong to God.[82]

He goes on to observe that as religions gather around notions of absolute truth and exclusive salvation, they actually become "an expression of the cultural richness of humanity and of living together in variety and diversity..."[83] Structuring his discussion around the Islamic concept of *tawhīd*, "an expression of the unity and uniqueness of God in human life," it is clear that he wants to dialogue with alternative religious views, but he will not compromise his strong conviction that Islam is the only true religion of God.[84]

Admittedly, it is difficult to make these distinctions, primarily because most inclusivists also hold to the supremacy of Islam as the one true religion of God. Even many Muslim pluralists will ultimately argue Islam presents humanity with the best religion and prospect for creating a truly just and religiously plural society. This is to be expected. If there are no significant elements within a religious tradition to convince its members it is worthy of their complete devotion, why remain within that faith?[85] These reflections will be revisited later, but for now, a concise look at the inclusivistic response is in order.

82. Gündüz, "Hegemonic Power," 127–28.

83. Ibid., 128.

84. Ibid.

85. Grace Burford picks up on this theme and uses it against Christian participants in a recent interfaith dialogue between Christians and Buddhists. In "Buddha Is So Great" (131) she queries, "If they were so taken by Buddhism, why did they hang on to Christianity?" Obviously, there are good reasons why Christians remain Christians, Muslims remain Muslims, and Buddhists remain Buddhists. An important point of dialogue is to discover what these are and explore them together. But the point is well

Inclusivism

"Inclusivism" designates a view where other religions are considered salvifically legitimate, but technically only on the terms of the religious believer's own faith. To clarify, *Christian* inclusivists claim people of other religions can be "saved" by being devout members of their respective religions, but that, ultimately, salvation comes only on the basis of Jesus' salvific work—whether they realize it or not.

From a Muslim perspective, inclusivism is usually expressed in the Islamic terminology of ethical "submission" and "obedience" to the commandments of God. For example, Shabbir Akhtar, after an extended section surveying Muslim-Christian dialogue, laments that the current "deadlock" in this dialogue "is an especially intractable one that is likely to endure for a long time."[86] Observing what he calls "authentic religiosity" in other world faiths, Akhtar seeks to go beyond this dialogical impasse by proposing that there are only two options for Muslims: to deny or ignore this "undeniable" religiosity outside of Islam (a problem he sees for exclusivism), or to find some way of *including* the religious other within the Islamic religion. Akhtar seeks to do the latter by examining the Qur'anic terms for "Islam" and "religion" (or *deen*).[87] He argues that according to the Qur'an, "the religion [*deen*] of Islam," which at its core is "submission [*islam*] to the will of God," goes back to "the very beginning of history."[88] So, while there is a clear and obvious distinction between Islam as an institutional, organized, and historical religion beginning in the seventh century, there are other religions that are salvifically related to Islam (in its "orbit") insofar as their followers are genuinely submitted to God. This is true even if these other religions only express limited, corrupt, and "irregular forms of Allah's varied grace." Thus, in his estimation, "[The Qur'an] nowhere restricts salvation (or, rather, religious success) to Muslims in the narrower sense of those who endorse Muhammad's claim to prophethood. The only conditions for obtaining God's forgiveness seem to be belief

---

taken and a challenge to every religious person. Why am I a follower of this faith and not another?

86. Akhtar *All Seasons*, 197.

87. As is often the case with transliterated words, this term is variously spelled, so each respective author's spelling will be retained throughout this section.

88. Akhtar, *All Seasons*, 198.

in the unity of God and his judgment coupled with the intention to perform good deeds."[89] By making this distinction, Akhtar believes he preserves the Islamic claim to be the sole true religion, while allowing for religious others to enjoy the eternal rewards of living in paradise under God's ultimate sovereignty.

Two similar examples of this inclusive differentiation (which seem to point back to W. C. Smith's earlier treatment of the subject[90]) come from Mahmut Aydin and Adnan Aslan. Commenting on Q. 42:13 ("The same religion [*dīn*] has He established for you as that which He enjoined on Noah . . . , Abraham, Moses, and Jesus"), Aydin argues,

> [T]he *dīn* that is established in this verse is the oneness of God, submission to God's will, obeying the orders of God's prophets, believing the book that God revealed to the prophets, God's angels, and the Hereafter. Hence, those who believe in these things need to understand *islām* not as an established religion but as an activity that expresses the above meaning.[91]

Thus, "revelation, a sacred book, prophethood, sacred places, the religious community, and law (*sharī'ah*) are not religion per se but its concrete forms . . . [that are] bound to time and place."[92]

In defense of this kind of inclusive vision, Adnan Aslan claims that "exclusivism was not an official approach of Islam. It has always accepted the possibility of salvation outside its borders."[93] Thus, what matters in salvation "is not one's formal affiliation to a religion but [a] personal inner decision."[94] To clarify further, Aslan goes on to assert, "those people who are outside the Islamic Faith might possibly be saved if, firstly, they accomplish the ethical and religious requirements of their own traditions, and secondly, when the truth is revealed to their inner being, they do not deliberately and consciously cover up that truth."[95] To summarize, "According to the Qur'an, *islam* is not only a

---

89. Ibid., 199.

90. For example, Smith (*Meaning of Religion*, 110) differentiates between Islam as "the name of a religious system [and *islām*], the designation of a decisive act," namely, submitting to God.

91. Aydin, "Challenge," 338–39.

92. Ibid., 339.

93. Aslan, "Religious Pluralism," 179.

94. Ibid.

95. Ibid., 184. This second condition appears to express a somewhat more restric-

name given to a system of faith or religion but it is also a name of an act of surrendering to the will of God. Any thing which bows to God's will voluntarily or even involuntarily is qualified as muslim."[96]

Having surveyed this view, we now turn to the fourth and final Muslim response to religious plurality, namely the pluralistic response.

Pluralism

In some important ways, pluralism does not stand on its own because ultimately all attempts to be truly pluralistic suffer from the tendency to collapse into some form of inclusivism.[97] And inclusivisms tend to collapse into exclusivistic claims for themselves since they all, in one way or another, argue that they are the "best" and "truest" way to approach religious plurality. In that sense, they argue others should also "see it their way" and use their inclusively pluralistic vision to approach properly the challenges of religious plurality. What, then, are the Islamic pluralists' claims?

One of the most important theses for pluralists revolves around the proposal that all world religions are roughly equal in their epistemological validity and salvific efficacy. They are all essentially concretized and instantiated (phenomenal) human responses to the ineffable and eternal (noumenal) God or the *Real*. Exclusive claims to truth and salvation should be abandoned or, at the very least, severely curtailed, for they only succeed in exacerbating the interreligious tensions and problems so evident in today's world. The best and only real way to solve these tensions is to approach one another as equals. In this way (and this way alone) true dialogue and mutual cooperation can take place interreligiously.

---

tive inclusivism than Akhtar's, illustrating that there are a wide range of inclusivisms in Muslim thought.

96. Ibid., 176.

97. From an Islamic point of view, one critique of Islamic pluralism has been briefly provided by Gündüz in "Hegemonic Power," esp. 127, where he notes that because "every religious system presents its followers with an understanding of a unique reality and truth by which alone salvation is possible . . . the pluralistic approach is contrary to the understanding of religion itself . . . , weakens the ties between religion and believers, and hence, damages the individual's piety."

Contemporary Muslim and Christian Responses to Religious Plurality

We will look at just one representative Muslim pluralist, Mahmut Aydin.[98] A major complaint Aydin has against exclusivistic religious claims is that he believes they inevitably lead to aggressively imperialistic and condescending attitudes towards other religions. And such attitudes are used religiously to justify all sorts of atrocious acts against other religions and peoples.[99] Speaking against both exclusivism and inclusivism, he notes,

> [I]nstead of arguing that there is only one true and absolute religion, or widening the boundaries of an absolute religion in order to include the followers of other religions, religious pluralism emphasizes the equal validity of every religious traditions [sic] to bring their adherents to salvation. In other words . . . , there are many true or valid religious paths through which people can be acceptable to God.[100]

Advocating this "rough parity" of religions, Aydin then summarizes what he sees as nine major benefits to holding this pluralistic vision before the world.[101] Only in this pluralistic way of thinking and acting can religions avoid what he deems the "barbarous and self-indulgent abuses of . . . absolute truth claims."[102]

Conclusion

Each of the aforementioned responses to religious plurality tends to produce a variable amenability (or sometimes hostility) toward the idea

---

98. He has previously been categorized as an inclusivist. However, since some of his statements (especially recently) are not merely inclusive, but more pluralistic, he is also grouped here. Because he has been heavily influenced by Christian pluralists like Wilfred Cantwell Smith and John Hick, it is not surprising that his theology of religions has become more pluralistic over time.

99. Aydin, "Religious Pluralism," 89–95.

100. Ibid., 96.

101. Ibid. 98–99. It is not important to lay these out here since three major benefits—1) avoidance of aggression, 2) avoidance of arrogance in the name of religion, and 3) mutual learning and acceptance—aptly crystallize his nine reasons.

102. Ibid., 99. One is tempted to ask at this point whether Aydin's own rather dogmatic claims might be used to neutralize all traditional religious claims to truth. This highlights one of the immediate problems with any attempt to claim all religions are roughly equal. If "true," it is only true from the pluralistic perspective and not necessarily from the perspective of the religions themselves.

of genuine interreligious dialogue. The difficulty with any such survey is avoiding the insidious trap of overgeneralization. Although there are many Christians and Muslims writing about the issues surrounding religious plurality, we cannot comprehensively survey or critique them. Most important to notice is that religious plurality is pushing Muslims and Christians, along with other religious peoples, to respond thoughtfully and creatively to this reality.

One of the most promising recent developments in this regard is the rise of interest in and commitment to Christian-Muslim dialogue. Such dialogue has yielded many insights about how best to respond to religious plurality. It has also highlighted a number of impasses and problems between Christianity and Islam that will be helpful to examine in order to place a dialogue between Pannenberg and Sachedina in its proper historical context. It is to such an examination and survey we will now turn in chapter 2.

2

Contemporary Christian-Muslim Relations: A Brief Historical and Thematic Survey

Christian-Muslim encounter is not new. It began in the earliest days of Islam's emergence in the Arabian Peninsula. The Qur'an shows that while Muhammad "did not have very much first-hand encounters with Christians,"[1] he was aware of Arabian Christianity. A review of Christian-Muslim relations between that nascent period and the present era reveals conquest, domination, subjugation, integration, deterioration, and reinvigoration within both religions.[2] Growing awareness of religious others and recent international events have created a renewed concern for Christian-Muslim relations. In Charles Kimball's words, "[Because] Christians and Muslims today comprise well over 40% of the world population . . . Christian-Muslim relations have become a central concern in our interconnected world community. Without question, the ways in which Christians and Muslims understand and relate to one another in the 21st century will have profound consequences for both communities—and for the world."[3] Consequently, this chapter surveys

---

1. Goddard, *History*, 34.

2. A comprehensive survey of these encounters goes beyond the scope of this chapter, and several excellent historical summaries of Christian and Muslim relations have already been produced to fulfill this task. One of the best of these is the previously cited Goddard, *History*. It broadly traces the history of these interactions from the earliest days of Islam all the way through to the end of the twentieth/fourteenth century.

3. Kimball, "Toward a More Hopeful Future," 379.

the last few decades of Christian-Muslim dialogue. By exploring these interactions, we will see that, although progress has been made, this growth is still "somewhat vulnerable" to regression.[4] We will also see that new resources are still needed to move toward greater understanding and cooperation between these two faiths.

Due to growing interest in Christian-Muslim dialogue, the volume of material for consideration is simultaneously encouraging and overwhelming. Consequently, choices for inclusion and exclusion inevitably have been made. In addition, we will look mostly at formal aspects of this dialogue. However, the crucial role *informal* interfaith dialogue— what Pope John Paul II called "a rich dialogue of life" and is now called "life dialogue"—plays in communities and cultures worldwide should also be noted.[5] Interactions between people of different faiths in the homes, businesses, and streets of our world today constitute the most important practical resource for interreligious understanding, appreciation, and cooperation, since such friendships and alliances are what make tolerant societies possible. But they can also become sources of hatred, oppression, and strife. Religious beliefs are especially powerful resources for uniting or dividing people. As important as these life dialogues are, a critical need for more formal interfaith interactions remains.

Thankfully, this pursuit has become an intentional component of several important transnational institutions, especially the World Council of Churches (or WCC) and the Roman Catholic Church. In addition, an increasing number of Muslims and Christian evangelicals are showing greater interest in actively participating in interreligious dialogue. We will begin by surveying the evolution of the Christian stance towards Muslims in the twentieth century.

---

4. Goddard, *History*, 186.

5. Concerning this "rich dialogue of life," Pope John Paul II said this in Syria in 2001: "Interreligious dialogue is most effective when it springs from the experience of 'living with each other' from day to day within the same community and culture" (cited in Borelli, "Christian-Muslim Relations in the United States," 322).

Meeting Faith to Faith:
A Recent History of Muslim-Christian Encounters

Before the twentieth century, many Christians explored Christianity's relationship to other religions in general and Islam in particular, thus interfaith dialogue did not begin in the twentieth century.[6] Nevertheless, these interactions were not usually considered part of the mainstream of the church's activities. In the twentieth century interfaith dialogue began to be more important for Christian life and witness.

For our limited purposes, we begin in 1910 at the World Missionary Conference in Edinburgh. Although the prevailing attitude was that Christianity was superior to other religions, changing undercurrents suggested other world religions were preparatory for the Christian gospel and possessed valuable aspects of goodness and truth. Christianity began to be seen as the fulfillment and highest form of religion. Thus, Christian mission was increasingly seen as a call for other religions to be completed or fulfilled through conversion to Christianity.[7]

A second conference, held in Jerusalem in 1928, was profoundly impacted by the horrific events of World War I. Not surprisingly, there was less optimism about the great Western culture Christianity had produced, and far more concern about Christianity's appropriate relationship to other world religions. Although no consensus was achieved,

---

6. For an excellent historical survey of these explorations, see Kärkkäinen, *Introduction*, 55–108. See also Goddard, *History*, 149–50, where he mentions G. E. Lessing, Friedrich Schleiermacher, and Ernst Troeltsch as all having seriously wrestled with the question of Christianity's relationship to other religions, especially Islam and Judaism. Netland, in *Encountering*, 23–54, also provides an engaging history of the important changes that took place during the Christian missionary era in the nineteenth century as it encountered other religions. He notes, "Ironically, even while the modern missionary movement was enjoying unprecedented success . . . dramatic changes were occurring in Europe that were to alter forever the Christian community's understanding of itself and its mission in the world. The crucial assumption that God had revealed Himself uniquely in the Bible . . . was being eroded by higher critical views of Scripture and the conclusions of Darwinian science. The distinctiveness of Jesus Christ was being challenged by the developing discipline of the history of religions. Common prejudices . . . were being undermined through extensive contact with the impressive cultures of China, Japan, India and Latin America" (ibid., 32). As a result, the Christian community was ripe for considering new perspectives on other world religions.

7. For a helpful summary of the concerns and conclusions of this conference see Netland, *Encountering*, 38–39.

the conference revealed a growing rift "between the Continental thinking, which tended to be more conservative, and the American position, which tended to focus on the continuity between religions."[8]

Ten years later in 1938 at Tambaram, Madras (India), the International Missionary Council (IMC) discussed Christianity's relationship to other religions. In preparation for the conference, long-time Dutch missionary to Java, Hendrick Kraemer, was commissioned to write what he called "the fundamental position of the Christian church" concerning the "attitude to be taken by Christians toward other faiths."[9] Astonishingly, the 450-page volume took only seven weeks to write and set off an immediate firestorm of controversy among conferees. Kraemer was responding to the growing popularity of the notion that while Christianity still represented the highest fulfillment of God's revelation, other world religions possessed significant goodness and commonality with Christian revelation and should be appreciated as such.[10] In contrast, Kraemer argued that while other religions possessed admirable aspects, they were hardly unfulfilled manifestations of the full flower of revelation within Christianity. Rather, crucial discontinuities highlighted the central importance of Christian mission to evangelize non-Christians. For example, concerning Islam Kraemer wrote,

> Islam . . . must be called a superficial religion. The grand simplicity of its conception of God cannot efface this fact and retrieve its patent superficiality in regard to the most essential problems of religious life. Islam might be called a religion that has almost no questions and no answers. In a certain respect its greatness lies there, because this . . . is a consistent exemplification of its deepest spirit, expressed in its name: Islam, that is, the absolute surrender to God, the Almighty.[11]

Kraemer goes on to call Islam "an unoriginal religion" with the peculiar ability to excel "all other religions in creating in its adherents a feeling of absolute religious superiority" that produces a "stubborn

---

8. Kärkkäinen, *Introduction*, 154.

9. Kraemer, *Christian Message*, v.

10. Kraemer was responding to William Ernest Hocking's *Rethinking Missions*, which was sympathetic to the fulfillment model made popular in the early twentieth century by John Nicol Farquhar's *Crown of Hinduism*.

11. Kraemer, *Christian Message*, 216–17.

refusal to open the mind towards another spiritual world."[12] Ultimately, "surrender to Allah, the fundamental religious attitude in Islam, has that same quality of absolute ruthlessness."[13] While Kramer apparently went on to moderate his views of Islam as he grew older,[14] the tone of this work was clear enough: Islam is unoriginal, superficial, close-minded, and ruthless. More generally, "Kraemer . . . saw other religions as human creations and in contradiction to God's revelation."[15] Obviously, this did not do much to foster interreligious dialogue between Muslims and Christians.

Despite the negative assessment of other world religions at Tambaram, the IMC would eventually play a crucial role in promoting interfaith dialogue in the latter half of the twentieth century. Just ten years later, in 1948, the World Council of Churches (WCC) was formed in Amsterdam, and nine years after that the IMC was integrated into the WCC, becoming the Commission on World Mission and Evangelism (CWME).[16] This provided a significant catalyst for Muslim-Christian dialogue.

The World Council of Churches

To organize the growing ecumenical spirit within Christianity, the WCC was formed. From the beginning, the WCC demonstrated openness toward the value and significance of other world religions, although not without controversy. They agreed upon initiatives to pursue a greater understanding of Christianity's role and relationship among other world religions. These eventually provided a more favorable atmosphere for conversations that formally emerged in the late 1960s and early 1970s.

These initiatives included the 1955 launch of an ongoing WCC-commissioned study entitled "The Word of God and the Living Faiths

---

12. Ibid., 220.

13. Ibid., 221.

14. See Race, *Religious Pluralism*, 14–16 and 23–24. See also Plantinga, *Christianity and Plurality*, 245–66, where later statements made by Kraemer mollify the harsh tone of this earlier work.

15. Sperber, *Christians and Muslims*, 7.

16. Kärkkäinen, *Introduction*, 155.

of Men," which explored new possibilities concerning Christianity's relationship to other world religions. There was a growing desire, especially at the CWME's Mexico City meeting in 1963, to move beyond Tambaram's negativism and promote dialogue as an important aspect of missions.[17] Eventually, at the 1971 meeting of the WCC Central Committee in Addis Ababa,

> The decision was taken to establish a separate sub-unit on dialogue with people of other faiths and ideologies [DFI]. This implied—after some hesitation—the structural recognition and greater importance of inter-religious dialogue and a formal separation from the sub-unit on mission which had carried the responsibility for most dialogues up to that point. In view of the scepticism of the partners in dialogue about whether dialogue might not be a new missionary advance, this was certainly a move to create confidence.[18]

Even before the creation of the sub-unit on dialogue (DFI), the WCC was actively fostering interreligious conversations, especially between Christians and Muslims. For example, in late January 1968, under the banner of the WCC, Protestant, Catholic, and Orthodox students of Islamic studies met with a group of Muslims at Selly Oak Colleges in Great Britain to discuss topics surrounding Christian-Muslim dialogue.[19]

The DFI organized two major international Christian-Muslim dialogues, the first in 1972 at Broumana, Lebanon, and the second in 1982 at Colombo, Sri Lanka. At Broumana, twenty-four Christians and twenty-two Muslims met to discuss "The Quest for Human Understanding and Cooperation: Christian and Muslim Contributions." It was intended to discuss ways Christians and Muslims could work together to tackle international problems. Not surprisingly, the issue of Palestine and the Middle East was raised, but so also were concerns over certain theological concepts like the nature of revelation and the doctrine of the Trinity. Nothing was resolved other than a mutual agreement that better Christian-Muslim relations were needed.[20]

17. Sperber, *Christians and Muslims*, 8–9.
18. Ibid., 251.
19. Much more could be said. For an outline summary of attempts to dialogue during the early years until 1975, see ibid., 25–31.
20. Ibid., 28, 92, 94.

Contemporary Christian-Muslim Relations

At the 1982 meeting entitled "Christians and Muslims Living Together: Ethics and Realities of Humanitarian and Development Programs," similar issues were raised and discussed. Overall, these meetings recognized the need for better relations but usually raised more questions and problems than answers and solutions. Ultimately, the majority of Christian-Muslim dialogues were regionally and locally sponsored and arranged. The reasons for this lack of larger international conferences are not entirely clear, but pragmatic issues like logistics and financial constraints played larger roles than interfaith conflicts.[21] These local conferences addressed many of the same questions and disagreements, often reflecting the particular contexts and settings in which the dialogues took place.[22]

These dialogues and attempts to foster Christian-Muslim cooperation were far from successful. A consistent set of themes and problems were raised and discussed, but little was achieved in terms of concrete initiatives for greater interfaith cooperation. In the synoptic words of Ovey Mohammed, "For the most part . . . , the meetings reflected the reality of conflict. . . . In essence, the Protestants wanted to address the issue of collaboration without conceding that Islam is a way of salvation. The Muslims argued that the Christian acknowledgement of Islam as a way of salvation is the only firm foundation for dialogue and collaboration. The DFI was not prepared to build the future of the Muslim-Christian relationship on such a foundation."[23]

21. Sperber (ibid., 74) suggests that the reason was primarily, if not solely, *financial*.

22. Major WCC-sponsored local dialogues were held in Cartigny (1969), Hong Kong (1975), Chambésy (1976, 1979), Beirut (1977), Bossey (1980), Porto Novo (1986), Geneva (for several consecutive years—starting in 1986—of consultative work with Christians and Muslims present), Dhyana Pura (1986), Kolymbari (1987), New Windsor (USA, 1988), Usa River/Arusha (1989), Canberra (1991), Glion (a trialogue with Jews as well as Muslims, 1993), Nyon (1993), Berlin (1994), and Hartford (Hartford Seminary, USA, 1999, 2003). For an outline summary of these dialogues, see ibid., 7–50.

23. Mohammed, *Muslim-Christian Relations*, 76–77. This negative assessment provides the (Catholic) author with a bridge to what he considers the more fruitful and positive experiences of dialogue between Islam and Roman Catholics flowing out of Vatican II. I would still suggest that the WCC's attempts to promote dialogue were a qualified success, even if little was resolved or tangibly accomplished—even within the WCC. As Kärkkäinen (*Introduction*, 151) points out, "Currently, there is sharp disagreement among the members of the WCC over how best to relate to other religions." Still, that these conversations were taking place at all was a huge step forward for Muslim-Christian dialogue.

While many of these WCC activities were occurring, historic and largely parallel changes were happening within the Roman Catholic Church, especially beginning in the period of the early-to-mid 1960s when the Second Vatican Council took place.[24] Additional changes in Roman Catholicism's attitude towards other religions in general and Islam in particular soon followed. We will now examine this remarkable period in Roman Catholic history.

Roman Catholicism

Given its sometimes bitter and troubled history of encounter with Islam, it may seem initially odd to centerpiece Roman Catholicism as critically important for the dramatic rise in Christian-Muslim dialogue in the latter part of the twentieth century. However, decisions made at Vatican II (1962–65) created more favorable attitudes toward interfaith interactions between Catholics and Muslims in the subsequent period.[25] In addition to the proceedings of the council, in 1964 Pope Paul VI established the Secretariat for Non-Christians and published the important encyclical *Ecclesiam Suam* ("His Church"), which discussed the importance of interfaith dialogue with non-Christians.[26] The decisions made at Vatican II are laid out in several documents produced by that

24. The exact relationship between the decisions of Vatican II and WCC as well as Protestantism's increasing openness to interfaith dialogue in general and Christian-Muslim dialogue in particular is complex. External sociological and ideological factors heavily influenced the movement of these Christian communities in the direction of amenable stances toward other religions. For a look at some of these, see Netland, *Encountering*, chs. 1 and 2.

25. Kärkkäinen (*Introduction*, 113–140) suggests doors opened earlier in Catholicism to the possibility of salvation being available to those outside the church through a 1943 papal encyclical entitled *Mystici Corpus* ("The Mystical Body"). Here Pius XII affirms only true Catholics are saved, but he seems to leave open to question the salvific status of those who desire salvation but have no access to the gospel. In the document he implies people with "a certain unconscious desire and longing" can be "ordained to the mystical Body of the Redeemer" but still not enjoy the full gifts and benefits that accrue to those who are active and overt members of the Holy Roman Catholic Church. In this respect, there is still *extra ecclesiam nulla salus* ("outside the church no salvation") but there may be those who are members of the church, "the mystical Body of the Redeemer," who either do not know it or have no means to affirm it expressly due to their contextual situation. For a closer look at this encyclical and its possible implications, see Sullivan, *Salvation outside the Church?*, esp. 133ff.

26. Dupuis, *Theology of Religious Pluralism*, 159–60.

landmark council. Of interest to this study are *Nostra Aetate* (NA), *Ad Gentes* (AG), *Gaudium et Spes* (GS), and *Lumen Gentium* (LG).[27] It is to these documents we now turn.

At the council, one of the most important changes concerned the church's relationship to the world. LG 8 revises an earlier understanding that seems to equate the church of Christ with the Roman Catholic Church alone. Instead of the older statement, "The Church of Christ *is* the Roman Catholic Church," it states, "The Church of Christ *subsists in* the Roman Catholic Church."[28] Thus, Catholicism's centrality is maintained, but others might be "related" to the Catholic Church even if not visibly members of it. This momentous change suggests there could be religious believers "who, through no fault of their own," did not hear about the fullness of grace found in Jesus and the fullness of religious life found in Roman Catholicism, but who nevertheless "are related to the church in various ways."[29]

Similarly, AG 9 states the purpose of missionary activity is to free adherents of other religions "from all taint of evil," restoring people to Christ. Thus, "Whatever good is found to be sown in the hearts of men, or in the rites and cultures peculiar to various peoples, is not lost. More than that, it is healed, ennobled, and perfected for the glory of God, the shame of the demon, and the bliss of men." There is a positive but tempered attitude toward aspects of other religions.

Concerning religious others, NA 2 states, "the church rejects nothing of what is true and holy in these religions," and affirms they "reflect a ray of Truth which enlightens all human beings."[30] Nevertheless, the document insists Christians must proclaim Jesus Christ as "the way, the

---

27. Flannery, *Documents*. The English titles are as follows: *Nostra Aetate*: "Declaration on the Relationship of the Church to Non-Christian Religions"; *Ad Gentes*: "Decree on the Church's Missionary Activity"; *Gaudium et Spes*: "Pastoral Constitution one the Church in the Modern World"; and *Lumen Gentium*: "The Dogmatic Constitution on the Church." All future references will use abbreviations of their Latin names.

28. Kärkkäinen, *Introduction*, 113; emphasis added.

29. These quotes come from LG 16.

30. Originally planned to address the question of Christianity's relationship to Judaism, according to Kärkkäinen (*Introduction*, 114) at the council there were "bishops from areas of the world [who] found themselves struggling with challenges from other religions," and so "it was decided that the scope of [NA] should be significantly enlarged" to accommodate and respond to this religious plurality.

truth, the life" because only in him can "human beings find the fullness of religious life" and through him alone "God has reconciled all things to himself."

GS 16 speaks about the Spirit's work and relationship to the cross and resurrection of Jesus, stating, "Since Christ died for all men, and since the ultimate vocation of man is in fact one, and divine, we ought to believe that the Holy Spirit in a manner known only to God offers to every man the possibility of being associated with this Paschal Mystery." This idea of being "associated" to Jesus through the Spirit's work becomes critical to understanding the exact relationship of other religions to the grace of Christ.

Thus, there is an attempt to affirm the traditional Roman Catholic position, preserving its role in salvation as well as Christ's supremacy, while still leaving space for God to be salvifically and revelationally at work through the Spirit in other religions. This point has been vigorously debated in the post-Vatican II period.

With regard to Islam, the council stated in 1965:

> The Church also regards with esteem the Muslims who worship the one, subsistent, merciful and almighty God, the Creator of heaven and earth, who has spoken to man. Islam willingly traces its descendents back to Abraham, and just as he submitted himself to God, the Muslims endeavour to submit themselves to his mysterious decrees. They venerate Jesus as prophet, without, however, recognising him as God. . . . Further, they expect a day of judgment when God will raise all men from the dead and reward them. For this reason, they attach importance to the moral life and worship God, mainly by prayer, alms-giving and fasting.
>
> If in the course of the centuries there has arisen not infrequent discussion and hostility between Christian and Muslim, this sacred Council now urges everyone to forget the past, to make sincere efforts at mutual understanding and to work together in protecting and promoting for the good and benefit of all men, social justice, good morals as well as peace and freedom.[31]

---

31. Cited in Goddard, *History*, 153. Borelli ("Christian-Muslim Relations," 322) points out that the phrase in this paragraph urging Muslims and Christians to "forget the past" was probably better understood by Pope John Paul II in his address in Syria in 2001 when he said, "For all the times that Muslims and Christians have offended one another, we need to seek forgiveness from the Almighty and offer each other forgiveness."

Ultimately, more positive attitudes in Roman Catholicism toward people of other faiths emerged. This had profound implications for other Christian denominations, opening the door to a radical new understanding of non-Christian world religions like Islam. Most post-Vatican II Catholics interpret these documents as explicitly granting salvific and revelatory value to other world religions. For example, Jacques Dupuis says concerning Vatican II, "The possibility of salvation outside the Church has been recognized by the Church long before Vatican II. . . . What in previous Church documents was affirmed . . . as a *possibility* based upon God's infinite mercy . . . is being taught by the council with unprecedented assurance."[32] In contrast, Gavin D'Costa, after an extended discussion of the documents, persuasively argues, "It is difficult to read the Conciliar documents as giving a positive answer to the question: can other religions, *per se*, in their structures be mediators of supernatural revelation and salvific grace? While it is true that there is no explicit negative answer, there is certainly no positive answer."[33] He believes this silence is probably "intentional" so the Church could uphold what is good in other religions while not necessarily affirming that they are also salvifically legitimate. He proceeds to note that even the very inclusive Rahner with his concept of the "anonymous Christian" admits these documents leave the question unanswered.[34]

Despite this debate, the majority of post-conciliar Catholics take an inclusive and even increasingly pluralistic view of other religions. In the words of Harold Netland, "Vatican II . . . clearly opened the door to a much more positive way of looking at other religions."[35] Due to numerous parallel and relatively proximal religious beliefs, the Christian desire to dialogue with Muslims after Vatican II became especially evident. We will now turn to this post-Vatican II period.[36]

---

32. Dupuis, *Theology of Religious Pluralism*, 161. As a sidebar, Dupuis' claim that the Catholic Church recognized the "possibility of salvation outside the Church . . . long before Vatican II" is far from established.

33. D'Costa, *Religions and the Trinity*, 105.

34. Ibid. For Karl Rahner's views, see "Importance of the Non-Christian Religions for Salvation," esp. 290–91.

35. Netland, *Encountering*, 44.

36. Because the section that follows is brief, for a further summary of post-Vatican II dialogues with a slightly different set of emphases see Sperber, *Christians and Muslims*, 299–315.

One effect flowing from Vatican II came from Pope Paul VI in 1975. Concerned the Catholic Church's passion for Christ-centered outreach was waning, he wrote *Euangelii Nuntiandi*, stating that evangelism is "incumbent by the command of the Lord Jesus, so that people can believe and be saved. This message is indeed necessary. It is unique. It cannot be replaced. It does not permit either indifference, syncretism or accommodation."[37]

Despite this document, the move towards interfaith dialogue and away from evangelistic outreach continued with the non-binding but important "Venice Statement" in 1977. This rejects "any action aimed at changing the religious faith of the Jews."[38] While not an official Catholic document, it marked "the first time that the Catholic Church abdicated any right to evangelization among a given group."[39] Nevertheless, it reaffirms "the Christian's right to proclaim the gospel and to seek the conversion of others" so long as it is done without coercion, and tries to strike "a balance between mission and dialogue" by affirming the active grace of God and the ongoing activity of the Spirit in the conscience of every person.[40] Thus, dialogue is an opportunity to see God at work in those of other faiths.

Perhaps one of the most significant Catholic documents produced after Vatican II is *Redemptoris Missio*, released by Pope John Paul II in 1990. In it he tries to clarify the fine line between affirming God's salvific activity (especially with respect to the Spirit) within other religions and the centrality of proclaiming the gospel to all. Promoting an inclusivistic concept of salvation, John Paul II affirms salvation is obtainable by those of other faiths, but ultimately, the fullness of salvation is found only and supremely in Jesus Christ. As Kärkkäinen summarizes, according to this document, "followers of other religions can find salvation, but such salvation is found finally and fully in Christ and his church. Dialogue is nevertheless commended by the pope as 'part of the Church's evangelizing mission.'"[41] Dialogue now becomes part of the Church's evangelistic mission, and this dialogue includes a search

---

37. *Euangelii Nuntiandi* 5, cited in Kärkkäinen, *Introduction*, 119.
38. Cited in Kärkkäinen, *Introduction*, 119.
39. Ibid.
40. Ibid., 119–20.
41. Ibid., 120.

for and recognition of the ways God's Spirit is working in the lives and claims of religious others.[42]

John Paul II was especially positive toward Islam, proclaiming openly to Muslims in 1985, "[Y]our God and ours is one and the same and we are brothers and sisters in the faith of Abraham."[43] He was also the first pope to visit a Mosque (in Damascus in 2000) and is credited by many to have upheld fundamental Catholic dogmas while still maintaining positive attitudes and having constructive dialogues with Muslims.

The overall result has been increasingly positive and open-ended dialogues between Muslims and Catholics. Still, recent leadership changes at the Vatican make it unclear where the current pope, Benedict XVI, stands on the value of ongoing Christian-Muslim dialogues. For example, speaking in Regensburg, Germany, on September 25, 2006, he used the following rather inflammatory quote from the fourteenth-century Byzantine Emperor Manuel II: "Show me just what Mohammed brought that was new, and there you will find things only evil and inhuman, such as his command to spread by the sword the faith he preached."[44] Understandably, this set off a firestorm of protest from Muslims and Christians, including Sachedina, who commented, "Pope Benedict's speech has done irreparable damage to Christian-Muslim relations. No amount of apology can undo the harm the irresponsible comments about Islam and its founder have done to the prospects of dialogue between these two Abrahamic traditions."[45] Later in the same post he says, "The world community needs interfaith dialogue today. But if religious leaders themselves demonstrate disrespect for other faith communities and stoop to insult their faith and reason, then it is doubtful there can ever be a dialogue between faith-communities. A precondition in a dialogue is equal respect to all parties in dialogue.

---

42. Besides *Redemptoris Missio*, several other Catholic publications have further clarified the relationship between mission, proclamation, and dialogue, but they all echo a similar theme, namely that proclaiming Christ's supremacy and interfaith dialogue are not mutually exclusive but constitute parts of a broader responsibility the church has to the world. For a survey of some of these documents, see ibid., 120–22.

43. Pope John Paul II's address to Muslims at a symposium on "Holiness in Christianity and Islam" in Rome, May 9, 1985, cited in Jukko, *Trinitarian Theology*, 95.

44. Benedict XVI, Regensburg Address. See the bibliography for the official English translation of the speech.

45. Sachedina, "Pluralism's 'Live and Let Live.'"

The moment one party assumes a moral high position it changes the dialogue to a monologue."[46]

To be fair, Benedict XVI's speech in its fuller context was more ecumenical, quoting from the Qur'an that "There is no compulsion in religion," and making the distinction between violent and non-violent forms of religious faith and practice. As papal spokesman Frederico Lombardi argued, the pope's primary intention in the speech was to promote "a clear and radical rejection of the religious motivation for violence."[47] Yet it lacked an irenic and affirming tone toward other world religions, especially Islam, for which Pope John Paul II was often recognized. Benedict XVI was quick to respond to the outcry with a number of conciliatory gestures, but many feared the damage was already done to the fragile bond wrought by decades of Christian-Muslim dialogue.

One positive development was an open letter written by a group of thirty-eight Muslim scholars inviting dialogue with Christians on the issues raised by this speech.[48] In *Christianity Today*, Woodberry summarizes the open letter's main points and then shares a distinctly evangelical perspective on Christian-Muslim dialogue, noting that "Meaningful dialogue does not require that the participants relinquish a witness concerning their faith. Nor does it mean we can't disagree about how they understand their history and faith. But it does require that we listen and learn what they really think. These 38 Muslim leaders have given us an extraordinary opportunity to do just that."[49] It still remains to be seen what long-term impact such papal comments will have upon Christian-Muslim dialogue. The ultimate hope is they will provide a springboard for future interfaith conversations. Encouragingly, in October 2007 another document responding to Benedict XVI's speech was written by Muslims to Christians, called "A Common Word between Us and You." It was signed by 138 Muslim authorities from 41 different nations and called for further dialogue together. In response to this document, in November 2007 Yale's Center for Faith and Culture (led by Miroslav Volf) produced a full-page add signed by a wide spectrum of Christians, entitled "Loving God and Neighbor Together: A

---

46. Ibid.
47. Cited in Meacham, "A Pope's Holy War."
48. See Ahmed et al., "Open Letter to Pope Benedict XVI."
49. Woodberry, "Can We Dialogue with Islam?," 109.

Christian Response to A Common Word Between Us and You," which sought to affirm points of common ground along with a mutual desire to dialogue with Muslims.[50] Since this latter work is written from an evangelical perspective, we will now survey some recent evangelical interactions with Islam.[51]

Evangelicalism[52]

Until recently, evangelicals remained largely uninvolved in interfaith dialogues. Not surprisingly, since Kraemer was perceived to be a paradigmatic representative of evangelical Christianity concerning Islam, formal discussions with Muslims were uncommon. Another reason for this absence was because, early on, usually only inclusivists and pluralists (using the older taxonomical system) were invited to the conversation. Since evangelicals were considered exclusivistic, the idea that they would care about, benefit from, and be beneficial to interfaith dialogue was not seriously entertained. Nevertheless, the evangelical scene is by no means monolithic. There is a broad spectrum of attitudes regarding other religions, especially Islam and Judaism, given their close relationship to Christianity. In fact, some evangelicals can now be classified as more christocentric and inclusive rather than ecclesiocentric and exclusive.[53] In addition, an increasing number of evangelical works have been produced on this subject, some of which we will now consider.

But before turning to particular evangelicals who are discussing dialogue between Christians and Muslims, two works exploring Christianity's relationship to other world religions will be noted, begin-

---

50. For the text of these two documents, see http://www.acommonword.com.

51. For a look at other (non-evangelical) leading Protestant and Orthodox dialogue partners over this period, like Anglican Bishop Kenneth Cragg, Orthodox Metropolitan Georges Khodr, and Protestant missionary and professor Wilfred Cantwell Smith, not covered here, see Goddard, *History*, 155–58.

52. Since "evangelical" and "evangelicalism" are not always clearly defined, see McDermott, *Can Evangelicals Learn?*, 21–39, for an examination of this issue along with an attempt to lay out some boundary markers.

53. Unfortunately, apart from what is covered below, it goes beyond the scope of this chapter to give a comprehensive survey of all types of evangelicals now active in Christian-Muslim dialogue.

ning with Gerald R. McDermott's *Can Evangelicals Learn from World Religions?* He argues,

> When evangelicals have considered the world religions, for the most part they have focused on the questions of truth (do all the religions teach the same essential truths? is truth propositional or ineffable?) and salvation (can non-Christians be saved?), not revelation (is there divine revelation in the religions?). Evangelicals' concern for revelation has extended only to the point at which it affects the question of salvation.[54]

Thus, McDermott's purpose is not to tackle salvific questions concerning other religions, but to provide a biblical and theological basis for expecting to find divine truths in them. If God reveals truth in other religions like Islam, those seeking to know God's comprehensive truth would want to search out opportunities for conversations with religious others to discover and embrace such divinely-given truths.

McDermott begins by surveying places in the Old Testament where God reveals himself to those outside chosen Israel. These show "the notion of God's people learning about God from those outside their traditions (in ways which help them better understand their own revelation) is not a phenomenon foreign to the Bible."[55] He then examines theological considerations for such a possibility. Of particular importance is the ongoing revelatory work of God's Spirit. Following D'Costa and others, McDermott observes that the Spirit's work cannot be detached from distinctly trinitarian theology, since

> Christ is the unique revelation of God. But the Holy Spirit is ever at work, as He was in the history of Israel before Jesus, to give understanding of the God Who was to send the Messiah and then give understanding of the Messiah Himself. He continues to give the church insight into the meaning of the Messiah—and some of those insights may come from reflection upon what the Spirit is doing in and with people outside Israel and the Christian church.[56]

Using this framework, McDermott develops Jonathan Edwards' concept of "types" to claim, "God planted types of true religion even in religious

---

54. McDermott, *Can Evangelicals Learn?*, 39.
55. Ibid., 90.
56. Ibid., 95.

systems that were finally false."⁵⁷ The example McDermott highlights is human sacrifice. It mimics God-instituted animal sacrifice, but even more, it points toward how "God outflanked the devil" by preparing "the Gentile world for receiving . . . this human sacrifice, Jesus Christ."⁵⁸

In short, "If there are types of true religion in the midst of religions that contain falsehood, and if these types are divinely implanted, then there is revelation from God even in the midst of religious error."⁵⁹ It may be "shadowy" and "incomplete" but it remains truth from God. Consequently, certain religions may contain "revealed types" of revelation that are neither general revelation (available to all human beings) nor special revelation (by which salvation through Jesus Christ is made known). They are particular to a religious community or practitioner and are similar to "little lights" and "scattered promises" given by the triune God.⁶⁰

While it is not fully clear why God provides extra-biblical, non-general revelation, McDermott shares several possible reasons for this non-salvific revelation. Perhaps God intends such truths to prepare adherents of other religions to be more receptive to the gospel once it is preached.⁶¹ They may also enhance the quality of life for those em-

57. Ibid., 106.
58. Ibid., 107.
59. Ibid.
60. Ibid., 114.
61. Ibid., 115. While pluralists usually say such revelation is *sufficient* for salvation, more ecclesiocentric evangelicals tend to see such truth as *preparatory* for the gospel, but still *insufficient* to save the religious other apart from some sort of additional special revelation. For a survey of something similar to the presence of this phenomenon of preparatory typological revelation for the gospel in recent missiological history, see Richardson, *Eternity in Their Hearts*, esp. 9–150. See also Richardson's *Peace Child* and *Lords of the Earth* for two extended concrete examples of these kinds of divinely inspired preparatory myths and typologies present within two culturally and religiously isolated people groups. Richardson calls these revelatory types "redemptive analogies," claiming they are planted by God in virtually every people group primarily as a means of preparing them to receive the gospel of Jesus Christ. Ironically, in his more recent and somewhat inflammatory *Secrets of the Koran*, 18, Richardson openly argues Islam is the only major world religion that lacks these kinds of divine redemptive analogies, saying that "Islam is unique among non-Christian religions. It stands alone as the only belief system that, due to its very design, *frustrates* anyone who seeks to use the redemptive analogy approach." I am not sure why he believes this since in my own study of Islam, there are many ways in which Muslim beliefs and practices serve as a prolegomena to Christian faith, as well as lead to a deeper faith in the one true God.

bracing them, even if they are not salvifically sufficient. Thus, they are expressions of God's goodness and love for humanity.[62] For Christians, typological truths can help them "restate more effectively [their] own Christian faith," and can "remind Christians of the best of their faith and help them sharpen their thinking about those truths."[63] These kinds of revelatory deposits might even illuminate Christian truths that Christians were not fully aware of. Ultimately, the practices and practitioners of other religions "can be used by the Spirit to induce repentance and awareness of God's judgment."[64]

McDermott applies this information in dialogue with several other religions including Islam. His conversation highlights five important ways he believes Islam reflects God's truth: 1) submission to God, 2) creation as a theatre of God's glory, 3) regular and theocentric prayer, 4) charity to the poor, and 5) faith and the public square, highlighting the importance of religious faith informing the civic arena of law-making and public policy.[65]

What is particularly refreshing about this thesis is the way it encourages interaction with religious others by expecting to find God's truth. In addition, it does not assume only error is present beforehand. Lastly, the salvific value of such truth can be reserved for future consideration without negating the affirmation of its presence and significance within other religions.

Another thinker in an evangelical theology of religions is Clark Pinnock.[66] While Kärkkäinen classifies him as "christocentric,"[67] one could also describe Pinnock as "pneumatocentric" or "Spirit-centric,"

---

62. McDermott, *Can Evangelicals Learn?*, 115. According to McDermott, this divine grace does not negate "demonic and destructive elements in the religions," but shows "in the midst of error there is truth that enlightens and helps."

63. Ibid., 116.

64. Ibid., 118. For an expanded answer to the question of why God provides these typological revelations in other world religions, see McDermott, *God's Rivals*.

65. McDermott, *Can Evangelicals Learn?*, 194–202.

66. Along similar lines, Pentecostal theologian Amos Yong also explores the role of God's Spirit in the religions of the world in *Discerning the Spirit(s)* and *Beyond the Impasse*, and so deserves mention, although his views will not be addressed further here. For a brief but helpful summary of Yong's perspectives on the Spirit, see Kärkkäinen, *Introduction*, 277–81.

67. Kärkkäinen, *Introduction*, 269–76.

for his recent work emphasizes the universal activity of God's Spirit in the lives of all peoples and communities.[68]

Pinnock lays out his pneumatological theology in *Flame of Love*. He encourages evangelicals to consider the possibility that God's Spirit is actively working within other religions. Pinnock admits his theology of religions is primarily motivated by an understanding of God as merciful and inclusive.[69] Thus, for him, the Spirit is "guiding, luring, wooing, influencing, drawing all humanity," not merely Christians.[70] The life-giving operations of the Spirit are cosmic and inclusive in scope, providing new ways to see God's work in all religions. Pinnock expands this by claiming,

> If the Spirit gives life to creation and offers grace to every creature, one would expect him to be present and make himself felt (at least occasionally) in the religious dimension of cultural life. Why would the Spirit be working everywhere else but not here? God is reaching out to all nations and does not leave himself without witness (Acts 14:17). Would this witness not crop up sometimes in the religious realm?[71]

Thus, Christian interfaith dialogue and mission is not merely for conversion, but for bringing a fuller understanding of Christ's gospel, which is already active through the Spirit in the religious sensibility of all human beings. As people respond positively to the Spirit's movement, they are drawn into relationship with God through what Pinnock calls the "faith principle."[72] Jesus remains the particular basis of God's saving work in humanity, but the Spirit applies his work more broadly in the life (and possibly death) of religious others.[73] In short, "Christ,

---

68. The term "pneumatocentric" comes from the Greek word for Spirit, "*pneuma.*" Pinnock may also be classified under older taxonomical system as a more "inclusive" evangelical.

69. An earlier work by Pinnock that deals more specifically with the issue of salvation and other religions is *Wideness in God's Mercy*.

70. Pinnock, *Flame of Love*, 216.

71. Ibid., 200–201.

72. Pinnock, *Wideness in God's Mercy*, 157–58.

73. I mention "death" here because Pinnock explores (unconvincingly in my estimation) what he sees as a strong possibility for all to receive a "second chance" to accept Christ after death. Concerning this, in ibid., 169, he argues, "Although the scriptural evidence for postmortem encounter [with Christ] is not abundant, its scantiness is relativized by the strength of the theological argument for it."

the only mediator, sustains particularity, while the Spirit, the presence of God everywhere, safeguards universality."[74]

Pinnock's work is valuable because it provides new ways to recognize God's active presence in other religions using a distinctly trinitarian framework.[75] Christological impasses, so prominent in evangelical theologies of religions, are not avoided, of course, but are at least postponed long enough to empower interaction with religious others. For evangelicals, the trinitarian issue will inevitably arise, since "the ministries of the Son and Spirit can, of course, not . . . be put in any kind of opposition. Rather they are to be seen as 'both-and.'"[76] In addition, trinitarian concerns will surface with Islam and its doctrine of God's absolute and undivided oneness (*tawhīd*). Nevertheless, concern for the Spirit's work invites the Christian dialogue partner to discover and discern the work of God in religious others. Coupled with McDermott's work on God's revelatory word being present through common grace and theological typologies, a new set of motivations arise for evangelicals to embrace actively a ministry of dialogue and witness with other faith traditions.

Besides McDermott's work on Islam, other recent evangelical contributions to Christian-Muslim dialogue can also be highlighted. In *Christianity at the Religious Roundtable*, Timothy C. Tennent laments that few conservative evangelicals have participated in recent interfaith conversations. Consequently, "People who stand outside the boundaries of historic Christianity are representing Christianity" to other religions in often inaccurate and theologically suspect ways.[77] One of Tennent's goals is to remedy this by providing transcripts of interfaith dialogues between an evangelical and adherents of Hinduism, Buddhism, and Islam. He seeks an exchange that is open, honest, civil, and true to the

---

74. Pinnock, *Flame of Love*, 192.

75. There are problems in Pinnock's views, but he highlights trinitarian resources evangelicals can consider and utilize for a theology of religions. Also, one need not agree with the wider salvific scope proposed by him to appreciate the pneumatological potential he offers for genuine interfaith dialogue. For a brief critique of Pinnock's views in *Flame of Love*, see Kärkkäinen, *Trinity and Religious Pluralism*, 103–5. For a more extensive and negative critique of Pinnock's views, particularly with respect to the soteriological breadth of God's mercy toward those outside the Christian faith, see Carson, *Gagging of God*, esp. 278–314, 351–52, and 518–36.

76. Kärkkäinen, *Pneumatological Theology*, 235.

77. Tennent, *Religious Roundtable*, 10.

historical aspects of each view. It is also presented as a challenge to other evangelicals "to engage in interreligious dialogue as committed Christian witnesses."[78]

In Tennent's conversation with Islam, he begins by tracing the historical contexts surrounding Islam's rise. He then lays out central tenets of Islamic faith, dialoguing with Muslims from Islam's three major branches (Sunni, Shi'a and Sūfī) to explore interactively potential problems and possibilities of Islam and Christianity's doctrines of God. Before the dialogue and after a brief overview, Tennent highlights several common beliefs between these two faiths, including many of God's attributes as well as the numerous sacred stories concerning Adam, Moses, and others. He also notes, "Islam shares common theological categories with Christianity, including concepts such as sin, righteousness, divine judgment, heaven, hell, forgiveness and mercy."[79] As extensive as these agreements are, Tennent decides to "focus primarily on the boundary between the Islamic doctrine of tawhīd and the Christian doctrine of the Trinity," since this "is where the real differences between Christianity and Islam begin to emerge."[80] This decision highlights the evangelical tendency to look for differences, more than common ground, with other religions. In past dialogues, the search for common ground took precedence over areas of conflict. But as will be argued later, the focus on commonalities may not always be the healthiest or most productive way to make significant dialogical progress. It is important to seek points of agreement among world religions, but deliberately avoiding conflict and attempting to smooth over or even deny real differences only produces a religious amalgamation that no longer represents any of the world's religions as they are actually understood and practiced by the vast majority of their adherents.[81]

---

78. Ibid., 33.
79. Ibid., 153.
80. Ibid.
81. This is especially the tact of Hick and others like him. For one of the most recent articulations of his views (which are constantly evolving), see *Rainbow of Faiths*. For a helpful and concise summary of Hick's major theses see Aslan, *Religious Pluralism*, 257–58. This is a transcribed interview Aslan had with Hick (and Nasr) in October 1994 at Hick's Birmingham, England home. For a fair and thorough critique of Hick's views (and others like him), see Netland, *Encountering*, ch. 7, esp. 221–46.

Tennent's dialogue highlights not only the challenge of addressing differences between Christianity and Islam, but also the difficulty of trying to be fair to the many internal variations and viewpoints within a particular religion. Thus, Tennent's claim that Christianity emphasizes the relational aspect of God, whereas Islam's doctrine of *tawhīd* emphasizes his transcendence in such a way that compromises his relationality, can be challenged by the Sūfī Muslim who claims that God can and must be "encountered not in the mind but in the heart."[82]

Ultimately, although the conversations appear to produce little change among the dialogue partners, key sticking points concerning the doctrine of God are clarified for both sides. As Tennent puts it,

> To those who regard dialogue with Muslims about the Trinity as a dead end, I would acknowledge, on the one hand, that this assessment gravely recognizes what a fundamental dividing line our differences on this doctrine produce. On the other hand, an ongoing dialogue is never a dead end. It is . . . a place where our paradigms can be challenged and where we can continue to grow and learn.[83]

Tennent also explores many touch points and tensions between Muslims and Christians concerning Jesus (referred to as *Īsā* in the Qur'an), particularly focusing on the Christian notion of divine incarnation. By choosing this kind of controversial topic, Tennent is overtly attempting to "stimulate the conversation" between dialogue partners and challenge what he sees as Islamic misconceptions of Christianity concerning Jesus.[84] In the end, Tennent's transcripts are helpful, even if painfully brief and lacking dialogical breadth.

As helpful as these aforementioned exchanges are, the number of them is few. Our hope and prayer is that by entering into discussion and dialogue with fresh challenges and insights, evangelicals can provide new directions and energies for interfaith collaborations with Muslims worldwide. Thus, it would be helpful to examine one recent example of dialogue involving Muslims and evangelicals entitled *Christian and*

82. Tennent, *Religious Roundtable*, 159. It can also be challenged by some of the apophatic theology of Eastern Orthodoxy concerning God's ineffability and transcendence. For one recent example of this kind of theology, see Zizioulas, *Being as Communion*.

83. Tennent, *Religious Roundtable*, 166–67.

84. Ibid., 178.

Muslim Reflections on Peace. The book is a compilation of papers presented at an interfaith conference between Christians and Muslims at Ondokuz Mayis University in Samsun, Turkey, three months before September 11, 2001. Setting the tone for the conference, Mehmet Nuri Yilmaz, Muslim Minister of Religious Affairs for Turkey, made the encouraging comment, "To me, it is not the presence, but the absence or inadequacy of healthy debate that will have serious negative consequences. Therefore, debate should not be seen as an obstacle to genuine dialogue."[85]

In the first half of this refreshing and innovative compilation of essays, prominent evangelicals explore topics pertaining to the promotion of peace between Christians and Muslims. Similarly, the second half exhibits the writings of Turkish Muslims addressing similar topics from distinctly Islamic perspectives.

Both evangelicals and Muslims in this volume emphasize the importance of Christian-Muslim dialogue to promote *interreligious* and international peace. For example, after surveying inappropriate ways Islamic scriptures and practices have been applied throughout history, Muslim scholar Israfil Balci notes that "religions, whose roots are peace, justice, tolerance, and compassion, can make a positive contribution to world peace. Our world needs more of this kind of dialogue. The qur'anic verses and many examples in the history of Islam show that dialogue is rooted in Islam."[86]

In the North American context, a conversation between Muslims and evangelicals is summarized in *Muslims and Christians at the Table*. This book lays out biblical and Qur'anic bases for Christian-Muslim dialogue,[87] describing some of the content of the extensive conversations that have taken place, dividing the topics into two basic categories, "theological and doctrinal" and "social."[88] While admitting their model is "particularly effective in the West," the authors argue "it can

---

85. Yilmaz, "Context for Reflection," xii.

86. Balci, "Islamic Approach Toward International Peace," 121.

87. For the biblical basis, see McDowell and Zaka, *At the Table*, 222–25. For the Qur'anic basis, see 229–32.

88. McDowell and Zaka, *At the Table*, 221. To provide examples of possible topics, they list out nineteen major theological and seventeen social subjects. In addition, the book lays out concrete guidelines for meeting together that can be adapted to other contexts on pp. 220 and 225–27.

work well in Muslim countries, too, because it is not threatening."[89] The primary goal is mutual understanding. Should conversion result, that is an additional blessing, but only a byproduct of an interactive exchange of claims from both faith traditions. In short, "The main idea . . . is to encourage face-to-face contact between groups of Muslims and Christians to learn from each other. . . . Through [the meetings], Christians and Muslims have built friendships, shared needs and family problems, shared meals, cried together, loaned money to each other and been drawn close."[90] It is these kinds of experiences between Christians and Muslims worldwide for which we hope and long.

Islam and Christian-Muslim Dialogue

The previous survey focuses upon Christian initiatives for interfaith dialogue, but Islam has also actively pursued interreligious conversations. What follows highlights some important Muslims interested in interfaith dialogue.[91]

Although slightly dated, an important work on this issue is *Christian-Muslim Encounters*, a transcribed summary of presentations made by Christian and Muslim scholars at a conference held June 7–9, 1990, at Hartford Seminary. It's purpose was "to initiate a fresh look at some of the issues that have shaped Christian-Muslim encounters over the centuries and in their contemporary manifestations, and to determine if we can begin to explore new modes of scholarship and forms of communication between the two faith communities."[92] Of particular interest to this study is the subsection entitled "Ideological and Theological Reflections," which falls under the "Contemporary Situation" of part 2. Here, several essays provide valuable insights into the potential pitfalls of Christian-Muslim dialogue,[93] and point to ways the conversation can continue to grow. In particular, Seeyed

---

89. McDowell and Zaka, *At the Table*, 228.

90. Ibid., 236–37.

91. For the sake of focus, only a few compiled Christian-Muslims dialogues will be subsequently noted.

92. Haddad and Haddad, *Encounters*, 2.

93. They are by Jacques Waardeburg (ch. 22), Kenneth Cragg (ch. 24), Harold Vogelaar (ch. 25), John Carman (ch. 27), and Seeyed Hossein Nasr (ch. 28).

Hossein Nasr's essay describes several issues he believes "remain crucial and need much further reflection by those theologians and religious scholars on both sides who are concerned with a deeper understanding between Christianity and Islam."[94] While basic issues like the nature of God, humanity, the end times, "and many other issues" are important, he argues "they have either been discussed in various sources already or can be resolved fairly easily . . . [and so] would not pose obstacles to mutual Christian-Islamic understanding."[95] Instead, he sees seven issues that are "more divisive and require greater theological attention at the present moment."[96] They are: 1) the particular way(s) in which God makes himself known to human beings in concrete space-time;[97] 2) the meaning of claims to finality in both Islam and Christianity;[98] 3) "the meaning and status of sacred scripture in the two respective traditions";[99] 4) questions surrounding the interpretation and translation of a special sacred language;[100] 5) the relationship of sacred law to society and public legislation, particularly with reference to human sexuality;[101] 6) questions about the historical aspects of the life of Jesus;[102] and 7) Christianity and Islam's relationship with both modernity and postmodernity.[103]

This article provides a natural segue into another book written about Nasr, by Adnan Aslan, called *Religious Pluralism in Christian and Islamic Philosophy*.[104] Aslan looks extensively at Nasr's Islamic views concerning the challenges of religious plurality, comparing them to

94. Nasr, "Comments," 457.
95. Ibid., 466.
96. Ibid.
97. Ibid., 457–58.
98. Ibid., 459–60.
99. Ibid., 460–62, quotation from 460.
100. Ibid., 462. Nasr highlights his concern here by noting that while "Arabic is the sacred language of Islam . . . , Christianity has no sacred language of its own."
101. Ibid., 462–63.
102. Ibid., 463–64. What Nasr is getting at is that Christology is deeply rooted in historiography and our ability to know today what actually happened in the distant past, and then to ascertain both the particular and enduring meanings and significances of those concrete historical events.
103. Ibid., 464–66.
104. The book was originally a doctoral thesis submitted by Aslan to the religious studies department of Lancaster University in the autumn of 1995.

John Hick's. Much of Nasr and Hick's "dialogue" centers around their general agreement over the idea that it is possible to experience God/the Real in very different ways, even apparently contradictory ways, but which can be understood as anthropologically and temporally conditioned alternative perceptions of the one undifferentiated Ultimate or Real. For Nasr, like Hick, the solution to the conflicts arising during interfaith dialogues "between Muslims and Christians should be sought in a type of epistemology which allows a single reality to be seen in two different ways."[105] If one rejects the validity of this both/and epistemology (as Aslan does), then not much is added to the table.[106] However, the book serves as an admirable example of how two scholars from Christian and Muslim backgrounds can be peacefully brought face to face to articulate their views.

Encouragingly, there is a growing Islamic interest in interreligious dialogue, and increasing numbers of Muslim publications affirm the need for such conversations. For example, in *Progressive Muslims* author Amir Hussain devotes chapter 10 to this issue.[107] After tracing some of Islam's history of being a religious minority in pluralistic settings, Hussain argues,

> It is important for . . . Muslim communities in general to return to the pluralistic vision of the Qur'an, and establish cooperative relations with other religious communities, particularly at this time. There are a great many negative stereotypes about Islam and Muslims, and it is only through dialogue that these will be slowly dismantled. And of course dialogue is also necessary for Muslims to learn about the beliefs of those around them. It is easy to be taught to hate Christians and Jews (as for example tragically occurs in Saudi Arabia) if there are few actual Christians and Jews in one's country.[108]

He then concludes, "God speaks to us in the Qur'an about God willing our differences and our disputes. Our differences . . . are not to be

---

105. Aslan, *Religious Pluralism*, 204.

106. I agree with Aslan's assessment in *Religious Pluralism*, 205–6, where he argues this type of epistemology is not helpful because 1) it is unclear what it could actually look like in a comprehensible way and 2) it appears to be either self-referentially, or at the very least, logically incoherent with respect to the independent reality of concrete historical events.

107. Hussain, "Interfaith Dialogue," 251–69.

108. Ibid., 267.

feared, denied, or eradicated. God teaches us through our differences. It is through dialogue that we learn about ourselves, about others, and, in so doing, perhaps also about God."[109]

Similarly, Ramadan's *Western Muslims* includes a chapter on "Interreligious Dialogue,"[110] in which he laments that those needing dialogue most, "those with the most radical views . . . , do not know one another, or reject one another," making dialogue "impossible."[111] However, the Qur'an explicitly states human diversity is God-ordained and a necessary benefit for all. Thus, "if there were no differences between people, if power were in the hands of one group alone . . . , the earth would be corrupt because human beings need each other to limit their impulsive desire for expansion and domination." In particular, "if there is to be diversity of religions, the purpose is to safeguard them all."[112] Ramadan admits other Qur'anic verses suggest eliminating religious others, but argues they must be read carefully to ascertain more appropriate meanings consonant with other more inviting passages. Thus, he believes there are four primary rules for successful interfaith dialogue:

> 1. Recognition of and respect for the legitimacy of each other's convictions. 2. Listening to what people say about their own scriptural sources and not just what we understand (or want to understand) them to say. 3. The right, in the name of trust and respect, to ask all possible questions, sometimes even the most embarrassing. 4. The practice of self-criticism, knowing how to discern the differences between what the texts say and what our coreligionists make of them, and deciding clearly what our personal position is.[113]

Beyond these guidelines, Ramadan contends there must also be a commitment to mutual cooperation because "Dialogue is not enough. . . . It is urgent that we commit ourselves to joint action."[114] As we talk, we will see we have much in common, especially our values and ethics. These mutual moral imperatives can become the basis for interfaith projects

---

109. Ibid., 267.
110. Ramadan, *Western Muslims*, 200–213.
111. Ibid., 201.
112. Ibid., 202.
113. Ibid., 210.
114. Ibid., 211.

of social transformation, bringing about a greater experience of divine justice for everyone.

These examples illustrate the increasing interest and priority contemporary Muslims are giving to interfaith exchanges, especially those forced to encounter other cultures and religions through the growing process of globalization. In short, there is an encouraging trend toward not only dialogue, but also social cooperation among Muslims and Christians.

Summary and Synthesis: Recurring Themes of Commonality and Conflict

The aforementioned survey reveals a small portion of the rich dialogues being carried out between Christians and Muslims worldwide. As a result, several themes revealing agreement, but also conflict, have repeatedly emerged across a broad spectrum of theological views. To appreciate the progress and problems that have arisen through these conversations, some of the major areas of accord and contention will now be thematically summarized.[115] To simplify and aid understanding, I have organized emergent themes into three main subjects, namely the theological, political, and ethical/praxiological. In the first section, a fourth category is also noted, namely the foundational theme of how best to begin and carry out Christian-Muslim conversations.

Consistent Conflicts and Barriers in Christian and Muslim Dialogue

Questions of Implementation and Representation

That dialogue has even taken place points to early groundwork done by many Christians and Muslims. These initial discussions raised concerns about who best represented Islam and Christianity, as well as the appropriate presuppositions, starting points, and ways to dialogue.

---

115. A comprehensive survey of the issues raised by Christian-Muslim dialogues is impossible to provide here. Fortunately, more comprehensive surveys are provided elsewhere by, for example, Brown, *Meeting in Faith*, and the already cited more recent and comprehensive work by Sperber, *Christias and Muslims*, which will be utilized extensively in this section.

Early dialogues were initiated rather hastily due to the political turmoil in Israel and the Middle East in 1967, so little preparatory thought was given to these issues. Only later were they more directly addressed.

Concerning representation, Sperber notes, "Unlike the Vatican, the WCC[116] had no official line which participants in the dialogues could adopt, and the individual member churches also found this difficult. On the Muslim side, in this respect, the end of the caliphate as the representation of all Moslems had had a negative effect."[117] The somewhat accidental result was that only certain segments of Christianity and Islam were represented. And sometimes these were quite unrepresentative of "the silent majority" in either religion.[118] Participants from both sides ultimately agreed a greater voice should be given to: 1) "mystics or militant Muslims," 2) those who "would simply like to live peacefully together in everyday life," 3) those who represent "regional differences and interests," and 4) even those "everywhere who have no close contacts with the other side and its world and are therefore indifferent to dialogue."[119]

Also important were issues of mutual trust and ulterior motives. In particular, Christian mission, social service, and proselytism were frequently viewed with suspicion by Muslims. Thus, "Muslims did not find it easy to encounter the Christians with trust. . . . In the dialogues, whenever it was a question of mission or aid projects, the Muslims levelled concrete accusations . . . that [Christians] were engaging in proselytism and deliberately encouraging Westernisation and secularisation."[120] Christians feared Muslims only wanted to impose Islamic law (*Sharī'ah*) to solve the world's problems, especially following the 1979 Iranian Revolution.[121] This might not have been so disconcerting were there not contemporary examples of what Christians saw as human rights violations and discrimination against "protected" non-Muslim minority groups (*dhimmī*) in states under *Sharī'ah*.[122] Ultimately, mutual

116. WCC = World Council of Churches.

117. Sperber, *Christians and Muslims*, 318.

118. As Sperber (ibid.) points out, Islamic thinkers (for example) were all "academically trained and open to dialogue."

119. Ibid.

120. Ibid., 322.

121. Ibid., 332.

122. Ibid., 326–27 and 332. This concern was raised primarily by Christians living

mistrust among participants "always boiled down to one thing: fear of discrimination by others and finally being overwhelmed."[123]

More could be said here, but these highlights provide a sufficient picture of the important foundational debates occurring during the dialogues. We will now turn to the more extensive arena of theological conflicts.

Theological Themes

Theological disagreements in dialogue are legion. After more than three decades of Christian-Muslim conversations, Sperber summarizes the situation this way: "Absolutely everything in the context of dialogue that has to do with theology and theological decisions is still very much disputed."[124] Some theological claims of Christians and Muslims can never come together without revising doctrines considered indispensable to the identity and meaning of each faith. For example, differences concerning each faith's conception of God were "greater and more unbridgeable" than other theological conflicts.[125] While Muslims show great respect for Jesus as a major prophet, the Christian conception of Jesus as the incarnated divine Son of God, given for the vicarious forgiveness of sin through his death on a cross and glorious resurrection from the dead, is simply blasphemous and incomprehensible to traditional Islam. Christianity's christological and pneumatological aspects inevitably give rise to distinctly trinitarian notions of God that have remained remarkably steadfast. In fact, "even modern [liberal] theology with its historical-critical assessment of the gospels would not change anything here."[126]

Muslims, with their seemingly immovable doctrine of *tawhīd*, God's indivisible, partner-free, transcendent oneness, were similarly

---

outside the West. Western Christians were much less negative about implementing *Sharī'ah* at a national level. Sperber (ibid., 334) speculates this may have been true because in the West, Islamic law is still "usually only an issue of private religious law" whereas Christians living under Islamic rule observed, "Muslim law has never worked as well in practice as is now being assumed in theory."

123. Ibid., 322.
124. Ibid., 341.
125. Ibid., 320.
126. Ibid.

"compelled to reject the Trinity and Christology as understood by Christians."[127] Thus, God's nature is contentious in Christian-Muslim dialogues, and "further rapprochement is improbable because the image of God is too closely linked with the identity of each of the religions."[128]

Another significant topic is the nature and authority of their sacred writings. For example, the Qur'an "was transmitted to Mohammed by God word for word and has to be accepted and understood accordingly—in the Arabic language." Christians, on the other hand, "had a much more nuanced understanding of revelation and took dogmatic, epistemological, historical and scientific questions into account." In particular, Christians often accused the Muslims of "completely ignoring the dimension of history."[129] Concerning textual authority, Muslims see the Bible as divine revelation, but as corrupted and distorted at important points. Thus, the Qur'an was given not only as the final revelation to humanity, but also to correct corrupted biblical teachings. Not surprisingly, Christians were less impressed with these claims, noting that the finality of God's revelation in Jesus blunts Islamic claims to revelatory ultimacy. Because Islam is "a post-Christian religion," the nature of the Qur'an and the prophet Muhammad has "always been a special challenge to Christianity." Thus, historical interfaith encounters have almost always "resulted in theologically opposite positions," and the dialogues reflected this.[130]

---

127. Ibid. The reasons for this rejection are more complex than simply appealing to *tawhīd*, and the need to avoid the sin of *shirk*, or idolatry, by ascribing supremacy to something or someone other than the indivisible God. In my "Contested Views of Christ in Christianity and Islam," 13–15, 23, I apply Pannenberg's theological method to pursue a christological debate between Islam and Christianity. There I argue certain unfortunate historical factors were the primary reason why Muslims rejected what they (wrongly) thought was the Christian doctrine of the Trinity. Only later when far more was at stake than just theology did Muslims actually come into contact with more biblically accurate and sophisticated forms of trinitarian belief. As a result, to maintain a distinctly Islamic identity and avoid either a return to the raw polytheism (from which their strictly monotheistic faith sprang) or suffer the fate of somehow being incorporated into the Christian religion, they were compelled to reject trinitarian notions by continuing to insist on viewing them through the clouded lens of their previous (mis)understandings.

128. Sperber, *Christians and Muslims*, 321.

129. Ibid., 320. This ignoring of historical aspects of divine revelation becomes especially important in the current debate between more traditional and more progressive Muslims.

130. Ibid., 93.

Another contentious area was Christian mission. Muslims were constantly suspicious that the dialogues were a disingenuous and subtle form of Christian mission intended to undermine Islam's supremacy. For them, Christian mission became "the greatest factor against dialogue."[131] While some Christians suggested suspending mission to ensure dialogue continued, most insisted mission was a central element of Christianity and therefore "part of religious liberty."[132] Muslims had trouble accepting this since they saw Christian mission as authoritarian, irrational, and psychologically manipulative, whereas "Islamic mission used rational arguments to convince people of so obvious a truth that one had to be a fool or malevolent, indeed almost inhuman, not to accept it."[133] To their credit, Muslims did continue to dialogue despite their many reservations.[134]

One of the basic questions explored was the meaning of being human. Christians debated the extent of human depravity and the involvement of the will in the process of redemption, but still emphasized the saving work of Jesus Christ and the need for God to rescue the believer through "sharing in suffering, and a liberation from sin, guilt and punishment."[135] Most Muslims had difficulty with these claims, noting that "death on a cross and the concept of original sin are absolutely inconceivable and completely unacceptable for Muslims."[136] For them, God's saving action was seen primarily in terms of "revealing and leading, and . . . liberating them for action and responsibility."[137] Thus, humanity's ability to make ethical choices was greatly emphasized over the inability to be righteous apart from divine grace and mercy.[138]

---

131. Ibid., 330.

132. Ibid., 331.

133. Ibid., 330. Over time this initial Islamic attitude of superiority did lessen.

134. To help understand why Christian mission is so disturbing to Muslims, Borelli ("Christian-Muslim Relations," 327) notes that "the word 'mission' functions in the same way among Muslims as the word 'jihad' does among Christians. Both are beautiful words, but in their use or perceptions there are implications of violence which are difficult to avoid."

135. Sperber, *Christians and Muslims*, 321.

136. Ibid.

137. Ibid.

138. There are other streams of thought in Islam concerning sin and the human condition much closer to Christian views. Woodberry ("Toward Common Ground," 23–31) explores some of these alternative perspectives.

Such claims give rise to corresponding soteriological questions concerning who is rightly related to God. Are Christians and Muslims "saved," and if so, how? If not, why not? On what bases can such judgments be made? Christians from more inclusive christocentric and especially theocentric pluralistic camps tended to affirm Muslims are saved without much reservation. Exclusivistic and ecclesiocentric Christians were more reticent to grant this soteriological status to Muslims. Muslims tended to see Christians in one of two ways: either as good-hearted but misguided believers in God clinging to an antiquated (but legitimate) system of belief that grants them salvation in a substandard but sufficient way, or as condemned souls in need of the true path of Islam. Either way, Islam was deemed superior. In Sperber's words,

> In general, even among the more open-minded Moslems, the theological starting point was as follows: Islam is the epitome of modernity, scholarly excellence, tolerance and democracy—and naturally the superior, only true religion which has been designed for world community and dialogue. . . . As Muslims understand themselves, a truly open dialogue can only lead to transferring to Islam. The Christian invitation to dialogue was immediately interpreted as a theological recognition of Islam.[139]

While there was little agreement among Christians over the salvific status of Muslims, Muslims consistently demanded anyone coming to the dialogue must grant them full soteriological legitimacy or there could be no conversation. Fortunately, this stance softened through the course of dialogue, making room for more ecclesiocentric and particularistic camps to participate. Nevertheless, this attitude remains strong among many Muslims.

Many other unresolved anthropological issues could be explored. For example, what is the appropriate place and role of men and women in society in general and in the sacred assembly in particular? But such issues may be better addressed in reference to questions about politics, ethics, and the treatment of minorities in Islamic and more secularized societies. Thus, we will now examine some contemporary sources of conflict between Christians and Muslims concerning Islamic law, human society, and secularism. As Sperber points out,

---

139. Sperber, *Christians and Muslims*, 319.

it has been repeatedly recognised that one quite fundamental difference between the two religions is that Islam's theological thinking is much more juridical and has therefore also from the very beginning developed concrete conceptions based on a legal framework for ordering the secular world. With this basic premise, secularisation as we know it in the Christian context is practically impossible.[140]

How should law be decided upon and applied in society? What is the basis for those laws, and which laws are meant to be applied to the sacred believing community versus humanity in general? How can this distinction be made? These questions provide a natural segue into the politically-oriented concerns arising from the dialogues.

Political Themes

Recent international events have made political dialogue between Muslims and Christians desirable, but also contentious. As was already noted, it was "the critical situation in the Middle East where the Six Days War in 1967 made it clear how necessary dialogue and understanding with Muslims would be."[141] Since then, there has been no shortage of situations needing Christian-Muslim dialogue and action.[142] And one of the biggest concerns surrounds the nature and appropriate application of *Sharī'ah*. Is this law timeless, time-bound, or a combination? If time-bound, in what sense? If timeless, then how can it be apprehended and applied by finite human beings in concrete time and space? Is it subject to criticisms of being unjust in light of current ethical trends, especially concerning women and religious minorities? If so, in what ways? If not, then is *Sharī'ah* a truly workable alternative to modern liberal and secular democracies? This raises the additional unanswered question: *which version* of *Sharī'ah* is the properly interpreted and applied one?[143]

---

140. Ibid.

141. Ibid., 317.

142. Besides the Israeli occupation of Lebanon and Palestine, the 1991 Gulf War, and the wars and issues stemming from the 9/11 attacks, Brown (*Meeting in Faith*, 59) also notes problems in South-East Asia where, "attitudes of exclusivism, of condescension or of hostility have characterized relations between Muslims and Christians."

143. None of these questions will be significantly addressed here. They are only

Because most Muslims tie religion and state together, Islam displayed far more interest in political issues during the dialogues.[144] Contemporary Christians, in contrast, usually distinguish more sharply between the state and religion. Consequently, politics quickly became a source of heated dispute. Sperber frames the debate this way: "Usually the Muslims wanted an Islamic state which *de facto* ruled out secularisation, whereas this caused Christians to think immediately of the *dhimmī* [protected minority][145] status and of holy war, so they therefore tended more to desire secularisation."[146] Apparently, it was difficult for many Muslims to accept the idea that *Sharī'ah*, at least if it was rightly applied in various contexts, was anything but perfectly just, creating the best possible society for the greatest number of people, Islamic and non-Islamic alike.[147]

---

raised to highlight the potential depth and complexity of both inter- and intrareligious dialogue on these and other closely related issues.

144. This close relation of religion and state is not a new phenomenon, of course. Christianity has exhibited similar propensities toward such religious and political amalgamations throughout history. In addition, many Muslims do not advocate a strict integration of Islam and the state. As Sperber (*Christians and Muslims*, 327) points out, "In Southeast Asia and to a certain extent in Africa, many Muslim participants were critical of the project of an Islamic state. They claimed that the results were often only pseudo-Islamic and that there had never been another really Islamic state since the early 'rightly guided' caliphs." Of course, this leaves open the idea that some "rightly guided" caliphs may again arise to reinstate the pure Muslim state in our modern times, so there is little comfort for secularists in such words.

145. To provide some clarification, Islam's political nature has historically helped it develop various legal, political, and social guidelines to address the question of tolerating, protecting, and regulating certain (acceptable) religious minorities living under the control of a Muslim-majority society. These "protected" minorities, called *dhimmī*, are typically allowed to exist and continue, so long as they abide by various limiting conditions. These conditions often vary from place to place, but usually include restrictions on having positions of influence and power in the governance of the greater society as well as any opportunities to expand and grow through religious proselytism. Frequently added to these restrictions is some sort of financial tribute (*jizya*), outlined from Q. 9:29, that is paid to the Islamic governing authorities. Thus, certain non-Muslims can remain within Islamic realms, but almost always at some significant cost to their own freedom, growth, and general opportunity in the society as a whole.

146. Sperber, *Christians and Muslims*, 326.

147. In *Christians and Muslims*, Sperber notes this common Islamic attitude. For example, she notes that in Hong Kong in 1975, "according to one Muslim speaker, in Mohammed's contract with the inhabitants of Medina there was an older model with equal rights for all. Amazingly enough, the speaker considered this model to a large extent to be a reality in Malaysia, where citizenship was linked with the Muslim faith

This confidence does not mean Muslims were unaware of the problems accompanying attempts to understand and apply *Sharī'ah* correctly. They knew in practice imposing Islamic law produced serious disagreements even among fellow Muslims. For example, at the discussion in 1988 at New Windsor concerning economic models in particular, "It was . . . almost impossible to define what was 'Islamic' because there were so many legal schools and traditions."[148] So Muslims were not blind to problems with *Sharī'ah*, but they tended to downplay or flatly deny concerns raised by Christians that aspects of this law may need fundamental juridical revision or perhaps wholesale rejection.

Concerning religious tolerance, Muslim "assessment of themselves as the most tolerant of all religions did not permit them to admit the discrimination against the Christian minority which is found in their legal provisions."[149] Both sides agreed religious minorities should be allowed "to exist and [have] religious liberty, but . . . even the precise juridical definitions of these terms created difficulties. We are still a long way from a multi-religious society that works."[150]

To summarize, there was little agreement reached in terms of political governance or legislative enactment and enforcement, along with its appropriate relation to religious belief and practice. The inability of Christians and Muslims to agree on the best way for the state and religion to relate to one another, as well as the particular aspects of legislative jurisprudence, fostered a mutual environment of distrust and stalemate with little hope for significant resolution.

---

and mission among Muslims was not automatically allowed" (176). And she shares that in Kolymbari in 1987, "a number of Muslims maintained that [under *Sharī'ah* law] non-Muslims had an equal legal status" as well as "freedom of worship" (180). However, after citing several practical examples of how in actual practice, this simply is not the case, she bluntly states, "Again, one is struck by a certain shortsightedness [among Muslim participants] which apparently did not recognise the inevitable, legal disadvantages for non-Muslims in an Islamic society and the pressure to convert."

148. Ibid., 181. This Islamic diversity, even at the local level, is further highlighted by Goddard (*History*, 192) when he speaks about the political views of various Muslims in South Africa, noting, "There is . . . a huge range of Muslim opinion within the relatively small Muslim community in [South Africa], and this is echoed and amplified many times across the Muslim world as a whole. . . . Complete consistency is rarely achieved in any one context, let alone across the whole of a worldwide religious community."

149. Sperber, *Christians and Muslims*, 327.

150. Ibid., 328.

Contemporary Christian-Muslim Relations

Closely related to political aspects of Muslim jurisprudence are ethical and practical concerns surrounding interfaith discussions on universal human rights, minority rights, as well as punitive codes and regulations. It is to these equally contentious issues we now turn.

Ethical and Praxiological Themes

To begin, there was talk about ethical commonalities between Islam and Christianity, but little agreement on cooperative endeavors.[151] The primary reason for this was the aforementioned Muslim suspicion toward Christian mission. Muslims were consistently distrustful of Christians who wanted to promote interreligious cooperation, even concerning the practice of interfaith dialogue itself. They felt such activities were merely subtle programs to manipulate religious others to embrace Christianity. Thus, the "rejection of every kind of Christian aid project remained unchanged even later on [in the dialogues]."[152] Muslims insisted Christians give Islam full salvific legitimacy to remove the notion of mission from the conversations, but for many Christians this question was still up for debate. Ultimately, little concrete progress was made.[153]

151. A recent exception is the agreement drawn up between the United Methodist Committee on Relief (UMCOR) and Muslim Aid, both humanitarian agencies concerned with helping those in times of crisis. Signed in June 2007, leaders of these organizations are adamant that humanitarian aid should be done for its own sake without any hidden agenda of bringing about religious conversion. Thus, cooperation was only made possible on this strictly outlined basis, and any attempts to persuade the recipients to embrace Christianity, Islam, or any other religion for that matter, was eschewed. To see the agreement and other details concerning it, consult http://www.umcormuslimaid.org/. As well, Kimball ("Toward a More Hopeful Future," 383) cites an example from 2003 when Jewish, Christian, and Muslim congregations in Toledo, Ohio, jointly built a Habitat for Humanity house.

152. Sperber, *Christians and Muslims*, 330.

153. Kimball ("Toward a More Hopeful Future," 384) laments the irony here by noting that, "With a little reflection, one can identify a range of societal issues where Christians, Muslims and others converge in their concerns and sense of responsibility. Achieving theological agreement should not be a prerequisite for cooperation." Kimball goes on to provide an example where he asks the reader to "imagine two researchers—a Southern Baptist from Georgia and a Muslim from India—working side by side at the Centers for Disease Control in Atlanta. Their research is focused on finding a cure for the devastating AIDS epidemic. It would never occur to these two . . . that they could not cooperate because of their theological differences as a Christian and a Muslim."

Another praxiological concern repeatedly raised during the conversations surrounds interfaith prayer and worship. Does interfaith prayer and worship constitute a unique experience of mutual respect and cooperation, or a syncretistic compromise of one's faith? According to Sperber, Christians were especially concerned about syncretism, and while "they consented to common prayers, meditations and devotions and to participating in the worship of others (deliberately not called common worship!), they did so more by force of circumstance and by setting theology aside for a while."[154] Ultimately, "theological clarification of this question was never achieved . . . [and] guidelines for common prayer or worship were [seen as] pastorally necessary but no one managed to produce them."[155] Thus, most of these discussions were dropped to pursue more fruitful avenues.

Concerning human rights in general and minority rights in particular, the interfaith exchanges generated enormous amounts of contention. For focus, just one aspect of Islamic family law—mixed marriages—will be highlighted.

Seeing interfaith marriages as an opportunity for a rich and continuous dialogue of life was not considered until later in the dialogues. In addition, it was recognized the potential that such marriages offered "should probably not be overestimated" because examples from Africa demonstrated "these marriages tend to be fairly superficial as far as religious dialogue is concerned."[156] In fact, in such Muslim-Christian marriages, "religious claims to absoluteness and mutual prejudice seem to *increase* rather than decrease as the years go by."[157] Nevertheless, it was believed that with coaching and communication aids such unique arrangements might yield significant long-term benefits for interreligious growth and understanding.

However, Christians in the dialogues pointed out that in mixed marriages Islam "discriminates especially against non-Muslim women" and significantly differs with Christianity over "family planning and children's upbringing," especially in the area of "religious education."[158]

---

154. Sperber, *Christians and Muslims*, 323.
155. Ibid.
156. Ibid., 334.
157. Ibid., 334–35; emphasis added.
158. Ibid., 334.

Such accusations were hard for Muslims to accept, of course. As Sperber points out, in response, "Muslims again maintained that Islam was perfect and its tolerance was unequalled in this respect, so that other religions could learn from it." [159] Apparently, only Christians noted instances where Muslims demonstrated their brand of tolerance by occasionally castrating Christian men who had "broken the rules" and married Muslim women.[160] In addition, both sides agreed that accurate and fair religious education for all children was a must, but little was resolved concerning "who should do the teaching about other religions."[161]

Beyond these concerns there was the ever-present conflict over religious minorities, whether Christian or Muslim. Muslims were quick to highlight settings like the Philippines where Muslims were oppressed and discriminated against by a Catholic majority.[162] Alternatively, Christians emphasized contexts like the Middle East, where Islamic rule often significantly limited non-Muslim religious groups, and Christians had even been forced to flee for their lives.[163] Ultimately, it was recognized such situations were not always strictly religious in nature and often had important, even decisive, alternative explanations for the problems minorities experienced.[164] Nevertheless, little was resolved concerning how best to approach the many challenges and problems of properly dealing with religious minorities.

Ultimately, the dialogues succeeded in demonstrating the complex relationships religion, politics, family order, ethics, and social justice often have with one another—and how contentious such topics can be. Despite the many disagreements, several areas of commonality arose and are highlighted below.

---

159. Ibid.

160. Ibid. Muslim men were free to marry Christian women without fear of similar reprisals. A laundry list of such offenses (on either side) need not be provided here. For a fascinating survey of some of the traditional and historical struggles in Islamic family law, especially with respect to the conversion and status foreign women and children, see Friedman, *Tolerance and Coercion in Islam*, 107–15.

161. Sperber, *Christians and Muslims*, 343.

162. Ibid., 143.

163. Ibid., 146.

164. Ibid., 147.

Emergent Themes of Commonality in Christian and Muslim Dialogue[165]

Theological Themes

There is no small debate over whether Christians and Muslims worship the same God. Sperber frames the issue this way:

> There is a certain range of attitudes on both sides. Whereas, at the beginning, some Christians claimed that Muslims did not worship the same God as Christians, later there was reference to the Abrahamic faith in one God . . . . On the other hand, many Muslims continued to consider that Christians were tri-theists, but the general trend among most of the Muslim participants in the dialogues was to view the Christians as monotheists with limitations, who naturally worshipped the same God as the Muslims but not quite correctly.[166]

So in a limited sense, the conversation partners were able to say that we are all worshiping the same God, but in terms of a general consensus that was as far as it could go, because "the image of God is too closely linked with the identity of each of the religions."[167] Nevertheless, common ground was found along the way. Thus, after "a number of dialogues, John B. Taylor summed up the common features: common creatureliness before God, common responsibility before God's judgment, the human being as God's representative and servant, [and] the struggle for a more just, better world."[168] To these could be added the mutual affirmation of humanity's need for divine revelatory guidance as

---

165. One difficulty with this section is that little is commonly held by all Christians and Muslims. As Sperber, (ibid., 86) notes, "an either/or approach to the question of truth is common to both religions and therefore conflicts are pre-programmed: the claims of one necessarily exclude those of the other." Thus, choices have to be made about what things really do constitute areas of commonality for Christians and Muslims. It is doubtful anyone from either religion could provide a comprehensive list of agreements everyone would uphold without some reservation or protest. Thus, the topics mentioned here are not offered for authoritative affirmation per se, but largely for future debate.

166. Sperber, Christians and Muslims, 321.

167. Ibid.

168. Ibid., 86.

well as a belief in our God-given dignity and inherently moral nature. And both see Jesus as a holy man and prophet.[169]

While more could be said, it is better to sketch broadly the outlines of common ground to avoid at least some of the contentiousness arising from the dialogues. With that said, political aspects of the dialogue yielding areas of common ground will now be explored.

Political Themes

Perhaps the one major area where Islam and Christianity came together centered around the problem of disestablishing religion from public life. Solutions given by each side were sometimes radically different, but the diagnosis was very similar: secularization had led to the marginalization of religion and the impoverishment of society as a whole. For Christians, there was a "departure from the secularism which had previously been preferred, a large amount of sympathy for the Muslims' problems, and concern for a multi-cultural society with different legal arrangements for different groups."[170] However, these agreements were reached by Christians who had no experience of living as a minority in a Muslim context and by Muslim minorities who "urgently demanded revisions of Islamic law and also saw a theoretic possibility for this, but also very clearly recognised the practical difficulties with a Muslim majority which had a different view."[171]

Thus, while some agreement was reached, many Christians (especially those in religiously minority contexts), continued to advocate strongly the secularization of all governments to avoid the governmental imposition of Muslim *Sharī'ah* upon the society as a whole, and not so much to disestablish religious influence from the public arena. In their experience, Muslim religious law only *theoretically* distinguishes between religious and secular realms of governance, but is rarely able to separate them in a manner resulting in religious freedom and equal-

---

169. The degree of christological agreement is hotly contested, but most admit the common affirmations shared here. For a discussion of Muslim and Christian views of Jesus, see Moucarry, *The Prophet & the Messiah*, esp. 127–216.

170. Sperber, *Christians and Muslims*, 209.

171. Ibid.

ity for all.[172] In short, "On one side, [there were] Christians who had already experienced *sharī'ah* or were immediately threatened by it and, on the other, the West which was not affected by the problem. The one group was dominated by pessimism and helplessness and the other reacted with incomprehension and reproaches."[173]

Ethical and Praxiological Themes

Despite the aforementioned challenges to cooperative activities and interfaith worship and prayer, such opportunities were explored and endorsed throughout the dialogues. In particular, "the point which encountered the greatest consensus was ecology, although it was restricted on the Muslim side to the prescriptions laid down in Islamic law for the economic context. Otherwise there was some lip service, especially from the Muslims, to social justice."[174] As was previously noted, early attempts to enact mutual projects of humanitarian aid were met with deep Islamic suspicion because Muslims "saw the Christian aid programmes simply as proselytism and wanted them terminated."[175] It was only much later in the dialogues that significant points of commonality were practically pursued. Eventually, both sides agreed upon a mutual list of global problems needing significant religious input. Sperber lists them as: "The concentration of wealth . . . and the growth of poverty, especially in Asia, the increasing urbanisation and criminality, unproductive expenditure on armaments, the disastrous effects of advertising, . . . the oil crisis, the wood crisis, the raw materials crisis and the population crisis—in short, the economic system as a whole with its sinful injustices."[176]

Through the course of the dialogue, mutually agreeable solutions to these issues were offered as well. They included "rejection of wastage in any form and thus also rejection of the consumer society, [and

---

172. Ibid., 183.

173. Ibid., 184. Sperber goes on to note the Copts in Egypt as just one example among many of those who are justifiably concerned about the imposition of Islamic law.

174. Ibid., 324.

175. Ibid., 324–25.

176. Ibid., 325.

a] commitment to combating environmental destruction."[177] But when it came to concrete proposals for enacting solutions, Muslims again tended to emphasize *Sharīʿah* as the panacea for all social ills, whereas Christians saw such provisions as "limiting or . . . subversive."[178]

Throughout the dialogues, the ultimate basis for pursuing common goals and ideals was drawn from the notion of "common humanity." As Sperber puts it,

> The fact that all participants are human beings with human and often very similar problems possesses an inner persuasive force that repeatedly overcomes theological reservations and unclarities on whatever side. Inter-religious dialogue and inter-religious cooperation are, in a sense, factual evidence of the relevance of 'common humanity', even though the expression continues to be rather unclear and disputed theologically.[179]

Because the actual practice of cooperation tends to be messy and imprecise, a technical definition was not needed to proceed.

On the topic of education, both sides agreed on its significance and on the need to expand curriculum to include other religious viewpoints. Exactly how this was to be done remained unsettled. Thus, "no final answers were given, just contributions to reflection and discussion."[180] Both sides also agreed that there was no such thing as "value-free" education, thus "educators and teachers have an ethical responsibility and it is better to make the influence of religions on education clearly visible."[181] This kind of concern begs for a more thoughtful theology of religions but no such theology was hammered out in the dialogues.

Ultimately, while progress continues to be made, the depth and success of these conversations remains somewhat preliminary. Consequently, significant mutual exploration is still required.

---

177. Ibid.
178. Ibid.
179. Ibid., 343.
180. Ibid., 344.
181. Ibid. Also noted by Sperber on this page was a need to include more women in the dialogues on education since so many educators of children are women.

Conclusion: Obstacles, Opportunities, or Both? Finding New Ways to Move Forward Together Again

We can ascertain from this succinct survey that there is a profound and increasing richness to these preliminary dialogues. And despite areas of mutual concern and affirmation, there are also significant and undeniable barriers to ongoing Christian-Muslim dialogue. In Jutta Sperber's words,

> It was, after all, always possible to identify common historical roots with Islam, whether they related to creation and judgement or to more practical questions, or even to the claims to absoluteness made for both religions. But, despite such common features, it should never be forgotten, as was quite accurately stated, that they relate in each case to quite different centres: Christ or Mohammed, the Bible or the Koran.[182]

Thus, the questions must be asked: Are these recurrent themes obstacles or opportunities for greater world peace as well as interfaith enrichment and cooperation? Can Christian-Muslim interactions make our world a better place? Such basic queries are not easily answered, and it would be sheer naiveté to think this treatment will somehow resolve the impasses and impediments still plaguing Christian-Muslim relations. Nevertheless, in Pannenberg and Sachedina we find promising resources for moving forward in Muslim-Christian conversations. To begin the process of mining these resources, their respective theologies of religions will be explored in the next two chapters, beginning with Pannenberg.

---

182. Ibid., 319.

3

God, History, the Future, and Religious Contestation: Wolfhart Pannenberg's Theology of Religions

We have traced recent Christian-Muslim dialogues, categorizing some of the challenges, opportunities, and responses to living in a religiously plural world. We have also seen the need for clearer and more viable Christian rejoinders to religious plurality. One of the most significant European systematic theologies to emerge in recent decades is by German Lutheran theologian Wolfhart Pannenberg. Especially noted for contributions in Christology,[1] anthropology,[2] and theology of science,[3] the publication of his three-volume *Systematic Theology*[4] represents something of a *magnum opus* for his life's work. For more than years forty years Pannenberg has expressed a deep concern for the relationship of Christianity to other world religions.[5]

Because of his concern for the demonstrable credibility and truthfulness of Christianity, Pannenberg has written extensively about religious plurality and Christianity's place and role among world religions. While he offers great insight and hope in this respect, it is especially surprising that, even with the culminating publication of his three-

1. Pannenberg, *Jesus—God and Man*.
2. Pannenberg, *Anthropology in Theological Perspective*.
3. Pannenberg, *Toward a Theology of Nature*.
4. Hereafter referred to by volume as *ST* 1, *ST* 2, and *ST* 3.
5. As early as 1962, Pannenberg was concerned about this issue; see his "Toward a Theology," 67.

volume systematic theology, Pannenberg never explicitly lays out an organized exposition of his theology of religions. As Finnish theologian and Pannenbergian scholar Veli-Matti Kärkkäinen notes, "what is somewhat disappointing about the *Systematic Theology* is that after the beginning chapters of the first volume, mainly dealing with methodological issues, Pannenberg does not develop the implications of his theology of religions, not even in his eschatology, which would be one of the loci most pregnant for doing so."[6] Consequently, his ideas must be carefully pieced together from a variety of sources produced during his distinguished theological career.

This chapter will lay out important aspects of Pannenberg's theological method and then construct his theology of religions before providing a brief critique. To aid in the task of drawing these resources together into a unified picture of a Pannenbergian theology of religions, we will begin by observing general and central distinctives in Pannenberg's thought that provide a backdrop for understanding his specifically Christian approach to religious plurality.

Crucial Aspects of Pannenberg's Systematic Theology: God, Truth, History, Anticipation, and the Future

Choosing one key distinctive in Pannenberg's expansive theological method is difficult and controversial. Several emphases have been proposed as controlling themes of his theology. In *The Postfoundationalist Task of Theology*, F. LeRon Shults notes three of the more commonly considered "ground principles" for Pannenberg's thought: reason (sometimes coupled with hope), history, and prolepsis or anticipation.[7] While these themes are certainly prevalent, Shults argues the true controlling principle in Pannenberg's writings is his understanding of God and how it reciprocally impacts and (re)forms every aspect of reality. As Shults puts it, "the attempt to understand and explain all things *sub ratione Dei* (under the aspect of their 'relation to God') is the basic principle in Pannenberg's approach."[8] If this provides insight into

6. Kärkkäinen, *Trinity and Religious Pluralism*, 81.
7. Shults, *Postfoundationalist Task*, 84–85.
8. Ibid., 92. I am inclined to agree with Shults' assessment, and the fact that Pannenberg himself writes the forward to this volume lends additional credibility to Shults' claim.

Pannenberg's theological perspective, then it is crucial to begin with his understanding of God's nature, for one's concept of God gives unity to all human life in particular and reality in general. Thus, "the single argument of the entire three-volume *ST* [is this]: the biblical trinitarian God is the best explanation for the human experience of being in a historical relation to the true infinite."[9]

The Importance of the Idea of God and Reality

For Pannenberg, the infinite, trinitarian God is the "all-determining reality."[10] This "requires that everything which exists should be shown to be a trace of the divine reality."[11] Since our concept of God gives the fundamental backdrop to all truth and existence, all of reality and all arenas of knowledge should be the concern of our theological understanding if we are to give adequate scope to the all-determining Christian God. Pannenberg puts it this way: "Theology as the science of God would then mean the study of the totality of the real from the point of view of the reality which ultimately determines it both as a whole and in its parts."[12] Thus, Barth, for example, was wrong in rejecting natural theology since it is not merely through special revelation that God is known and understood.[13] God is also known in nature for he is its source and sustainer, as well as the giver of divine revelation in human history. Thus, God's character and plans are revealed through the unfolding particular episodes of concrete history. In short, God is the Lord of *all* history, not merely specialized sacred history. In addition, Pannenberg's trinitarian emphasis aids his theology of religions by providing a way to represent the particularity of Jesus in history and the universality of the Spirit's work (and so the triune God as a whole) in the on-going sustenance of and revelation in creation.

This idea of God being the true infinite and all-determining reality who makes all of history the grand stage of his self-disclosure is intimately coupled with Pannenberg's systematic method of doing theol-

9. Ibid., 104.

10. Pannenberg, *Philosophy of Science*, 303.

11. Ibid.

12. Ibid.

13. For Barth's view as he defended it in a debate with Emil Brunner, see Brunner and Barth, *Natural Theology*.

ogy. There is a strong sense of *reciprocity* in his theological approach.[14] Human beings are historically situated and inherently finite in their understanding of reality (the *anthropological* nature of human life), yet they (and all things) are subject to the sovereign creative power of God through whom all things find their relation (the properly *theological* aspect of all reality). Thus, Pannenberg seeks to do his theology with a view from above *and* below. Anthropology is the inescapable arena for doing theology, while God remains the all-determining source of reality and truth. Consequently, we are not merely describing human beings as human beings, we are describing God's relationship to humanity in our historical and earthly existence. For example, in speaking of his christological method in particular, Pannenberg states,

> Only methodologically do we give precedence to arguing from below. . . . In truth, material primacy belongs to the eternal Son, who has become man by his incarnation in Jesus of Nazareth. Rightly understood, then, the two lines of argument from above and from below are complementary. Is, then, the relation between theology and anthropology a circular one of reciprocal conditioning? In fact, regard for reciprocal conditioning of concepts of God and concepts of human nature and destiny is a methodological premise. . . . The circle here, if we may call it such, is not the vicious circle of a logically defective argument that assumes what it must prove. Rather, we have here a relation of real mutual conditioning between an idea of God and a human self-understanding.[15]

Thus, we must "start from below," firmly located in time and space. Nevertheless, if God exists and has made the whole universe, then the very ground of our situated being finds its total existence in God. By having a concept of God that enables human beings to explain comprehensively and coherently all of reality, illuminating the meaning and purpose of human life and history, Christianity shows (at least proleptically and provisionally) the superior explanatory power its particular concept of God has over and against all other competing concepts of God and reality.

---

14. For an explication of reciprocity in Pannenberg, see Shults, *Postfoundationalist Task*, 165–77.

15. *ST* 2:289–90.

God, History, the Future, and Religious Contestation

How is this idea of God demonstrated to be superior and thus "true" so far as we can see? Pannenberg provides a set of concepts coupled with the idea of truth to present what he sees as a compelling answer to this question, namely coherence, history, and prolepsis. We will take these three ideas in turn, looking first at Pannenberg's notion of coherence and its complex but critical relationship to truth.

Truth as Coherence

Pannenberg's ideas about coherence come with important modifications that distinguish them from more traditional coherence theories of truth.[16] Instead of relying on internal coherence as the best test of truth, Pannenberg expands his coherentism to include not merely internal coherence, but also coherence with other areas of knowledge (like physical science, sociology, anthropology, etc.) that stand outside the particular scope of the topic (theology in this case) being presented and developed. This causes him to identify areas of direct and implied correspondence between theology and other fields of human knowledge. Thus, Pannenberg carries out this project of demonstrating truthfulness through coherence with a view to both internal aspects of consistency and external points of correspondence with other disciplines. In this way, Pannenberg's drive to find a more expansive and comprehensive form of coherence moves him to attempt two vitally interrelated projects in his systematics. We will begin a more thorough explanation by first looking at internal coherence.

Truth as Internal Coherence

For Pannenberg, the truth of theology is dependent upon the format and nature of its presentation. The more internally integrated, systematic, and coherent, the more the theological project demonstrates it is *true*. As Pannenberg states,

> [T]he systematic presentation of the content of Christian doctrine is already related as such to its truth claim. It tests the truth

---

16. For a look at one such theory, see Rescher, *Coherence Theory*. For an updated version of Rescher's coherentism, see his *Pluralism*. Another recent example is Lehrer, *Theory of Knowledge*.

> of what is presented. If truth can only be one, the things that are regarded as true will not contradict one another, and they can be united with one another. To this extent a systematic presentation of the articles of faith directly involves their truth and the ascertainment of their truth. . . . [T]he truth of the content is linked to the systematic presentation itself.[17]

While the temporal presentations and methods to achieve such unity may be significantly altered through time, the principles of the internal agreement of Christian doctrine and its agreement with basic rules of reason remain "permanently valid."[18] The teachings themselves, if true, must cohere with one another, for that is the nature of God's unified truth. Thus, coherence is not so much a *result* of systematics as it is a *prior condition* that underlies all truly theological revelations. In short, "the inner coherence that comes to light in the process cannot be external to the doctrine itself. It undoubtedly precedes its demonstration in the systematic presentation, but we can know this only on the basis of the presentation."[19] And while this systematic construction of Christian doctrine cannot guarantee the truth of its content, it does offer an important criterion for determining its validity and truthfulness.

Truth as External Correspondence

As important as internal coherence is for truth, it still "cannot conclusively decide the truth question."[20] A second element is needed in systematizing Christian doctrine. The truth lies objectively within the divine teaching of Christian theology, but can be missed because the coherent presentation must connect to the general reality lying behind it. Thus, another aspect of Pannenbergian coherence involves "the element of 'correspondence' to the object, the actual truth, which is a basic epistemological aspect of the concept of truth."[21] If theology seeks to elucidate a truly comprehensive concept of God, then Christian doc-

17. *ST* 1:19.
18. *ST* 1:20.
19. *ST* 1:22.
20. *ST* 1:23.
21. *ST* 1:24. The idea of truth as correspondence has come under a barrage of postmodern scorn in recent years. For one possible defense, see Groothuis, *Truth Decay*, 83ff.

trine and the question of God's reality cannot be detached from the nature of the universe and arenas of human knowledge lying outside theologically proper boundaries. As Pannenberg observes, "if the theses of Christian doctrine do not make the world's questioning of the reality of God . . . a question that is put to its own Christian truth consciousness, then these theses will not make contact with worldly reality but will hover above it and will not, therefore, be true."[22] All truth must connect to and cohere with what is known outside of Christianity to be actually true. Even the questioning of God's reality is grounded in God himself since he is creator of all. In short, good Christian theology must "present, test, and if possible confirm the claim. It must treat it, however, as an open question and not decide it in advance."[23] Even the raw subjectivism of some recent Protestant dogmatics cannot obliterate the universal nature of truth because "*my* truth cannot be mine alone. If I cannot in principle declare it to be truth for all . . . then it pitilessly ceases to be truth for me also."[24] Truth *in principle* is comprehensive because it finds its source in God who rules over and is in all. Christians should confidently allow their claims to be tested if they are certain God and his truth lies behind all reality. But no matter how compelling one's presentation is, no matter how obvious something appears, because of our finite and situated state, "all such knowledge will always be preliminary so long as time and history endure. . . ."[25] By being humbly open to public testing and scrutiny, one's perspective on truth can be strengthened, modified, and even radically altered in light of new information arising from the ongoing dialogue of ideas.

This notion of truth becomes vitally important for Christianity's relationship to other world religions. Such dialogue asks how one can decide between conflicting perspectives about God and reality. For Pannenberg, the best way to decide is to demonstrate one's concept of God and reality is consistent, comprehensive, and has greater explanatory power than all competing views put forth by alternative religions and philosophies. And this is ultimately demonstrated by the systematic and dialogical presentation of those views through time.

22. *ST* 1:49.
23. *ST* 1:50.
24. *ST* 1:51.
25. *ST* 1:16.

To summarize, truth in God's world, by its very nature, must remain public—open for all to examine and consider. If the earth really is God's, then truth must cohere with all right knowledge of and in that world. And yet it must also remain provisional because it will never be fully revealed until time's culmination. In short, because personal experience is always conditioned by finitude, claiming "unconditional, independent certainty is forcibly to make oneself, the believing I, the locus of absolute truth."[26] Instead, if Christians want to avoid "irrational fanaticism,"[27] they cannot presuppose the truth of Christian dogmatics prior to a systematic and critical presentation of such claims. Thus, the theological project becomes a systematic presentation of the coherent nature of the Christian concept of God in light of all human experience and knowledge. As such, the goal of systematics becomes the demonstration of the systematic theological presentation's internal coherence as well as its broader coherence with all human knowledge—whether science, sociology, psychology, anthropology, or the like. But this demonstration of truth as coherence happens by way of hypothetical reasoning as well as basic assertions about the nature of ourselves and the world in which we live. In so doing, the theologian offers "a model which, if it is tenable, will 'prove' the reality of God and the truth of the Christian doctrine, showing them to be consistently conceivable, and also confirming them, by the form of the presentation."[28] Of course, this presentation is restricted by the finitude of the one(s) explaining/presenting it to the world, but nevertheless, "the different models of Christian teaching, for all their limitations, still have the function of an anticipatory presentation of the truth of God for the definitive revelation for which the world is waiting."[29]

Truth and History

If Christians must face the historically situated nature of their truth claims, how can they say their theology is *true* in the provisional present? And what is the relationship between truth and history? Pannenberg

26. *ST* 1:47.
27. *ST* 1:47.
28. *ST* 1:60.
29. *ST* 1:60.

deals with this issue primarily in an essay entitled "What Is Truth?" Here, after exploring important differences and similarities between Greek and Hebrew notions of truth, Pannenberg emphasizes there is a "radical historicness"[30] involved in all human thought. Consequently, it becomes difficult to know

> whether our view of the world is truer than that of other peoples and cultures. Thereby it becomes questionable where truth is to be found at all. If reference to the unity of everything real is essential to truth, then it cannot simply deal with our present world. Its unity should instead also embrace other peoples and cultures of distant times, for whom the whole of reality presented itself differently from the way it does for us today. . . . In this situation, unity of truth can now only be thought of as the history of truth, meaning in effect that truth itself has a history and that its essence is the process of this history. Historical change itself must be thought of as the essence of truth if its unity is still to be maintained without narrow-mindedly substituting a particular perspective for the whole of truth.[31]

This attitude of seeking ever increasing unity through incorporating a constantly expanding view of God, reality, and truth becomes particularly important in dialogue with other cultures and religions. Thus, a Hegelian dialectic process is involved in acquiring and comprehending truth. Pannenberg's use of Hegel is explicit when he asserts truth progresses in history through an ongoing process whereby "All preliminary stages will be driven beyond themselves by their inner contradictions."[32] It is this drive against contradiction that moves interreligious dialogue beyond a quest for similarity and toward an antagonistic search for truth by weighing and considering competing and contradictory claims.

Ultimately, "truth as such is understood not as timelessly unchangeable, but as a process that runs its course and maintains itself through change. . . . What a thing is, is first decided by its future, by what becomes of it."[33] Thus, "the truth of the whole will be visible only

30. Pannenberg, "What Is Truth?", 20.
31. Ibid., 20–21.
32. Ibid., 21.
33. Ibid., 22.

at the end of history."³⁴ Elsewhere Pannenberg summarizes the idea this way: "Each individual experience finds definition only in relation to a context that for its part stands within a larger context until we arrive at the totality of all experiences and events. Hence individual meaning always finally depends on the total meaning of all experience and consequently on the totality of all events and reality that can be the object of experience."³⁵ Consequently, at any point in time, the claim for the meaning, significance, and truth of an event or experience can only be ultimately confirmed when history is completed and the individuated part is placed into the context of the whole. This makes history—secular and sacred—critically important, since only in light of the total catalogue of unfolding historical events can the significance and meaning of any one event be revealed. Thus, an ever-growing, cross-cultural and trans-temporal awareness of human history, not merely an atomistic glimpse at individuated historical events, is what aids in ascertaining the truth value of particular claims about God and reality. This provides the methodological motivations behind Pannenberg's constant use of the history of ideas, events, and movements to bolster truth claims throughout his systematics. Thus, as Shults argues, "an emphasis on history must be incorporated in any valid interpretation of Pannenberg,"³⁶ and Stanley J. Grenz calls Pannenberg's theological method "historical argumentation," noting that for Pannenberg "truth emerges from the flow of historical debate. The historical sketches . . . are not superfluous, then, but are integral to the development of his own position."³⁷

Ultimately, history matters so much for Pannenberg because it is not only the means of supporting his truth claims, but also the unfolding self-revelation of God to humanity.³⁸ Therefore, he makes the initially startling claim, "History is the most comprehensive horizon of Christian theology."³⁹ But this can only be true if in history the "theological presentation of God is central," and so "finds its unity in being

---

34. Ibid.

35. *ST* 3:590.

36. Shults, *Postfoundationalist Task*, 90.

37. Grenz, *Reason for Hope*, 13.

38. Pannenberg first began to develop this claim in a volume he edited and contributed to, called *Revelation as History*.

39. Pannenberg, "Redemptive Event and History," 15.

testimony to the deity of God."[40] Thus, moving back to theology proper, history only makes unified sense in light of our notions of God and what he appears to be doing through the comprehensive sweep of time.

Given the universal drive in Pannenberg's idea of God, pushing for the provisional present to be contextualized into the framework of history's whole makes sense. But it also presents finite humans with a dilemma concerning absolute truth claims. If all time has not passed, can we still claim what we know in the incomplete and finite present is actually true? Pannenberg acknowledges this requires a virtuous and humble recognition that our understanding in time remains forever transient and "falls short of full and final knowledge of the truth of God."[41] Consequently, our statements about theological truth must be humbly made, yet this "does not make our statements indifferent."[42] They can and should be made passionately, but there is always room for discussion and revision in view of new historical information since, "On account of the historicity of our experience and the openness of its contexts to the future . . . we have to think of the total meaning as still incomplete."[43] Only at time's end when history is consummated in God will we perfectly see how every particular event was a crucial part of God's comprehensive self-revelation. In Pannenberg's words, "History will thus be a demonstration of God, though only at its end."[44] Thus, all Christian truth claims remain hypothetical and testable until the full eschatological revelation of God's kingdom. Meanwhile, they must be examined as they stand, as truth claims that might actually be true *or* false. Consequently, "mindless acceptance does not honor them as propositions; the treatment of their truth claim as worth testing does."[45] But due to humanity's finitude, all truth claims remain inherently debatable until time reaches its zenith in God's eschaton.

---

40. *ST* 1:59.
41. *ST* 1:55.
42. *ST* 1:55.
43. *ST* 3:590.
44. *ST* 1:245.
45. *ST* 1:58.

Truth and Anticipation/Prolepsis

Given that only by knowing the context of the whole of history can any one event in history be given its proper significance and meaning, is there any hope to know, promote, and defend the truth *now* if its ultimate confirmation and unity are only realized in the completed future? Could it not be argued there is consequently no basis to claim Christianity is true *in the present*? At this point, Pannenberg introduces a unique means of solving this dilemma by using the idea of prolepsis or anticipation and the resurrection of Jesus Christ to supplement his epistemology.

The answer to this problem "lies in the proleptic character of the Christ event. That is to say, the resurrection of Jesus is indeed infallibly the dawning of the end of history . . ."[46] Thus, "In Christ, the eschaton has already appeared. Therefore it seems that history, at least in the sense of universal historical process, is finished. Christ is the end of history. . . . [H]istory as a whole is made possible for the first time because the end of history is already present."[47] Christ's resurrection becomes the "daybreak of the eschaton" for all humanity, and the "universal historical scheme itself is forced open."[48] Consequently, Christians, through faith in Christ, *already* provisionally participate in the future resurrection that will culminate in Christ's eschatological return. The proleptic nature of the Christ event and "understanding of the destiny of Jesus was the basis of primitive Christianity's, and especially of Paul's overwhelming certainty of truth. Can we still make this our own?"[49] Yes, says Pannenberg, but this certainty rests upon two critical things. First, it relies upon the fact that an "apocalyptic hope of resurrection still contains truth for us; i.e., whether it can still be reproduced within our understanding of the being of man in the world."[50] Pannenberg believes this is possible since everyone has an "openness . . . to question

---

46. Pannenberg, "What Is Truth?," 24. This theme of prolepsis in Christ appears very early in Pannenberg's thought. These aforementioned words were first printed in a 1962 German article, cited in ibid., 1, and in his essay "Redemptive Event and History," which was first delivered as a lecture in 1959.

47. Pannenberg, "Redemptive Event and History," 36.

48. Ibid., 37–38.

49. Pannenberg, "What Is Truth?," 25.

50. Ibid.

beyond death."⁵¹ Secondly, we can only base our certainty of truth upon the Christ event if we "still understand the resurrection of Jesus as a historical event which happened at a specific time: as a reality, and not a mere hallucination."⁵²

If we can demonstrate these things are realities, then the future of truth's confirmation still remains open since Christ's return currently remains in the future, and yet truth *en toto* has been proleptically revealed in him such that we can know it provisionally as a unified whole. Consequently, the completed and timeless Greek and the incomplete and historical Hebrew notions of truth "become one for the first time only in Jesus Christ."⁵³ Jesus Christ becomes the firm foundation for truth's unity. Through Christ's resurrection, the eschatological whole irrupts into the partial present solving the dilemma of historical incompleteness.⁵⁴ Still, the total fulfillment of what began in the resurrection (to be revealed in God's eschaton) remains unrealized in the contingent present. Yet "with Jesus the end is not only . . . seen in advance, but it has happened in advance."⁵⁵ It is not merely a vision of the future reality that is to be actuated in God's eschatological kingdom, it is the inauguration and in-breaking of the fulfilled future into the incomplete present. The future is not only something coming, it is something already currently known and realized. In short, "If Jesus has been raised, then the end of the world has begun."⁵⁶

To summarize, we are bound in time, relativized and conditioned by our "situatedness," and yet this need not make "the relativity of our experience and reflection" the condition of truth itself.⁵⁷ Truth remains absolute in God, but it is not yet fully realized to those still in time. Only through time's culmination will the truth be fully revealed and vindicated in and by God. We can only determine the true meaning of

---

51. Ibid.

52. Ibid., 26. Because of the centrality of the literal and historical resurrection of Jesus of Nazareth to his argument, Pannenberg provides a fairly extensive defense of the historicity of the literal bodily resurrection of Jesus. For a look at this defense, see *ST* 2:343–63. See also his *Jesus—God and Man*, 88–105 and 108–14.

53. Pannenberg, "What Is Truth?," 27; see 26–27 for a concise summary of Pannenberg's argument.

54. *ST* 1:247.

55. Pannenberg, *Jesus—God and Man*, 61.

56. Ibid., 67.

57. *ST* 1:54.

things if our determination rests upon an anticipation of a total appearance of the whole in the future. As this future unfolds, these anticipations are changed and modified through our ongoing experience of the progressive history and plan of the one true and faithful God. We see what is reliable and unreliable, but only provisionally. Nevertheless, that completed and holistic future has already dawned and irrupted into the present through Christ's resurrection. Thus, Christians make truth claims informed and empowered by the proleptic presence of the risen Christ within the body of the church. Still, only in the eschaton will all competing understandings be finally settled by God. This introduces one more central feature of Pannenberg's theology of religions, namely the eschatological aspect.

Truth and the Future

Because Pannenberg places so much weight on prolepsis in truth's ultimate confirmation, it is not surprising that the eschaton becomes a crucial issue to address. A significant portion of *ST* 3 lays out his eschatological vision. There Pannenberg claims that one of the distinctive marks of God's future kingdom is humanity's unity beneath Christ's lordship. So, the proleptic aspect of Christ's resurrection that bears the greatest significance is his unity with God the Father. This oneness will be most evident in the eschaton when everything is unified in God's transforming love. And this makes sense since the sovereign God has the reconciling power to bring all things into communal unity. The movement of God's unfolding history is toward an equality of human fellowship and intimacy with the all-determining Power that created all things and longs to draw all things into a great society of eternal love. Pannenberg links this to God's image in humanity by noting that "the positive aim of rule [over creation] . . . is not mere coercion [but] to bring unity and peace. The destiny of human beings to be images of God would then be fulfilled in the reconciliation of the world through the coming of the Messiah."[58] Only then will the human race be "renewed and united under the reign of God" showing "the image of God in human beings . . . has a 'societal structure.'"[59] This divine image in human-

---

58. Pannenberg, *Anthropology*, 531.
59. Ibid.

ity corresponds to "the Trinitarian life of God," since this relation will be "fulfilled in the human community and specifically in the community of God's kingdom . . . in which all dominion of human beings over one another will be eliminated."[60] Because the church serves as the proleptic, eschatological community under the Lordship of God, its presence upon earth reminds human beings of this coming consummation when all will be one in God's eschatological kingdom. This fellowship is "more than just a promise because it rests on an event of fulfillment [Jesus' resurrection] that has taken place already. Nevertheless, this event is not yet complete. It also carries a reference to future completion."[61] The Holy Spirit gives all believers a foretaste of this eternal, timeless, divine fellowship, lifting them beyond themselves toward the power of the future. In short, "By the Spirit the eschatological future is present already in the hearts of believers."[62] Rather than closing off present forms and notions of truth, Jesus opens up the future by bringing time's completed end (the not yet) into the incomplete present (the now) in the form of anticipation. This provides believers with a real (though conditioned) experience of eternity in the temporal now through the ecstatic work of the Spirit who lifts us beyond ourselves and the present into eschatological fellowship with God. Is this offer of divine fellowship limited to explicit confessions of Christ? For Pannenberg, while Christ remains the standard and guarantor of salvation, "what counts [for those outside Christianity] is whether their individual conduct actually agrees with the will of God that Jesus proclaimed. The message of Jesus is the norm by which God judges even in the case of those who never meet Jesus personally."[63] Thus, this future eschatological transformation will not merely include those within the visible church of God. It will also be "the fulfillment of human society" as a whole.[64] And that fulfillment is manifest primarily in the unity of all humanity under God—proleptically demonstrated by the church in the present age as it participates in the future life of God through the sacraments and the Spirit's ecstatic power. As Pannenberg puts it, "the church is the people of God, a pro-

60. Ibid., 531–32.
61. *ST* 3:550–51.
62. *ST* 3:552.
63. *ST* 3:615.
64. *ST* 3:580.

visional representation of the future of humanity as it is reconciled with God in his kingdom."[65] Christ's proleptic body does not always fulfill its intended role in the present and can even sometimes obscure God's plan for humanity. Thus for Pannenberg, there may be people who are "longing for the kingdom of God," but unfortunately, "can no longer see [that kingdom] in the church's life."[66] Consequently, the truth is still in Jesus, and Christianity's God is still Lord of the universe and the source of all truth, but some outside Christianity may also be part of God's eschatological fellowship. Naturally, this has important implications for his theology of religions.

In summary, theological truth is demonstrated in the coherence of the presentation made on the basis of the concept of God and reality. And this coherence is not merely internal, but must also be externally related to the whole history of ideas and events in a way that gives illuminating explanatory power to the human condition. Given life's situated nature, one's knowledge and understanding of any portion of history is necessarily finite and conditioned. The true and comprehensive significance of any particular event or concept can only be fully seen in view of the completed whole of history. However, Christianity is uniquely situated to remain open to this holistic future because Jesus' resurrection, through the ecstatic power of the Holy Spirit who lifts us out of the finite present into the eternal age to come, proleptically reveals the totality of the future in the unfinished present. Only at the end of all things when God's eschatological kingdom is revealed in all its fullness will his unified truth and undisputed reign be vindicated to all mankind. In the mean time, the church provides a crucial anticipatory (although still imperfect) picture of the intimate and eternal fellowship all creation will enjoy in God's eschaton.

I have treated Pannenberg's interrelated concepts of truth, history, and prolepsis (coupled with important aspects his eschatology) at length for a specific purpose concerning his theology of religions. Because they play a crucial role in both the method and the motivation for all interreligious dialogue, they required closer examination before proceeding to the actual process of religious dialogue and the relationship of Christianity to other religions.

---

65. *ST* 3:433.
66. *ST* 3:525.

Pannenberg's Method for a Theology of Religions: God, Religion, and the Nature of Humanity

As discussed, Pannenberg sees the task of understanding Christianity in the context of other religions as a critical aspect of demonstrating its truthfulness and bolstering its credibility. This conviction becomes sensible when understood in the total context of history—a history representing God's revelatory unfolding of himself to humanity. Thus, the idea of religion and the religious nature of people in general provide a crucial backdrop for any theology of religions. In developing his theology of religions, Pannenberg expends much effort historically tracing various concepts poured into the idea of religion in chapter 3 of *ST* 1 and in his *BQ* 2 essay "Toward a Theology of the History of Religions." It is to these two treatments we now turn.

The Concept of Religion

Pannenberg's exploration of the idea of religion, true to his theological method, traces important aspects of its long and complex history. We pick up the subject in the modern period with its many challenges for Christianity. By this time, a crucial question about religion and religions arose that was not previously a major issue, because "For the older Protestant dogmatics the plurality of religions posed no problem for the truth of Christianity. True and false religion could be differentiated according to the standard of the Word of God."[67] If some alternative religious belief or practice was inconsistent with biblical teaching, it could simply be considered false on the basis of the authority of God's Word. In the modern period, however, that view was increasingly difficult to uphold. As Pannenberg notes, "The task is this: How can theology make the primacy of God and his revelation in Jesus Christ intelligible, and validate its truth claim, in an age when all talk about God is reduced to subjectivity, as may be seen from the social history of the time and the modern fate of the proofs of God and philosophical theology?"[68]

Attempts to make Christianity the supreme religion produced several proposed bases, but they tended to compare themselves to a general

---

67. *ST* 1:129.
68. *ST* 1:128.

concept of religion, making Christianity "the 'religion of religions.'"[69] Other religions were therefore "inadequate forms" of religion in general.[70] Eventually, because some religious views (like some forms of Buddhism, for example) are technically atheistic, the idea of religion became detached "from the concept of God" altogether, resulting in "a purely anthropological definition of religion."[71] And while these definitions were not "totally false" since they did describe certain dimensions of human religiosity, they still could not provide a general, satisfactory, and universal concept of religion.[72]

During this period there was a strong drive to abstract a universal principle of religiosity and describe what might be called "the essence of religion." The history and philosophy of religion became separated "with the repudiation of total conceptions of the course of religious history."[73] Eventually, "the so-called *comparative* approach to religious history" sought to find "similar motifs in different religions."[74] This had the grievous result of "shrinking genuine *historical* interest in religion."[75] Thus, a "phenomenology of religion" arose that detached "the forms in which religious life is expressed from their historical contexts," treating such connections as "inconsequential."[76] As a result, there was less interest in the actual history of religions and more concern for abstracting general principles from religions, leading scholars astray from what religion really is. The more abstracted from their concrete historical situations these principles became, the less these scholars were "able *empirically* to distinguish between superficial and essential mutualities."[77] This is not to say such observations are worthless, but it shows that they "can at best provide only a preliminary anthropology of religious experience."[78] A more complete theology of religions must attend to the unique and concrete historical expressions of particular religions.

69. *ST* 1:129–30.
70. *ST* 1:130.
71. *ST* 1:137.
72. *ST* 1:138.
73. Pannenberg, "Toward a Theology," 72.
74. Ibid., 73.
75. Ibid.
76. Ibid.
77. Ibid., 75.
78. Ibid., 77–78.

Otherwise, it "necessarily leads to violent distortions of the phenomena and to the affirmation of deceptive mutualities that have no basis in the concrete intentionality expressed in the religious phenomena."[79]

Religions, then, must be understood as dynamically embedded in the historical matrix of space and time. Unity is grounded in the unity of deity, not in an extracted abstract essence that cuts across the spectrum of all religious experiences and claims. Pannenberg summarizes his argument this way:

> In view of the continuing plurality and competition of the gods and beliefs, it is an illusion to think we can formulate a concept of religion that is not characterized by a specific standpoint in the history of religion. . . . If an appropriate definition of the concept of religion demands recognition of the primacy of the self-declaring deity vis-à-vis the religious relation of worship of this deity and fellowship with it in worship, in formulating the concept, we cannot ignore the plurality and antagonism of deities and views of deity. This fact, however, does not cancel out the existence of a single concept of religion.[80]

Since religions are concerned with the nature of *deity*, they are fundamentally *theological*. True to his commitment to reciprocity in theological method, Pannenberg notes, "Theology has both a critical and a constructive task. A theology of religion must be critical of the reduction of the concept of religion to anthropology."[81] Thus, one of Pannenberg's major tasks in *Anthropology in Theological Perspective* is to explain how purely secular anthropologies of religions do not adequately understand the nature of human religion as the pursuit of God's *reality* and not merely a reductively atheistic anthropological *idea* about God and reality. Due to philosophical, historical, and even theological reasons, the "'new anthropology' became the basis for the secular culture that arose after the end of the confessional wars of the sixteenth and seventeenth centuries. This culture developed in detachment from the Christian churches."[82] Consequently, there was an implicit "disregard of the theological question concerning the human person."[83] So, the solu-

79. Ibid., 78–79.
80. *ST* 1:149.
81. Pannenberg, "Response," 296.
82. Pannenberg, *Anthropology*, 17.
83. Ibid., 18.

tion is not to ignore modern anthropology, doing Christian theology in a walled-off, pietistic, and compartmental way, separated from the concerns and perspectives of modern life. Instead, Pannenberg argues:

> [T]he only conclusion theologians should draw from this situation is that they may not indiscriminatingly accept the data provided by nontheological anthropology and make these the basis for their own work, but rather must appropriate them in a critical way. This kind of critical appropriation is necessary in dealing with nontheological anthropology because . . . the relations between anthropological findings and the subject matter of theology have in large measure been lost from sight. . . . [A] critical appropriation . . . is also possible if the God of the Bible is indeed the creator of all reality.[84]

However, this process does not *presuppose* God's existence beforehand. It merely sees anthropological data as potentially helpful in the comprehensive process of demonstrating God's reality as the best explanation for all that exists.

Essentially, Pannenberg wants to move away from a purely *secular* interpretation of religions and reality. He would like to see Christianity's perspective be an option in the public arena alongside other religions and sciences. Thus, Christianity becomes another science, another alternative and competing way of knowing and understanding the world. But starting from purely secular religious concepts results in explanations of religion that "contradict the witness of the religions themselves."[85] Nevertheless, "Defining the nature of religion [still] does not answer the question of its truth."[86] And observing that human beings are inherently and incurably religious is not sufficient to prove the truth of religion either, because "from [humanity's] religious disposition there does not follow the truth of religious statements."[87] Simply to describe what religious adherents are doing or what beliefs they are claiming is insufficient for understanding them *as they really are*. To treat their truth claims as secondarily important in one's search to find a unifying concept of religion does no justice to the actual way religions

---

84. Ibid., 18–19.
85. *ST* 1:151.
86. *ST* 1:151.
87. *ST* 1:156.

make universal truth claims for themselves.[88] Furthermore, arguing *religious* truth claims are fundamentally different from normative public truth claims and are only derived from subjective human desires and needs is to misunderstand or misrepresent what religions actually claim for themselves. Appeals to subjectivity in religion do not help since subjectivity tends to wall itself off from all reality, and therefore does not accurately represent the idea of God as the comprehensive and all-determining reality who is the very ground of all human subjectivity.

The Nature of Religious Progress

The result is this: claims made by competing religions are fundamentally different. Thus, "the many and frequently contradictory religious statements regarding gods and their working cannot be accepted as true merely on the ground that we are all referred to a sphere of the holy."[89] A strong disposition to be religious is one important aspect of human experience pointing toward the existence of deity, even if it is an insufficient criterion by itself to make a definitive judgment. The best way to explore the question of truth in religion is "in the sphere of experience of the world, as the world, including humanity and its history, shows itself to be determined by God."[90] So Pannenberg agues,

> [T]he question of the divine reality cannot be settled independently from dealing with particular and antagonistic claims of the different religious traditions. . . . But in what sense, then, can we speak of "genuine revelation of God within the history of religions"? Hardly in the sense that the different truth claims of the religious traditions may be accepted equally: they cannot, because they fight each other.[91]

This gets to the heart of Pannenberg's theology of religions. Religion is the contested search for the best (*truest*) explanation of reality as we know it in light of the particular religious concept of God and ultimate reality. Elsewhere, Pannenberg expands the idea this way:

---

88. Pannenberg is clearly responding here to the project of Hick and others like him.

89. *ST* 1:157.

90. *ST* 1:159.

91. Pannenberg, "Response," 314.

> The history of one deity was always that of conflict with competing deities and truth claims.... But this did not rule out in principle the possibility that the contours of the deity might emerge in the process of competition.... In view of the extensive spread of the religions that sprouted from this root [of Israeli Monotheism], does that not mean that the history of conflicts between the gods was the path to the development of the unity of the divine reality which has finally produced a religious situation embracing all humanity?... Is, then, the unity of the divine reality the true object of the struggle of religious history?[92]

In the contested struggle for truth, a religion's ability to unify within itself other competing viewpoints through integration and even supersession, using its own internal resources (called the syncretistic process), demonstrates its dynamic creativity and explanatory power. In Pannenberg's view, "Christianity affords the greatest example of syncretistic assimilative power."[93] As religions encounter one another, "they run into conflicts... which can be smoothed out or peacefully settled in various ways: by the relativization of the universal claim of one's own as well as of the alien religion to merely that of a given circle of devotees; by means of interpretation or . . . even cultic fusion; and, finally, by displacement."[94]

In *ST* 1, Pannenberg illustrates his meaning using Israel's Old Testament concept of God, noting that "Jewish belief did not involve a total rejection of all other gods. Yahweh is confessed as the one God, but he is identified in some sense with El, the Canaanite God of creation, and later with the Persian God of heaven."[95] Thus, "from the standpoint

---

92. *ST* 1:148.

93. Pannenberg, "Toward a Theology," 87.

94. Ibid., 88. This sounds remarkably like the historical thesis about truth, justice, and rationality that MacIntyre develops and defends in *Whose Justice, Which Rationality?* In an unpublished article entitled "Tradition on Its Way," I critically explore the many parallels as well as key differences between Pannenberg and MacIntyre concerning the idea of truth.

95. *ST* 1:179. For those uncomfortable with such a notion, modern missionary activities show how certain aspects of deity in other religions can be revised and taken up into the idea of the Christian God without compromising his being. In fact, the parallels in the concepts of deity discovered in some non-Christian religions are sometimes quite remarkable. In this way, a local name for a certain god can sometimes be used in Bible translation in such a way as to be "taken over" by a Christian belief and understanding that provides a fuller picture of God who was known about but perhaps

of the faith of Israel, not everything connected with the belief in God in other religions was reprehensible."[96] The Jewish idea of God was able to redefine and then incorporate other notions of deity into itself successfully through time, demonstrating its superior dynamism and assimilative power.

Christianity's success in this process also reveals its superiority to other religions because Christ's proleptic revelation of God's future reign leaves it open to revision and growth, while simultaneously giving it a solid basis for making holistic truth claims. Religions and sects that "finitize" their views of God, locking them into a particular time and place, close themselves off to any future revelations and eventually become stagnant, lifeless, and sterile. Thus, "non-Christian religions perceived the appearance of the divine mystery only in a fragmentary way because they were closed to their own transformation, to their own history."[97] In contrast, "The sustaining power of Christianity to endure in world history lies in its openness to the future, a feature rooted in . . . divine revelation as promise. A religion that lives by promise toward the future can cope with the vicissitudes of the historical process better than religions related to the past-oriented myth of primordial time."[98] As such, "the characteristic contribution of Christian theology to the history of religions should consist not in some sort of construction developed from the standpoint of Christian dogmatics, but rather in working with an unprejudiced openness to create space in the history of religions for the appearing of the divine mystery *and* for its debatability."[99]

Ultimately, religious claims "should be tested . . ." to see if "the divine mystery expressed in a religious phenomenon is able to illuminate the reality of existence . . . *then* and . . . in *contemporary* experience,

---

previously worshiped in ignorance or in an incomplete way (cf. Acts 17:23). This does not detract from the fact that some of these gods are demonic and unredeemable, of course. But it does point out the sometimes ambiguous task of translating and contextualizing the gospel into a radically foreign culture and worldview. For an African perspective on this process of contextualization, see Bediako, *Christianity in Africa*. For a look at the process carried out by the early church apologist Justin Martyr, see Tennent, "Was Socrates a Christian?"

96. *ST* 1:179.
97. Pannenberg, "Toward a Theology," 115.
98. Pannenberg, "Response," 304.
99. Pannenberg, "Toward a Theology," 117.

and therewith to confirm its claim to open up an access to the divine mystery."[100] In addition, "[T]he testing of the truth claims which religions make with their statements about the existence and work of the gods does not take place primarily in the form of academic investigation and evaluation but in the process of religious life itself. The standard is not external to the deity itself.... Does God prove in actual experience to be the power that he is claimed to be?"[101] Thus, claims for deity are evaluated *internally* based on the experience of the world in light of the understanding a particular religion has about God (or the gods).

As humanity's experience of the world unfolds, cultures and religions inevitably mingle and clash, bringing about historical changes. These changes cannot be accounted for merely by sociological, political, and economic explanations. History continually demonstrates the crucial role religious conceptions about God (or the gods), human nature, and reality play in historical transformation and progress. To consider these dynamics as secondary and reactive to secular changes in culture is to ignore the actual nature of history. Rather than ruling out religious explanations beforehand, they must be given fair consideration as one of the possible (and even likely) reasons for historical change. As Pannenberg observes, "A theology of world religions that wants to be true to the empirical situation in the way the religious traditions confront each other must not evade or play down the conflict of truth claims. If we look to the history of religions in the past, there was always competition and struggle for superiority on the basis of different truth claims."[102] In the final analysis, we must answer this crucial question: Do "the gods of the religions . . . show in our experience of the world that they are the powers they claim to be"?[103]

A Pannenbergian Theology of Religions

To summarize, when the *truth* of a religion is in question—that is, "whether the gods in whom its adherents believe prove to be gods"[104]—

---

100. Ibid., 118.
101. *ST* 1:159–60.
102. Pannenberg, "Conflicting Truth Claims," 103.
103. *ST* 1:167.
104. *ST* 1:168.

God, History, the Future, and Religious Contestation

there are, according to Pannenberg, three important points for dynamic appraisal of truth value. The first criterion is this: "The confirmation or nonconformation of religious assertions, and especially of the belief in the existence and work of deity, is experienced and established in the first instance by the adherents of the relevant religious fellowship. . . . If the expected confirmation does not eventuate, there will not be an immediate forsaking of the deity."[105] However, a "tension between faith and experience" will arise.[106] This tension is also produced by the responsibility older generations have to pass on the faith to subsequent generations as well as "when belief in the deity is brought to those who thus far have not belonged to the circle of worshipers of this deity."[107] This is an internal crisis of belief that primarily seeks resolution within the fellowship of the faithful.

Second, the need for confirmation or disconfirmation of truth claims about the deity often arises from "the competitive pressure of the truth claims of other deities which claim the same sphere of experience of the world as proof."[108] This occurs cross-culturally when cultures collide with one another, as well as intra-culturally when alternative views vie for wider adherence.

Third, for claims about the deity to be validated, historical changes should also bring about positive changes in the understanding of the deity so new light is shed on the power and nature of that deity as well as the nature of the world in which we live. There is a reciprocal relation where religious believers seek to understand and interpret the meaning of history as an ongoing disclosure and "demonstration of his deity to

---

105. *ST* 1:168.
106. *ST* 1:168.
107. *ST* 1:168.

108. *ST* 1:168. It is this fact that makes the epistemological clash between Islam, Christianity, and secularism (for example) so consistent—and contentious at times. Each of these worldviews tends to make exclusive truth claims about the world in which we all live and about the way things actually are and should be. Since these universal visions do not always agree with one another (or even, as we must all admit, within themselves) these alternative perspectives produce constant contestations about the existence, meaning, relevance, and the nature of God (and other derivative theological concerns), for believers and unbelievers, insiders and outsiders alike. The question as to how any particular religious person should respond to the religious and nonreligious other within these contests is one of the critical subjects of this current study.

them."[109] This is God's revelation—"the manifestation of divine reality even within the unresolved conflicts of religious and ideological truth claims."[110] But because it is necessarily interpreted in time by believers, our understanding of God "does not always correspond to the truth," necessitating further divine self-disclosure over time.[111] Whether or not a certain conception of God (or the gods) survives through time suggests the dynamic power of that particular God and the success of his believers to understand and explain him to others. The more a believing community's worship corresponds "to the true God and his revelation," the more it can be characterized as true worship, and the more interpretive power those views provide for our current experience of the world.[112] But in terms of testing truth claims, "The method of *theology* and of theology of religion and religions is to test religious traditions by the standard of their own understanding of the divine reality. . . . Does it, in other words, provide an interpretive approach to reality which gives insights into the way it is experienced in practice?"[113]

Because these criteria are internally related to each community of faith, even if they inevitably intersect and interact with those outside their community, "no basic objections can be made against the fact that theology within the Christian tradition concentrates upon a theology of Christianity, provided that the assumption of the superiority of the Christian revelation to other religious traditions remains in principle open to discussion and is not isolated from criticism."[114] Thus, we need to know what we believe about God and his world, defending it to others as truth, while simultaneously recognizing that our limited and historically conditioned understanding of truth is still open to further modification, correction, and even rejection. This is especially true since unfolding history is the stage upon which God continues to disclose himself to the world in such a way as to demonstrate more clearly his divine purposes and power. In so doing, God corrects and revises incomplete and finite views of his infinite greatness.

109. *ST* 1:170.
110. *ST* 1:171.
111. *ST* 1:170.
112. *ST* 1:172.
113. Pannenberg, *Philosophy of Science*, 320.
114. Ibid., 323.

God, History, the Future, and Religious Contestation

Meanwhile, we face a variety of perspectives on God, because we encounter "the Absolute, the true Infinite . . . in the medium of worldly experience and its finite contents."[115] Therefore, "the one infinite power is divided up into many powers for those who try to learn its nature through its manifestations. But these many powers are simply particular aspects of the one Infinite. We are still aware of the unity of the divine."[116] Consequently, the process of interreligious dialogue is a process of mutual sharing and discovery, but often times it focuses on differences in perspective. There are, of course, places of common belief and practice that point to the unity of deity present to all humanity. In fact, Pannenberg sees the common practice of righteous human behavior as the best indicator of a person's attitude and relation toward the future of God. But what is most interesting in dialogue is not only the coherence of the theological presentation, but also the many places where sharp disagreements, especially concerning religious concepts of God and/or ultimate reality, occur. Herein lies the most potential for progress in theological knowledge and understanding. If God is the Lord of all history and is revealing his ways and nature through time to all, then theological development comes not only in the form of Christianity's incorporation and interpretation of historical events, but also in terms of finding out what God has done and is doing throughout the world in the hearts and minds of human beings from a wide variety of religious perspectives. Granted, the resurrection of Jesus Christ has opened Christians up more fully to the future reality of God's lordship over all, giving them a clearer picture of the truth, but that does not rule out their need for a greater and more comprehensive knowledge of God and his unfolding revelation in the whole of human history. The situated nature of human existence necessitates an admission that current understandings can and will be superseded by the future unveiling of God in history—since it is and will remain in the final analysis *his* story. In short, "According to the witness of the Bible the deity of God will be definitively and unquestionably manifested only at the end of all time and history."[117] At that culminating moment all will finally be made clear in God's eschatological kingdom. He will unambiguously

---

115. *ST* 1:179.
116. *ST* 1:180.
117. *ST* 1:54.

show himself to be the sovereign God over all. In the meantime, the church has a crucial role in representing God's kingdom upon earth.

Although not fully revealed until the eschaton, God's kingdom is still proleptically present and active through the church. By the Spirit's ecstatic power it is lifted beyond itself, pointing toward the eschatological communion of all humanity with God in his coming kingdom. As Pannenberg puts it, "The church is not yet the kingdom of God; it is a preceding sign of the future fellowship of humanity under God's reign."[118] So, it represents a provisional anticipatory picture or sign of the eschatological destiny and goal God has in store for all of humanity, making it "an eschatological community."[119] Thus, the church is meant to represent the unified divine eschatological fellowship of all humanity, and "Christian mission thus presupposes the church's sense of election,"[120] for the calling and task of not only teaching and imparting the gospel, but also impacting and even sometimes directing the political and secular ordering of society to the glory and honor of God. Therefore, the church is uniquely and corporately elected not only to be separated from the world's ways, but also to perform an inclusive mission *to* the world's peoples. Consequently, election is not exclusive but rather inclusive in its goal and nature since God wants to include everyone and everything in his eschatological fellowship.[121] Even in world history, divine election plays an important role. In a world where strife and war have become the norm, God's chosen people are to be a picture of unified fellowship, "called on to offer a model of his kingdom."[122] Unfortunately, the church sometimes obscures its eschatological and elected nature, but it can never wholly destroy it since it participates in something—and Someone—beyond itself. This ecclesiological failure can even drive God's elect out and away from the church's corruption and ungodliness. And yet in their failure and subsequent judgment, God is always able to bring good out of evil and conception out of destruction, renewing the church and society by his providential grace and lordship, which will only be fully revealed in the eschaton when

---

118. *ST* 3:16–17.
119. *ST* 3:32.
120. *ST* 3:509.
121. *ST* 3:523.
122. *ST* 3:524.

God, History, the Future, and Religious Contestation

Jesus returns to redeem and rule the earth for God's glory through the Spirit's power. Pannenberg summarizes:

> [T]he sign of the divine rule in the life of the church is often distorted to the point of unrecognizability. May there not be, then, subjectively justifiable grounds on which to remain aloof from the church? Does this not mean that some of those who do so, or who turn away from the church, act out of disenchanted longing for the kingdom of God that they can no longer see in the church's life?[123]

Thus, those outside the official church might still be related to God and his kingdom as proleptic participants in the coming eschatological fellowship. The wideness of God's love suggests a wideness in his mercy for those outside the fellowship of the Christian church. Again, in Pannenberg's words,

> It is true enough that the event of a personal encounter with Jesus through the Christian message and a response of faith to it cannot be the universal criterion for participation in salvation or exclusion from it if we take seriously what the NT says about the love of God for the world that embraces all people. Many have never been reached by the proclamation of the gospel. For them the fact of personal encounter with Jesus through the church's preaching, which depends on contingent and historical factors, cannot be decisive for eternal salvation. In their case what counts is whether their individual conduct actually agrees with the will of God that Jesus proclaimed. The message of Jesus is the norm by which God judges even in the case of those who never meet Jesus personally. Christ guarantees a share in eschatological salvation with the fact that all people, whether Christians or not, have the chance of participation in the kingdom of God that Jesus proclaimed . . .
>
> What, then, is the advantage of Christians at the future judgment? The advantage is that in the person of Jesus they *know* the standard for participation in eternal salvation and hence also the standard of judgment. . . . [T]hey can also be sure already of future participation in salvation.[124]

Are none in danger of condemnation, then? Pannenberg cannot escape clear Scriptural testimony here when he concedes, "In view of

---

123. *ST* 3:525.
124. *ST* 3:615–16.

the plain NT statements on the matter we certainly cannot rule out the possibility of the eternal damnation of some."[125] Nevertheless, there is in Pannenberg a strong drive toward the unification of all things under the all-consuming, all-encompassing God. And this self-admittedly moves him toward a more universal picture of salvation: "[Since] the Christian claim aims at the *finality* of revelation as well as of salvation, . . . it also includes a tendency towards 'universal salvation.'"[126]

Ultimately, God alone will resolve all contested truth claims when time is consummated and he comes to full reign in the eschaton. In the mean time, Christians enjoy the proleptic presence of the risen Christ who has brought that future eschatological reality into the now, giving Christians an anticipatory taste of this completed future in the partial present.

This presents a highly inclusive picture of humanity unified at the end of the age under the sovereign lordship of the one, all-encompassing God made known through Jesus Christ. Thus, Christian mission ideally points toward this grand eschatological fellowship with God as it proleptically demonstrates it in the present. In the meantime, dialogue serves to produce greater unity and understanding between the adherents of all religions as together we carry on a contested debate for the truth and continue to correct and expand our knowledge of God and his world.

A Trinitarian Theology of Religions

One last area of concern in Pannenberg's theology of religions remains. Recall that he argues that the inter- and intra-religious concept of God is centrally important in religious contestation and our ability to explain successfully the history and experience of our world. Because Pannenberg is working from within Christianity, it is appropriate to delve briefly into his uniquely trinitarian theology since this is so distinctively Christian in nature, and since he makes the Trinity a thematic centerpiece of his systematic theology. In fact, as Robert Jensen puts it, without this emphasis "the structure of Pannenberg's doctrines of

---

125. *ST* 3:620.
126. Pannenberg, "Response," 315.

Christ and God would have to be altered radically."[127] And the way he develops his trinitarian theology provides surprising resources in our search for a more comprehensive picture of God and his possible presence within the beliefs and practices of other religions. It is this trinitarian idea of God we will now briefly explore.

That Pannenberg insists on developing a distinctly trinitarian view of God may initially be surprising with respect to a theology of religions. At a time when many ecumenical Christian theologians are "downplaying" trinitarian aspects of God, Pannenberg brings an emphatic voice into the interfaith dialogues, insisting the historical self-disclosure of God reveals not only his infinite attributes and characteristics, but also his distinctly *trinitarian* nature. Crucial in this revelatory respect is Jesus of Nazareth—particularly his resurrection as a concrete literal fact of human history. Without the words, life, death, and especially resurrection of Jesus seen holistically, the development of trinitarian belief becomes unlikely. However, historical events make trinitarian belief seemingly inescapable. Because of the importance of Jesus in the development of this doctrine, Pannenberg makes a surprising move in his discussion of God in *ST* 1. Rather than beginning with God's unity and then trying explain his "three-ness," Pannenberg begins with the tri-unity of God and only afterwards moves to resolve the question, "If God is three, then how can he also be one?" Traditional theology has almost always started with God's oneness and then tried to solve the problem of his tri-unity. But since the historical Jesus reveals a triune God, our first concern must be the concrete events supporting that belief. Only then can we revisit the question of God's unity. Pannenberg summarizes the reason for his ordering this way:

> The moment it appears that the one God can be better understood without rather than with the doctrine of the Trinity, the latter seems to be a superfluous addition to the concept of God even though it is reverently treated as a mystery of revelation. Even worse, it necessarily seems to be incompatible with the divine unity. Only in this setting can biblical exegesis and historical criticism be used to destroy trinitarian teaching.[128]

---

127. Jensen, "Jesus in the Trinity," 190.
128. *ST* 1:293.

Ultimately, from our knowledge of Jesus' life, as well as all of human history, we can most sensibly conclude the universal God is best understood as *trinitarian*.

Recall that human history is often the antagonistic record of competing views of truth vying to demonstrate their greater truthfulness and rationality. Within this competition, areas of commonality alongside points of contention move the intercultural and interfaith discussions forward toward the truth. Consequently, the idea of God's triune nature becomes a critical point of interreligious contention and Christian distinction.

The distinctive nature of the contestation for the truth of Christianity's God and truth's relationship to history, interfaith dialogue, and a theology of religions does not stop there. Pannenberg's theology of religions also emphasizes the Spirit's work in conjunction with the Father and the Son. Rejecting the *filioque* clause, where the Spirit proceeds from the Father and the Son and so tends to be subordinated to them, he argues that the Spirit is "constitutive for the fellowship of the Father with the Son."[129] As an equal member of the triune Godhead, the Spirit plays a critical role in God's creation that goes far beyond the bounds of the church. Elevating creatures beyond themselves ecstatically into the life of God, the Spirit gives eschatological life to believers, as well as dynamic life to all creation. This thematic use of the Spirit in Christian theologies of religions is not new, but Pannenberg, like Gavin D'Costa, refuses to sever the Spirit's intimate link with the Father and the Son in the intertrinitarian life.[130] Therefore, while the Spirit lifts people beyond themselves toward life in God, the Son and the Father are present where the Spirit is, even if only ambiguously. Consequently, there is no contradiction between the universal work of the Spirit and the historical particularity of Jesus.[131] This is important since recent theologies of religions have tended to detach

---

129. *ST* 1:268.

130. D'Costa (*Religions and the Trinity*, 11) notes that wherever the Spirit of God is present, "there too is the ambiguous presence of the triune God . . ."

131. Kärkkäinen (*Trinity and Religious Pluralism*, 90) summarizes this point well by observing that "pneumatology represents universality while Christology in a sense becomes the point of tension between the historical particularity and the eschatological universality, though not in an exclusive way, but rather in a way that opens up Christianity for dialogue with others."

the Spirit's work from the work of the Son and the Father. Dialogue becomes a search for the activity of the divine wherever we may find God in all his trinitarian fullness.

To summarize, we agree with Grenz who observes,

> Pannenberg's understanding of the relationship of Christianity to the religions moves from his fundamental conviction that the Christian conception of God is superior to the understandings of the ultimate reality found in other religions, whether ancient or contemporary. He is confident that this assertion can be demonstrated by rational inquiry, which in turn becomes the task of systematic theology. At the same time, that very conception of God as the Triune One, when properly understood, provides the foundation for dialogue among the religions.[132]

Thus, Pannenberg argues the idea of a trinitarian God is the best way to explain the nature of reality and the totality of our experience within that reality. The trinitarian God not only arises from Christian theology, but it has profound explanatory power that spills over into discussions about religion in general and other religions in particular. Thus, the triune concept constitutes a crucial aspect of a public and unashamed Christian theology for the twenty-first century. Rather than explaining away trinitarian ideas about God, Christians can challenge peoples of alternative faiths to come to grips with this kind of God. Whether or not the gods of other religions actually turn out to be the sovereign and all-determining God of the universe can only ultimately "be decided by God, not us."[133] However, we must dialogue with peoples of all perspectives to gain a richer understanding of God's all-encompassing truth. In so doing, we hold out hope that our understanding of God and his world will be enriched, challenged, expanded, and revised in view of an increasingly comprehensive picture of his total self-revelation to all humanity through the unfolding course of time and space.

---

132. Grenz, *Reason for Hope*, 209.
133. Pannenberg, "Religious Pluralism," 103.

Summary, Critique, and Conclusions

Strengths

The strengths of this Pannenbergian approach to a theology of religions are many. For our purposes, I will mention only four. First, Pannenberg's desire to make religious truth claims the subject of public, rational discourse is a much-needed corrective to the privatization of religious views so prominent in much contemporary thought. In an age where secularism increasingly assumes that it is neccesary to ignore or consciously exclude religious perspectives from the public marketplace of ideas, Pannenberg's sweeping work pushes itself into the mainstream of current thought, touching significantly on disciplines of modern science, history, sociology, psychology, philosophy, as well as a host of others.

Second, Pannenberg seeks to take religious claims at face value rather than press them into some foreign framework that reinterprets their universal truth claims as some sort of abstract and amorphous concept of religious relation. The competing and sometimes incommensurable claims of various religions can be seriously examined for what they are—definite claims about the nature of the world and ultimate reality. And these claims are made by living religions with concrete and historically embedded ideologies and practices that can be openly tested and considered by all.

Third, Pannenberg's views about truth, revelation as history, and his theological musings surrounding the work of the triune God in creation make him open to genuine exchange in interreligious dialogues. Because all humans are finite and because God reveals himself in all of history—not merely in specialized sacred history known only to the faithful—the need for expanding one's understanding and knowledge is programmatic if one's comprehension of God is to grow. Thus, there is genuine humility and room for mutual integration, enrichment, and correction during interfaith conversations.

Finally, Pannenberg's creative use of the Trinity without sharply separating the three divine persons provides fresh resources for a distinctly Christian theology of religions that takes the claims and practices of other religions seriously, but still retains a normative theological role for the particular work of the Son alongside the universal work of the Father and the Spirit. Rather than making the triune persons largely separate and sometimes even apparently contradictory with one another, all are present and working to reveal and draw all people to the one true God, a God who shows himself through history to be distinctly *triune*. Consequently, in Christian theology, knowledge of God is not merely speculative, but revealed in the concrete history of Jesus, who provides the fullest and clearest picture of God as he really is.

Concerns

Despite these laudable elements, problems also emerge. For focus, only seven will be mentioned here. First, from an evangelical perspective, Pannenberg's highly selective and sometimes skeptical use of Christian Scripture is troublesome. Any Christian theology of religions that does not give more place and attention to Scripture leaves itself open to a certain level of inadequacy. This is especially frustrating with respect to passages that appear to speak against universalistic pictures of salvation and suggest more negative assessments of the truth claims found in alternative religious views. Pannenberg would have done well at least to touch on some of the issues surrounding such exclusivistic passages.

Second, and closely related, there is a disturbing tendency towards universalist salvation that does not only do an injustice to the Scriptures but also to the claims of other religions. If the salvation of all is ultimately subsumed under the Christian God alone, what is the reason for contestation? Why persuade others in the first place? To his credit, Pannenberg addresses this concern, but does so in an unsatisfactory way. If Christ is the norm for salvation, why do other religions make similarly universal salvific claims that clearly exclude a biblically sound christological aspect? Herein lies one problem with inclusive views of salvation. If most will be saved on the basis of Jesus' work, why do so many religious others appear to be so utterly opposed to embracing Christ and Christianity? Many of Pannenberg's central christological claims would be roundly condemned by the vast majority of religious adherents who hold tenaciously to the truth of their respective faith traditions.

A third problem relates to Pannenberg's lack of critical interaction with postmodern concerns. This is particularly grievous given the emphasis Pannenberg places on reason, the objectivity of history, and universal truth. While I am no fan of relativistic postmodern thought, the problems it raises concerning knowledge and the adequacy of human reason are real and should, at bare minimum, be addressed. Pannenberg's near silence on these matters is exceptionally disappointing and unfortunately leaves him open to the charge of irrelevance in the postmodern climate. As Kärkkäinen observes, "in order for Pannenberg's proposal to make sense to contemporary philosophical and theological discourse, he should subject his theological method to critical dialogue with those who disagree about the method."[134] But this is precisely what he fails to do in any significant way. This is a double irony given his drive to demonstrate the comprehensiveness of theology to address (positively and negatively) every current thought form. To be credible, aspects of postmodern thought must be included in this project of interactive critique and analysis, something he fails to provide.

Fourth, methodologically, the idea that religions are best understood as communities continually involved in a common search for universal truth is interesting and may well describe some religions (like Islam, for example), but probably not all. This makes his theology of religions rather one-sided and open to the characterization of being more Western in its orientation. Again, this is okay for what it represents, but can it really be called a "universal" vision for all current and historical religious perspectives? This point alone is contentious and far from self-evident.

The fifth concern is closely related: Is interfaith dialogue really a common quest for truth for all participants? Pannenberg seems to think it is, but it is not hard to imagine dialogue partners with other very different primary conversational agendas. Perhaps truth would be a concern, but it need not be primary in interreligious conversations. Religions have a large range of reasons and motivations behind what they believe and do. The quest for truth may or may not be high on that list. For some forms of Buddhism, for example, the idea of truth, far from being the goal, must be subsumed into and finally overcome in one's pursuit of enlightenment—an enlightenment that can only be obtained through a rigorous process of *eliminating* all notions of deduc-

---

134. Kärkkäinen, *Trinity and Religious Pluralism*, 92.

tion, distinction, desire, and difference. In such a religious program, a Pannenbergian concept of truth would actually become a *barrier* to the ultimate goal of its adherents. So again, Pannenberg's pursuit of truth is distinctly Christian in its orientation. It may also be distinctive of other world religions, but certainly not all. Thus, his offer of a universal method for interreligious dialogue is probably better understood as one type of conversation to be carried on in the midst of many others with alternative religious agendas and concerns.

Sixth, and closely related to the previous two critiques, Pannenberg offers criteria for determining which religion provides the best and most comprehensive explanation of reality and human experience under their relation to God, but it is hardly apparent that his criteria are universal for all religious evaluation. Some religions would likely find Pannenberg's points of evaluation wholly inadequate or skewed towards a Christian (or perhaps Western?) perspective. In fact, religious traditions typically have a wide range of criteria for determining faithfulness to the tradition. Usually these are internal to the tradition, even if they claim to be comprehensive ways of seeing, understanding, and interacting with reality. The truth of God may be a concern, but not necessarily the only or even primary one.

Seventh, there seems to be a lack of clarity concerning how dialogue partners can successfully discern between divine and demonic aspects of revelation in history. If God can be found in other religions, what are the criteria enabling us to see his presence within the shadow of sometimes humanly and demonically clothed theology, ideology, and praxis? Little is said about problems like the corruption of sin or the need to be vigilant in the relentless pursuit of the one true God. How, then, are we to understand and evaluate certain events and claims that mitigate against a Christian (for example) concept of God? And if the eschaton will ultimately show how all events in history fit together into the plans and purposes of God, what current basis do we have for passing moral and epistemological judgments upon historical events, practices, and truth claims? Regarding this, Pannenberg has not explicitly provided enough resources.

Ultimately, most of these concerns point to the fact that while Pannenberg claims to offer a universal, neutral method for interfaith dialogue, he more likely offers one possible way in which to dialogue with those of other faiths. And while it may be a fruitful method, it does not necessarily offer the best avenue for interreligious exchange. As an evangelical Christian, I find myself impressed by and exceptionally warm toward much of Pannenberg's project. In addition, many Muslims would find affinity with a significant portion of Pannenberg's program for a theology of religions, but that hardly qualifies it as a universal method for interreligious dialogue. It seems better to recognize his method as one possible program to be dialogically tested alongside a myriad of others as we seek to live together peacefully and morally in a religiously plural world.

Despite these aforementioned concerns, Pannenberg provides rich resources for a specifically *trinitarian* theology of religions, incorporating all the best of current theological views into his highly integrated and systematic presentation. The elements included in this chapter can help Christians dialogue both humbly and confidently with other world religions in a relentless pursuit of God. In addition, the many similarities between Islam and Christianity lend themselves to a spirited interreligious dialogue of the kind Pannenberg envisions. The next chapter will continue this kind of dialogue by examining the views of Islamic scholar and ethicist Abdulaziz Sachedina.

4

Islam, Tolerance, and Democracy: Abdulaziz Sachedina's Ethically Inclusive Response to Religious Plurality

Before beginning, I must confess that I am something of an outsider to Islam. Although endeavoring to represent Sachedina's Islamic response to religious plurality accurately, I was not raised a Muslim and do not embrace Islam as an insider. In addition, other Christians have done a better job of understanding and entering into the Islamic world. This confession is offered as both a word of caution and an expression of encouragement. It is a word of caution because this treatment may not fully or fairly represent a truly Islamic viewpoint.[1] It is also an expression of encouragement because the goal of understanding and embracing religious others in ongoing dialogue is not so much a destination point as it is an orientational process that never reaches any humanly predetermined end. Where I fail, others will follow bringing greater clarity, completion, and continuation. I, too, will move on in this journey with the hope of gaining greater understanding and appreciation for Sachedina's perspectives in particular and the many virtues of Islam and its followers in general.

---

1. This would not be Sachedina's fault, but mine alone. In addition, it should be noted that any claim to be presenting a truly Islamic perspective must be qualified by the open recognition that there is no one singular form of Islam that accounts for every concrete expression of the Muslim faith. As Ng Kam Weng (*Quest for Covenant Community*, 2) puts it, "We need to recognize that there are many 'Islams' rather than just a generalized Islam."

However, beyond this, an outsider's view can sometimes provide perspectives that insiders have become less aware of or even blind to. For example, Sachedina admits that a major challenge to seeing a more democratically plural Islam was "to become an outsider to [his] own community" so he could "explore more expansive vocabularies and notions of value understood by other communities."[2] Only then could he begin to re-envision the Islam within which he was raised and educated. Thus, those standing outside a certain viewpoint, both intra- and inter-traditionally, can provide important alternative perspectives and resources to those within their respective traditions.[3] It is with the aforementioned "outsider's" confession, as well as the hope of growing in my own understanding of the Islamic other, that direct attention can be given to Sachedina's vision of a future world society that is religiously plural and democratically peaceful.

Sachedina has been concerned about issues of politics and ethics throughout his distinguished career. One of his most important recent contributions to Muslim interreligious relations is *The Islamic Roots of Democratic Pluralism*.[4] Here Sachedina argues that Islam provides rich resources for a pluralistic, peaceful, democratic, and publicly moral society. Representing his fullest presentation of these ideas thus far, we will now examine this book more closely, supplementing it with other primary and secondary resources.

Sachedina's Ethical Inclusivism

While I classify Sachedina as ethically inclusive, the precise details of his perspective yield insights into Islamic source texts, as well as a hopeful vision for peaceful and plural communities. Sachedina begins

---

2. Sachedina, "Freedom of Religion and Conscience," 1. This unpublished lecture will hereafter be abbreviated as FRC.

3. This is similar to the process explored by MacIntyre in *Whose Justice? Which Rationality?*, esp. chs. 18–20, where he argues that when cultures and religious traditions clash the ensuing appropriation of internal and external resources from one's own and other traditions sometimes helps to solve internal problems a tradition faces. For a sophisticated postmodern epistemological appropriation of MacIntyre's work, see Murphy, *Anglo-American Postmodernity*.

4. Sachedina also recently published a brief lecture entitled *The Role of Islam in the Public Square*.

by noting that secularist approaches to plurality do not adequately account for how important religion is for most human beings, as well as how religions provide the "moral imperatives needed to maintain social cohesion."[5] Admittedly, some recent examples of Islamic governing systems have been exclusivistic and "divisive," giving fodder to those claiming that these "religiously inspired [Muslim militants are] massed against the liberal and democratic values of the West."[6] And while such responses are not justified, they become inflamed by secularist attempts to exclude religion from public life. Thus, "the rise of religious militancy in various parts of the world is a growing reaction to the secularist denial of any religious inspiration for movements on behalf of peace and human rights."[7] Ultimately, this extremist expression fails to account for the Muslim distinction between religious adherence and the governmental rule of law. Thus, Sachedina wants to "arrest the breakdown and corruption of political order [arising from the misuse of religion by a vocal minority] by rediscovering and promoting a common moral concern for peace with justice."[8]

For him, the growing pluralistic "religious sensibility" among all people can lead humanity to more tolerant and universal creeds, moving religious adherents "beyond an exclusionary and consequently intolerant institutional religiosity."[9] But what troubles Sachedina most is the "lack of serious analysis about the concept of religious pluralism among religiously oriented Muslim groups," preventing "a healthy restoration of interpersonal and intercommunal relations in the Muslim world."[10] Sachedina rejects exclusivistic religious ideologies and historically traces some of the sociopolitical and religious intolerances and atrocities. Nevertheless, he realizes seriously practiced religion always has horizontal, societal dimensions that cannot and should not be fully privatized. Thus,

---

5. Sachedina, *Roots*, 4.

6. Ibid., 5.

7. Ibid., 8. On p. 3 Sachedina calls this secularist exclusion of religion in public discourse the "'disestablishment' proposition."

8. Ibid., 6.

9. Ibid., 7.

10. Ibid., 11.

> Here we arrive at the key problem for contemporary religiosity: what is left of religious commitment and conscience if religion is debarred from dealing with issues relating to justice and peace? Social responsibility . . . has always been a major motivation for the cultivation of shared ethical concerns and objectives that are prerequisites to the very possibility of a just social order.[11]

These "shared ethical concerns and objectives" can become the basis for just and free societies. In particular, Sachedina argues that within Islamic sources, especially the Qur'an and the authoritative traditions (*hadith*), lie rich assets for creatively developing pluralistic societies. On these bases, he is convinced Muslims will eschew governmental violence to promote Islam, and instead will strive for free, moral, and plural societies that can not only live with, but even appreciate and embrace religious others. This transformative perspective will arise not because it is desirable from increasingly popular pluralistic perspectives on human rights, but because the Qur'an expects and demands it.

His method of interpreting the Qur'an and *hadith* utilizes four traditional aspects of textual interpretation. These include (1) attention to literary and linguistic aspects of the text, (2) determining the text's historical context, (3) concern for intra-textual reference to clarify meanings, and (4) an explanation of the passages in the authoritative *hadith*.[12] He also uses traditional and contemporary commentaries from Sunni and Shi'ite scholars to elucidate possible meanings of difficult Qur'anic passages.[13] By paying close attention to these interpretive aspects, Sachedina hopes to demonstrate "how history impacts hermeneutics of the Qur'an [and how historically] scriptural resources were retrieved and manipulated to justify one or the other interpretation that impacted the reality of religious diversity in terms of interfaith relations in Muslim societies."[14] Consequently, more inclusive visions will

---

11. Ibid., 10.

12. Ibid., 18.

13. The use of resources from both major branches of Islam is intentional and important since Sachedina comes from a Shi'ite background and thus could be dismissed by Sunni Muslims on that basis alone. Significantly, according to a biography of him from http://www.giffordlectures.org, although he was "born Shi'a, [Sachedina] has served as an imam in the Sunni mosque in Charlottesville, Virginia." This concretely demonstrates the kind of inclusiveness Sachedina seeks to encourage in fellow Muslims.

14. FRC, 6.

emerge from the pertinent resources resulting in more democratically pluralistic Muslim societies.

Especially important for this task is the Qur'an, since "There is no other text that occupies a position of such unquestionable and absolute authority for Muslims."[15] If Sachedina can show inclusive religious plurality is explicitly supported by the Qur'an, he believes this provides a compelling impetus for more pluralistic visions of Islamic society to be taken seriously by all Muslims. After laying out these initial aspects of his study, Sachedina explains how Muslim sacral texts provide the basis for "an inclusiveness [that leads] to a sense of multiple and unique possibilities for enriching the human quest for spiritual and moral well-being."[16]

The People Are One Community

Sachedina begins the second chapter of *The Islamic Roots of Democratic Pluralism* by noting religious plurality is "a byproduct of snowballing technological advances in transportation and communication."[17] Thus, people can no longer live in isolation from one another. Sadly, intercultural and interreligious encounter has not always been peaceful. Especially troubling for Sachedina is an exclusivism where "Each tradition, armed with its self-awarded patent on divine revelation, seeks supremacy rather than accommodation when confronted with an alien faith."[18] Thus, religious exclusivism remains one of the greatest enemies of an inclusiveness that might provide humanity with a viable religious plurality in the new global arena. For him, "The essential point to consider is whether religious communities are willing to recognize one another as spiritual equals, each entitled to its own distinctive path of salvation."[19] Sachedina advocates a conciliatory stance between exclusionary exclusivisms and extreme pluralisms like those of John Hick. Sachedina is admittedly drawn to Hick's thesis, describing it as "sound and practicable" as well as "realistic and conducive to outwardly bet-

15. Sachedina, *Roots*, 26.
16. Ibid., 23.
17. Ibid., 22.
18. Ibid.
19. Sachedina, *Role of Islam*, 6.

ter relations between dialogue participants."[20] But, he still realizes there are practical problems with Hickan pluralism because of the deeply entrenched belief in the "rightness" of one's own religion.[21] By affirming that other religions provide tradition-specific ways of salvation, Sachedina believes he finds a middle (inclusive) way to formulate the issue. Thus, "religious inclusiveness [will begin] to emerge as an important ingredient of international relations policy."[22]

To counter self-righteous exclusivisms that condemn all religious others, Sachedina cites the well-known verse, "The people were one community [*umma*]; then God sent forth the Prophets, good tidings to bear and warning, and He sent down with them the Book with the truth, that He might decide the people touching their differences" (Q. 2:213). For him, this passage expresses three central truths: (1) humankind is "one community" since it is created by God, (2) religious particularity arose through the process of sending various prophets to particular places and times, and (3) each religion was given its own special book of revelation to help resolve differences among faith communities.[23] The latter two points highlight the particular aspects of divine revelation, whereas the first emphasizes the theologically *universal* notion of

---

20. FRC, 18–19.

21. The problems he sees with Hick are broader than the practical. For example, in FRC, 20, Sachedina questions Hick's assertion that an exclusive religious truth claim is inherently arrogant. He goes on to say, "Given the fact of irreducible religious diversity," little is achieved by a project that requires such diversity to be glibly glossed over in the hopes of "forging a common ground among different peoples." And since "there is no empirical evidence for the [Hickan] claim that religions all share a common goal *except in the realm of moral demands*," it is better to pursue a "mutual respect and harmony founded on common moral terrain." Emphasis added.

22. FRC, 19. It should be reemphasized that Sachedina's claim is made in the context of an Islamic history and setting, and thus is directed more toward a particular type (or perhaps types) of religious excusivism than it is toward religious exclusivism in general. Along these lines, Sachedina (FRC, 21) says, "It is not necessary to conclude that truth-claim exclusivism will almost certainly grow to hate those with whom one fundamentally disagrees. The challenge is to find ways of channeling the disagreements to develop respect [for] one another's views while still believing that one is right and the other is wrong." This is important to note since it will be argued in chapter 6 that every form of religious inclusivism and pluralism ultimately collapses into its own unique form of religious exclusivism. Thus, it is the *stance* and *attitude* (rather than the taxonomical category or specific "ism") that matter most when dialoging with religious others.

23. Sachedina, *Roots*, 23.

humanity—the people as "*one* community." In FRC,[24] Sachedina adds an additional facet, namely that God must intervene to provide a decisive resolution to the particularities that have arisen in history.[25]

According to Sachedina, from its inception Islam has been an inherently public religion, and so "has been accurately described as a faith in the public realm."[26] Nevertheless, as public and universal as Islam is, this "publicness" does not rule out the possibility of a clear and vital distinction between private aspects of religious faith and public aspects of societal security and unity. The way the Qur'an creates space for this private expression of faith must be revealed without compromising or rejecting the place of divine justice and ethical norms in public and political structures of society.[27]

The space for distinguishing public and private aspects of religious faith is firmly grounded in a Qur'anic term Sachedina calls the "primordial" or "noble" nature (*fitra*).[28] This nature provides the requisite rational capacity and free will that enables all people to grasp and fulfill God's moral expectations. While the Qur'an does not say humans are made in the "image of God" as the Bible does, the parallels here are remarkable.[29] Thus, not surprisingly, the *hadith* mentions Adam, for

---

24. "Freedom of Religion and Conscience"; see note 2 above.

25. FRC, 9.

26. Sachedina, *Roots*, 24.

27. The use of the word "divine" here is intentional since secular ideologies often reject the value or even possibility of divinely delivered norms of jurisprudence as an aid to creating peaceful and moral human societies. But because this space between the public and private arena is not always clearly discernable in the concrete situations of real life—especially when it comes to issues like religious apostasy—this creates what Sachedina calls "tensions" between public and private aspects of religious belief.

28. Sachedina, *Roots*, 28. "Noble nature" is used by Sachedina in *The Role of Islam*. In FRC, 10, he calls it a God-given "innate capacity" that guides and enables a person to move toward desired (moral) goals.

29. Sachedina takes this concept of *fitra* from Q. 30:30, where it states that God created humankind with "God's original [nature or *fitrat allah*]" set upon it. The main biblical passages highlighting human beings are created in God's "image" and "likeness" are Gen 1:26–27; 5:1 (using the Hebrew words *tselem* and *d^{e}mûwth*); 1 Cor 11:7 (*eikōn* in the Greek); and Jas 3:9 (*homoiōs* in the Greek). The actual meaning and constitution of that image and likeness (*imago dei*) in humanity has been vigorously debated and variously described throughout the history of Judeo-Christian theological reflection. For one recent example providing a fresh Christian perspective on the issue, see MacFarland, *Divine Image*.

example, was created in God's image.[30] In fact, in an earlier essay, entitled "Freedom of Conscience and Religion in the Qur'an,"[31] Sachedina explicitly links the *fitra* with secular and especially Christian theories of moral conscience. There he argues, "The question of conscience in the Qur'an is connected with the idea of *fitra*, the innate disposition created by God as a necessary medium of universal guidance."[32]

More will be said about the significance of this innate capacity, along with the Muslim concept of the heart (*qalb*) later on. For now, Sachedina only highlights that the God-given *fitra* constitutes the primary basis for the Qur'anic claim that human beings are all part of one universal community. Although the verb here is in the past tense, "*were* one community," it is often translated in its present tense, "*are* one community." Sachedina chooses the present tense to emphasize that this oneness was not merely some past reality, but is a current reality for all humanity.[33] Endowing every person with a primordial moral and rational nature (*fitra*), God provides a constitutional basis "for the development of a 'global ethic'" where "peoples of diverse spiritual commitment" can "build a working consensus of values and goals."[34]

Sachedina builds upon this by pointing out Qur'anic passages that clearly teach the salvific legitimacy of other monotheistic religions, but then laments that such passages were effectively obscured by Islamic doctrines of "supersession" and "abrogation."[35] Unfortunately, supersession was created during Islam's formative stages to solidify an exclusive religious identity for the community, helping to distinguish it from

30. For reference to this, see *Sahih al-Bukhari: Ararbic-English*, vol. 8, p. 160 (bk. 74, ch. 1, trad. 246).

31. This essay is ch. 3 in Little et al., *Human Rights*, 53–90. For a concise historical review of the development of the concept of conscience in Western and Christian thought, see Little et al., "The World's Religions," 218–25. This is a slightly revised version of a similar section in ch. 1 of the earlier *Human Rights*.

32. Sachedina, "Freedom of Conscience and Religion," 57. Later (p. 65) Sachedina says that "*fitra* is the capacity to exercise rational choice in the matter of faith." This highlights his emphasis upon the universal human ability to be rational and consciously choose good over evil, something Christian theology usually seats in human intellect and will. So, *fitra* is more than a moral concept of conscience—knowing what is right and wrong. It also includes the ability to express that knowledge through concrete moral action.

33. Sachedina, *Roots*, 28.

34. Ibid., 28.

35. Ibid.

competing traditions.³⁶ Later, the need for identity and distinction also provided a basis for "aggression against and exploitation of those who did not share this sense of solidarity . . ."³⁷ Tragically, the concept of a "holy war" (*jihād*), where sacred authority could provide the community with the justification for such aggression and oppression, soon followed.

In addition to supersession, the concept of abrogation (*naskh*) was added, where a later Qur'anic verse could "override" or cancel out previously revealed passages.³⁸ Consequently, when certain verses suggested the legitimacy of other religions, abrogation was extensively employed for similar (and ultimately illegitimate) sociopolitical reasons—to help preserve the long-term integrity, identity, and security of the newly formed and forming Islamic community. Thus, history deeply impacted (and continues to impact) the Muslim understanding of itself and its sacred texts both positively and negatively. In FRC, Sachedina summarizes the idea this way:

> Muslim scripture captures the real experience of the early community struggling to regulate relation between tolerance and exclusive truth claims that provided the people [with] its unique identity among communities of [the] faithful. . . . Remarkably, different periods of Muslim history have generated different interpretations of the Qur'an in consonance with the social and political conditions that faced the community. During the heyday of the Muslim empire's political ascendancy some Qur'anic passages were used to determine tolerant attitudes toward other faiths. . . . In contrast, in the age of colonialism other passages of the holy book provided justifications for war against non-Muslim powers and their representatives.³⁹

---

36. For example, Sachedina (FRC, 29) suggests, "It is not far-fetched to suggest that debates about Islam superseding Christianity and Judaism, despite the explicit absence of any reference to it in the Qur'an, must have entered Muslim circles through the most thorough going Christian debates about Christianity having superseded Judaism."

37. Sachedina, *Roots*, 29.

38. Ibid., 29–30. While not called abrogation, Christianity employs a similar concept with respect to certain Old Testament passages and practices regarding their relationship to the New Testament era.

39. Sachedina, FRC, 6.

Unfortunately, inattention to historical process in Muslim hermeneutics has often led to inadequate and inaccurate interpretations (and applications) of its sacred texts.[40]

Instead, there are better ways to understand these verses in context—ways that not only avoid contradictions, but also largely eliminate the need to appeal to the controversial doctrines of supersession and abrogation.[41] Thus, it can be demonstrated that the Qur'an is universal and unified, a divine but historically influenced revelation given through Muhammad that reaffirms the same basic message previously revealed by God to other prophets in history. Differences can be accounted for by recognizing that particular times and places required different ways of communicating the same unchanging message—that people need to submit to the absolute oneness of God (*tawhīd*) and do what is right. If there was any place for abrogation, it was only with respect to "specific legal injunctions revealed in particular verses but apparently repealed . . . by other verses" due to changing historical circumstances in early Islam.[42] In particular, verses advocating initiating hostilities against unbelievers cannot abrogate those that speak about the salvific legitimacy of other Abrahamic faiths. In their contexts, these "hostility verses" deal with specific situations particular to their historical settings and would rarely be repeatable today.[43]

Concerning the various prophets and their respective revelations, if the *fitra* is endowed with all that is necessary to know and obey God's will, then revelation comes primarily to "clarify and elucidate matters that are [already] known through human intellect."[44] Therefore, claiming ignorance is illegitimate, even if earlier revelations (through Jesus and Abraham, for example) were later corrupted and distorted.[45] In

40. In a July 27, 2007, post to the *Washington Post*'s On Faith, Sachedina calls this inattention to historical process "a crisis of interpretation" in contemporary Islam that must be vigorously and immediately remedied by Islamic scholars.

41. Sachedina (*Roots*, 29–30) notes that "modern scholarship of some prominent Muslim jurists has provided incontrovertible documentation that all 137 putatively abrogated verses are in fact still valid."

42. Ibid., 32.

43. FRC, 26.

44. Sachedina, *Roots*, 33.

45. The Islamic doctrine of corruption (*tahrif*) is often employed in cases where Old and New Testament teachings differ from Qur'anic teachings. Concerning this, Sachedina (FRC, 31) claims that the "substance" of Jewish and Christian revelations

short, the *fitra* is present in every person before God sends prophets to specific communities at specific times and places. Consequently, everyone is obligated, "regardless of their particular religious affiliations, to live harmoniously with one another and work toward justice and peace in the world."[46]

Developing the concept of a universal community of humanity, Sachedina is not content to simply claim that primordial human nature situates every human being in a horizontal relationship of tolerance, since "Toleration does not require active engagement with the other."[47] Rather, the goal for religious plurality is to understand and even rejoice in those of different religions. And such active interreligious dialogue can serve "as a working paradigm for a democratic, social pluralism in which people of diverse religious backgrounds are willing to form a community of global citizens."[48] To promote such a community, Sachedina insists the "intrinsic redemptive value of competing religious traditions" must be affirmed.[49] Without this stance, exclusive attitudes easily become tools through which one religious tradition justifies the oppression and even violent persecution of others.

He supports this claim by noting divine revelation comes to people through the vehicle of language such that it becomes expressed in indicative and imperative sentences that are "propositional." However, "what ultimately comes to be regarded as revelation by the community of the faithful is an individual experience of something believed in rather than stated as creedal belief."[50] As Q. 4:163 says, the essential (what Sachedina calls "constitutive") truths underlying the various expressions of religious revelation are given throughout history to various

---

"has remained recognizable despite the neglect and alteration it has suffered." In the Qur'an, claims of textual corruption seem to be especially directed toward the Jews. For a brief survey of pertinent passages, see Moucarry, *Prophet*, 47–51.

46. Sachedina, *Roots*, 35.
47. Ibid., 35.
48. Ibid., 35.
49. Ibid., 36.
50. Ibid., 36. It appears here that Sachedina is giving some recognition (although perhaps not explicitly) to Friedrich Schleiermacher's claim that religious experiences result in attempts to describe those experiences linguistically. In this way, truth claims are made that lend themselves to exclusivistic and propositional understandings of what Sachedina describes as a "multidimensional encounter with the living God." For a look at Schleiermacher's views in more depth, see his *On Religion*.

prophets. And God makes these truths available to everyone so that no one can claim he is unfair. Nevertheless, these particular revelations "should serve only to delineate the conditions and methods of applying the constitutive principles."[51] Methods of application vary, but timeless and universal axioms remain unchanged. True religion (*dīn*)—what Sachedina describes as behaving "duly before God"—is ultimately expressed by means of *submission and surrender* (the true meaning of the word *islām*, with a lowercase *i*) to God.[52] Therefore, although Q. 3:85 clearly states, "Whoso desires another *dīn* than *islām*, it shall be not be accepted of him; in the next world he shall be among the losers," this need not require that the *institutional and formal religion of Islam* as it has come to be expressed and known concretely in history is the only legitimate expression of *dīn*.

Thus, religious traditions express praxiological variations, but ultimately retain a recognizable core of common principles that stand behind such diverse expressions. The Qur'anic basis for affirming other religious expressions emerges from verses 109:1–5, which end with, "To you your religion, and to me my religion!" Consequently, those claiming the superiority of their religion ignore the Qur'an's pluralistic thrust and deny its claim that God appointed to Jews, Christians, and Muslims their own respective "path and a way" (Q. 5:48). This passage goes on to state "if God had willed, He would have made you but one community," but he chose not do so in order that we would "compete" with one another to do good deeds.[53] The decision of many Muslim commentators to give these verses reduced import using abrogation reveals their failure to consider seriously other more pluralistic readings of the Qur'an.[54]

Laying this groundwork, Sachedina believes he provides a good basis to claim that the Qur'an has a pluralistic attitude, especially concerning Jews and Christians (Q. 2:62). He then argues that because Islam provides the most comprehensive political vision of any world religion, and given its Qur'anic pluralism, it offers "the only thoroughgoing religious critique of international public order with its secular-

---

51. Sachedina, *Roots*, 38.
52. Ibid., 38.
53. Ibid.
54. Ibid., 40.

ist and liberal presuppositions."[55] This is especially true since the *fitra* provides a theological basis for a universal human disposition to know and do what is right. Thus, no one can claim ignorance when speaking about universal notions of morality.[56] Ethics, then, becomes the most promising sphere for developing an ideal and truly *public* social order, because, "No matter how religions might divide people, ethical discourse focuses on human relationships."[57] The key to success is not the creation of an orderly society so much as a *communal* society with a free, ongoing, and genuine exchange of mutual moral norms. As all members of society continue to interact and reason with one another as equals under their Sovereign Creator, only then can these common ethical principles be codified in legislative bodies reflecting universal ideals of peace and justice.[58] And only then can peace be translated into action. Otherwise, law and faith become disconnected and tremendous resources for good are left dormant and underdeveloped.[59]

How can a coherent picture of Qur'anic pluralism be presented? How can verses utilized by fundamentalists to justify "holy war" (*jihād*) be reexamined in light of more pluralistic ones? First and foremost, historical aspects of these passages have been largely ignored. This "failure to assess honestly the impact of history on the development of the normative Muslim tradition" has negatively affected its ability

55. Ibid., 42.

56. Again, we see a close parallel to the Christian notion of conscience, the seat of moral discernment. However, Christian theology is more pessimistic in its assessment of the post-fall state of universal human conscience. Thus, the New Testament talks about conscience (using the Greek word *suneidēsis*) in a variety of negative ways— "weak" (1 Cor 8:7), "defiled" (Titus 1:15), "evil" (Heb 10:22), and "seared" (1 Tim 4:2)—as well as positive ones—"blameless" (Acts 24:16), "good" (1 Pet 3:16), "clear" (2 Tim 1:3), and "perfect" (Heb 9:9). Conscience seems to be some sort of innate human ability to discern right from wrong. But the Bible suggests that this ability has been defiled and damaged by sin, requiring correction and cleansing (Heb 9:14). Significantly, Islam also talks a great deal about sin and the ways in which the human heart (*qalb*) can become veiled and hardened to the truth and moral life of God.

57. Sachedina, *Roots*, 43.

58. Ibid., 43.

59. In a moment it will become obvious where this comment is directed—toward the fundamentalist Muslim movement. This whole section represents the major source for the descriptive term "ethical inclusivism," since it is specifically in the ethical arena that Sachedina believes every *fitra*-endowed human being is a valuable member of a society where people can publicly and freely express, debate, and rally for the legitimacy and even supremacy of their moral vision.

to make proper sense of and positively impact the modern situation.[60] Any solution must "begin with an understanding of how faith relates itself to history and how the normative tradition interacts with human conditions."[61] Consequently, these texts must be placed in their contexts and re-envisioned to draw out contemporary meanings and relevance. Otherwise, "Any rash application of these ordinances today . . . without first ascertaining the objective situational or circumstantial aspects (*mawdūd'āt*) of the rulings could lead to a faulty assessment of the changed circumstances of Muslim power."[62] Thus, some "past juridical decisions have become irrelevant in the modern system of international relations, and they are thus unable to shed light on the pressing task of recognizing religious pluralism as a cornerstone of interhuman relations."[63]

Without this ongoing program, Islam becomes locked within the past, unable to understand adequately or respond properly to the vicissitudes of history, leading to its own demise.[64] And this is precisely what is happening to Islamic fundamentalism.[65] In their zealous attempt to *preserve* truth, they only succeed in marginalizing it (and themselves) from the changing contemporary scene.[66] Sachedina wants Muslims to reply vigorously and thoughtfully to this challenging landscape, because "for now . . . it is only the fundamentalist form of Islam that claims to offer an alternative to secular ideologies."[67] The problem is especially acute since fundamentalists often assert that non-Muslims are *completely incapable* of ordering a morally free society because they reject the only possible standard for implementing human government—the

---

60. Sachedina, *Roots*, 45.

61. Ibid., 47.

62. Ibid., 49.

63. Ibid.

64. This kind of isolationism also results in the moral and intellectual impoverishment of others who might benefit from the divine truths and moral norms embedded within Islam.

65. After exploring other possible terms, Sachedina (*Roots*, 52) lands on "fundamentalist" because he finds it "a far more intelligible designation for 'all [contemporary] religiously motivated individuals, drawn together into ideologically structured groups, for the purpose of promoting a vision of divine restoration.'" He is quoting here from Lawrence, *Defenders of God*, but gives no page number.

66. Sachedina, *Roots*, 50–51.

67. Ibid., 51.

Qur'an *as they interpret it*.⁶⁸ Consequently, revelatory knowledge is considered "entirely non-rational . . . [a set of] immutable principles . . . of social and political organization, applicable irrespective of time and place."⁶⁹ This attitude tends to result in a thoughtless "anti-Westernism" that fails to appreciate the many contributions Western thought makes to Islam—and vice versa.⁷⁰ It also stunts Islamic growth. By grounding a universal ethic in the *fitra*, Sachedina affirms (against this sole fundamentalist reliance on revelation) every person's ability to know and fulfill justice. Therefore, even godless secular people and societies retain *some* ethical norms that serve as crucial minimal starting points for creating just and pluralistic communities.⁷¹

The following section lays out the historical and political aspects of the modern world that led to the rise of militant Muslim fundamentalism, including Islam's failure to respond adequately to "the vicissitudes of the modern nation-state."⁷² This resulted in an inability "to recognize the impact of complex ethnic, economic, political, and social relationships in intercommunity conflicts."⁷³ Consequently, "Contemporary Islamic ideology is going through an epistemological crisis that must be addressed from within by Muslim intellectuals."⁷⁴ Sachedina hopes, for the sake of Islam and world peace, that such an undertaking is well under way, especially concerning the pluralistic question so forcefully asserting itself in today's multi-religious context. Without this project, Islam may fail to create "the necessary tools to further the development

68. Ibid., 58.

69. Ibid., 60.

70. For example, Ramachandra (*Faiths in Conflict?*, 9) points out that, "Far from the East being East and the West remaining West, the two have borrowed from, and interacted with, each other for centuries."

71. Sachedina, *Roots*, 60. This claim enables Sachedina to broaden the scope of those invited to be part of the moral discourse. Now it is not merely monotheists and religious peoples who can be a part of the process. The *fitra* is found in every human being and so manifests itself in even secular people, although some have certainly forsaken and ignored the *fitra* more than others. About this, in FRC, 34, he says, "according to the Qur'an, human beings endowed with moral cognition must work together to create a just society. Hence, there is no difference between Abrahamic and non-Abrahamic traditions, when it comes to extend[ing] the necessary respect for other religions without abandoning one's own faith."

72. Sachedina, *Roots*, 54.

73. Ibid., 56.

74. Ibid., 57.

of institutions with an authentic, unmistakable Islamic identity," and end up "trying to pass off a cosmetically Islamized counterfeit."[75]

Compete with One Another in Good Works

Having argued for this universal ethical human constitution grounded in the *fitra*, one question still remains: how can moral virtue and divinely grounded justice be pursued? In chapter 3 of *Roots*, Sachedina gives a preliminary rejoinder. He opens with the Qur'anic passage calling every religion to "compete with one another in good works" (Q. 5:48), and then addresses one of the burning issues concerning contemporary Islamic states: the *dhimmī*, or protected minorities, under Muslim rule. Tracing the history of protected minorities, Sachedina notes the story—at least concerning Christians and Jews—is an uneven mixture of remarkable pluralistic communities and dismal paternalistic subjugations.[76] Quoting extensively from and arguing against a discriminatory document of dubious origins called the "Pact of 'Umar," Sachedina claims that the most respected sayings of Muhammad show that protected minorities were to be treated with utmost respect and fairness.[77] In fact, Sachedina even argues that, "By virtue of explicit recognition of common ground shared between Muslims and the people of the Book, Islam never harbored a widespread belief that Jews and Christians are to be denied salvation if they do not first convert to Islam. Unlike the early Christians, the early Muslims felt no need to establish their sociopolitical and religious identity at the expense of another community."[78] Only later historical practices ignored and abused statutes for administering justice to and promoting the welfare of protected minorities.

---

75. Ibid., 61–62.

76. Ibid., 63–65. It was only when the dubious "Pact of 'Umar" was instituted that clear forms of religious discrimination arose. For a look at some of the history of Islamic treatment of protected minorities, see Friedman, *Tolerance and Coercion in Islam*, esp. 34–86. Concerning the more discriminatory period of the Middle Ages, Friedmann (ibid., 4) notes that "Muslims can take comfort in the commonly held view that the living conditions of non-Muslims under medieval Muslim rulers were significantly better than those imposed on Jews and other religious minorities by their Christian counterparts."

77. Sachedina, *Roots*, 65–67.

78. Ibid., 69.

For Sachedina, any call to interreligious competition must assume the presence of the *fitra*, for it alone provides the ontological backdrop for a pluralistic ethic where all people can "compete with one another in good works." Thus, "all humans are endowed with an innate scale with which they can weigh rightness and wrongness."[79] In light of postmodern scholarship, many have been tempted to deny universal ethical norms, but for Sachedina, if the *fitra* exists, moral standards are not arbitrary but specific and universal. These standards are best found inductively, rather than deductively, since general principles are best ascertained through their concrete manifestations. Nevertheless, "moral reasoning could become blurred if not fortified by belief in the transcendence, in obedience to the ultimate authority to whom 'shall you return, all together' (K. 5:48)."[80] Thus, morals should be applied in the real world, forming the basis for speaking and living out "an ethical language that can be shared cross-culturally in the project of creating a just society" so they will become intelligible to the idioms of alternative cultures and religions.[81]

Another challenge religions face when addressing a democratic secular society arises from the nature of the ethical norms they espouse. Frequently, religious values are "seen as a threat to secular democracies when [they] challenge the secular values that increasingly promote self-gratification as the primary human imperative."[82] In addition, religions have checkered histories of political power plays against religious, cultural, and racial others. Thus, unease often arises over the melding of public policy and religion, especially when religions make exclusivistic claims against "the religious other."[83] Particularly grievous to Sachedina has been the inability of Muslim social ethics "to provide the moral and spiritual weapons needed to combat oppressive state force and to generate civic participation or communal cooperation."[84] The deplorable result has not only been oppression of minorities, but endless cycles of international wars and intranational strife.

79. Ibid., 71.
80. Ibid., 72.
81. Ibid., 73.
82. Ibid., 73.
83. Ibid., 74.
84. Ibid., 75.

Cooperative participation to establish and enforce moral codes need not require a strictly secular regime where religious faith is pushed towards private arenas of life. Rather, it is necessary to espouse "a non-secularist model of religious tolerance," for this is the Islamic way—one that refuses to privatize religious norms and ideals.[85] Of course, it is not merely Islamic, but also *Abrahamic* to link church and state. Belief in "an ethical God who insists on justice and equality in interpersonal relations" produces an "indispensable connection between the religious and ethical dimensions of personal life [that] inevitably introduces religious precepts into the public arena."[86]

This integration has not been without problems—some of them quite serious. Sachedina traces the history of religious and political relationships in Islam, noting that the "role of adult Muslim believer, not that of citizen, was the only inclusive political role" for Islamic governance.[87] The resulting problem was defining Islam's place in the changing contexts of arising modern nation-states. While the Qur'an offers clear ethical guidelines for a just society, it does not offer enough detail to deal with every specific contingency of contemporary life. Thus, despite the Qur'an's pluralistic impulse toward individual responsibility, moral judgment, and personal freedom, most Muslim leaders failed to appreciate these in a way that breaks away from traditional and exclusionary formulations of Islamic rule and law. Consequently, "the *Sharī'a* . . . has grown increasingly inflexible" and the "value of the Islamic tradition as a resource for policy in the modern world still awaits intelligent articulation."[88]

Much formulation, consultation, and instantiation of possible alternatives is needed to exemplify a freely democratic and religiously plural Muslim state—one that persuasively emerges from Islamic sources. Again, the source of such reasoning is grounded in the *fitra*, the basis for engaging in "*jihād* (struggle and striving)" to be moral and pursue the moral well-being of one's neighbor by competing with one another

---

85. Ibid., 77–78.

86. Ibid., 78. This linking of state and religion is not unique to Abrahamic religions. Most of human history demonstrates the propensity of religions to be closely integrated with public and political governance.

87. Ibid., 80.

88. Ibid., 81.

in good works.[89] Societal success depends upon more than "matters of commerce and market relations, . . . it also presupposes a shared foundation of morality and binding sentiments that unite autonomous individuals who are able to negotiate their own spiritual space."[90] Thus, the *fitra* gives moral freedom to human beings that transcends particular religious adherence. This pre-revelatory provision of God is coupled with the ethical aspects of his special historical revelation through the prophets. And they agree with one another "because, according to the Koran, their source is one and the same: God."[91] Sachedina summarizes his point this way:

> God has endowed human beings with the necessary cognition and volition in their *fitra* to further their comprehension of moral truths. Moreover, the distinction between evil and good is ingrained in the human personality in the form of a prerevelatory, natural guidance with which God has favored human beings. . . .
>
> Guidance from God is an exaltation of individual conscience as opposed to forcible, collective conformism; hence, the responsibility for the salvation of each Muslim lies in his or her own hands rather than in any religious authority. God provides a general direction, a spiritual predisposition . . . [that] is further strengthened through prophetic revelation. The Koran repeatedly shows . . . this form of guidance is universal and available to all who aspire to become godfearing and prosperous.[92]

Revelation is supplementary, but not primary, since the *fitra* already includes the capacity for moral discernment and fulfillment. Revelation aids those who already seek the good, but those rejecting ethical living are held accountable by God apart from their knowledge of special revelation. Thus, "certain moral prescriptions follow from a common human nature and are regarded as independent of any particular spiritual beliefs."[93]

It is the Qur'anic notion of *fitra*, then, that forces Muslims to reexamine the verse, "No compulsion is there in religion" (Q. 2:256). For Sachedina, differentiating between religious commitment and a

89. Ibid., 82.
90. Ibid., 84.
91. Ibid., 85.
92. Ibid., 85.
93. Ibid., 88.

broader societal moral accountability only makes sense in light of a divinely-endowed libertarian view of human free will.[94] This broader ideal may be intimately linked to the religious perspective, but is not dependent upon a personal faith in that religion for its basic understanding and execution by the individual. Thus, "no compulsion" not only extends to the "people of the Book" but to everyone, for "all human beings must have the basic right to exercise free choice in this matter [of religious faith]."[95] Thus, this verse "seems to be saying that a person cannot be deprived of civil rights on account of a religious conviction, no matter how distasteful it might be to the dominant faith community."[96] Nevertheless, while persons are free to choose religiously, universal moral standards discernable through the *fitra* are objective and universally binding. They exist for the good of all and are the guarantor of "true human well-being. In enforcing [these] basic moral standard[s], resort to compulsion is legitimate."[97]

This compulsion is sometimes necessary because the human heart does not always seek after God. In Islam, the heart is intimately related to the *fitra*, and Sachedina describes their relationship to each other and to moral discernment this way:

> The heart (*qalb*, plural *qulūb*) in Koranic usage is the "seat of consciousness, thoughts, volitions and feelings." Hence, the heart is the physical locus of the *fitra*, that inherent capacity that is affected by the choice made in the matter of faith. When a person rejects faith, the heart becomes veiled and is deprived of its ability to understand the moral situation. The heart thus functions as a faculty for distinguishing truth from falsehood,

---

94. This assertion is articulated in the midst of a Muslim debate between Ash'arite and Mu'tazilite notions of human freedom. The Ash'arites, akin to some of the more Calvinistically Christian views of human freedom, claimed that God's sovereignty overrides the human will when responding to divine guidance. The Mu'tazilites, on the other hand, "emphasized complete responsibility of human beings [and so] upheld the concept of human free will" (ibid., 87). Sachedina holds to a Mu'tazilite view because the Ash'arite "interpretation [of human freedom] rules out the notion that human beings can freely affirm religious faith" (ibid., 89). For a look at this debate from a Christian perspective, see Basinger and Basinger, eds., *Predestination and Free Will*.

95. Sachedina, *Roots*, 91.

96. FRC, 15.

97. Sachedina, *Roots*, 95–96. Still, according to Sachedina (FRC, 18), "the dominant community needs to leave the public space non-coercive and cognizant of other communities' rights to follow their religious practices without any impediment."

good from evil, the beneficial from the harmful. It discovers the benefit of revealed guidance . . . .[98]

Thus, the *fitra* provides the moral norms necessary for the heart (*qalb*) to respond, but if a person chooses in his or her heart to forsake the benefits of following God's righteousness, some external limitations must be enforced to protect not only overall social stability and welfare, but also to prevent the individual from destroying him or herself through ongoing sinful and rebellious acts. Therefore, it is possible to differentiate between freely chosen individual religious adherence, and universal moral standards grounded in the moral constitution (*fitra*) of every person—standards that need to be affirmed and enforced in any pluralistic *and truly moral* society.[99] To summarize,

> Since no authority can coerce an individual to believe or accept a particular faith, human beings are free to negotiate their personal faith and its consequential connection to a community. . . . Whereas in the matters of private faith the position of the Qur'an is "non-interventionist" . . . , in the public projection of faith, the Qur'anic stance is based on coexistence among faith communities, even if one among them enjoys majority in terms of membership and political power.[100]

---

98. Sachedina, *Roots*, 91. The notion of heart here is similar to a Christian understanding of heart and conscience, where they both become the seat of moral discernment and play a role in ethical volition. Sachedina makes this connection explicitly in ibid., 92. Just as the heart can become "sick" (Q. 8:49), "veiled" (Q. 18:57), and "hardened" (Q. 2:73–74) in Islam, the conscience can be "seared" (1 Tim 4:2), the heart can be "darkened" (Rom 1:21), "unbelieving" (Heb 3:12), and "hardened" (Heb 4:7) in Christianity. The *Roots* discussion here is similar to an earlier discussion by Sachedina in "Freedom of Conscience and Religion," 69–70.

99. To clarify this relation, Sachedina (FRC, 11) notes that through the *fitra*, "God provides general direction, a spiritual predisposition that can guard against spiritual and moral peril (if a person hearkens to its warnings); this natural guidance is further strengthened through prophetic revelation." However, the "rejection of revelatory guidance . . . does not necessarily deprive conscience of its cognitive capacity and practical impact. Thus, when God denies guidance to those who do not believe in divine revelations (Q. 19:104), the denial pertains to the procurement of the desirable end of becoming godly, not to the initial guidance that is originally engraved upon the hearts of all human beings through the *fitra*." Consequently, all people are without excuse before God at the final judgment.

100. FRC, 18.

Ultimately, "the final judgment in the matter of faith rests with God alone . . . [and] coercion is exclusively the domain of the 'Master of the Day of Doom' (K. 1:4)."[101] Still, the Qur'an is concerned about creating just and moral societies for everyone, and this becomes the political responsibility of all public servants in these societies. This produces what Sachedina calls "an inherent tension" when a plurality of faith communities have competing, rather than complementary, public moral agendas.[102]

Historically, Islam developed a pre-modern paradigm called the "millet system" to deal with the tension created by religious minorities (*dhimmī*), "granting each religious community an official status and a substantial measure of self-government."[103] Unfortunately, this system eventually resulted in discrimination and an attitude of Islamic superiority toward non-Muslims "because the Sharī'a never accepted the equality of believers and non-believers," even though this runs "contrary to the pluralistic spirit of the Koran."[104] This stance also extended to Muslims who practiced their Islam in a manner deemed unworthy or aberrant by those in power. Inevitably, questions about religious heresy and apostasy arose. Are these a state or religious concern—or something of both? How does apostasy endanger and undermine the social order, especially in Islam, where "the Koran presents comprehensive commandments in which moral and civil are not always easy to distinguish"?[105]

Sachedina explores apostasy carefully, noting the Arabic word (*irtdād*), translated as "apostasy" in English, "meaning 'rejection' or 'turning away from,' was historically applied to the battles that were fought against those Muslims who had refused to pay taxes to the Islamic political authority after the prophet's death."[106] Thus, unlike Christian notions of apostasy emphasizing issues of religious belief, Muslim ideas about apostasy were concerned about communal sub-

101. Sachedina, *Roots*, 95.

102. Ibid., 96.

103. Ibid., 97. The "millet system" was specific to the Ottoman Turkish system, but serves as a concrete historical example of one way in which Muslims attempted to deal fairly with non-Muslim minorities, or *dhimmī*.

104. Ibid.

105. Ibid., 98.

106. Ibid., 99–100.

version and rebellion against the established political order. Tensions arose because although the Qur'an advocates religious plurality, early in history, "the social ethics delineated by the Muslim jurists regarded pluralism as a source of instability in the Muslim public order."[107] A society emerged where apostasy was treated harshly, sometimes even with death. No vital distinction was made between matters of religious freedom (that are relatively private and do not significantly disrupt or endanger society in general), and matters where acts of "sedition that cause discord and threaten unity" are publicly promoted.[108] Only in the latter case can apostasy be severely penalized and "countered ... with violence if necessary."[109] Ultimately, Sachedina calls this ambiguity and tension a "self-evident problem" for Islam, leaving decisions concerning when apostasy threatens the state's integrity and unity up to those in power: "The Muslim civil authority has the ultimate responsibility for using its discretionary power to assess the level of discord created by a public declaration of an apostasy and to lay down the appropriate measures to deal with it."[110] Nevertheless, these authorities "must con-

107. Ibid., 100.
108. Ibid., 101.
109. Ibid. In *Role of Islam*, 18, Sachedina states that while the Qur'an prescribes several specific consequences for certain moral infractions, "no defined punishment" concerning apostasy is supplied. In addition, he notes in "Freedom of Conscience and Religion," 78, that "The question of apostasy is particularly important for understanding the discrepancy between the Qur'anic emphasis on religious liberty ... and the intolerant, sometimes even harsh, attitude of Muslim jurists concerning the treatment of apostates.... [W]ith the exception of apostasy, no legal penalties are provided for offenses against religion as such; they will be dealt with in the hereafter. This exception in regard to apostasy stems from the inability of classical jurists to distinguish the admittedly complex relationship between a moral and a religious action." Later (ibid., 83) he argues against the death penalty for apostasy since such a punishment "is in direct conflict with the Qur'anic spirit of religious liberty." In FRC, 3, he encouragingly notes that "recent rulings in the matter of apostasy are refreshingly against [the] death penalty because the penalty is derived from the traditions rather than the Qur'an, where one's rejection of Islamic faith after having accepted it is regarded as a sin against God, and hence, beyond the jurisdiction of Muslim political authority." Thus, in Sachedina's estimation, the Qur'an itself, in places like Q. 2:217, argues that apostates will ultimately be dealt with by God in the life to come, taking the punishment outside the realm of the temporal and making it an issue for God and God alone.

110. Sachedina, *Roots*, 101. While there may be some discomfort here, this same type of discretion is exercised in religious matters by secular states as well. For example, the belief among Jehovah's Witnesses that blood transfusions are religiously offensive to God sometimes appears to conflict with the state's compelling interest to protect

scientiously shoulder the burden of proof and show the Muslim community... that any decision to use compulsion in matters impinging on a person's faith is in no way aimed at changing that person's belief, but simply at enforcing basic moral and civic requirements."[111]

Thus far we have explored Sachedina's claim that modern Muslims desperately need to give greater attention to historical aspects of Islamic faith and its sacred texts. This has special urgency due to recent world events that show how Islam is being exploited by radical ideologies to promote violently exclusionary forms of Islam that run counter to the Qur'an's pluralistically inclusive tenor. Consequently, Sachedina provides a vigorous and historically sensitive reinterpretation of the Qur'an highlighting its more inclusive and pluralistic character—something he argues is truer to its original intent. In addition, Sachedina couples this with the additional Qur'anic concept of the *fitra*, enabling Muslims to maintain a vital distinction between personal freedom in matters of religious faith and political governance, compulsion, and enforcement in matters of universal moral standards. Thus, in today's context, "The Islamic heritage must guide rather than govern a modern nation-state."[112] The form of governance will reflect modern political and national structures, but its application must still be guided by Islamic visions of just and moral societies.

Having laid out Sachedina's basic argument for a Qur'anic pluralism, we can now turn to another aspect of his inclusively Islamic vision for society, something he calls "forgiveness toward humankind."[113]

---

the lives of minors, but at the same time, it also has the responsibility to uphold the importance of parental authority and religious freedom. Religiously motivated people and movements can, to varying degrees, threaten political stability but still appear to be in the right, as appears to be the case in modern Myanmar (Burma), for example. However at other times, such movements can be dangerous to the order of society in a clearly negative sense, as for example, when white supremists, motivated by a twisted form of religious zeal for a "pure" race, seek to kill all those who do not exhibit the right "color" or genetic heritage. Thus, some of these cases require exceptional wisdom and grace, no matter who rules the state.

111. Sachedina, "Freedom of Conscience and Religion," 85.

112. Sachedina, *Role of Islam*, 21.

113. What follows in this chapter is closer to a laundry list than a tightly integrated set of propositions leading to a single conclusion. The one thread that runs through the discussion is that of *forgiveness*.

Forgiveness toward Humankind

Sachedina begins this chapter by lamenting that, despite Qur'anic verses highlighting God's mercy and compassion (like Q. 2:178, which calls Muslims who "wish to pardon the murderer" "honorable"), traditional Islamic law overemphasizes vengeance. With its exclusive claims, Islam has exemplified a propensity to vilify those who reject its statutes and doctrines—sometimes leading to "outright condemnation to hell," and at other times fostering "a call for *jihād*—a holy war."[114] In short, "the denial of a God-given right to religious freedom [in historical Islam] has fostered antipluralistic attitudes among religious extremists."[115]

Complicating Islam's history of retribution are harsh and vengeful precedents set long ago. Largely overlooking pluralistic aspects of the Qur'an, Islam has demonstrated a fair propensity for violence. Citing Q. 2:178, Sachedina argues Islam has "untapped resources" that can provide new emphases on ministries of compassion and forgiveness toward those who have done wrong.[116] In particular, the *fitra* enables us not only to obey and serve God, but because God is merciful, the *fitra* also empowers us to return to God and beg for forgiveness. The individual can then be healed from the damage caused by doing evil. However, forgiveness is not merely a vertical exercise, but also a horizontal one where forgiveness and kindness are extended to the offending other, since this is how God acts toward humanity. This kind of forgiveness, "rather than an endless cycle of violence, can restore relationship among enemies."[117] This attitude is also displayed in Qur'anic notions of fair retribution which seek to allay "the natural human tendency to an excessive penalty."[118] Thus, rightly understood, the Qur'an is a rich and compelling spiritual resource for fair retribution, restorative social justice, and humble reconciliation—a reconciliation of people with God and one another.

According to Sachedina, working against this Qur'anic call to forgiveness and reconciliation are two particularly "grievous sins . . . ,

---

114. Sachedina, *Roots*, 103.
115. Ibid., 103.
116. Ibid., 104.
117. Ibid., 105.
118. Ibid., 105.

arrogance (*istikbār*) and jealousy (*hasad*)."[119] Both cause conflicts and a desire to have and be more than one ought. Arrogance especially leads to attitudes of self-righteous superiority and an exclusivism that justifies violence against religious others. For Sachedina, to overcome arrogance, conflicting divergent interests of individuals and social groups should be recognized as vital aspects of human interdependence, and be granted some level of legitimacy.[120] Similarly, jealously leads to aggression and coercion of others, which can only be remedied through a "social interaction which fosters a sense of interdependence, thereby reducing violence among individuals."[121] This leads to "sincere repentance and public apology" which becomes a "prelude to the just resolution of conflict."[122] Thus, humble forgiveness and respectful social interaction—not harshly coercive and excessively revengeful responses to societal harm—become the cornerstones of functional and peaceful pluralistic societies.

Concerning just governance, Islam has always emphasized that ethical social orders must include a responsible system of political leadership. But this responsibility brings a danger of mismanaging power, particularly for what Sachedina calls "ideological states" like Islam. This is especially problematic when the legitimate power to administer social justice is concentrated in the hands of only a few.[123] To avoid abuse, safeguards ensuring the just and benevolent rule of law must be in place, since justice is the primary counterweight to satanic arrogance and jealousy. And this justice must extend not only to fellow Muslims ("brothers in religion"), but also to non-Muslims, for although they are not "brothers in religion," they are still "equals in creation."[124] In Sachedina's words,

> This is the foundation of Muslim civil society: the privilege of citizenry attaches to Muslim and non-Muslim alike, both sharing equality in God-given dignity. . . . It [is] a violation of law and religion to discriminate against a fellow citizen simply because he or she happens to be a non-Muslim.

119. Ibid., 107.
120. Ibid., 108.
121. Ibid.
122. Ibid., 108–9.
123. Ibid., 109.
124. Ibid., 110.

If this is the teaching of Islam, then where does this religiously generated discrimination against the other come from? According to the Koran, the source of this socially depraved conduct is the worship of Satan, who was the first being to utter the statement that has become the source of all human conflicts: "I am better than he!" (K. 38:76).[125]

The solution to social discord is not only forgiveness, but social engagement. Consequently, "retributive punishment is worth pursuing only to the extent that it leads to reconciling . . . the victim and the wrongdoer, and rehabilitating the latter after his or her acknowledgment of responsibility."[126] This leads to more peaceful and stable societies, and remedial punishment has an even greater goal—the reconciliation of the wrongdoer with *God*, turning him or her back into the "middle way."

Before turning to the difficult subject of *jihād*, it should be noted that Sachedina says very little in *Roots* about the process and importance of interreligious dialogue for seeking not only reconciliation and forgiveness but also the affirmation of universal moral norms from which just, peaceful, and pluralistic societies are formed and reformed. For that discussion, we must turn to the more recent FRC.

Here, Sachedina begins his reflection on interfaith dialogue by affirming that "differences [between world religions], even as they appear irreconcilable, are [an] indispensable part of each community's unique collective identity. No community, however enlightened, is willing to abandon its exclusive religious identity and its claim to salvation."[127] Unfortunately, most contemporary dialogues have "essentially remained academic" and even been used by brutally oppressive and discriminatory regimes to advance political agendas.[128] Thus, their importance has been limited. For Sachedina, the central starting point for any interfaith dialogue is an affirmation of religious pluralism, something vehemently

---

125. Ibid.

126. Ibid., 111.

127. FRC, 2. Later (p. 18) he directly addresses the issue of what he calls "John Hick's revisionist-pluralist theory that stifles the acknowledgment of profound disagreements or affirmation of the truth of one's own beliefs and practices."

128. FRC, 2. As two national examples of this kind of political chicanery he cites Saudi Arabia and Iran, where, in his estimation, "their record of human rights violations in the matter of free exercise of religion, their patterns of discrimination, intolerance and persecution is deplorable."

rejected by most Muslim scholars because they believe it would "take away the unique claim of Islam as the only religion that is acceptable to God."[129] Instead,

> Recognition of religious pluralism within a community . . . promises to advance the practical principle of inclusiveness in which the existence of competing claims to . . . religious truth need not precipitate conflict within religiously and culturally varied societies. Quite to the contrary, such an inclusiveness should lead to a sense of multiple and unique possibilities for enriching [the] human quest for spiritual and moral well-being in other than their own religious tradition.[130]

This search for a "common moral and spiritual terrain" to find "solutions to the problems of injustice, oppression, and poverty" results in the *Qur'anic requirement* for "Muslims to sit in dialogue with their own tradition to uncover a just approach to religious diversity and interfaith coexistence."[131] It also requires Islam to converse with religious others. This conversation is possible, even when exclusive truth claims are made, since fundamental disagreements, far from leading to hate, can actually lead participants to mutual appreciation, respect, and genuine learning from the other. Thus, "An interreligious dialogue that claims that all religions are essentially saying the same thing, or doing the same thing, or both, will in all likelihood base itself on a superficial comparison of relevant texts or praxis, and is, therefore, inadequately open to discuss and understand the complexity and diversity of religious creeds and practices."[132]

According to Sachedina, religious differences are so intractable, the Qur'an is clear: "in the final analysis, it is only God who can put an end to disputes based on these irreconcilable differences created by [the] particularity of human religious experience under different prophets and revelations."[133] Still, the necessary pursuit of common

---

129. FRC, 4. Sachedina means the independent salvific value of other world religions *must* be affirmed for dialogue to be fruitful. Otherwise, "the community of nation-states [will be] faced with endless violence and radical extremism propelled by [an] uncompromising stance in the matter of exclusive religious truth" (FRC, 2).

130. FRC, 7.

131. FRC, 10. I emphasize "requirement" since this is Sachedina's wording.

132. FRC, 21.

133. FRC, 21.

Islam, Tolerance, and Democracy

ground in long-term peaceful interpersonal relations remains, and these are forged and strengthened through dialogues with people from diverse religious and cultural backgrounds—not merely "people of the book."[134] Sachedina envisions this dialogue in the following way:

> As the religious communities of the global village draw closer in mutual confrontation and even understanding, the time has come for religiously sensitive scholars to retrieve the ethical and the spiritual resources of their respective religious narratives that are conducive to the revitalization of . . . discourse among the peoples of the world's religions. The moral and social problems confronting peoples of the world today make it imperative that . . . all religious communities will have to put their collective efforts in upgrading their [particular] discourse to [a more universal] idiom that would permit cooperation between diverse groups without denying the fundamental source of their religious identification.[135]

Having covered interreligious dialogue in Sachedina's thought, we can now return to the controversial issue of *jihād*, especially as it relates to Islamic relations with non-Muslims.

A long-standing debate in Islam (as well as in recent interfaith discussions) concerns the meaning and contemporary significance of the Arabic term *jihād*. As Sachedina admits, "the [traditional] notion of *jihād* poses a challenge to Muslim pluralists. The requirement of *jihād* against unbelievers and hypocrites in the Koran seems to support the view that Muslims must destroy other faiths and peoples to create an Islamic society—*dār al-islām*."[136] But Sachedina argues that, Qur'anically speaking, there are more peaceful (and perhaps even more compelling) ways to understand the idea of *jihād* and the passages calling for Muslims to subjugate, exterminate, and eradicate "unbelievers." Primary to this discussion is Q. 9:124, which calls believers to "fight those unbelievers who surround you." Sachedina believes the tension of Qur'anic voices—some calling for compassion and some for battle—is best understood in a "moral-religious and political" context only "prevalent in seventh-century Arabia."[137] Thus, the call for war against

---

134. FRC, 34.
135. Sachedina, "Universal and Particular Discourse," 37.
136. Sachedina, *Roots*, 112.
137. Ibid., 113.

unbelievers was likely concerned with a need for protection and a way to deal with aggressive and troublesome enemies threatening Islam's survival. In addition, the call for *jihād* against other Muslims "to impose doctrinal unity . . . is religiously as well as morally troublesome [since] religious commitment is freely negotiated between God and humanity."[138] Even though Muslim jurists adopted terms like "abode of Islam" and "abode of war" early on, Qur'anically, it would have been better to divide the world into abodes of belief and unbelief instead. This makes spiritual practices and beliefs conditions of the heart, but avoids attaching any sacred nature to objects and pieces of land, for example.[139] For Sachedina, contemporary *jihād* is best understood not as a struggle against visible enemies, but something closer to this:

> *Jihād*'s . . . purely religious signification includes a struggle against one's own baser instincts. This inner *jihād* has been declared by the Prophet as the "greater *jihād*," whereas the external combat is identified as the "lesser *jihād*." The ability to forgive requires a *jihād* against one's anger and resentment in order to restore one's spiritual station by participating in the divine attribute of forgiveness.[140]

Unfortunately, because of Islam's intimate connection of governance and religion, internal aspects of *jihād* were eclipsed by more political notions of fighting external enemies. Thus, jurists eventually used *jihād* politically, moving away from the Qur'anic posture of *defending* Islamic communities from outside aggression, toward more offensive strategies for *advancing* Islam through armed conquest, coercive conversions, and religious subjugation of the vanquished.[141] Again, this ignored clear Qur'anic passages forbidding religious compulsion and oppression of minorities.[142] It also failed to allow "separate jurisdictions

---

138. Ibid., 114.

139. Ibid., 116.

140. Ibid., 113.

141. This process, deemed the "politicization of religion," is by no means restricted to Islam. As Sachedina notes in *Role of Islam*, 10, "All world religions, at one time or another, have succumbed to secular pressure and have subordinated their core spiritual-moral message to the political ambitions of their particular communities. Such marriages of convenience between exclusive faith communities and political power has actually led to the disestablishment of the universal ethical and legal foundations of various religious traditions."

142. Sachedina, *Roots*, 117.

for religious and moral acts," and did not make nuanced Qur'anic distinctions between personally religious and publicly moral matters.[143] Sachedina is *not* saying *jihād*—the use of arms—is never justified for Islamic communities and nations. It is legitimate when Islam is militarily threatened, but "It is not all unbelievers who are the target of force, but unbelievers who demonstrate their hostility to Islam by persecution of Muslims."[144] Thus, such a course is meant to retain communal unity and is to be accomplished with clear moral and political guidelines.[145]

Although related to Islamic *jihād*, Sachedina has thus far left questions of internal civic protest and governmental overthrow largely unaddressed. Nevertheless, he tackles them in the section entitled "The Ethics of Self-Determination."[146]

According to Muslim tradition, for rebellion to be legitimized, it must include a communal aspect. Otherwise, an individual or small group of individuals are merely acting from self-interest. In addition, this community must be primarily "concerned with the preservation of Islamic values," making it a "public mandate," rather than a "private initiative."[147] Unfortunately, the juridical history of Islam does not say much against the indiscriminate use of power to support insurgent causes. However, it does highlight that "the primary concern of the entire community when rebellion occurs is to find ways of reconciling the contending parties and reestablish order."[148] Precedence is given to maintaining unity and stability, but the notion of restorative justice has been neglected by the jurists. For Sachedina, Q. 49:9 shows that "Just as private individuals must engage in personal *jihād* and show proper restraint in self-defense, public officials must also wage their institutional

---

143. Ibid., 117.

144. Ibid., 115.

145. Ibid., 119. On 119–21 Sachedina explores these guidelines historically and then concludes with this summary statement: "Any *jihād* that leads to meaningless destruction of human life and ignores concerns for peace with justice is non-Koranic *jihād*" (121).

146. Ibid., 121. While this section is more directed toward issues of intra-Islamic conflicts, it matters to Sachedina's overall thesis since traditional ways of seeing insurgent minority movements have often ignored Qur'anic injunctions to seek just reconciliation between warring factions as opposed to indiscriminately destroying the other.

147. Ibid., 122.

148. Ibid.

Contemporary Muslim and Christian Responses to Religious Plurality

jihād to ensure that social and political institutions reflect Koranic justice."[149] And this goal "to establish 'peace with justice' must be taken seriously by all responsible human societies on earth."[150] Thus, it is not merely a Muslim concern but a universal one.

The Qur'an does give authority to governments to maintain communal stability and unity by putting down rebellious groups and individuals—even by appropriately forceful means. However, according to Sachedina,

> At no point does the Koran endorse the community's use of political power to compromise freedom of conscience, which is an inalienable right through the very creation of the *fitra* in humankind. The state would forfeit its claim to be Islamic if it were to coerce people in the matter of the God-human relationship. Consequently, the case of apostasy in sacred law must be reinterpreted to allow for pluralism to emerge as a permanent feature of political life.[151]

All of this underscores the way *jihād* was supposed to be understood and applied. Unfortunately, an improper comprehension and use of *jihād* has entered the imagination of many Muslims today. A better way to understand the term encompasses the need to strive and fight for "peace with justice in order to advance horizontal relationships," rather than improperly using it to justify "the perpetration of extreme violence in the name of God."[152] Reconciliatory justice and peace are more consistent with God's compassionate and forgiving way of dealing with human beings. Why, then, does the Qur'an sometimes endorse using violence to restore justice? And why doesn't God resolve all differences by sovereignly making humanity into a single, unified community? Sachedina answers this way:

> Human existence . . . is caught up in contradictory forces of light and darkness, guidance and misguidance, justice and injustice. Although not born in primordial sin, human beings are subject

---

149. Ibid., 124.

150. Ibid.

151. Ibid., 127. Sachedina's point here is that, based upon the pluralistic injunctions of the Qur'an, a new understanding and legal application of apostasy must be sought by contemporary Muslims.

152. Ibid., 127.

to weakness, temptation, arrogance, narrow-mindedness, and, self-interest....

In this struggle, religion is the fount of inspiration. It inculcates ethical responsibility and personal accountability for one's actions. Furthermore, it generates incentives to correct one's social misconduct by emphasizing consequences of moral choices. The religious belief in the hereafter prompts human beings to identify actively with the cause of justice and work for it.[153]

There is still a place for retributive justice, but the ideal society is one where moral duties are upheld, religious freedoms are in place, rigorous intellectual interactions are celebrated, and personal and corporate accountability are exercised with compassion, forgiveness, truth, and righteousness. Since this kind of society is impossible without working against corrupting human tendencies that lead to unrighteousness, "the struggle against injustice was the sole justification for engaging in *jihād*."[154]

To close his argument, in the epilogue of *Roots* Sachedina observes that making past time-dependent juridical judgments into timeless, changeless, divine principles of justice hinders Islam's ability to deal adequately with the vicissitudes of contemporary life, handicapping it from significantly impacting future societies except, perhaps, as a counter-cultural oddity. Thus,

> Any community that treats past human intellectual endeavors of understanding and applying the revelation as sacred, and hence immutable, end up actually closing what Muslim scholars have aptly described as "the gates of independent reasoning" (*ijtihād*) in matters of law.... Every age needed its Muslim scholars (*mujtahid*, the one who practices *ijtihād*) to freshly interpret the revelation without departing from its original message.[155]

---

153. Ibid., 129.

154. Ibid., 130. This struggle in tension with the Qur'an's legitimizing of governmental authority to maintain order is what Sachedina calls "Koranic activism." For a more in depth exploration of the subject of *jihād* by Sachedina, see his "Justifications for Violence."

155. Sachedina, *Roots*, 133. This is the process of "contextualization." In "Islamic Theology," 34, he highlights this crucial activity of transmitting divine truths through the course of time and historical changes this way: "without contextualizing certain juridical-ethical judgments about Muslim-Christian relations within their social-political setting..., we cannot begin to expound a new Islamic theology of interfaith relations that could further non-discriminatory co-existence among peoples of differ-

Elsewhere, he says, "A non-critical approach to the 'situational aspects' that dominated past juridical decisions, which have become irrelevant in the modern system of international relations, could not be expected to offer relevant solutions to the pressing problem of recognizing religious pluralism as a cornerstone of interhuman relations."[156]

He also notes that none of the classical Muslim jurists considered their judgments to be divine in nature. Their adherence to the virtue of humility made such an attitude antithetical to the spirit of their ongoing project of re-appropriation. It is this same project Sachedina engages in to expound a religious plurality that is Qur'anic in nature and yet avoids "relativizing religions to the point of creating an esperanto religion."[157] By emphasizing shared ethical imperatives in all religions and the universal moral nature of the *fitra* inherent in every person, Sachedina believes he provides a fresh Islamic and specifically Qur'anic basis for societies that exhibit values of peace, justice, *and* genuine religious freedom and variety.

One question still remains—and it stems from Q. 3:110, which states Islam is "the best community ever brought forth to human beings, commanding the good, and forbidding the evil, and believing in God." Can Muslims claim to be "the best community" and still pursue religiously plural and democratic societies? In response, Sachedina insists, "The status of being the best [is not connected] with a self-righteous presumption of the need to convert others; rather, it ascribes the status of the best to a community charged with the responsibility of instituting good and preventing evil."[158] In fact, the opposite is true. Part of this responsibility, obscured by Islam's felt need in its early history for a consolidated religious identity, was to "create a just society in which peoples of different religions would coexist in peace and harmony."[159] The best society still includes the call to believe in God, of course, but

ent faiths."

156. Sachedina, "Islamic Theology," 36.

157. Sachedina, *Roots*, 134. By using the phrase "esperanto religion" here, Sachedina is referring to a common essential religion that is somehow derived from and representative of all. The word is usually capitalized in English ("Esperanto") and comes from a late nineteenth-century (failed) attempt by L. L. Zamenhof (who called himself, "Dr. Esperanto") to create an artificial international language derived from words common to all of the major European languages.

158. Ibid., 135.

159. Ibid.

this belief is "strictly personal," whereas "enjoining good and forbidding evil... is defined in terms of social-ethical responsibility to other humans."[160] Thus, the latter is public in nature, while the former is private—although it has numerous public ramifications. However, "the moment [personal] religion is coerced, it breeds hypocrisy."[161] This inevitability renders the idea of a "best" society grounded upon some governmentally mandated requirement of ascribing to "a comprehensive shared religious doctrine... inconceivable."[162] How can the "best" society be riddled with governmentally coerced and enforced religious hypocrisy?[163] Thus,

> The thesis that Islam does not make a distinction between the religious and the political requires revision in light of what has been argued in this volume. Even the all-comprehensive sacred law of Islam, the Sharī'a, presupposes the distinction between the spiritual and temporal, as it categorized God-human (*'ibādāt*) and interhuman (*mu'āmalāt*) relationships respectively. God-human relations are founded upon individual autonomy and moral agency regulated by a sense of accountability to God alone.... Interhuman relations, in contrast, are founded upon an individual and collective social-political life, with personal responsibility and social accountability.... This latter category of interhuman relations has customarily provided Muslim governments with the principle of *functional secularity*.... The same principle rules out the authority of Muslim governments to regulate religious matters except when the free exercise of religion for any individual is in danger.[164]

This is all based upon the fundamental premise that all human beings, endowed with the *fitra*, are "equals in creation." Thus, Islam provides our contemporary world with a compelling communal vision of private

160. Ibid.
161. Ibid.
162. Ibid.

163. Here Sachedina seems to be drawing from an earlier (1988) work, Little's "Western Tradition," where Little suggests that all religious belief is inherently *voluntary* by nature. Little describes it as "the irreducible voluntariness of religious belief" (p. 29) and says, "enforced religion contradicts and perverts the essential voluntariness of genuine religious commitment" (p. 25).

164. Sachedina, *Roots*, 137. Emphasis added to highlight the unique concept of secularity Sachedina is promoting, one that is religiously free, but also ethically informed by religious ideals and norms.

and public values that promote justice, moral responsibility, and social renewal through interpersonal restoration wrought by extending divine forgiveness and mercy to one another.

Ultimately, Sachedina's vision for Islam is one where independent reasoning (*ijtihād*) is in a continual reciprocal relation of fresh interpretation, application, reinterpretation, and reapplication.[165] It is a vision where people from all creeds and nationalities can live, work, and converse together peacefully in a society pursuing ethical justice while allowing real space for religious liberty. According to Sachedina, it was Muhammad's prophetic vision, and it is his own for contemporary Islam as well.[166]

Critical Reflections and Analysis: Kudos, Questions, and Concerns

As with any treatment of this magnitude, it is difficult to assess adequately the intricate details of Sachedina's nuanced proposal. In addition, because I am not a Muslim or Islamic scholar, the more comprehensive task of analyzing the many historical, linguistic, and juridical details concerning Islam must be delegated to more competent experts from within Sachedina's own faith community. Still, some critical observations are in order.

First, Sachedina's creative proposal for a more pluralistic reading of the Qur'an that opens up private space for religious freedom without forsaking a moral basis for just governance is a welcome contribution to an Islamic theology of religions. Making the *fitra* the foundation for moral insight and shared ethical vision is intriguing. In addition, the insight that genuine religious belief is inherently personal and must be freely chosen is extremely important for opening up sacred space

---

165. According to Sachedina in "Islamic Theology," 33, the success of this process is dependent upon the commitment of Muslims and others to "understand the [sacred] text [of their faith tradition] and the historical context of the religious truth" accurately, as well as to have a good understanding of the contemporary world—both in general and as an individual and a community within a particular concrete setting. This is very similar to the criteria Ramadan lays out in *Western Muslims*, where he seeks to provide a blueprint for Muslims to live well and thrive in the Western context while at the same time maintaining and integrating their distinct religious identity with their new (inter)national identity.

166. Sachedina, *Roots*, 139.

Islam, Tolerance, and Democracy

between the enforcement of public moral standards and the allowance of private religious belief and practice. Given recent and historical intolerances demonstrated by some of the more vocal and marginally influential elements within Islam, Sachedina's concept of "functional secularity" in Muslim governance coupled with a Qur'anically grounded religious plurality provides new resources for helping Muslims (and others) re-envision Islam's future. The impetus for affirming religious plurality in terms of the salvific legitimacy of other faith traditions is not based upon (post)modernity's pluralistic impulse so much as it is encouraged by the Qur'an itself. Thus, rather than co-opting a strictly secular plurality, Sachedina argues for *Qur'anic* plurality.

The obvious benefit of Sachedina's work is that he provides fellow Muslims with a non-violent, inclusively pluralistic framework that is compellingly persuasive because it is thoroughly grounded in authoritative Islamic texts. And yet it is also thoughtfully critical, interacting with historical and traditional understandings of these texts in ways that demonstrate his familiarity with all major streams of Muslim hermeneutics. This helps circumvent the argument of Muslim conservatives who claim that any move toward religious plurality and democratization in Islam is a capitulation to the spirit of the age and a move *away* from Qur'anic teaching.

One possible criticism against Sachedina is noted by reviewer Andrew Bacevich, who says his work is not only "short, dense, and bone dry," it has little hope of significantly influencing the larger Muslim community.[167] In his own trenchant words, "Even if we stipulate that this . . . imaginative remapping of the Koran *ought* to invalidate contrary readings, it would remain the height of folly to expect large-scale change in actually existing Islam to result anytime soon."[168] However, this kind of criticism is closely akin to saying that all early attempts at articulating religiously plural ideals in America (like those of Roger Williams) were futile because of local majority opposition from religious and political leaders (like John Cotton), as well as the long history of Christian integration and interpenetration with political governing authorities in the Old World. Naturally, the contexts and opportunities in today's world are very different, but attempts to articulate new religiously pluralistic visions are no less significant since they cut a

167. Bacevich, "Encountering Islam," 55.
168. Ibid.

wake against the rushing current of traditionalist and fundamentalist visions of Islam—visions using religious language, texts, and history to justify deplorably oppressive and unjust political and social orders. In addition, Sachedina's proposal taps into and legitimizes the majority of peaceful and pluralistically minded Muslims, who know something is wrong with the Islam envisioned by traditionalist and fundamentalist interpreters, but who may not be completely clear as to what is amiss or even where to turn their religious and political loyalties in public protest. So, I am not sure Bacevich's criticism is all that substantive.

In fact, by Sachedina's account, far from being novel, this pulse of Qur'anic pluralism was never absent but only ignored, missed, and misinterpreted throughout much of Islamic history. It remained within the sacred texts waiting to reemerge and be reemphasized when the time was ripe. Perhaps contemporary political and pluralistic attitudes were important catalysts, but this does not mean such impulses are now being externally imposed upon the text.[169] This also demonstrates the interpretive resilience and rich internal resources historically extended world religions like Islam possess when faced with new challenges through time.[170] Thus, Sachedina's use of the Qur'an and his demon-

169. It may seem ironic that Sachedina acknowledges the impact history has had on Islam's inability to see the Qur'an's pluralistic bent, but then proceeds to imply his own analysis of the Qur'an is not merely another historically conditioned example of gathering certain texts that support the current pluralistic spirit of the age. He could very well be found guilty of the same kind of myopic appropriation he argues against with respect to the traditional jurists. However, I am not sure that Sachedina would deny the impact contemporary thought has had on his thinking. In fact, this kind of "historically impacted" interpretation is unavoidable, even as one seeks to minimize the biases it tends to create. Neither am I convinced this reduces its credibility or importance. Rather, it may well be that current global sensibilities have highlighted the rich pluralistic resources already present within the sacred texts of Islam in nascent but as yet not fully developed forms. This kind of highlighting can occur during intercultural and interreligious dialogues as well, where one faith tradition reminds another of vital resources that were always present, but for various reasons became obscured and neglected. In this way, Sachedina's vision is perhaps best characterized as a *rediscovery* and *recovery* of authentic Islam—at least as he envisions it from the earlier Meccan period as opposed to the later Medinan period.

170. MacIntyre fans will immediately notice that this argument comes from *Whose Justice? Which Rationality?* There, he convincingly argues (and historically seeks to demonstrate) the ultimate success of any intellectual tradition (secular or sacred) is based upon its ability to demonstrate to its members (and outsiders) its superior explanatory power through the reinterpretation and reapplication of its sacred texts and traditions in the face of internal and external epistemological and ethical challenges

stration of its inescapable historicity is laudable among the cacophony of Islamic voices claiming to represent pure, unadulterated, ahistorical, and Qur'anic Islam.

However, something must be said in response to Sachedina's claim that the influence of concrete periods in history upon spiritual insight and the understanding of sacred texts is sufficient to explain critical differences between the creeds and practices of world religions. Any detailed and careful examination of these yields not only a remarkable catalogue of common beliefs and customs, but also a huge array of incommensurate and contested perspectives. It is difficult to see how Sachedina's appeal to historicity and the contextual nature of divine revelation can adequately account for all of the competing and apparently contradictory claims. Some appear irreducibly irreconcilable, and may be why doctrines of abrogation (*naskh*) and corruption (*tahrif*) arose so quickly and prominently within Islamic tradition. Sachedina's attempt to minimize the need for such problematic doctrines is commendable, but ultimately leaves too much unresolved and passes too easily over central differences that have provided so much fuel for inter-religious conflicts.

Another praise-worthy aspect of Sachedina's proposal is his emphasis on the importance of religious resources in providing society with public ethical norms for legislative creativity. His critique of secularism's attempts to disestablish religious influence from public policy-making is crucial, for he is surely correct to note religion remains centrally important to the vast majority of the world's population. Excluding it from the public arena severely impoverishes society and marginalizes a huge segment of the populace. It may also inflame those who feel left out and unheard by those in power. By publicly including religious concerns, such alienating feelings are more likely to be curtailed.

Beyond issues of marginalization are the blessings of enrichment. Religions are rich receptacles of ethical resources for the legislative goals of just and cohesive societies. Their disuse or misuse by past and

---

it inevitably encounters through time. It is also based upon the tradition's syncretistic ability to utilize materials from other traditions to reenvision itself not only in contemporary contexts, but to explain more plausibly the problems and even successes of alternative traditions as well. Such increasingly comprehensive explanatory power gives devotional weight and credibility to the respective members of the various competing traditions.

present governments does not invalidate them at all. Careful appropriation of such assets is always a struggle in the life of any religion. But this appropriation raises the valid concerns many secularists have about their content and the ways they have been utilized by immoral and corrupt leaders.

Perhaps the first concern along these lines is raised by the universal way Sachedina talks about ethical norms. He is openly assured such moral norms exist and are readily discernable by any and all rational human beings. Several things can be said about this. First, recent postmodern critiques of universal moral norms and truth claims may or may not be intellectually convincing, but given the propensity of many today to believe relativistic notions of morality and epistemology, surely some interaction with postmodern concerns would be appropriate, especially if Sachedina is trying to convince secular governments to include religious perspectives as a vital foundation for their legislative corpora.

Another concern is that Sachedina's vision leaves me wondering, what constitutes good works? And more practically, what do we do when there are strong inter- and intra-communal disagreements about moral perspectives? How can these be resolved, especially since history shows such disputes are rarely resolved by simply *talking* about them with one another? In fact, some aspects of Muslim jurisprudence raise grave concerns in my mind. Sachedina is surely right in making ethics the basis for creating free and just public orders, but the *actual content* of those ethical norms and the *prescribed temporal punishments* for violating them are less obvious. Granted, the widespread moral confusion in many societies today is vividly indicative of secular humanism's failure to recognize or produce any transcendent or coherent moral vision. But any move to instantiate Islamic law in the West, with all of its attendant and lingering concerns over women's rights, minority political and religious freedoms, and laws regulating judicial access, business commerce, family life, Islamic leadership, along with a host of other greater and lesser legal affairs, like alcohol and pork consumption, appears to be exceedingly problematic.

Obviously, Sachedina is speaking first to Muslims, many of whom already sit under some form of Islamic rule of law (*Sharī'ah*). But since he also writes in and to a North American audience and appears to be speaking to the West, I would like more details on some of the democratic laws that might be enacted and enforced in a Sachedinian society. After surveying his writings on this subject, I am still left pondering how a pluralistic Muslim society might actually look. And I am still not satisfied with or comforted by the thought of living as a Christian minority in this kind of Islamic state.

A closely associated issue concerns Sachedina's treatment of the ambivalent relationship between religious practice, civil unity, and social order. As Sachedina admits, one of the greatest challenges for a publicly expressed religion like Islam is discerning what duties are specifically religious and subjectively based (and so granted a significant degree of individual freedom), and which duties are publicly critical for the continued stability, security, and unity of a given society. Muslim history shows this struggle was seldom resolved to anyone's satisfaction, even within strictly Muslim communities. How will these things be clearly discerned and kept separate? What should the punishments, if any, be? Is conversion to atheism, for example, akin to treason? What about converting to Christianity, Hinduism, Buddhism, or agnosticism? Is evangelism an inherent threat to public order?[171] History shows these are not idle musings, but genuine practical concerns. Particularly disconcerting here is the question of *apostasy*.

Sachedina's somewhat glib abdication to the government to hammer out the details of what constitutes apostasy and how it impacts society as a whole is puzzling. Perhaps he believes embracing the notion of allowing private space for freedom of religious belief and practice will make governments less apt to punish religious conversions and other acts of religious alteration, but much of Islamic history is not on his side.[172] As a Christian, I believe a more realistic view of human

---

171. In Singapore, for example, because Muslims tend to get upset when Christians and others seek to convert them, as a peacekeeping gesture it is technically illegal to "proselytize" them. In this case, mission and evangelism are outlawed on the basis of the recipient community's own reaction, not necessarily on the potentially inflammatory behavior of the evangelist. And as a recent court case demonstrates, this injunction is not merely theoretical. Two otherwise law-abiding Singaporean Christians were sentenced to several months in a Singaporean jail for anonymously handing out religious tracts in residential mailboxes that condemned Islamic belief in favor of a Christian view of salvation.

172. Friedmann (*Tolerance and Coercion in Islam*, 121–59) gives a very helpful extended survey of the early historical development of Islamic law concerning apostasy, although he openly states that he "is not concerned with the modern Muslim views on apostasy" (121 n. 1).

nature and its propensity to become corrupted by great power and an abundance of possessions is pertinent here. If religion is the dominant unifying force in such a community, it is easy to see why apostasy easily becomes a governmental concern—not because it should be, but because governments *want* it to be. By demanding religious conformity, freedom and its perceived threats to governmental power and social stability are minimized—or so the argument goes. Without a clearer presentation of precisely what apostasy is and how it can be handled as a distinctly *religious* concern rather than a problem of social sedition and rebellion, I remain uneasy about Islamic concepts of religious freedom, especially in Muslim-majority contexts.[173] As such, this issue will be addressed further in chapter 6.

Closely related are concerns about economic systems and methods of governing society. As Ebrahim Moosa points out, Sachedina's vision is given

> without specifying the political context from which he speaks. From his tone one intuits that his context is irenic. For this reason one must concede that these principles might play out very differently in less stable political contexts. It might have been helpful if the author had said something about liberalism, neoliberalism, globalization, despotism, and capitalism, since theology is mediated by these political and economic master narratives.[174]

Recall that Sachedina writes *Roots* specifically to Muslims, whereas in the earlier essay, *Human Rights*, he writes for a broader western audience. Thus, his call for a universal plurality based upon ethical common

---

173. Christianity has also been guilty of handling apostasy poorly in its own history. However, from New Testament passages like Matt 18:15–17 and 1 Cor 5:1–5, it is clear that apostasy was never intended to be handled by political rulers, but by church leaders. And the punishment was essentially no more than public condemnation before the congregation and then banishment from the fellowship of believers—not exile or removal from society as a whole. In addition, 2 Cor 2:5–11 suggests it was ultimately to be a *restorative* gesture in hopes the apostate may one day repent and be brought back into full fellowship with the community of believers once again. This admittedly revises the Old Testament vision of dealing with apostates in several significant ways. Space limits any further exploration of these complex issues other than to mention that they remain difficult tensions in societies where religion and government are intimately linked—as they were in Old Testament Israel and still are today in many Islamic nations.

174. Moosa, "Abdulaziz Sachedina," 173.

Islam, Tolerance, and Democracy

ground inherent in human nature seems more muted than it is in the earlier essay. Perhaps it is because the Qur'an only explicitly accepts certain world religions (like Christianity and Judaism) while remaining silent about others. It may be too large a leap for some Muslims to consider polytheistic Hindus, for example, as possessors of salvation, important conversation partners, and active moral participants in a pluralistic social order.[175] The concept of universal morality is still present in *Roots*, but the vagueness and ambiguity of how Sachedina's just, peaceful, and—most importantly—religiously free society will actually look in a variety of potential contexts leaves too many unanswered questions. Sachedina must provide more content-oriented and structurally specific material to allay legitimate social concerns.

Additional questions surround problems of the human heart. Since, "when a person rejects faith, the heart becomes veiled and is deprived of its ability to understand the moral situation," and if "the heart thus functions as a faculty for distinguishing truth from falsehood, good from evil, the beneficial from the harmful,"[176] this has potential for significant abuses. Power-hungry rulers wanting to "help" misguided people might dictate and enforce what they claim is "best" for their subjects. Such a view of the heart opens the door to the idea that some people are more able to see and know what is good and evil, true and false, beneficial and harmful. For Sachedina, this could inevitably mean only committed Muslims would know what is "best for all" in any given society.

I am not suggesting this can be wholly avoided, however. Moral distinctions among people *do* exist, and the notion that God gives greater capacity for understanding and practicing what is true and right to those who seek him is hardly unique to Islamic thinking. As Paul points out in Rom 1:18ff., the basis for moral discernment and understanding is giving thankful glory and honor to God and living a righteous life. Consequently, potential abuses notwithstanding, that people

---

175. Perhaps this is true, but in the Pancasila form of government in Indonesia, the largest Muslim-majority country in the world, Hinduism and Buddhism (as well as Christianity) are officially recognized and seen as religions believing in God. This example shows there is no necessary or decisive barrier to interfaith recognition and cooperation between Muslims and Hindus (as well as Buddhists, Jews, and Christians) in Muslim-majority societies.

176. Sachedina, *Roots*, 91.

seeking a moral vision for society should do so with a heart for God and righteousness seems correct. And Sachedina's call for humility in this process does provide a safeguard against potential abuse by those in power.[177] All of this highlights the need for extreme care and caution in making certain religious commitments the standard for moral discernment in public discourse.

A stronger system of checks and balances is needed to guard against the inimical human tendency to use power abusively. While Sachedina does address the problem of sin, his treatment seems too optimistic considering the historically well-documented negative propensities of human nature. This is especially the case since Sachedina is attempting to provide an Islamic basis for pluralistic, just, and free human societies. In fact, Christianity's doctrine of human depravity played a significant role in the conception, construction, and implementation of the political system of "checks and balances" found in the United States. More specific proposals are needed to avoid some of the potential abuses of political and religious power. Along with Sinasi Gündüz, I wonder whether the long and uneasy history of religion-state relations is better seen as religion wrestling with its societal role as it seeks to be true to itself and make itself relevant within non-religious ideological movements.[178] Perhaps Islam's failure to create truly golden societies is related not only to humanity's "darker side," but also to the inherently difficult and ambiguous relationship between human culture and divine mandates.

Similarly, because Sachedina puts great stock into his concept of the *fitra*, it would be good to look more thoughtfully at the Mu'zilite/Ash'arite debate over the nature of human freedom. While Sachedina does note this debate concerning the nature of the *fitra*, he clearly takes the typically contemporary Islamic position that humanity was not "born into sin." Furthermore, he appears to take this position primarily because it helps his argument, and not necessarily because it is a better way to understand the Qur'an on the subject.[179]

---

177. As we will see in chapter 6, this has important implications for all interfaith dialogue that affirms transcendent moral values and exclusive religious truth claims.

178. Gündüz, "Hegemonic Power," 124.

179. For more on this debate as well as ways in which Christian and Muslim beliefs about human nature are parallel with one another, see Woodberry, "Toward a Common Ground." As Woodberry points out on p. 30, if human nature is more

Islam, Tolerance, and Democracy

Also, Sachedina does not adequately explore alternative interpretive paradigms for various passages and key concepts he uses to bolster his claims. Translations are notoriously ambiguous, especially concerning controversial terms.[180] For example, Yohanan Friedman does an exemplary job exploring numerous alternative possible meanings in Islamic tradition and the Qur'an concerning the passage, "No compulsion is there in religion."[181] In contrast, Sachedina only occasionally mentions alternative perspectives. What is especially disappointing is not so much that he has not done enough research; on the contrary, he is a scholar of the highest order and has certainly done extensive analysis of the pertinent material. However, as they stand, his writings do not sufficiently demonstrate this scholarly breadth. Given the controversial nature of the subject and its relative importance, more interaction with other points of view is needed. It would raise the persuasive power and credibility of his arguments, especially for Muslims holding alternative perspectives. This is essentially a request for Sachedina to make more explicit the reasons for adopting his particular ontological, epistemological, and hermeneutical perspectives concerning the best way not only to understand ethics and human nature, but also to elucidate the historically and theologically complex and reciprocal relationships between the Qur'an, the *Sunna* and the *Sharī'ah*.[182]

---

radically flawed than some Muslim anthropological theology suggests, then the nature of the solution may be very different as well. This undercuts Sachedina's claim that human beings not only possess the ability to know what is right and wrong, but they also have the internally unaided power to perform righteous actions.

180. This is especially pertinent since Islam officially teaches that Qur'anic translations (like those used in Sachedina's book) are not technically God's authoritative word since only the Arabic version holds this position of honor. Granted, translation is a de facto necessity if interlinguistic communication is to be achieved, but my point remains. It is only in an abundance of possible translations that the meanings of particularly difficult and controversial terms and passages can be adequately explored.

181. Friedman, *Tolerance and Coercion in Islam*, 87–120.

182. This is the great adventure that many contemporary Muslim thinkers have been compelled to embark upon in view of the new global climate. Thus, many Muslims have recently responded to the formidable challenges that modernity and postmodernity create for premodern Islamic theology and its relationship to traditional Islamic law. For an extremely helpful summary of the various strategies and schema contemporary Muslim thinkers have adopted to address such challenges, see Johnston, "Muslim Theologies of Human Rights." Johnston (p. 154) places Sachedina in a group of Muslim scholars "who argue that the relationship between Islamic theology and law must be totally rethought." Johnston describes this rethinking as a

Although I have been somewhat critical, I remain intrigued and excited by the prospect of interreligiously pursuing a project of a Sachedinian sort. The toll of religious disestablishment in much of the West is only beginning to manifest itself. To be not merely a political critic, but to offer a vision of justice, tolerance, engagement, and embrace is something every serious religious adherent should applaud. And this aspect of societal critique raises another point of concern, namely Sachedina's claim that only Islam can provide a thorough-going critique of secularist society. Putting aside possible accusations of arrogance or triumphalism, I would counter this claim by noting that the most strident and pertinent critiques of modern secular societies have often come from *within* those societies.[183] This makes sense since, as Sachedina believes, the most effective critics and visionaries are those who come from within a community in need of radical reform and revision. In addition, other religions have provided non-secularist critiques of moral and structural problems in contemporary secular societies. Nevertheless, Sachedina's point is not without warrant. Critical outsiders often see what those from within miss or even refuse to admit. Thus,

---

"hermeneutical turn" (p. 164) in Muslim theology that is used in two basic ways. The first way, what Johnston calls, "*Maqāsid al-sharī'a* in a traditionalist setting," looks for conservative ways to adapt the *Sharī'ah* to contemporary contexts, but largely leaves the traditional judgments intact and unmodified. Thus, "in practice, there seems to be little room for adaptability" (p. 169). The second way, what Johnston calls "The *maqāsidī* strategy of human rights in Islam," involves "an epistemological turn toward a relative empowerment of reason over revelation supplemented by the hermeneutical decision to follow the spirit of the sacred texts—here the ethical principles—over the various formulations of past *ijtihād*." This allows such thinkers to evaluate the ways in which times have changed and how the legal principles that arose in response to former times can be reevaluated and reapplied to contemporary issues and contexts. The way in which this method is actually carried out varies greatly, but in Johnston's insightful analysis, "The watershed issue is over epistemology and hermeneutics" (p. 179), as well as the ontological status of ethical imperatives and ideals. It is not my intention here to give an extensive summary or analysis of Johnston's work, but merely to highlight the fact that Sachedina departs from more traditional Islamic theology and hermeneutics in significant ways. As such, it would have been helpful for Sachedina to make this departure, and his reasons for doing so, much more explicit in his writings. Had he done so, it would have helped to bolster his arguments in particular and his credibility in general.

183. It can also be argued that secularism is itself a kind of pseudo-religion, offering its own religio-political vision for what society should be. At the very least, it certainly is a tradition along the lines of MacIntyre's presentation. For a closer look at this thesis, see MacIntyre, *Three Rival Versions*.

Islam's critique of secularism should be taken seriously and assert itself more forcefully as a prophetic voice against the moral confusion and decadence so prevalent in many of these societies. But it is probably better to see this kind of Islamic critique as one important and unique voice alongside many others, rather than claiming it offers "the *only* thoroughgoing religious critique of international public order with its secularist and liberal presuppositions."[184]

Historically and sociologically, Sachedina claims that early in their history, Christians needed "to establish their sociopolitical and religious identity at the expense of another community."[185] In response, I would suggest that the reasons for Christianity's insistence on supremacy are complex and may have contained such aforementioned aspects, but at the core, Christian claims to supremacy were not motivated by a need for "sociopolitical and religious identity" so much as they were inescapably grounded in the person and ministry of Jesus, especially with respect to his resurrection from the dead.[186]

Concerning its early history, Sachedina repeatedly argues for this same kind of sociopolitical explanation for Islam's tendency to show intolerance for non-Muslims as well as Muslims who did not conform to the religious and political vision of Islamic authorities. Perhaps this is the case, but, as it does when applied to Christianity, such an explanation borders on sociological reductionism, ascribing religious exclusivity to a need for communal identity and consolidation alone. More should be said to provide plausible explanations for why Islam so quickly became what it did in the generations immediately following Muhammad's death. A more careful analysis of this formative period would add significant weight to Sachedina's project.

Another critique centers on Sachedina's frequent claim that "The *fundamental problem*, as reflected in the classical formulation of Muslim political identity, is religious authoritarianism founded on an exclusive salvific claim, which runs contrary to the global spirit of democratiza-

---

184. Sachedina, *Roots*, 42; emphasis added.

185. Ibid., 69.

186. Muslim denials of the resurrection have been a point of spirited debate during recent interfaith dialogues. These denials arise mainly from Q. 3:54–55 and esp. 4:157–58. For two creative (re)interpretations of these passages from a Christian perspective that persuasively argue that the resurrection of Jesus need not be denied by Muslims, see Moucarry, *Prophet*, 137–38; and especially Cumming, "Did Jesus Die on the Cross?"

tion emerging through the acknowledgement of religious pluralism."[187] With all due respect to Sachedina, attributing the problem of violence to exclusivism is too reductionistic to be very helpful. Millions of exclusivistic believers of many religions—Islam included—do not advocate the use of arms for propagating their faith, suggesting that the situation is more complex and less centrally related to exclusivism *per se*. It is more likely (as Sachedina himself already pointed out) some exclusivists have used religion to justify neocolonial, imperialistic impulses to conquer and rule the world—all in the name of God and religion. It might be claimed that the motivation for such a political end is "for God's glory," and for the good of all, but this does not explain the extremely complex and multifaceted relationship religion has with both human culture and political ideology. This problem is not new, of course, and for this reason Tariq Ali argues Islamic fundamentalism is not a religious problem, but a political, sociological, and ideological one.[188] In short, there are underlying rationales and reasons, sometimes not fully understood by even its most fervent promoters, that are clothed and articulated in religious language to motivate huge numbers of people to strive for world domination—all in the name of God and humanity's greater good. Sachedina's indictment of exclusivism is probably best understood as indicting a particular form of exclusive ideology that is carefully wrapped in a veil of (pseudo)religiosity.

Finally, while attempts to move Muslim fundamentalists away from the dangers of militant exclusivism are to be applauded—loud and long—Sachedina's inclusivistic vision still fails to be open enough to the fact that all major religions make exclusive claims for themselves that are simply not commensurable. The attempt to move Christians into the "*muslim*" camp under the banner of "*islām*" (submission to God) fails to answer several even more important questions. If I, as a Christian, have "submitted my life to God," what does this submission actually entail? Is it on God's terms? My terms? The Qur'an's terms? Traditional Islam's terms? The Bible's terms? And how would I know which of these was actually speaking for God? If my faith tradition (Christianity) teaches submission to God is only possible under the salvific Lordship of Jesus Christ, then claiming me for "*islām*" hardly

187. Sachedina, *Roots*, 41; emphasis added.
188. Ali, "Theological Distractions."

qualifies as an argument either way. And the way Sachedina has ethically framed the salvific question is inherently skewed toward a traditionally Islamic view of soteriology—and away from a (more evangelically conservative) Christian one.

I am not trying to be harsh, but I question the pluralist tendency to assume religious exclusivism is *inherently* dangerous and detrimental to the tasks of dialogue, compromise, and mutual learning. As I will argue in chapter 6, virtually every pluralistic and inclusivistic vision ultimately collapses into some form of exclusive claim for the truth of their position. Sachedina's inclusive vision necessarily hinges upon the concept of doing good works, not only to demonstrate one's right relationship with God, but actually, in some important sense, to *attain* that right relationship. Evangelical Christianity's emphasis on a right relationship to God being established by God's grace through faith in the finished work of Jesus Christ takes strong issue with Sachedina's rather exclusive claim.

Admittedly, one of the daunting challenges for exclusivists is to present a religiously distinct and conservative vision of reality that does not exclude or demean the other, but instead openly tolerates, invites, and even embraces them whenever possible. This embrace comes not through coercion or manipulation, but rather from a powerful internal resource vitally present within the religious tradition itself. By letting the other truly be the other instead of demanding they come with certain preset notions of what dialogue can or cannot say or do seems more consonant with the Christian religion I seek to represent with humility.[189] Ultimately, I believe the best way to benefit and grow from the religious other is to meet that other as he or she actually stands—with all of his or her passions, convictions, questions, and comments.

---

189. Sachedina claims in his more recent FRC that he has made genuine space for these religious claims to exclusive truth, but he still seems to struggle with allowing exclusive ideology into the arena of interreligious dialogue. Thus, he appears to be somewhat inconsistent on this particular point in his writings. Given the recent expressions of lethal hatred within exclusivistic Islam, it is not surprising Sachedina is reticent to affirm an exclusivist religious perspective. But even more than this concern over exclusivism, his Qur'anic exegesis drives him toward an ethical inclusivism that tends to overtake many of the exclusive claims that Christianity, for example, makes for itself—especially the claims surrounding the person and work of Jesus Christ.

Conclusion

For all of my questions and comments, I still have great hope that more pluralistic visions like those of Sachedina's will increasingly be argued for and promoted among Muslims. Given Islam's firm adherence to the divine authority of the Qur'anic texts, as well as its dependence upon the stipulations laid out in the *Sharī'ah*, the move to "pluralize" Islam through a careful reexamination of those authoritative sources is wise. Coupled with a conscious quest for forgiveness and reconciliation, political action, genuine dialogue, and peace and justice with and for all, such a reassessment provides a powerful impetus for Muslims and religious others to find more ways to live and thrive together peacefully as "equals in creation."[190]

In conclusion, Sachedina's vision of a just and plural democratic society calls for serious cooperative endeavors from all thoughtful and concerned communities and individuals, whether Muslim, Christian, or otherwise. In the words of progressive Muslim scholar Farish Noor, "It is often stated that Islam is a religion of peace, and this is true, but only if we realize that this peace can only be realized when Muslims [and non-Muslims] acknowledge the fundamental humanity they share with others."[191] With this I wholeheartedly agree. If Christians and Muslims constitute the vast majority of adherents among the world's religions, any serious attempts at cooperative endeavors between them and other religions will benefit the long-term welfare of ourselves, our families, our nations, and our world.

Having laid out Sachedina's distinctively Muslim response to the challenges and opportunities afforded by religious plurality, a comparative analysis between his view and Pannenberg's will be provided next. In particular, areas of agreement and discord will be highlighted, with a view to seeing more clearly the problems and promises present within these two creative responses to the wide array of belief systems now existing and interacting in close proximity with one another.

---

190. I am referring here to *Roots*, 110, where Sachedina utilizes this concept from Muslim caliph 'Alī b. Abī Ṭālib.

191. Noor, "Victory of Islam," 324–25.

5

Pannenberg and Sachedina in Critical Conversation: Conflict, Cooperation, and Convergence

Having explored Pannenberg's Christian, and Sachedina's Islamic theology of religions, this chapter gives further analysis by comparing and contrasting the views of these two thinkers. By pointing out areas of commonality and convergence, as well as conflict and contention, a clearer picture of their potential resources for encouraging future Christian-Muslim conversation and cooperation will emerge. We will commence by making a few general remarks concerning the general scope of Pannenberg and Sachedina's overall projects before delving into the particulars.

Purpose and Scope of Pannenberg and Sachedina's Projects

Sachedina writes primarily to convince *Muslims* that Islamic moral norms need not be abandoned to support religious freedom in pluralistic societies. Thus, he focuses on Qur'anic resources since Muslims see these as divinely trustworthy, arguing other religions are Qur'anically sanctioned, legitimately salvific expressions of God's universal moral vision. Consequently, unlike Pannenberg, he does little to develop a broad-scope theology of religions.

Pannenberg's attempt to provide an all-inclusive vision of what theology is intended to be and do in the hands of the systematic theologian drives his material to encompass history, philosophy, science, sociology, and anthropology. In short, unlike Sachedina's very focused theology of religions, Pannenberg's broad comprehensiveness is built within and inherent to his theological enterprise. Because of this, it is tempting to praise Pannenberg's vision on the basis of its breadth alone. However, Sachedina's scope becomes a strength rather than a weakness, making it more accessible to the reader. Indeed, Pannenberg has been criticized for being obscure and inaccessible at times. As William Placher notes concerning Pannenberg, Jüngel, and Moltmann,

> For whom is Pannenberg writing? I am told that in some German circles Pannenberg and Jüngel are considered "real" theologians while Moltmann is viewed as a bit of a popularizer. In [America], on the other hand, even Moltmann seems sometimes too technical, maybe just too difficult, for many students and pastors. . . . So one worries whether in [America] Pannenberg's work presupposes too much interest in metaphysics and the theological tradition to attract the academy's attention, and is just too difficult to make much of an impact in church circles. To say that, one hastens to add, may be more of a criticism of us [as Americans] than of him.[1]

Sachedina, on the other hand, writes more simplistically than Pannenberg. This empowers understanding, gaining adherence that relatively obscure and complex perspectives may not enjoy. Still, Pannenberg's range of scholarship is clearly his strength as he seeks to bring all knowledge under the holistic sphere of theological reflection and systematic synthesis because the Christian God is the sustainer, determiner, and Lord of all.

Sachedina's emphasizes Islamic revelatory resources and their anthropological implications, whereas Pannenberg offers a more general theological model. Pannenberg describes this distinctively Christian model as "a model which, if it is tenable, will 'prove' the reality of God and the truth of the Christian doctrine, showing them to be consistently conceivable, and also confirming them, by the form of the presentation."[2] Thus, it could even be said that Sachedina's project

---

1. Placher, "Revealed to Reason," 194.
2. *ST* 1:60.

fits *within* Pannenberg's model of providing greater credibility and explanatory power by seeking to demonstrate the internal coherence of Islam's sacred texts, along with their correspondence to and interaction with problems and needs of contemporary societies. In doing so, he potentially provides Muslims with more compelling reasons to consider their faith to be true.

Having made these more general observations, a more detailed analysis of these two theologies of religion can be explored, beginning with key areas of common ground and convergence.

Areas of Agreement: Commonality and Convergence

God as Holy and Sovereign Lord and Creator

One of the most important areas of commonality between Pannenberg and Sachedina is their view of God. Unfortunately, Sachedina does not focus on theology proper, but maintains a background belief in the universal greatness, majesty, and holiness of God that firmly undergirds all he envisions. Thus for him, like Pannenberg, God is the sovereign, all-powerful creator of the universe. He is the righteous judge of all and uniquely created human beings to understand and reflect his rational and moral nature. Every person is divinely endowed with moral conscience (the *fitra*) and the rational capacity to respond to that conscience. Thus, no one is morally unaccountable at the eschatological judgment when everything done on earth is revealed and either rewarded or punished by God.

In this sense, Sachedina likely agrees with Pannenberg's notion (laid out by F. LeRon Shults) that everything and everyone exists "*sub ratione Dei*, (under the aspect of their 'relation to God')."[3] We are created by God, and our existence depends upon and is grounded in him. Thus we are morally sensitive and rational creatures, and this implies that we are morally free and morally accountable.[4]

---

3. Shults, *Postfoundationalist Task*, 84–85.

4. The anthropological aspects of Pannenberg's theology are more expansive than what is noted here, but for focus, only those that are relevant are included. For a more extensive look at these, see *ST* 2, esp. chs. 8 and 9.

Consequently, there is a universal drive in both Islam and Christianity that seeks to bring all of creation under submission to God's sovereign will. Sachedina and Pannenberg see their respective religions as all-encompassing and universal, and this stems from their views about God's sovereignty and his independent nature as it contrasts with a dependent world. Religion cannot be excluded from the world, for it flows from the worship of the one true God who created, cares for, and communicates with it.

For example, Sachedina states that because of Islam's view of God as Lord over all creation, it "has been accurately described as a faith in the public realm."[5] Elsewhere, he puts it thus: "[Belief in] an ethical God who insists on justice and equality in interpersonal relations" produces an "indispensable connection between the religious and ethical dimensions of personal life [that] inevitably introduces religious precepts into the public arena."[6] Religious and public realms are impossible to separate completely. Similarly, Pannenberg declares, "Christian faith, like any religion that takes itself seriously, has to claim recognition and influence as a normative basis on which to shape every sphere of human life, not just individual conduct, but life in society as well, including matters of law and politics."[7] Much like Sachedina's vision for a plural and religiously influenced society, Pannenberg envisions such a society from a Christian perspective, noting that,

> Christian awareness is now on the point of outgrowing the antagonisms of the denominational age and hence the historical reasons for making religion a private matter. A renewal of the social sense of Christians as the "people of God" beyond all confessional differences, tolerance and respect for other forms of faith, and above all a new sense of being close to the Jewish people and associated with it might well initiate a new epoch in shaping the relation between Christianity and the public order.[8]

---

5. Sachedina, *Roots*, 24.

6. Ibid., 78.

7. *ST* 3:482.

8. *ST* 3:482–83. Pannenberg argues here that recent historical tendencies to make religion "a private matter" were based upon "the antagonisms of the denominational age." As interesting (and debatable) as this contention is, especially as it relates to Islam and its refusal to be pushed to the margins of the state, it goes beyond the scope and concern of the current chapter and so will not be examined here.

Thus, for both men, there is no legitimate way to exclude religious commitment from the public arena since God remains sovereign Lord of all.

In addition, both argue space must be made for religious freedom and plurality in modern societies. The sacred and the secular must be distinguished but not separated from each other. Religion must be a public aspect of any good society, but this aspect must not only be the perspective of the majority faith tradition. Sufficient space for the religious freedom of all must be granted and celebrated. Sachedina provides this space by arguing that the universal moral *fitra* enables human beings to form pluralistic societies shaped around common ethical norms.[9] He also notes that true religious devotion is inherently personal and voluntary and consequently cannot be coerced. Thus, any society wanting to encourage genuine religiosity must also make space for religious freedom.

In principle, Pannenberg agrees with these aforementioned ideas, but in a distinctly Christian way. He links God's image in humanity not only to moral aspects of conscience, but especially to God's intertrinitarian life. This image leads human beings to pursue an ethical social life characterized by "unity and peace" among all people because it directly reflects the communal nature of God.[10] In addition, he emphasizes the "relativizing" role the church plays concerning the secular state.[11] The state often tries to usurp its inherently temporal nature and God-given role of providing social structure by attempting to become what the church already is—an eternal and holy community that already participates in the sovereign eschatological rule of God. By reminding the state of its inherently provisional nature, the church keeps the state from absolutizing itself and becoming tyrannical in its attempts to take the place of God.[12] The eschatological nature of church fellowship automatically creates space between sacred and secular arenas of human society. This space is created in a twofold manner. First,

---

9. Sachedina, *Roots*, 60.

10. Pannenberg, *Anthropology*, 531.

11. I am using secular here (along with Pannenberg) in a way that does not require the disestablishment of all public religious input. Thus, "secular" in this context merely means distinct and distinguishable from the church, but not necessarily divested of religious influence. For a helpful look at different types of secularism(s), see Ramachandra, *Faiths in Conflict?*, 146–47, where he distinguishes three main types.

12. *ST* 3:56.

based upon Christianity's need to be open to the historical process of God's self-revelation, it must "create space in the history of religions for the appearing of the divine mystery *and* for its debatability" across religious boundaries.[13] Thus, it must continually invite interreligious dialogue and interaction to discover God's unfolding truth throughout all of human history, and not merely the history known to Christianity. Second, this space is created as the church points out to the political and social order that there is a perpetual "distinction between what is provisional and what is definitive, between what is secular and what is spiritual."[14] Consequently, the church reminds the public social order that it is not absolute and must be open to change and input from various religious perspectives. Inevitably, secular states cannot escape their need for "religious or quasi-religious basis and justification . . ."[15] Therefore, "The thesis that the state is totally free as regards religion is thus an illusion."[16] Because God is active in all human history and religiosity, the invitation to free, open, and publicly influential dialogue is a vital part of any healthy political structure. Still, state and church must never be confused. If conflated into one another, the state "will be exposed to the temptation to misuse the Christian name for the achieving of goals of very earthly power politics, along with what may easily be unscrupulousness in the use of ends that seem adapted to attain these goals. . . . But the church is also in danger of divine judgment if it fails to accept coresponsibility for the renewing of the political order."[17]

To conclude, then, Sachedina's political emphasis on providing space for religious freedom and Pannenberg's theological and dialogical emphasis are related to their respective political contexts. Ongoing interreligious interaction in societies is assumed by Pannenberg, just as the apparent lack of it in many Islamic contexts provides the impetus in Sachedina to fight for it. Pannenberg writes to secularized and plu-

---

13. Pannenberg, "Toward a Theology," 117.

14. *ST* 3:482.

15. *ST* 3:482.

16. *ST* 3:482. Ramachandra (*Faiths in Conflict?*, 151) notes that, "By claiming the ultimate loyalty of its citizens, the essentially religious character of the modern state is revealed." He goes on to point out, "This affective dimension to nationalism is nurtured by religious myths and rituals" that use such things as quasi-religious stories of patriotism, heroism, flags, emblems, and songs.

17. *ST* 3:510.

ralistic communities in Europe and the Americas, directing his appeal toward religious aspects of interfaith dialogue. In contrast, Sachedina tries to convince Muslims that Islamic states need not be inherently anti-pluralistic. For him, this is a political and religious issue. Ultimately, they are both vying for pluralistic visions of peaceable and unified societies that incorporate religious freedom and diversity, but their starting and focal points are different.

One additional area concerning God's nature is that of coherence. Because God is unified and rational, coherence plays a vital role in demonstrating the truth of one's faith tradition. Pannenberg pursues coherence by seeking to present a theological perspective that is internally consistent, and also coincides with and explains the nature of our world. The more consistent a faith tradition is with itself and other arenas of knowledge, the more likely it is to be *true*.

Although Sachedina never explicitly makes a connection between God's sovereign rule and the need for coherence in one's faith tradition, it is significant that Sachedina is deliberately slow to use abrogation or supersession to explain potentially contradictory elements in the Qur'an concerning other religions. His notion of a rational, consistent God influences his pursuit of a coherent picture of Qur'anic revelation. It could be argued that this is something of a stretch. After all, Sachedina makes it clear that his reluctance to appeal to these doctrines relates primarily to his contention that they were improperly used by the early Islamic community to justify oppression and exclusion of religious others—and that they continue to be used this way in some segments of contemporary Islam. Still, his views of rationality and the need for a coherent revelation are certainly grounded in his understanding of God's unified nature. This principle leads Sachedina to argue that revelations given by God to Jews, Christians, and Muslims are historically situated, and so vary in many ways from each other. However, these revelations all embody a consistent set of what he calls "constitutive principles" from God.[18] The core message is the same, even if the respective revelations display variety based upon historical particularity.[19]

---

18. Sachedina, *Roots*, 38.

19. One more thing could be briefly added concerning Sachedina's drive for coherent comprehensiveness—namely his use of authorities from both Sunni and Shi'ite scholars to give a broader basis for his argument that the Qur'an explicitly affirms religious plurality.

Pannenberg also sees truth as a unified whole because it comes from God. However, his emphasis on historical process and eschatology highlights the *progress* of divine revelation. This progress points toward a single unified fellowship for all creation in the eschaton of God, but unlike Sachedina, stress is less upon the perceived *continuity* of God's message to humanity through time.

Ultimately, because of their views of God, both are keenly aware of the need for religious belief and practice to be both private *and public*, influencing every arena of human experience and knowledge. This yields a religious faith that affirms the universal nature of truth and ethical norms. These are not merely mythical notions expressing existential human aspirations. Rather, they are claims that are concretely testable as true or false, right or wrong. And this has tremendous ramifications for their respective theologies of religions.

The Historical Nature of Divine Revelation

A second point of convergence highlights the inherently historical nature of God's revelation to humanity. Pannenberg's emphasis upon history with respect to divine revelation is well-documented. In addition, he sees truth as necessarily all-encompassing in nature. Thus, for something to be true, it must be unified and comprehensively incorporate all that is known and understood in human experience and knowledge. At the same time, truth is radically historical in nature since it is necessarily embedded and expressed within the changing course of events in space and time. So important is history to Pannenberg's theological project, Stanley Grenz characterizes his method as "historical argumentation. . . . Truth emerges from the flow of historical debate. The historical sketches . . . are not superfluous, then, but are integral to the development of his own position."[20] So, the historicity of God's revelation is central to his theological program.

Likewise, Sachedina emphasizes this notion. For example, concerning the historical nature of God's revelation he states, "Failure to assess honestly the impact of history on the development of the normative Muslim tradition" has negatively affected its ability to make proper

---

20. Grenz, *Reason for Hope*, 13.

Pannenberg and Sachedina in Critical Conversation

sense of and impact positively the modern situation.[21] He continues, "The Koran remains in the hands of humans who have to decide how to make it relevant to their moral-spiritual existence at a given time and place in history."[22] A third comment makes the point inescapable: "A search for answers to the questions [about how best to interpret certain sacred passages] has to begin with an understanding of how faith relates itself to history and how the normative tradition interacts with human conditions."[23]

Rather than claiming divine revelation comes to humanity naked and unadorned, both men recognize the historically conditioned and limited anthropological nature of humanity's understanding and application of divine revelation. To understand properly and apply such revelation, we must give due attention to its historical aspects. Failure to do so puts us in danger of making our current (and therefore limited) understandings definitive and universally absolute. We are therefore likely to miss important aspects of revelation and misapply them in contemporary contexts. The result is an impoverished and stunted view of truth and morality that is unable to cope with changing realities and needs in today's world. As Sachedina puts it, when understood this way, revelation is seen as "entirely non-rational . . . [a set of] immutable principles . . . of social and political organization, applicable irrespective of time and place."[24] Instead, only a clear concept of history and its impact on God's particular revelation to specific communities in specific places and times enables us to reapply and ascertain how truth from that time becomes truth for us in our time.

One additional aspect in Sachedina's theology of religions bears mentioning: his claim that differences in special revelation (especially concerning Christianity, Judaism, and Islam) can be accounted for by historical process and particularity. God is one, and his revelation is therefore consistent through time. History conditions revelatory content, but the central message remains the same. As Sachedina, puts it, revelations to specific communities "should serve only to delineate the

---

21. Sachedina, *Roots*, 45.
22. Ibid., 46.
23. Ibid., 47.
24. Ibid., 60.

conditions and methods of applying the constitutive principles."[25] The principles are timeless and unified since their source is in God, but the "conditions and methods" vary significantly.[26]

Similarly, Pannenberg affirms that the "radical historicness" of all human experience and knowledge cannot be fully transcended. But rather than perceiving this as a weakness, Pannenberg clearly sees an opportunity. If truth is historically constituted and conditioned, our comprehensive search for truth "cannot simply deal with our present world. Its unity should instead also embrace other peoples and cultures of distant times, for whom the whole of reality presented itself differently from the way it does for us today.... In this situation, unity of truth can now only be thought of as the history of truth, meaning in effect that truth itself has a history and that its essence is the process of this history."[27] Thus, revelation and history are even more intricately related. Divine revelation is not merely influenced by historical situatedness. Instead, history is a comprehensive disclosure of Godself. Truth is historical and therefore so is God's true revelation. Thus, knowing history as a whole is crucial to understanding God's comprehensive character and purposes. Part of the Pannenbergian push for interreligious dialogue is a push for greater knowledge of human history as it unfolds in every time and place. Apart from the historical claims and understandings of other religions, it is impossible to understand the vast matrix of God's self-revealing and unfolding plan throughout all of history. By arguing together for our respective truth claims, clearer views of God potentially emerge, and we can see more of the whole in the partial present. Even more than this, our conversations move us beyond the present so that "all preliminary stages will be driven beyond themselves by their inner contradictions" and toward the eschatological and completed future of God's eternity where all apparent tensions concerning the history of truth will finally be resolved and overcome.[28] In short, "the truth of the whole will be visible only at the end of history."[29] Thus, history gradually proves itself to be a revelatory vindication of God's

---

25. Ibid., 38.
26. Sachedina's general argument along these lines is found in ibid., 32–38.
27. Pannenberg, "What Is Truth?," 20–21.
28. Ibid., 21.
29. Ibid., 22.

all-determinative nature, but full vindication will only be evident in the eschaton.[30] Consequently, "As the revelation of God in his historical action moves towards the still outstanding future of the consummation of history, its claim to reveal the one God . . . is open to future verification in history, which is yet incomplete, and which is still exposed, therefore, to the question of its truth."[31]

Openness to the future is important not only for Pannenberg, but also for Sachedina who notes that a failure to recognize the historical nature of God's revelation resulted in a failure among Islamic fundamentalists "to recognize the [historical] impact of complex ethnic, economic, political, and social relationships in intercommunity conflicts" among other things.[32] Attention to historical process opens up new possibilities to interpret and apply historically embedded truths of divine revelation—at least for all future presents.

Closely related to this are concerns about the anthropological nature of all human knowledge and morality. It is to these issues we now briefly turn.

Human Ethics and Human Nature

Any ethical vision for society must have an adequate understanding of human nature and what makes us morally rational, sensitive, and capable beings. Inadequate views lead to flawed moral social visions. For Sachedina and Pannenberg, ethics form the basis for unity in societies. And this basis must be religiously informed since religions provide the best and most comprehensive embodiments of moral norms.

For Pannenberg, like Sachedina, the basis for acceptance into God's eschatological fellowship is ethical in nature. Speaking about those outside Christianity, he says, "What counts is whether their individual conduct actually agrees with the will of God that Jesus proclaimed."[33]

---

30. In the meantime, for Pannenberg, Christians have unique access to the whole of history constituted in the future through the proleptic revelation of God through Jesus Christ, especially in his resurrection from the dead. In Pannenberg's own words in *ST* 1:247, "The future of God is not merely disclosed in advance with the coming of Jesus; it is already an event, although without ceasing to be future."

31. *ST* 1:257.

32. Sachedina, *Roots*, 56.

33. *ST* 3:615.

Given his inclusive view of Jesus as a divine prophet and his claim that the core message spoken to all prophets through history is the same, it is even possible that Sachedina could openly agree with this statement.

Similarly, Sachedina's entire project is centered around the premise that humans have a universal moral nature (the *fitra*) that provides the ethical and social basis for human community as well as salvation before God. Every person is accountable to the Creator. In FRC Sachedina notes that the "existence of similar human conditions in other cultures and the universally recognizable laws of nature that regulate interaction between religion and history, faith and power, ideology and politics, suggest the common moral and spiritual terrain that human beings tread in their perennial search for solutions to the problems of injustice, oppression, and poverty."[34]

For Pannenberg, there is a similar universal "human religious disposition" supporting the idea that everyone and everything finds its explanation and ground of being in God.[35] Humans are inescapably caught up in a religious quest. However, the unique nature of each quest must not be lost in a drive to abstract a concept of religion detached from actual historical religious claims and manifestations. In short, "It is an illusion to think we can formulate a concept of religion that is not characterized by a specific standpoint in the history of religion.... We cannot ignore the plurality and antagonism of deities and views of deity."[36] They must be taken at face value and not pressed into some vague and abstract concept of religion.

One point of interest here is Sachedina's claim that if God wished, he could have made humanity completely unified, but that this was not his sovereign will. By *ordaining human diversity*, God motivates human beings to "compete with one another in good works" and challenge each other to see God's truth in increasingly expansive and universal ways through the eyes of cultural and religious others who may see his being and purposes in different (but complementary) ways. This claim is similar to Pannenberg's that truth must be publicly contested. This might be understood as a mere contest of truth claims, but it certainly includes praxiological and ethical dimensions of truth that demon-

---

34. Sachedina, FRC, 10.
35. *ST* 1:156.
36. *ST* 1:149.

strate moral and practical consistency between philosophical and theological claims for truth and their ethical implications. Thus, Sachedina's interreligious competition to outdo one another in good works can be roughly seen as another way to contest for the truth of one's religion. It not only matters what you *claim* as true, it also matters what you *demonstrate* as true—a concrete ethical correspondence to conceptual truth claims. Thus, religious contestation includes not only a drive to display a comprehensive coherence of true doctrine (orthodoxy), but also a corresponding comprehensive coherence of right moral living (orthopraxis).

This inclusive vision for human communities pursuing truth and living ethically points to another area of common ground between Sachedina and Pannenberg. Both put forth religiously inclusive visions for humanity, although respectively Islamic and Christian in nature. We will now explore the common points of these two distinctive inclusivisms.

Inclusive Theologies of Religions

Both Sachedina and Pannenberg share a vision of human destiny that includes people from every tribe, tongue, and nation. And while both approach a theology of religions from different religious bases, the criteria they use for determining the ultimate destiny of the human race and the signs of humanity's right relationship to God are strikingly similar.

As previously mentioned, Pannenberg openly states that "a personal encounter with Jesus" through the proclamation of the gospel cannot be the sole criterion for participation in the divine eschatological fellowship of all humanity "if we take seriously what the [New Testament] says about the love of God for the world that embraces all people."[37] What matters most is "whether their individual conduct actually agrees with the will of God that Jesus proclaimed."[38] Thus, Pannenberg's theology, like Sachedina's, is ethically inclusive, but in a distinctly Christian way. For Pannenberg, Jesus' life and especially resurrection provide the ontological and soteriological bases for humanity's eschatological fellowship with God. The church represents a proleptic irruption of the

37. ST 3:615.
38. ST 3:615.

eternal eschaton in the provisional present, but sometimes obscures this through its poor ethical and social example. In Pannenberg's words, "the divine rule in the life of the church is often distorted to the point of unrecognizability."[39] Consequently, some leave the church not based upon unrighteousness or a desire to forsake God's truth, but due to their "longing for the kingdom of God that they can no longer see in the church's life."[40]

Beyond specifically Christian aspects of Pannenberg's theology of religions, the parallels to Sachedina here are obvious. For Sachedina, true religion (*dīn*) is expressed morally by those who may or may not be members of institutional Islam, but who nevertheless demonstrate through their righteous lifestyle that they live in a state of submission and surrender (*islām* with a lowercase *i*) to God.[41] For him, the Qur'an embodies the most accurate ethical (and theological) vision known to humanity. Still, for both, the standard for acceptance is ethical living rather than adherence to a particular set of propositional creeds. Such creeds are important for their respective faith traditions, but the soteriological standard for divine salvific inclusion remains primarily, if not completely, *ethical and moral* in nature.[42] Ultimately, God will judge the world with a righteousness that cuts across denominational and religious barriers of time, place, and dogma. This brings us to eschatological aspects of Pannenberg and Sachedina's theologies of religions.

Eschatology and the End of All Things

Pannenberg's eschatological vision is far more developed than Sachedina's. Again, this is a result of design. Pannenberg's emphasis on prolepsis and the Hegelian claim that individual parts of history can only be rightly understood in light of the whole of history requires a more extended look at eschatological aspects of a theology of religions,

39. *ST* 3:525.
40. *ST* 3:525.
41. He makes this argument primarily on in *Roots*, 38.
42. Sachedina is likely much more conservative in his estimates concerning the overall number of people who are ultimately acceptable to God. In his methodological drive to make God the all-determining and sovereign Lord of all, Pannenberg tends to border on universalism in salvation—although in *ST* 3:620 he admits that on the basis of clear scriptural warnings, he cannot be a full-fledged universalist.

for only from the perspective of the future can complete sense of the past and the present be made. Therefore, Pannenberg discusses the eschaton extensively in his systematic theology.

In contrast, Sachedina's interests are more concerned with contemporary political and practical aspects of religious plurality. Nevertheless, he does not ignore eschatological aspects of his ethical and political vision of a democratically free, moral, and religious society. He explicitly notes that, concerning contestations between religious factions and faiths, "in the final analysis, it is only God who can put an end to disputes based on these irreconcilable differences created by [the] particularity of human religious experience under different prophets and revelations."[43] Core differences between religions can only ultimately be resolved by God's direct intervention into human affairs when he fully reveals his kingdom rule in the age to come.[44]

Similarly for Pannenberg, eschatology holds the key to the resolution of all religious contestation. Thus, "the deity of God will be definitively and unquestionably manifested only at the end of all time and history," when all historical disagreements are divinely resolved.[45] Meanwhile, God's people (with varying degrees of clarity) provide a proleptic vision of the eschatological fellowship every human being will enjoy with God in the eschaton. Thus, "Christ guarantees a share in eschatological salvation with the fact that *all people, whether Christians or not*, have the chance of participation in the kingdom of God that Jesus proclaimed."[46] This is a distinctly Christian vision of the eschaton, but it still bears a striking resemblance to Sachedina's inclusive vision of a unified societal fellowship based upon the universal constitution of human beings created by God with a noble, moral nature (*fitra*).

Having noted areas of convergence and commonality, we can now turn to critical points of difference.

---

43. Sachedina, FRC, 21.

44. This is very similar to Muslim Alwi Shihab's ("Christian-Muslim Relations," 70) contention based upon Q. 34:24–26 that "Our Lord will gather us together and will in the end decide the matter between us in truth and justice. And He is the one to decide, the One who knows all."

45. ST 1:54.

46. ST 3:615; emphasis added.

Important Areas of Contestation: Finding Truth at the Borders

Since these thinkers hail from Islam and Christianity, there are some obvious areas of difference. These center around the doctrine of God (trinitarian versus a monotarian), the ultimate means and basis of salvation, and especially the person and work of Jesus of Nazareth. In addition, there are more subtle differences that also provide places for examination and exploration in future Christian-Muslim dialogue.

God's Basic Nature: Indivisible or Triune?

For Pannenberg, on the basis of the historical revelation made known in Jesus, God's nature is distinctly and inescapably *triune*. Alternatively, Sachedina's Islamic notion of *tawhīd* declares God's nature is *indivisibly one* and brooks no partners. In fact, because the Trinity is historically revealed in Jesus of Nazareth, Pannenberg gives precedence to God's inherently triune nature, making his *unity* a theological problem for Christians, rather than vice versa.[47]

Given these apparently incompatible views of God's nature, more Christian-Muslim interaction is needed here. This is especially important since Sachedina, on the basis of his Qur'anic exegesis, has no trouble affirming Christianity's salvific legitimacy. If Muslim theology rejects a triune God based upon *tawhīd*, Sachedina must clarify how he passes so easily over what many Muslims proclaim to be patently offensive and blasphemous. Does he do so by assuming theological corruption (*tahrif*) by Christians through time? Does he think orthopraxy trumps orthodoxy, and if so, how and on what basis? Given Qur'anic condemnations of ascribing partners to God and corresponding accusations of idolatry (*shirk*) alongside potentially harsh punishments for idolaters, can this be legitimately downplayed or ignored?

This highlights how Pannenberg believes historical progress and a clearer understanding of God unfolds through a process of religious interaction and contestation about God or the gods. For him, critical points of difference must not be ignored, declared insignificant, or

---

47. As Pannenberg notes, this is a reversal of the traditional way in which theology proper has been dealt with in Christian systematics. For a helpful summary of the significance of this move in Pannenberg, see Kärkkäinen, *Trinity*, 128–31.

considered harmful to peaceful societies. Rather, competing claims are one of the most important aspects of interreligious interaction, for they become potential resources for historical unity whereby God is better known and seen as one. In Pannenberg's words,

> The history of one deity was always that of conflict with competing deities and truth claims. . . . But this did not rule out in principle the possibility that the contours of the deity might emerge in the process of competition. . . . In view of the extensive spread of the religions that sprouted from this root [of Israeli Monotheism], does that not mean that the history of conflicts between the gods was the path to the development of the unity of the divine reality which has finally produced a religious situation embracing all humanity? . . . Is, then, the unity of the divine reality the true object of the struggle of religious history?[48]

Pannenberg suggests unity is the ultimate object of religious contestation because the one true and all-encompassing God is revealed in the history of such competition. Thus, not only ethics can unite societies, but also arguments about what God is really like and what he requires of humanity. In the eschaton, this divine unity will be fully realized, but until then interreligious conflicts will occur. In the process, these conflicts are variously resolved, but they must not be ignored or easily explained away. They should be interreligiously explored, for progress is forged through conflict and not merely through finding common ground.

Soteriologically, points of difference include the nature of salvation, the idea of prolepsis, and the centrality of Jesus' literal and historical resurrection from the dead. It is to these points we will now give some attention.

Salvation, Prolepsis, and the Resurrection of Jesus

Given his limited focus, Sachedina says very little about the identity or nature of Jesus Christ beyond his status as a prophet. Nevertheless, the christological issue cannot be avoided since Jesus' person and work play a central and proleptic role in Pannenberg's understanding of salvation.

---

48. ST 1:148.

From earlier discussions, it may appear Pannenberg is merely an ethical inclusivist, making human salvation dependent upon good moral behavior. But this does not do justice to the broader context of his theo-, christo-, and eschato-centric soteriology.[49] For Pannenberg, full human salvation is not afforded by moral behavior, but by Jesus' historical resurrection. Through the resurrection, Jesus not only unambiguously confirms his identity as the Holy One of God, he also brings an irruption of God's complete, timeless, and eternal eschaton into the incomplete present. Pannenberg calls this irruption a proleptic, anticipatory taste of eternity that is already complete in the timelessness of God, but not yet fully known and experienced by humanity in time. Thus, salvation is both a now and a not yet. The believer currently participates (but only in a proleptic and provisional way) in the eschatological fellowship of God that all will completely and inexhaustibly experience at the decisive end of the age when he reconciles all things to himself in Jesus. This assures believers they are already part of that eternal fellowship while still keeping them open to the future. It also prevents them from making any specific place or moment in time the sole source of divine authority. Thus, the resurrection of Jesus is what Pannenberg calls "the dawning of the end of history."[50] Without it, Jesus' claims to deity are not confirmed and there is no demonstration of God's completed eternity breaking into the partial present. Consequently, salvation is wholly dependent upon Jesus, even for those who do not overtly call him Savior and Lord, for Jesus is the basis and opening point for the eschatological fellowship humanity will enjoy with God in eternity.[51]

In this light, we must reaffirm that Sachedina is an ethical inclusivist. Soteriologically, inclusion in the life and blessings of God is based upon moral aspects of human behavior grounded in the *fitra*. Thus, moral behavior is "remembering" the moral rectitude already inherent to human nature, making Sachedina's inclusive vision is both anthropo-

---

49. In chapter 1, I characterized S. Mark Heim's theology of religions as "eschatocentric." The kind of eschatocentrism I am referring to here is different from Heim's and so should not be confused with it.

50. Pannenberg, "What Is Truth?," 24.

51. The Spirit is also part of this process whereby the individual is ecstatically lifted outside the self and drawn into the communal fellowship of God opened up by Jesus Christ. As Pannenberg puts it in ST 3:552, "By the Spirit the eschatological future is present already in the hearts of believers." In this way, salvation is distinctly pneumatocentric as well as theo- and christocentric.

and ethico-centric. And yet, these features cannot be moved outside of the realm of God's absolute sovereignty. He created human beings inherently moral, giving them the rationality and will (innate capacities) to do what accords with his righteous will.

Pannenberg is certainly concerned about human morality and its salvific impact, but his inclusivism is probably better understood as eschatological inclusivism since the focus of inclusion is centered less around ethical aspects of human life and more around the eschaton of God when all time and creation will be subsumed into his eternal kingdom. The emphasis is on God and his revelation in history, especially through Jesus and his resurrection. The focus is also theological, but in a different direction, moving from God's future that stands in eternity outside of time, back towards humanity who remains temporally situated.

This emphasis upon the eschaton of God serves as a transition into the next topic of concern, namely the people of God and the kingdom of mankind.

The People of God and the Kingdom of Mankind

Recall that for Pannenberg, the distinction between church and state lies primarily in the eschatological nature of the church and the provisional nature of the state. For Sachedina, the distinction lies primarily in the universal endowment of the *fitra* upon every person, as well as the inherently free nature of genuine religious commitment. According to Pannenberg, since God reveals himself through time in all people, religious plurality offers Christians the opportunity to hear from God through the lives, teachings, and claims of other religious viewpoints. So Pannenberg and Sachedina seek to make space for religious and secular others, but they do so by emphasizing different aspects of human existence.

Sachedina creates space by discussing the constitutionally moral aspect (*fitra*) of every human being as God's creation, as well as a concept of religious commitment that requires individual religious freedom to be encouraged. He also explains how the Qur'an speaks pluralistically about other religions, especially Judaism and Christianity. This serves as an impetus for Muslims to grant full freedom of worship for these two faiths.[52]

In addition to Pannenberg's celebration of diversity by welcoming interfaith dialogue to discover, clarify, and challenge religious truth claims and their comprehensive explanatory power, social space for religion is opened up through the ontological and unsurpassable difference between the proleptic and eternal church as the people of God and the finite and temporal state as the kingdom of humanity. The state is related to the eschatological kingdom of God by establishing "justice and peace" in society.[53] Such a society is an anticipatory sign of God's eschatological kingdom where communal justice and peace reign. However, because government does not enjoy the unique ontological relationship the church does, "this-world utopias of a form of social fulfillment that will be achieved by human action can count as only very imperfect expressions of the hope of a future consummation of humanity."[54] In contrast, the church, through the resurrection of Jesus Christ and the ministry of the Holy Spirit, already participates in the eternal and completed eschatological reality that has dawned in finite time. When God finally comes to reign without equivocation, the state will be unnecessary. The proleptic and eschatological church constantly reminds the state of its provisional and limited character. Thus, by their very nature, there is always impassible space between the people of God and the kingdoms of mankind. All attempts to confuse or fuse them ultimately prevent either from fulfilling their God-ordained callings. Religious freedom is needed for the church to be the church and the state to be the state.[55]

52. Sachedina's offer of freedom is wider than this, but he uses the *fitra* and the Qur'an's affirmation of Judaism and Christianity to open up Muslims to the possibility that other faith traditions might also be granted full freedom of worship.

53. *ST* 3:51.

54. *ST* 3:586.

55. This discussion summarizes Pannenberg's treatment of this issue in *ST* 3:27–57. This space between the state and the church is distinctly *Christian*. How it can be opened up between the state and other religions (who presumably are not ontologically open to the future in the same way as Christians) is not clarified by Pannenberg and so remains something of a mystery. Of course, he never set out to provide such an explanation for religions other than Christianity. In addition, his theology was not intended to give any kind of detailed description of the means by which human societies could be politically unified and yet religiously free and diversified, as Sachedina is more inclined to envision. Still, the idea of a proleptic and eschatological

The Purpose of Interfaith Dialogue

Although hinted at already, Pannenberg and Sachedina have different emphases concerning interfaith dialogue. Sachedina focuses more on creating a universal ethic leading to legal formulations and political governance for a just and plural society that enforces moral norms but also empowers religious freedom. As he puts it, interfaith dialogue should be seen "as a working paradigm for a democratic, social pluralism in which people of diverse religious backgrounds are willing to form a community of global citizens."[56] The goal of dialogue is a community forged through discovering areas of common moral commitment.[57] While this implies interfaith dialogue should focus upon moral visions for functional and just societies, some reference to religious claims lying behind moral prohibitions and commendations must be provided.[58]

---

ontological space between church and state is an intriguing aspect of a specifically (Pannenbergian) Christian notion of society. In fact, Pannenberg contends that it is precisely for this reason that, "Distinguishing church and state has become typical of the cultural tradition influenced by Christianity" (*ST* 3:52). The idea that the state is inherently provisional does suggest some ways in which a differentiation between religions and their freedom of worship and political governance might be examined and applied. It should also be noted that the church is similarly provisional in the sense that it is only needed until the eschaton arrives in all its fullness, but its present participation in that eschatological future through the Spirit-empowered sacramental presence of the risen Christ draws it out of the finite and provisional present and toward that harmonious and unified future. Human government, by its very nature, enjoys no such ontological relation to the eschatological future and so can make no claim to embody a political culmination of all places and times.

56. Sachedina, *Roots*, 35.

57. Ibid., 43. Sachedina does give recognition to the issue of contention in interfaith encounter, admitting that due to the intractable nature of many religious disagreements, "in the final analysis, it is only God who can put an end to disputes based on these irreconcilable differences created by [the] particularity of human religious experience under different prophets and revelations" (FRC, 21).

58. It is not clear that this search for common moral norms will end up being anything but contentious and divisive on its own. Arguments over the content of legislative prescriptions extend not only to what is right and wrong, but also to what are the most appropriate consequences for any given crime. Now of course, it should not be ignored that there are enormous numbers of legal codifications that are easily seen to be common to both faith traditions. However, at the seams, there is potential for enormously divisive discussions. In my opinion, Sachedina does not provide us with a clear enough way to deal with and resolve these kinds of fundamental disagreements. This may be less of a problem with Sachedina and more of a problem with the finite nature of human communities.

Pannenberg's interest in dialogue includes this kind of project, but is wider in scope. For him, interreligious dialogue should be primarily concerned with pursuing a more comprehensive knowledge of the truth in every field of study. This quest not only seeks common ground with religious others, but pays careful attention to religious *differences*, attempting to explore, discuss, and argue more thoroughly about such conflicts. This is especially true with respect to theological claims about God or the gods. By a (Hegelian) dialectical process, "All preliminary stages will be driven beyond themselves by their inner contradictions."[59] New syntheses then move us toward the future where fresh truth claims are publicly tested for their coherence and explanatory power in light of contemporary human knowledge and experience.

Mutual Resources for a Viable Pluralistic Society

Now that areas of difference and convergence have been briefly explored, we will highlight some resources Sachedina and Pannenberg's theologies of religions provide to potentially move Christian-Muslim dialogue forward. We will also address how they aid in the formation of pluralistically democratic and religiously free societies united around common religious ideals of peace and justice, beginning with Sachedina's ethically inclusive theology of religions.

Resources in Sachedina's Theology of Religions[60]

The first aspect showing significant promise for Christian-Muslim dialogue and intercommunal cooperation is Sachedina's insight into the libertarian nature of genuine religious belief. Even apart from his concept of the *fitra*, this notion is crucial for creating public space for religious freedom, both as a function of the political structures of the society and as a function of those religious traditions that are integral parts of that society.

Encouragingly, recognition of the need for religious freedom has recently been echoed by other Muslims writing on Islam and de-

---

59. Pannenberg, "What Is Truth?," 21.

60. One need not agree with all aspects of Sachedina's theology of religions to benefit from and embrace some of its features.

mocracy. For example, Abdolkarim Soroush argues, "There is no such thing as forced adoration, love, and testimony. True faith is contingent upon individuality and liberty."[61] Citing the Qur'anic prohibition of any "compulsion in religion" (Q. 2:256), he contends,

> The heart of a religious society is freely chosen faith not coercion and conformity.... To compel individuals to confess a faith falsely; to paralyze minds by indoctrination, propaganda, and intimidation; and to shut down the gates of criticism, revision, and modification so that everyone would succumb to a single ideology creates not a religious society but a monolithic and terrified mass of crippled, submissive, and hypocritical subjects.[62]

This freedom leading to genuine religiosity is too easily ignored when governments push for a stability of conformity to consolidate and extend their control over society.

Closely related is Sachedina's ethical and anthropological understanding of the *fitra*. This concept, coupled with the notion of the heart (*qalb*), has remarkable similarities to Christian ideas about human beings being created in God's image. Such anthropological perspectives provide starting points for Muslim-Christian dialogue about what it means to be human and what virtues God wants human beings to develop and pursue. Such conversations are especially needed since thoughtless postmodern ethical and epistemological relativism is becoming increasingly vogue not only in Western societies, but also in other parts of the world. The resulting intellectual, moral, and social confusion and impoverishment have created an existential longing for new and more substantial ways to understand our human condition. Anthropological views should be openly examined and discussed as a vital part of the process of societal reorientation. It should not ignore postmodern critiques, but since all attempts to eschew metanarratives inevitably collapse into some other (often hidden or unrecognized) form of metanarrative, it behooves us to reconsider coherently comprehensive views of moral virtue, human nature, and the ultimate goal or *telos* of human existence.[63]

61. Soroush, *Democracy in Islam*, 141.

62. Ibid., 141–42.

63. I am consciously borrowing the language of Alasdair MacIntyre from his books *Whose Justice, Which Rationality?* and *Three Rival Versions of Moral Enquiry*, where he repeatedly talks about the importance of the concept of a *telos* or "goal" in

Similarly, Sachedina's emphasis on the inherently public nature of religious truth claims sourced in a sovereign God works against secularism's attempts to privatize all religiously motivated ethical and epistemological assertions. The tragic irony of such attempts is at least threefold.

First, disestablishing religion from public life creates what secularism is trying to avoid—religious zealotry and reactionary politics attempting to destroy current political governance. When not listened to, especially concerning things nearest and dearest to them, people tend to become bitter and angry. They can more easily be incited to join with violent and revolutionary movements that give them a sense of empowerment and significance that was robbed of them by secularist tyranny.[64]

Second, by eliminating all public religious influence, secularism often becomes a pseudo-religious tyrant, dictating what its citizens can and cannot do and believe. In the process, secularism must supply moral and ideological justifications, not only for religious exclusion, but also for its own legal and social values. It must find them somewhere, often turning to watered-down, vague, abstracted principles left over from previously embraced religious ideals detached from their original contexts.

This leads to a third problem, namely moral impoverishment. Because societies inescapably need moral bases for cohesiveness and for public projects of justice, secular states that banish all religious input cut themselves off from a priceless store of moral and ethical insight and practice proven to be valuable for the formation and maintenance of genuinely good and enduring societies.[65] Religions provide commu-

---

rational and moral enquiry.

64. This is not a religious phenomenon only. This kind of revolutionary reactionism is prevalent in history whenever people are suppressed and denied basic rights to freedom and opportunity, religious or otherwise.

65. Granted, these same religions have also shown themselves to be a rich resource for moral atrocities and intellectual retardation, but I would argue such appropriations are, more often than not, ideologically and culturally influenced from *outside* of these respective faith traditions. In this sense, religion has been co-opted by an outside influence to justify an unrighteous and anti-religious end. I should also state that on the basis of their sacred texts and internal religious resources, some of these faith traditions are more prone to these kinds of ideological and moral misappropriations than others, but that argument goes beyond the scope of what we are trying to accomplish

nities with rich moral ideals and lasting social identities that continue to persevere and reinstantiate themselves across cultures, places, and times. These are the resources governments need the most to actualize social cohesion, genuine justice, and lasting peace and stability. This is not to say these societies will be monolithic. Freedom, especially of religion, is an inherently diversifying force, but if these religions are genuinely tapping into their moral and communal resources, they provide powerful motivations for an authentic social unity that celebrates human and religious plurality—one that is dynamically produced from within the members of society rather than hierarchically demanded and coerced governmentally from the top down.[66]

Thus, the need for religions to bring their most treasured claims for moral and social life into the public arena has never been greater in our increasingly postmodern and secular age. Sachedina's insistence on this is a desperately needed corrective to help stem a growing tide of religiously detached and therefore morally impoverished secular governments.

In this light, Sachedina's emphasis on politics and the need to find a practical and pluralistic ethic for human societies is a most welcome aspect of his theology of religions. It is too easy to rely upon theoretical models and ideals rather than actual daily dialogues of people from all systems of belief and practice living out their lives with one another in community. In this sense, Sachedina's refusal to provide a clear model for forging religiously plural and morally just societies may be intentional, since they can only be worked out at the ground level. By providing Muslims with a Qur'anically-sanctioned view of Christianity and Judaism (and other world religions by extension), it is hoped that the door for such conversations between Muslims and religious others will open wide. Only then can societies reflect the peace, justice, plurality, and freedom God intends them to exhibit. Along these lines,

---

here and so must be relegated to another study.

66. This kind of dynamism witnessed in American democracy (at least until recently) is mentioned by Alex de Tocqueville in his landmark work, *Democracy in America*, and is subsequently highlighted by Ramachandra (*Faiths in Conflict?*, 158) when he points out that "The moral cohesion of a political community cannot rest on the force of law alone, and the health of any community will finally depend on the moral character of its individual citizens. Democracy does not arise in a vacuum. It requires disciplined citizens if it is to thrive; citizens nurtured in a culture that prizes not only the love of freedom but voluntary self-restraint."

Sachedina's desire to let religious claims remain as they are provides the only possible way to create a genuinely plural context for religious freedom to thrive and dynamically transform society from the grassroots level.[67]

Another resource Sachedina provides for Christian-Muslim dialogue is his reemphasis upon the inherently historical nature of all revelation. He recognizes Islam's need to be open to new interpretations of sacred texts so they can be more understandable and appropriately applicable in contemporary contexts. With some radical branches of fundamentalist Islam claiming to provide timeless and authoritative understandings and applications of divine texts to further violent and revolutionary agendas against secular and religious (sometimes even *Muslim*) others, it has never been more urgent for thoughtful Muslims to give greater attention and voice to historically sensitive interpretations and reapplications of their sacred scriptures that directly speak against these kinds of dangerous and exploitive misappropriations of authoritative materials.

Sachedina's creative explanation and exploration of Islamic *jihād* and apostasy is an excellent example of this kind of careful concern for the impact history has upon our understandings and (re)employment of religious truth claims and moral ideals. By looking at such controversial notions historically and contextually, it is easier to see and appreciate alternative and perhaps even more textually faithful renderings of such terms for our contemporary world.[68]

One final resource in Sachedina bears mentioning, namely his assiduous and innovative examination of Islamic mercy and forgiveness over and against today's more commonly applied notions of ret-

---

67. As was already noted, Sachedina seems to struggle some with this aspect of his presentation, and he is not always consistent in his sanctioning of exclusive religious claims without revision. This is most likely due to the current propensity of some branches of Islam to use these kinds of exclusive truth claims to motivate Muslims politically and even militantly to dominate and exclude religious others.

68. For example, *jihād* can be understood primarily as what Muhammad called a "greater *jihād*," which, according Sachedina (*Roots*, 113) is primarily concerned with the Muslim's "struggle against one's one baser instincts.... [Thus] the ability to forgive requires a *jihād* against one's anger and resentment in order to restore one's spiritual station by participating in the divine attribute of forgiveness." In the same way, apostasy can be reexamined and, at the very least, be definitively removed from the historically suspect realm of being a capital offense.

ribution and revenge. By highlighting the Qur'anic context in which retribution and revenge are placed—a context of restoration and resolution, Sachedina encourages Muslims to inculcate the more intentionally Islamic religious values of administering justice mercifully, punishments restoratively, and moral enforcement compassionately and kindly. In this way, current tendencies in certain radical Islamic sects to emphasize revenge and retribution can be challenged by the Qur'anic emphasis on God's infinite compassion and mercy.[69] Again, this redirected emphasis provides another critical tool for Muslims to allay recent fundamentalist moves toward violently radicalized Islamic teachings.

Resources in Pannenberg's Theology of Religions[70]

To begin, Pannenberg's emphasis upon the total sovereignty and lordship of God provides the backdrop for many of the promising resources for future interfaith conversations. Because all things find their existence under God, one is immediately struck by Pannenberg's emphasis on religious truth claims as historically public assertions that increasingly cohere with and correspond to all arenas of human knowledge. All things find their existence and meaning in the all-determining God, yet everything has a limited degree of ontological independence and freedom from God. Consequently, attempts to wall religious claims off from public concern are not only ill-advised, they are virtually impossible.

Because all history is *his* story, it becomes the continuous revelation of God's purposes and character to humanity—at least until the eschaton. Thus, God is not only revealing himself in Christianity's history, he is revealing himself through every person and every religion extended through time. When time is complete, all contestations concerning the truth will ultimately and definitively be resolved. "Truth is thus historical and eschatological."[71] Meanwhile, this truth must be argued for and

---

69. Some of the verses in the Qur'an emphasizing this gracious and kind aspect of God's character include Q. 2:178; 3:31; 39:53; along with many others.

70. As with Sachedina, one need not embrace Pannenberg's theology of religions wholesale to benefit significantly from aspects of his views.

71. Kärkkäinen, *Trinity*, 127.

demonstrated in history through the process of dialogical interaction and contestation with as many alternative points of view as possible. This allows honest exploration of the many competing and even radically different points of view, since truth is found through a process of affirming commonality *and* resolving critical differences produced by intra- and interreligious tensions and contradictions. This spirited exchange results in ever-increasing understanding and insight into God's nature and plans for everything and everyone. But such interactions can only be real if religious truth claims stand *as they are* without revision. They cannot be pasted over or blurred into one another, but must be understood as genuinely competing ways of seeing the world and our experiences of it in light of our unique concepts of God. Through contestation, some paradigms evince more sustained explanatory, integrative, and assimilative (what Pannenberg calls "syncretistic") power than others. But this power can only be demonstrated if each view is contested on its own merits and not pressed together with other traditions into some sort of abstract amalgamation of "common core" beliefs and practices. Religions, then, are potentially valuable contenders for truths that challenge others to grow in their understanding of God and his world. Interfaith dialogue is necessary if truth, especially theological and religious truth, in more of its fullness is to be apprehended.

This idea of revelation as history leads to another aspect of Pannenberg's theology of religions, namely that God has historically revealed himself to be distinctly *trinitarian*, especially through Jesus. This understanding of God and the economic role the Trinity plays in human history is central to Christianity and its ultimate (theological and missiological) relationship to all other religions, cultures, and peoples. Thus, creation reflects and is sustained by a specifically *triune* God. Of all claims about God and gods in other religions, the trinitarian claim is particularly unique, lying at the borders of interreligious contestation. If the most crucial theological truths lie within points of greatest contest and difference, then nowhere is this truer than Christianity's concept of God as Trinity. Consequently, any truly Christian theology of religions must openly address, argue for, and listen to others' arguments concerning the truth or falsehood of this central claim.

Pannenberg is no exception, being one of the most thoroughly trinitarian theologians of his time. In fact, in *ST* 1, Pannenberg places the doctrine of the Trinity *after* the chapter on revelation and the nature of divine disclosure and *before* the chapter on God's unity. Because God revealed and continues to reveal himself in history as *triune*, the whole of Pannenberg's systematics is trinitarian in nature. The historical revelation of God in Jesus *drives* Christian theologians to pursue distinctly triune understandings of God and his world. Because systematic theology is supposed to demonstrate coherently and comprehensively the truth about *God* as he reveals himself to humanity in history, the Trinity becomes the structuring principle for his entire systemic theology, permeating every topic of discussion. Otherwise, God as he actually reveals himself in history is ignored or seen as irrelevant to a proper knowledge of him and his world. In Pannenberg's words, "The moment it appears that the one God can be better understood without rather than with the doctrine of the Trinity, the latter seems to be a superfluous addition to the concept of the one God . . . . Even worse, it necessarily seems to be incompatible with the divine reality."[72] Kärkkäinen puts it thus: "Trinity is not just *a* topic in the Christian dogmatics, nor an appendix to the discussion of the one God. Rather, the only way to give an account of the Christian God is to speak of Father, Son, and Spirit."[73] To combat this unfortunate tendency in most classical and contemporary systematic theologies, Pannenberg explicitly claims his systematics are intentionally "more thoroughly trinitarian than any example I know of."[74] Therefore, his "delineation of the doctrine of God does not come to an end with the conclusion of [*ST* 1]. The entire presentation of the Christian faith constitutes the development of this doctrine. At every juncture, therefore, he returns to the discussion of the triune God."[75] God has acted in history (the economic Trinity) in trinitarian ways to reveal that he is triune in nature (the immanent Trinity). Thus, to speak about God without speaking about his triune nature is to speak about him incompletely and insufficiently.

Pannenberg works this triune economy out in a variety of ways. First, God the Father is related to creation by virtue of being its good and loving Creator and Sustainer. His love is expressed in eternity toward the Son and is mediated through the Son. This love for creation and the Son is complementary, since "The creatures are objects of the

72. *ST* 1:291.
73. Kärkkäinen, *Trinity*, 128.
74. Pannenberg, "God's Presence in History," 263.
75. Grenz, *Reason for Hope*, 78.

Father's love as they are drawn into his eternal turning to the Son. In other words, they become the object of the Father's love because the eternal Son is manifested in them."[76]

Nowhere is Jesus' Sonship more clearly revealed than in his uniquely historical incarnation, an event that "is no alien thing" since Jesus is the source of creation's distinctiveness from God the Father in the first place.[77] Ultimately, his resurrection definitively confirms his claims to divine Sonship as well as his eternal distinction from the Father and the Spirit. In short, "The Easter event definitively decided the personal identity of Jesus as the Son of God, but in light of that event, he was the Son of God from the very beginning of his earthly course, and even from eternity."[78]

Because the Son is distinct from the Father, he "is the origin of all that differs from the Father, and therefore of the creatures' independence vis-à-vis the Father."[79] The Father can only be the Father with the Son. Thus, Jesus opens up an ontological basis for otherness in God that is expressed creatively—as a distinct creation dependent on God for its existence and sustenance, but possessing real (although mediated and limited) independence as well. Creatures are sustained by God because "God alone has unrestricted duration. All limited duration derives from him."[80] The infinite God necessarily contains in himself all that is finite. Otherwise, he would not be truly infinite. Thus, the finite, by its very essence, depends upon the infinite for its presence and continued existence. This gives rise to the human tendency to be religious and search after God or gods.

The Spirit is also involved in this process since God is *trinitarian*, not merely *binitarian* in nature. He provides the basis for unity in the Godhead. In describing the way in which the Son creates independence for creation, Pannenberg states, "even as the Son moves out of the unity of deity [by his free self-distinction from the Father], he is still united with the Father by the Spirit, who is the Spirit of freedom (2 Cor. 3:17). . . . The freedom of the Spirit links the two in free agreement."[81] Thus,

76. ST 2:21.
77. ST 2:386.
78. ST 2:319.
79. ST 2:22.
80. ST 2:33.
81. ST 2:30. Pannenberg is very critical of the *filioque* clause later added by the

"If the Spirit were not constitutive for the fellowship of the Son with the Father, the Christian doctrine of the deity of the Spirit would be a purely external addition to the confession of the relation of the Son to the deity of the Father."[82]

Crucial for this discussion is Pannenberg's treatment of the Spirit's trinitarian ministry in creation, not merely in the Godhead. Several aspects could be noted, but for our purposes, his dynamic activities of giving life to all things and lifting everything out of itself into mutual interdependence upon God and others are particularly important since "creatures share in the life of the Spirit only by moving out of their own finitude."[83] The Spirit prevents creaturely independence from becoming a source of destruction through separation from the life of God. With respect to human beings, the Spirit enables human reason to see particularities within creation as well as "the unity that holds together what is different."[84] By "ecstatically" lifting us outside of ourselves, the Spirit enables us to be "aware of the presence of truth and totality in the individual."[85] The Spirit becomes our source of personality and awareness of "otherness" outside of ourselves so we can see our distinctiveness alongside our interdependence and interrelatedness. And this becomes an expression of the triune image of God within humanity: "We are already lifted above ourselves by the Spirit of God and are thus enabled to accept our own finitude. . . . Only by accepting our finitude as God-given do we attain to the fellowship with God that is implied in our destiny of divine likeness. In other words, we must be fashioned into

---

church in the West to the creedal statements about the Spirit's relationship to the Son (and the Father). This Latin phrase, meaning "and the Son," claims the Spirit proceeds from the Father *and the Son* (*filioque*). In Pannenberg's mind, this addition suggests the heretical doctrine of subordinationism where the Spirit (and Jesus) are derived from God the Father, but not coequal or coeternal with the Father. For Pannenberg's critique of subordinationism, see *ST* 1:275ff.

82. *ST* 1:268. Pannenberg is obviously using the Hegelian concept here of "self-differentiation," whereby identity is gained by defining the self in connection with, but also in distinction from, the other. In this way, the Father depends on the Son to be the Father, the Son depends on the Father to be the Son, the Spirit depends on the Son and Father to be their constitutive fellowship, and the Son and the Father depend upon the Spirit to maintain constitutively the unbreakable unity between them in the Godhead.

83. *ST* 2:34.
84. *ST* 2:197.
85. *ST* 2:197.

the image of the Son, of his self-distinction from the Father."[86] This ecstatic ministry of the Spirit creates religious awareness of finitude in human beings and so, according to Grenz, gives rise to variable temporal expressions of religiosity.[87] The Spirit ecstatically lifts not only believers, but all creation out of itself, moving it toward the eschatological unity of fellowship with God who made all, is all, and is in all. According to Kärkkäinen, "A key here... is the principle of continuity: the same Spirit of God who brings about the new life in Christians and the Christian church is the same Spirit that is the life-principle of everything that exists."[88] This provides the broader basis for seeking fellowship with all humanity, not merely with other believers, since our anthropological and creational unity reflects our eschatological destiny with God. In short, "Human consciousness in its ability to be itself among others has a thoroughly 'ecstatic' structure, and precisely in this way it is given life by the Spirit."[89] The Spirit's ecstatic ministry is not merely manifest in the present, but draws everything toward the eschatological future in God. Thus, "The goal of the Spirit's dynamic is to give creaturely forms duration by a share in eternity and to protect them against the tendency to disintegrate that follows from their independence.... The working of the Spirit constantly encounters the creature as its future, which embraces its origin and its possible fulfillment."[90] In this way, there is a universally proleptic aspect of the Spirit's ministry.

This careful integration of Father, Son, and Spirit leads to an interesting conclusion about God's work in creation and human history. For Pannenberg, recent pluralist writers' tendencies to detach the universal ministry of the Spirit from the particular work of the Son forsakes God's unity as he has revealed himself, and misses the way the Trinity is universally at work in the particulars of concrete space and time.[91]

86. *ST* 2:230.
87. Grenz, "Commitment and Dialogue," 204–5.
88. Kärkkäinen, *Trinity and Religious Pluralism*, 89.
89. *ST* 2:452.
90. *ST* 2:102.
91. In *Meeting of Religions*, Gavin D'Costa argues from a distinctly Roman Catholic perspective against this pluralist tendency to separate the Spirit and the Son in such a way that they are no longer acting together in creation. According to D'Costa, some pluralists appear to set the members of the Trinity in opposition to each other rather than displaying them as working harmoniously together. In contrast to this tendency, D'Costa states that wherever the Spirit is present and at work, "there too

Thus, where the Spirit is working, so are the Father and the Son—not in contradictory or competitive ways, but in ways that demonstrate their perfect fellowship and unity. And the triune God is drawing everything and everyone to himself. In Kärrkäinen's well-put words,

> On the basis of his understanding of trinitarian relations, according to which the Spirit is to glorify the Son and through the Son give honour to the Father's claim of unique lordship, Pannenberg is able to maintain that everywhere in relations where the divine mystery is at work, the Son is too. Now it may be that there are distortions and misrepresentations present in religions, but still the Son, as the mediator of all creaturely existence, is 'behind' this quest for meaning and truth. And the same Spirit of God, who lifts up creatures, especially human beings, above themselves to share in the divine life, is at work in correlation to the Son.
>
> This pneumatology represents universality, while Christology in a sense becomes the point of tension between the historical particularity and the eschatological universality, though not in an exclusive way, but rather in a way that opens up Christianity for dialogue with others.[92]

Dialogue is no longer just concerned with who belongs to the community of the faithful, but becomes a search to find God in all his fullness as he increasingly makes himself known among all nations and peoples. Ultimately, ambiguity about God's purposes and how his triune nature presents itself to all humanity through world religions will only be removed at the eschaton. Meanwhile, dialogue seeks to discover his ongoing trinitarian revelatory work in all aspects of history. Until time's end, we seek understanding through our agonistic interactions with one another, striving to know truth in its ever-growing eschatological wholeness.

---

is the ambiguous presence of the triune God, the church and the kingdom" (p. 11). Thus, for D'Costa, it is not only the triune God in his fullness who is present where the Spirit is at work, God's church and kingdom are (ambiguously) present as well. Similarly, Kevin J. Vanhoozer, in his article "Does the Trinity Belong ?," after laying out Pannenberg's triune understanding of God, says, in reference to Panikkar and others like him, "Whereas Panikkar and other pluralists try to weaken the ties that bind the Spirit to the Son, a reading of the 'expanded economy' that takes account of the diverse relations of Father, Son, and Spirit, would, I believe, configure the Spirit as the deputy of Christ rather than as an independent itinerant evangelist" (p. 66).

92. Kärkkäinen, *Trinity and Religious Pluralism*, 89–90.

Along these lines, central to Pannenberg's project of interfaith exchange is his use of prolepsis, Christ's resurrection, and its eschatological implications. Because Christ brings the completed future into the provisional present, Christians can see particular historical events in the context of the whole. However, this glimpse is only proleptic, an anticipation of the fullness that is yet to come. Thus, Christians have a confident basis for the exclusive truth claims they make, namely the proleptic presence of Christ who brings the complete power of the future into the incomplete and provisional present. But they also have a basis for humility since this holistic truth from the future is only currently present provisionally. History is still unfolding. God has not fully vindicated himself or his people, thus we cannot see as clearly or interpret as accurately God's unfolding history as much as we would like. Only in the eschaton when God is fully revealed will our visions of truth be comprehensively clear.

Therefore, we are forced to admit our dependence, not only on God for insight into his world and its people, but also upon other people and religions to provide insights and perspectives we could not possibly gain in isolation. In short, this eschatological emphasis on prolepsis encourages Christians to display both confidence and humility in their interfaith conversations. As Kärkkäinen observes,

> Since it is only at the eschaton that the truth of any religious claim can be finally established, the dialogue process becomes a real *process*. The religions themselves, not only their claims, are provisional in nature. At best, they approach the truth. Therefore, any kind of haughty claim for superiority of any religion can hardly stand the criticism of an honest dialogue. On the contrary, even the final result of dialogue cannot be guaranteed beforehand. Provisional truth by definition is open to corrections and adjustments.[93]

We dialogue not only to contend for and share our notions of the truth. We dialogue together to discover where the truth might lead us, challenge us, surprise us, assure us, confront us, and revise our understandings of God and his world. Without this, we close ourselves off from God's future and can no longer adequately "cope with the vicis-

---

93. Kärkkäinen, *Introduction*, 244. Pannenberg is not against *any* claim to superiority. Rather, he is against *haughty* claims to superiority, for pride inevitably blocks one's ability to hear and appreciate new understandings of God's truth.

situdes of the historical process."94 The goal of this historical process is the final vindication of God's nature and purposes for all creation.

Until then, the church in society is a provisional proleptic picture of that ultimate *telos* and character. By being a unified community of human beings exhibiting the primary characteristic of God's trinitarian being, namely relationality and love, the church provides human society with an ontologically real, living, and anticipatory sign of the intimate fellowship humanity will enjoy with God and one another in the eschaton. Politically peaceful and just human communities and societies imperfectly demonstrate the heart and nature of God and his desire for every human being—to be in eternal and unbroken communion with one another and with himself as their loving Creator and Lord. We are to love one another, for we are all creations of the one true trinitarian God, even if we do not acknowledge him as such. However, in Pannenberg's own words,

> Only the eschatological future of God will consummate this revelation of His love in the consummating of creation for participation in God's own eternal life. . . . Only the eschatological consummation . . . can remove all doubts concerning the revelation of the love of God in creation and salvation history even though the love of God has been at work already at each stage in the history of creation.[95]

All humanity is made in love by God in order to love—God and one another. Our sin and drive for an unhealthy independence get in the way of that eschatological purpose, but they cannot ultimately destroy or thwart it.[96] And in our ongoing pursuit of peaceful and just human societies in space and time, whether we consciously know it or not, we dimly reflect the eternal communal realization God desires and will bring about at time's culmination.

Now that some of Pannenberg and Sachedina's theological resources for interfaith dialogue have been explored, we will synthesize these materials into a more useful form.

---

94. Pannenberg, "Response," 304.

95. *ST* 3:645. This "participation [of creation] in God's own eternal life" is described (in the final paragraph on 646) as "the incorporation of creatures . . . into the unity of the trinitarian life." Thus, it is a unified fellowship that is inherently *trinitarian*.

96. Pannenberg makes this point earlier in *ST* 3:584. For a fuller look at Pannenberg's hamartiology and doctrine of sin, see *ST* 2, ch. 8, esp. sections 3 and 4.

Contemporary Muslim and Christian Responses to Religious Plurality

Preliminary Synthesis of Mutual Resources[97]

While some of these materials will be common to both theologies of religions, they need not be in order to be dialogically useful. For example, the claim that the Christian idea of a triune God is an important resource for interfaith dialogue is controversial. Nevertheless, I will argue in chapter 7 that this area holds great promise for future interreligious conversations between Christians and Muslims. Having noted this, there are several aspects of these theologies of religions that can be emphasized and synthesized here.

First, Sachedina's emphasis on the libertarian nature of genuine religious belief is crucial to fruitful interfaith exchanges of divine and human ideals and virtues. Without such an understanding of religious and human freedom, tolerance is a farce and plurality only superficially expressed at best. In addition, the constitutionally moral nature (*fitra*) of every human being gives societal room for interreligious and interpersonal ethical and rational discourse. Coupled with a Christian understanding of humanity created in God's image and the corresponding moral understanding and conscience, much space is provided for everyone to discuss ways to live together justly and peacefully. Because all people have been made with this divine ethical imprint, they are all capable of defining, upholding, participating in, and contributing to an increasingly good society and community.[98]

Pannenberg's insight into the provisional (although divinely mandated) role of the secular state gives additional room for distinguishing and keeping separate the governance of a society and the religious affections and practices of its people. Religion and state governance must never be collapsed into each other, for not only does history show the inevitable abuses of such an arrangement, but from a Christian perspective they are inherently and essentially incompatible at crucial points. The state is provisional and temporary, whereas the church proleptically participates in and expresses the eternal eschatological power

---

97. The synthesis provided here is intentionally introductory and provided as a preview for how some of these resources will be developed more fully in the chapters that follow.

98. As will be explored further in the following chapter, this affirmation is not unqualified. The human tendency to sin and forsake the morally righteous nature of his or her being becomes a significant and perpetual barrier to the creation of such societies.

of the divine future for all creation. The church perpetually challenges the state, reminding it of its inescapable provisionality. It also provides society with concrete perspectives and examples of true justice and interpersonal peace in and through time.

Sachedina and Pannenberg's emphasis on the historically conditioned (and for Pannenberg *constituted*) nature of God's revelation forms a powerful tool for encouraging interfaith dialogue between world religions. Historical aspects and contexts of revelation must be better understood and explored, not only within traditions, but also between them as they continually modify their explanatory visions of God/the gods and his/her/its/their truth(s) to the members of the community and to those of other faiths over time. In so doing, these traditions open themselves up to opportunities that the unfolding future brings into the present, enabling them to confront and correct false and damaging perspectives and practices.

Sachedina uses these historical insights to develop new ways of understanding Islamic *jihād*, apostasy, and mercy that blunt more fundamentalist conceptions. He also uses them to encourage Muslims to see religious others (especially Christians and Jews) as possessing genuine, although time-bound and culturally conditioned, revelations of God. Consequently, dialogue becomes more than an attempt to convert the hearer. If God revealed himself in other world religions, sending them prophets unique to their time and situation, Muslims might gain from them divine revelatory insights that could benefit modern societies. Thus, Sachedina provides a Qur'anic basis for conversing with and appreciating religious others.

For Pannenberg, despite the historical particularity of Jesus, God continues to reveal himself throughout time. Thus, dialogue provides opportunities to apprehend more and more truth in its comprehensive fullness since truth is manifest not only to Christians, but to all people everywhere. Through interreligious interaction, we have the potential to see more clearly God's unfolding revelation of Himself to all.

This affirms that religious truth is God's truth and must be publicly proclaimed and implemented. True dialogue is not reserved for the academy alone, but must be publicized through continuous interactions of common people engaging one another day after day in the concrete contexts of human life.

In addition, both emphasize the need to let religious truth claims stand as they are, without imposing on them a foreign and pluralist framework. Only then can they be accurately appreciated and examined, and accordingly understood, modified, rejected, accepted, and questioned through interfaith interaction. More than this (and contrary to most pluralists), points of religious *discord*, as much as areas of accord, become the places where the most interesting discussions and progress are potentially made. By letting people argue for the truth of their perspectives as they stand, insights into the nature of God and his world can continually be (re)cognized, (re)discovered, (re)emphasized, and (re)applied.

From a distinctly Pannenbergian Christian perspective, one additional crucial resource for interfaith dialogue concerns the idea that God is triune in nature and action. How this trinitarian framework can be brought into ecumenical and interreligious dialogue will be more thoroughly addressed in chapter 7, but for now it must be recognized as one of the most important conversation topics in a genuine interfaith exchange between Christians and Muslims, not to mention those of other faiths and ideologies.

Finally, both men highlight the eschatological nature of dialogue, since only at the end of the age will God definitively show himself to be Lord, resolving all conflicts and misunderstandings regarding our religious, ethical, and epistemological claims. Pannenberg expands this eschatological aspect of interfaith interaction by claiming that all people are inexorably drawn by the Spirit toward a perfect and unbroken fellowship with God the Father that will only be fully realized in the eschaton. Nevertheless, the provisional nature of human existence in time and space opens the way to explore places where religions might be misguided and deceived as well as accurate in their understanding of God, reality, and creation. Only in God's eschaton will he be shown true while everyone and everything else will be revealed as somehow limited and deficient. Meanwhile, from a distinctly Christian perspective, the proleptic presence of God's completed future is opened up in the provisional present through the ecstatic ministry of the Spirit and Christ's resurrection from the dead. Since it is the living body of Christ, the church provides the world with a proleptic yet provisional picture of God's eschatological purposes for all of creation—an eternal and unified fellowship of all with God.

Summary and Conclusion

To summarize, these aforementioned resources can be categorized in a number of ways. They are *theological* because they are concerned with truthfully and faithfully representing the nature and purposes of God. They are *political* and *social* since they are publicly directed toward human societies and seek to deal with the appropriate structure and governance of such communities. They are *historical* in that they give careful attention to the ways history constitutes, influences, and impacts our understanding and application of religious truth claims, ideals, and practices. They are *anthropological* because they provide distinctly religious perspectives on the constitution and purposes of human existence and experience in this world. They are *ethical/praxiological* by presenting the world with a concrete set of moral norms and customs that can make our world a more peaceful and just place in which to live. They are *epistemological* in that they confront the modern ethos of intellectual relativism with a bold affirmation of universal public truth that is rationally embodied and argued for within and between religious communities that are successfully extended through the long march of time. They are *faithful* because they allow religious truth claims to be argued for and adhered to as they actually stand without prior revision or amendment. Lastly, they are *eschatological* since they give open and unapologetic recognition to the provisional nature of their claims along with the need for God to intervene decisively in human history to bring about a definitive and ultimate revelation of himself as Lord of all.

Given these resources from Sachedina and Pannenberg, the task of pursuing new avenues for Christian-Muslim dialogue remains. Where do we go from here? What aspects might generate the most interesting topics of discussion and debate? How can Muslims and Christians provide ongoing and significant input for greater expressions of peace and justice in modern human societies? These and many more issues will be more thoroughly explored in the following chapter.

6

Problems and Possibilities of Religious Plurality Revisited: A Contemporary Vision for the Pluralistic Now and Not-Yet

The vision provided here is unashamedly and inescapably *Christian*. And while insights and resources from Pannenberg and Sachedina's theologies of religions are utilized, I do not embrace all aspects of their views. Nevertheless, the rejection of certain portions does not diminish the many benefits to be appropriated from what they say about God, religion, human nature, and society. Thus, this chapter represents an interactively critical employment of their theologies of religions. As Pannenberg argues, part of forging a biblical theology of religions involves conversing with alternative and conflicting viewpoints. Such perspectives will be explored as they become relevant to the discussion, beginning with pluralist claims concerning the biggest barrier to interfaith dialogue and the best ways to initiate interfaith interactions.

Barriers to Interfaith Dialogue: Challenging Pluralism's Claims

Many pluralists assert the primary barrier to peaceful coexistence and successful promotion of interreligious understanding and cooperation between Muslims and Christians is religiously exclusive attitudes. To suggest, for example, that Islam, is *the* truth and only way to salvation while all other religions are variously deficient and corrupt is to impede

Problems and Possibilities of Religious Plurality Revisited

insidiously any pathway to fruitful mutual associations. This exclusive perspective is blamed for a variety of historical and contemporary problems in interreligious relations. Pluralism is touted as offering the only viable way to resolve all interfaith quarrels. Hugh Goddard, for example, proposes several reasons why "evangelicalism has a significant negative impact on Christian-Muslim relations in many different parts of the world."[1] These include 1) having a high view of biblical authority, 2) a high view of Christology, 3) a conflated and simplistic view of Christianity and its relationship to Western civilization, and 4) a strong tendency toward Christian Zionism, "which gives rather uncritical support to the state of Israel."[2] Similarly, Mahmoud Ayoub argues, "The most urgent goal toward which both communities *ought* to strive is . . . the mutual acceptance of the legitimacy and authenticity of the religious tradition of the other as a divinely inspired faith."[3] For him, this is "a *fundamental requirement* for honest and constructive dialogue" and "should *always* guide our efforts" in this interfaith conversation.[4] In addition, "Muslims and Christians *must* accept each other as friends and partners," something that "implies the admission . . . that both Christianity and Islam have . . . the moral and spiritual resources to guide their followers to the way of salvation."[5]

Ironically and somewhat inconsistently, after insisting upon these dialogical prerequisites, Ayoub then contends that traditions should "speak for themselves" and "not remake the other in their own image as a precondition for acceptance."[6] Unfortunately, this demand that Christians and Muslims recognize beforehand the salvific legitimacy of one another's faith traditions simply begs the question, since a critical aspect of honest interreligious dialogue is debating that very assertion. Requiring this prior affirmation dictates the terms of the discussion, something pluralists say they are trying to avoid in genuine dialogue.

This tendency is a major shortcoming of many pluralist and inclusive treatments of interfaith dialogue today. In their zeal to create

---

1. Goddard, *History*, 190.
2. Ibid.
3. Ayoub, "Goals and Obstacles," 315. Emphasis added to demonstrate the "ought-ness" and rather deontological nature of Ayoub's statements.
4. Ayoub, "Goals and Obstacles," 315; emphasis added.
5. Ibid.; emphasis added.
6. Ibid., 316.

more peaceful and fruitful interactions, they fail to see the unsupported preconditions required to welcome someone to the religious roundtable. Many of these prevent religious adherents from making exclusive claims at the outset, thereby excluding large numbers of potential dialogue partners who still believe their faith is the "best and truest." This results in impoverished discussions and artificially created experiences of peace and unity that cannot be sustained long-term and do not include the vast majority of their respective faith adherents.

Of course, some of these preconditions are appropriate since certain ways of coming into dialogue are necessary to provide some degree of safety and civility. If, for example, free religious practice and expression involves the extermination of all who disagree, then the deeper value of protecting human life trumps freedom of religious speech and especially practice. Thus, a commitment not to kill one another would be one important prerequisite to interfaith dialogue.[7] What is most concerning about a position like Ayoub's, for example, is its myopic tendency to assume pluralism somehow avoids dialogical prerequisites, when it clearly does not. This is one of the major critiques leveled against pluralism. Promoting itself as neutral and accepting, it often (tacitly and perhaps even unknowingly) demands certain beliefs and attitudes be affirmed before one can join interfaith dialogue. Thus, pluralism becomes what it tries so hard to avoid: a dictatorial religious ideology created to keep certain religious others away from the conversation. If one does not believe that all roads lead to God/the Real or that Islam and Christianity offer roughly equal ways of obtaining salvation, then one is deemed detrimental to future dialogue, and excluded from the discussion. As Jürgen Moltmann notes concerning Paul Knitter,

> [He] appears to claim the ability to adequately describe the pluralistic framework as the *solely valid* foundation for dialogue between religious traditions. For a Christian, this seems to me to concede essential points in their self-identity without really arguing the grounds for these concessions. A pluralist theology of religions can be no less imperialistic than the Christian

---

7. Sachedina, "Pluralism's 'Live and Let Live'" notes this aspect of needing certain prerequisites for interfaith dialogue when he says, "A precondition in a dialogue is equal respect to all parties in dialogue. The moment one party assumes a moral high position it changes the dialogue to a monologue . . ." To clarify, he is speaking primarily in terms of mutual respect here, not so much about believing that one's religious perspective is better than another's.

> theologies of religion that Knitter wants to overcome.... In addition, are only those religious communities which accept the conditions of dialogue as suggested by the "pluralistic theology" worthy of dialogue?[8]

Thus, pluralists argue everyone *ought* to embrace their position to produce a peaceful world. This is a different demand than finding enough common ground to live side by side in religious freedom. The struggle is finding appropriate and workable limits of tolerance. But the demand to ignore or modify central truth claims to promote interpersonal communion and community ends up being an insufficient and unsupportable basis for lasting cooperation. It is a partnership based upon sentimentality rather than reality, a precarious foundation indeed. As Miroslav Volf argues, "Since truth matters and since a false pluralism of approving pats on the back is cheap and short-lived, we will rejoice over overlaps and engage others over differences and incompatibilities so as to both learn from and teach others."[9]

Ultimately, pluralism's attempt to provide a compelling vision for more beneficial interreligious interaction collapses into another kind of exclusivism. In Heim's insightful words,

> To accept the affirmation of their faith given by the pluralistic theologies, those of other religions need to agree first that it is actually still their faith which is being affirmed when it is in the translated form these theologies give it. Second, they need to be willing for their religious life to be cast in the mold pluralistic theology has set for it....
>
> If those in other traditions are not willing to adopt these categories, they seem to lose dialogical parity that pluralistic theologians earlier so strongly demanded for them.[10]

In short, if religious others are not willing to converse on pluralist terms, they are seen as less than equals in the dialogical hierarchy.[11]

---

8. Moltmann, "Is 'Pluralistic Theology' Useful?," 155.

9. Volf, "Living with the 'Other,'" 5.

10. Heim, *Salvations*, 108–9.

11. Heim (ibid., 109) recalls a situation where a non-pluralist Jewish dialogue participant was told by a pluralist, "With your views, you shouldn't be involved in dialogue." In the course of the exchange another participant suggested that only thoroughly pluralist thinkers could be a part of "authentic dialogue." Heim concludes his thoughts on this exchange by noting, "Here it would seem that the old lamented triumphalist attitudes of Christians remain in vigorous health, if in different forms."

Similarly, inclusivism claims to legitimize religious others, but then seeks to subsume them into a subcategory of the religion from which the inclusivism springs. Rather than letting others remain the other, they are redefined and claimed to become, often anonymously or unwittingly, "one of us." Using the salvific categories of one's own faith tradition, central aspects of other religions are redefined and incorporated into the schema of one's own. Thus, both traditions are reordered and redesigned to fit a new conception of what it means (for example) to be "saved."[12] Often the new concept is neither true to the religion of the other, nor faithful to one's own. It becomes a "third way" of seeing the situation.

As already shown, both Sachedina and Pannenberg's theologies of religions are inclusive in nature. For Sachedina, this inclusivism is ethicocentric and based upon the moral expression of submission to the will of God. The criteria for divine acceptance are morally discerned and demonstrated by religious and non-religious individuals who live lives that conform to God's righteous will. Not surprisingly, his standard is decidedly *Islamic*, and does not give much room for alternative religious conceptions of ultimate goals.[13] Sachedina attempts to allow religious claims to stand without revision, but blunts the force of this effort by arguing Islam, Christianity, and Judaism must consider one another efficaciously salvific if interreligious dialogue is to succeed. Ultimately, Sachedina's inclusivism encourages interreligious dialogue between Muslims and religious others, but still struggles to let them stand as truly other.

---

12. One of the great difficulties in using such categories for all religions is that the very notion of salvation as it is commonly understood in Christianity, Judaism, and Islam is not easily translated into the concepts and eschatological goals of other religions. If, for example, the goal of religious practice is not personal communion with a God, but being swallowed up and completely incorporated into the impersonal world soul, then it becomes difficult to universalize a religious category for what every religious person, regardless of their faith tradition, seeks to become or obtain. This highlights one of the most important difficulties religious pluralism (not to mention inclusivism) has to overcome: How can incompatible religious views be ultimately reconciled with one another, if at all?

13. For some, the goal of religion is not a life of righteousness per se, but enlightenment and a corresponding *emptying* of the mind and *elimination* of all concepts of desire and otherness, including logic and moral distinction. Such emptiness eschews universal categories of morality and rationality as ultimately *detrimental* to attaining this enlightened idyllic state of nonbeing.

For Pannenberg, the inclusion of humanity in divine eschatological fellowship is also partially morally determined, but this fellowship will demonstrate a soteriological breadth that reveals God's sovereign and all-encompassing nature. Thus, it is an eschatocentric inclusivism distinct from Mark Heim's.[14] Like Sachedina, Pannenberg's inclusivism has problems and limitations.[15] Still, Pannenberg's strength lies in his ability to give real room for religions to interact as they actually exist without demand for revision. Since only in the eschaton will everything be clarified and God be fully vindicated, until then all religions have their place and make their claims in an ongoing contest for a greater knowledge of God/Reality. Such interactions are necessary, for only in the process of dialogue can God's comprehensive truth be increasingly revealed and understood in time. Nevertheless, for Pannenberg, religious otherness will be swallowed up in that decisive eschatological moment when God reveals himself to be God without equivocation. Dialogue is necessary in the provisional present, but ultimately, all arguments and confusion will cease.

Therefore, Pannenberg is unashamedly Christian, arguing for the exclusive Lordship of Christianity's God. Likewise, Sachedina is unapologetic in his claim that Allah is the exclusive Lord of all and the sole determiner of humanity's final destiny. Consequently, both theologies tend to become exclusive in their claims, even while trying to give room for other possible claims. One problem not always adequately brought out is this: what can be done to arbitrate between truth claims about God's nature and reality that are, as they stand, *contradictory*? Can all such claims be explained away by historical conditioning and situatedness? Is it really possible to embrace simultaneously the dual affirmations that God exists and does not exist? This highlights the fact that pluralism and inclusivism try to give room for religious others as they are, but end up creating new exclusive perspectives they believe warrant universal acceptance and adherence. As Netland observes,

---

14. Heim's eschatologically inclusive vision is laid out in *Depth of Riches* and summarized in ch. 1.

15. For example, Pannenberg wants to argue that God's sovereignty will ensure the complete salvation of almost everyone through his fellowship with humanity in the eschaton, whether or not people believe or want such an end to be the case for them. Could this not border on a coercive kind of salvation that fails to give adequate respect to the free and independent choices of God's creatures?

> Pluralists appear to be nonjudgmental about the beliefs and practices of the religions. But appearances can be deceiving. . . . It is difficult to come up with a genuinely pluralistic model that is coherent and does not privilege any particular religious perspective. What sometimes seems to be an open pluralism can in reality be a covert kind of inclusivism, so that what initially appears to be a very accepting posture toward other religions really involves understanding and accommodating religious others within the framework of one's own tradition, which remains normative. . . . This is not really pluralism but merely an especially generous form of inclusivism.[16]

Likewise, inclusivists define others on their own terms, incorporating them into their own tradition, regardless of their assent. So inclusivism and pluralism have a tendency to collapse into another (often more subtle) form of *exclusivism*.

Replacing one exclusivism with a more amiable form solves only one small aspect of interreligious interaction—one that need not be an inherent part of exclusivism's attitude towards religious others. Is it not better to take every religion at face value and interact with candor and frankness? Admittedly, some forms of exclusivism do contribute to mutual distrust, active rejection, and even aggressive destruction of religious others. History is replete with disturbing examples of aggressive misuse of religious fervor. As C. S. Lewis notes, the worst kind of zealots are motivated by religion. Thus,

> It seems that there is a general rule in the moral universe which may be formulated "The higher, the more in danger." The "average sensual man" is certainly, by ordinary standards, a "lower" type than the man whose soul is filled with some great Cause, to which he will subordinate his appetites, his fortune, and even his safety. But it is of the second man that something really fiendish can be made. . . . It is great men, potential saints, not

---

16. Netland, *Encountering*, 213. Netland therefore calls these theologies "pseudopluralisms." It is this kind of pluralistic tendency to collapse into inclusivism that Heim capitalizes on in *Depth of Riches*. There he openly admits that he is "a convinced inclusivist." (p. 8). Thus, his vision is still inclusive since he convincingly agues that all pluralisms end up being inclusive rather than truly pluralistic in nature. However, he claims that his proposal it is the most "pluralistic" of all Christian inclusivisms provided thus far. He may be correct in this claim, but his hypothesis is fraught with serious problems and unanswered questions. For a fair but critical analysis of Heim's thesis, see Kärkkäinen, *Trinity and Religious Pluralism*, 145–52.

little men, who become merciless fanatics. Those who are readiest to die for a cause may easily become those who are readiest to kill for it.[17]

He goes on to observe,

> [The fanatical principal] encourages a man to think that his own worst passions are holy. It encourages him to add, explicitly or implicitly, "Thus saith the Lord" to the expression of his own emotions or even his own opinions.... For the Supernatural, entering a human soul, opens to it new possibilities both of good and evil. From that point the road branches: one way to sanctity, love, humility, the other to spiritual pride, self-righteousness, persecuting zeal.... If the Divine call does not make us better, it will make us very much worse. Of all bad men religious bad men are the worst.[18]

Thus, a more important question demanding an answer is, "Are exclusivistic religious attitudes largely to blame for the religiously-sanctioned hatred and aggression in the contemporary world?" Granted, virtually all religiously aggressive people are exclusivists. Why else would they so adamantly propagate their faith, going so far as to die, conquer, and kill others to do so? Perhaps, but this (mis)use of religious faith is related more deeply to external ideologies than exclusivist faith traditions. The problem is not exclusivism per se, but the inappropriate use of exclusivistic religious fervor to obtain unrighteous ends.[19]

---

17. Lewis, *Reflections on the Psalms*, 28. Lewis was not addressing *Islamic* religious fanaticism here, but the perceived fanaticism of some of the Jewish poets expressed in the so-called "imprecatory" psalms of the Old Testament. Nevertheless, the general principle described by Lewis is hauntingly and tragically accurate, especially in the light of certain recent world events.

18. Ibid., 31–32.

19. I am not questioning the sincerity of all leaders of such movements here. Many leaders have (ab)used religion for their political and economic advantage, but others have displayed great passion without any such discernable ulterior motives. Thus, violent ideologies are often the basis for such movements, and oftentimes these leaders are not fully aware of the ways they have been influenced (and often *misled*) by these viewpoints. The primary impetus for activist and quietist expressions of religious faith is almost always the historical/political situations religious people find themselves in. Sachedina, in "Activist Shi'ism in Iran, Iraq, and Lebanon," carefully explores this notion with respect to Shi'ite Muslims, tracing the history of their movement from quietism to activism during the past 150 years. He notes that in Iran, for example, "conditions under the shah [in the 1960's and 1970's] were the sine qua non for the emergences of political activism among the previously quiescent Shi'ites of Iran. The

Perhaps Islam is a religion of peace. But that claim is potentially obscured by the actions of Muslims who define peace in terms that bring the threat of subjugation to all standing outside their particular community. And this community is often not an open Islamic fellowship, but a tribal and clannish one demanding an interpretation of Islam that rejects all who do not support their narrowly sectarian vision.

Thus, Islam suffers from the refusal of some of its leaders to reject radicalist visions of Islam. By being co-opted by fanatical ideologies, the meanings of important Islamic sacred texts are cast in doubt. What are the merits of suggesting Qur'anic materials support such violent agendas? Are there better ways to frame interpretive parameters? If so, what are they and who are the best promoters of alternative visions for Islam? The way authoritative texts are read and understood significantly matters, making Sachedina's project all the more vital for Islam's interreligious future. The silent majority of Muslims refusing to speak against radically fundamentalist views of their faith give complicit approval to such demonic ideologies and practices carried out in the name of Islam's God. As Liyakatali Takim puts it, "The silent majority syndrome has to end simply because Muslim acquiescence . . . has encouraged an extremist expression of Islam."[20]

Ultimately, religious exclusivism need not be rejected to ensure more peaceful and just societies. Thus, when Muslim scholar Sinasi Gündüz asks, "Is the absolute truth claim of religions an obstacle for sound inter-religious relations based upon mutual trust and

---

Shi'ite religious leadership seized upon this potential for activism in the growing disillusionment with rapid modernization . . ." (p. 419). Such activism can be either legitimate or illegitimate. Unfortunately, the ease with which religion can be used for illegitimate opposition and violent expression is well-documented. While it goes beyond the scope of this treatment to pursue such an ideological connection in any significant way, for a helpful brief exploration of it, see Gündüz, "Hegemonic Power," esp. 123–25.

20. Takim, "Conversion to Conversation," 343. Granted, the refusal to speak out is often motivated by fear and a desire to remain alive. Many current Islamic fundamentalists are very clear about their intentions to silence, by any and all means, those who would oppose them. So, I do not wish to ignore the genuine risks involved in defying and contradicting those who would rather exclude than embrace the other. However, if no one speaks out, the silence will ultimately be even more deafening and dangerous. In the famous words of Edmund Burke, "All that is necessary for the triumph of evil is for good men [and women] to [say and] do nothing."

Problems and Possibilities of Religious Plurality Revisited

understanding?"[21] he soundly answers "No," since the "absolute truth or salvation claim of a religion does not require one to see the other(s) as an enemy or to be disrespectful."[22] In short, it is not an inherent source of religious or social enmity. He also reminds us that

> Religious traditions with their differences contribute much to the cultural richness of humanity. In order to preserve and perpetuate this richness, adherents of different religions should live together (though they may argue with each other on various subjects . . .) without modifying their religious concepts and discourses due to the pressure of the hegemonic powers and ideologies.[23]

Given the reality of religious plurality, how and where do we begin to interact? And how do Pannenberg and Sachedina help us in this process? More focused attention will now be given to these issues.

Expanding the Boundaries: Learning from and Speaking with Others

Although I have been critical of pluralism and inclusivism, much can be learned from them. They highlight several important dialogical starting points worthy of consideration. These include: 1) the need to dialogue with and a desire to listen to and understand, rather than just preach to, ignore, or even destroy the other; 2) the need to come to the conversation humbly, willing to admit that our finitude makes it impossible to know all truth; 3) the need to affirm that God's grace and gifts are not restricted to members of one's own tradition (even if one contends the fullness of salvation is still restricted); and 4) the need to pursue cooperative efforts for peace and justice among all peoples, regardless of cultural and religious affiliation. To these four aspects I would add the additional need to allow religious others to speak about and contend for their faith (within some basic parameters of safety and civility) in ways that are faithful to that tradition. Thus, the pluralist demand to forego all exclusive claims must be rejected.

---

21. Gündüz, "Hegemonic Power," 127.
22. Ibid.
23. Ibid., 128.

Contemporary Muslim and Christian Responses to Religious Plurality

All these dialogical affirmations point to one central need: to engage and interact continually with those *different* from ourselves. As Bernard Adeney puts it, "In order to have real dialogue [with others], we need the ability *not* to understand them. We must see them as strange before we can really see them at all."[24] By being isolated and protected from others, we are not only walled off from their benefits and blessings, we are restricted by our own finite and sin-tainted resources. Of course, being in community with others subjects us to their limitations and distortions as well, but by broadening our resource base we are more likely together to allay these limitations and corruptions. And we are more likely to remain open and attuned to God's unfolding plans and purposes for humanity's present and future. Thus, there are both benefits and risks in genuine interfaith dialogue. Avoiding the risks may seem temporarily safer, but this security prevents us from fully discovering and appropriating even greater potential benefits.[25]

We will expand upon each dialogical need, seeing how they might be enhanced and supplemented by Pannenberg and Sachedina's theologies of religions, beginning with the affirmation that listening and understanding are primary goals of interreligious interaction.

Listening to, Learning from, and Forgiving the Other[26]

Conservative evangelical Christians often do most of the talking and nearly none of the listening in crosscultural and interreligious conver-

---

24. Adeney, *Strange Virtues*, 140.

25. There are dangers in encounter as much as there are dangers in isolationism. Encounter, even between relatives and friends, can lead to violence just as surely as vilifying those who are "not like us" can. Enemies can be both well-known and unknown. So we must be careful in assuming knowledge of the other will inevitably or automatically lead to an embrace and acceptance of that other. Sometimes intimate fellowship and understanding leads to open hostility and rejection—as in so-called "family feuds." Nevertheless, two things are clear concerning attempts to remain cut off from relationship with those who are different. First, in today's interconnected world, it is increasingly difficult to retain a protected status. Even the most remote people groups are being confronted with the need to respond to and deal with the global realities of what has been called a "shrinking planet." Secondly, even if one could theoretically remain secluded from the outside world, it is far easier to vilify, demonize, and hate those who are unknown than it is to hate and seek the destruction of one's sister and brother, father and mother, counselor and friend.

26. In what follows, although I will utilize many aspects of their theologies of re-

sations. As Millard Erickson argues, if evangelical Christians want to influence others more effectively today, "We will need to enter into the other person's perspective, to think from his or her presuppositions. It means that we will have to listen . . . rather than just talking, which tends to be an occupational disease of both clergypersons and sometimes of lay Christians."[27] The central need for listening and learning in dialogue cannot be overemphasized for the notoriously monological.

Again, before dialogue begins, some preconditions must be observed. Primary to these is a firm commitment to civility and respect. But before dialogue can commence, it may also be necessary to step back and consider something even more basic to relationship, namely *forgiveness*. As Alasdair MacIntyre demonstrates, the conversation of traditions we join has a *past* as well as a present and a future. In the course of that history, things have been said and done to one another that require a conscious decision to offer and receive forgiveness.[28] Forgiveness often requires interpersonal processing, and may involve considerable initial investments of time and energy, but the long-term benefits are significant.

Sachedina's exploration of Qur'anic mercy and its restorative thrust provides a distinctly Islamic basis for extending forgiveness and pursuing reconciliation between Muslims and Christians. This mercy is grounded in God's gracious character. In addition, the God-given *fitra* enables us to experience forgiveness from him when we fail to love and obey him fully. As we are healed and experience his mercy and forgiveness, we are able to extend God's graciousness to others who have offended and sinned against us. Failure to enact the restorative

---

ligions, I will not remain restricted to Pannenbergian and Sachedinian resources for interfaith dialogue, but will examine other resources and possibilities as well.

27. Erickson, *Postmodernizing the Faith*, 155.

28. Concerning this, Friedmann (*Tolerance and Coercion*, 4) has the following encouragement for Muslims: "Rather than denying the existence of certain intolerant elements in medieval Islamic thought, modern Muslims might instead admit that such elements exist, while at the same time exercising their power to reject these and embrace the more liberal and tolerant principles in their tradition. Some modern Christian institutions have already taken this way: they grapple with their historical guilt for acts such as the massacres perpetrated by the Crusaders or for the excesses of the Spanish inquisition by decrying . . . 'the hatreds [and] persecutions . . .' rather than embarking on futile attempts to deny their historicity."

and merciful kindness of God is a failure to obey and be like him.[29] God is the source of mercy as well as the enabler of people to experience it with others.

Similarly, the example of Jesus provides the basic motivation for Christians to offer forgiveness to others. When he was being crucified unjustly on a cross, Jesus spoke to the Father about his enemies this way: "Father, forgive them, for they do not know what they are doing."[30] Elsewhere Jesus teaches that Christians are called to love and pray for their enemies and those who persecute them. This graciousness is based upon the character of God the Father who "causes his sun to rise on the evil and the good, and sends rain on the righteous and the unrighteous."[31] Seeking peaceful relations with others, even those seeking to take one's life, is a particularly Christian concern. As Paul wrote, "If possible, so far as it depends on you, be at peace with all people."[32]

By working through the process of forgiving one another together, we are more likely to form genuine bonds of peaceable loyalty and friendship, even when we are compelled to "agree to disagree" with one another. This initiates and further supports the critical process of intercommunal listening to and learning from one another.

Humility in Dialogue

Closely related to forgiveness is the companion trait of *humility*. If anything is to be learned from one another we must listen—something that is nearly impossible without humility, the recognition that one is not omniscient, infinite, or perfect. Although one can claim a true knowledge of God and his purposes, one cannot claim that such knowledge is comprehensive and non-amendable, for that assumes having infinite omniscience.[33] Sachedina affirms this idea and follows his treatment of

---

29. By way of a reminder, these arguments are found in Sachedina, *Roots*, 102–9.
30. Luke 23:34.
31. Matt 5:44–45.
32. Rom 12:18.
33. Christian apologist Francis Schaeffer used to say Christians can have "true truth" even if they cannot have "exhaustive knowledge" about God. In *Escape from Reason*, 22, he says this about biblical truth in particular: "We have from the Bible what I term 'true truth'. In this way we know true truth about God, true truth about man, and something truly about nature. Thus on the basis of the Scriptures, while we

Qur'anic forgiveness with the topic of humility (versus arrogance and jealousy). He sees it as vital to one's ability to forgive, learn, and grow through interaction with the religious other. He also sees humility as the surest way to avoid the human tendency to resort to aggression and hatred of the other. It opens up a sense of need for others that leads to "social interaction, which fosters a sense of interdependence, thereby reducing violence among individuals. Furthermore, it requires them to realize that . . . resentment degrades others and causes them moral injury."[34]

In addition, Pannenberg points out people are made in the image of a triune God. This suggests that although people have limited independence through the differentiating work of Jesus from the loving Father, they are also dependent and finite. Consequently, they reach out to the truly infinite and independent God through the ecstatic ministry of the Holy Spirit who lifts them out of independence into dependence upon God and one another in love. This is universally true, whether or not the person is a Christian. As people are lifted out of their independence, they can see the values and truths others provide through their experiences of God's unfolding purposes and plans in time. Humility comes through recognizing this dependence upon God for existence, sustenance, goodness, and truth. It also comes from acknowledging our finitude and the provisionally historical nature of divine revelation. To comprehend and apprehend all truth, we would need to be omnipresent, omniscient, and infinite. Because revelation is historical, we can only grasp the whole of it when we know it in its totality. Speaking with people from other places (and times through examining history) enables us to see God's revelation more comprehensively. Of course, only in the eschaton can every particular event be placed into the context of the whole, revealing its unambiguous meaning and truth value. Until then, humility admits that our conceptions of truth in time and space are revisable in light of new and more comprehensive information and experience.[35] And humility moves us to interact, learn from,

---

do not have exhaustive knowledge, we have true and unified knowledge."

34. Sachedina, *Roots*, 108.

35. Pannenberg's use of prolepsis to grant Christians a degree of certainty that comes to them from the completed eschaton of God through the power of the Spirit and the resurrection of Jesus, does not negate this provisional aspect of human knowing. The need for perspective from others, in the present and from the annals of his-

and even disagree with others who may possess vital aspects of God's all-determinative truth that we have missed, ignored, and even denied. Thus, people are opened up to the possibility that they are not only right or wrong, but also perhaps uninformed and ignorant of certain facets of God and his creation.

The Gifts of God to the Whole Human Race

Closely related to humility and our need to forgive and learn from one another is the affirmation that human beings need one another to provide love, care, mutual enrichment, and moral and intellectual accountability. Anyone who has honestly examined other cultures and world religions must affirm the presence of remarkable moral and spiritual values in addition to profound truths.[36] The presence of enduringly successful societies and communities adhering to very different religious perspectives gives evidence that alternative world religions cannot completely be products of demonic deception and folly. They must display and embrace aspects of God's grace, even if they are obscured and distorted by sin and human finitude.[37] Thus, religions are

---

tory, remains critically important in the dialogical process of knowing and living out the comprehensive, all-encompassing truth of God. And this dialogue is not merely religious in nature, but should include experts and scholars in all fields of human knowledge in an ever-increasing attempt to draw together more and more aspects of human understanding into a comprehensive, coherent, and holistic theological system.

36. As MacIntyre demonstrates in *Whose Justice, Which Rationality?*, any enduring religious worldview must have sufficient truth and explanatory power—a rich deposit of resources from history and tradition—in order to survive and thrive in the world for any length of time. Pannenberg makes very similar claims about the successes and failures of religious traditions to continue to thrive and gain adherence through time.

37. The issue here is one of divine *revelation*, and not so much *salvation*. That debate relates to questions—using Christian and Muslim categories—of what it means to be "saved," as well as how it is that one can obtain it. This critical question should be a continual topic for Christian-Muslim relations even as it is an intrareligious debate within these traditions. Since an answer to this question takes us beyond the scope of our concern here, see Okholm and Phillips, eds., *Four Views on Salvation*, for a closer look at the Christian debate on this subject. With respect to the question of revelation, there is much debate among Christians about whether or not other religions can possess divine revelation not yet revealed to Christians. Are they merely obscured, distorted, and underemphasized, or does God really reveal new truths in other religions and religious others? Lindbeck (*Nature of Doctrine*, 49, 54, 67) suggests that it may well

not completely evil, but neither are they wholly good. In addition, as an evangelical, I would unapologetically argue that some religions express more of God's truth moral character than others. No rough parity is promoted here. Otherwise, we would have very little to talk about and accomplish in interfaith dialogue.

As a Christian, I am unashamed to affirm the truth and moral life of Jesus far exceeds similar claims made by all other religious leaders and systems. Otherwise, I would not remain a Christian. Nevertheless, my sin and finitude corrupt and shroud my own understanding and moral sensibility. Thus, I cannot deny there are rich resources available to one another through mutual interfaith dialogues that have yet to be appreciated and explored. And these resources have a *theological* basis for their presence since *God alone* is the source of all that is good, and since human beings are created in his image. Consequently, they possess divinely bestowed gifts and abilities that graciously enrich others, no matter where they are, who they are, and what religious or cultural tradition they are a part of. These gifts are variously expressed through people of great knowledge and understanding, through those who vividly display righteous moral norms and ideals, through people with artistic vision and skill, through musicians, athletes, leaders, servants, and individuals gifted in communications, through those who reflect God's beauty, love, and strength, and through those who possess exceptional creativity and wisdom.[38] Thus, God's goodness is demonstrated in and to the whole of humanity, and not only to Christians. "He causes his sun to rise on the evil and the good, and sends rain on the righteous and the unrighteous" (Matt 5:45). He shows kindness to all people by

---

be that divine truths previously unknown to Christianity are present within other faith traditions. However, I am inclined to agree with McDermott (*Can Evangelicals Learn?*, 117), who argues that the finality of revelation in Jesus Christ suggests that "'new truths' must be new understandings of that revelation rather than ideas that go beyond what is already contained or suggested in that revelation. Consequently, revelation in the religions may give Christians new ideas about how to understand Christian revelation better, and these ideas may have never been thought of by Christians in the previous history of the church—or at least by those who have left written remains." Sometimes it takes the challenge and insight of an outside perspective to overcome the obscuring power of intratraditional limitations and shortsightedness.

38. This is by no means a comprehensive listing of possible ways in which human beings as divine image-bearers can genuinely benefit from and enrich one another. It is provided only as a preliminary reminder of the innumerable ways in which humans are intended to be used by God to bless and appreciate each other.

giving them "crops in their seasons," and providing them with "plenty of food" and filling their "hearts with joy" (Acts 14:17). "He himself gives all men life and breath and everything else," and "God did this so that men would seek him and perhaps reach out for him and find him, though he is not far from each one of us. For in him we live and move and have our being" (Acts 17:25, 27–28). Human beings are to reflect this wideness in God's abundant kindness by serving and blessing one another, regardless of creed, color, or culture.

Recall that Pannenberg provides a basis for people's critical need for one another through his concept of revelation as history and his claims about the comprehensive nature of God's truth. If human religiosity is grounded in the trinitarian structure of human existence and a longing for knowledge of God, then religion becomes a contested interaction of religious truth claims about God and his creation. All revelation from God is inherently historical in nature, and the truth and significance of a particular event can only be fully known in view of all historical events. Without interfaith interactions, we not only miss God's desire for us to benefit from mutual human enrichment, we also miss certain aspects of his truth. Only by pursuing an increasing knowledge of God's world and its people (past and present) can we see more of God's truth. This need for time's completion highlights Pannenberg's concept of prolepsis and the way in which both Jesus and the Spirit provide a foretaste of the completed eschaton in the provisional present. Thus, Christians know something of the eschatological wholeness that will be experienced in the eschaton, but they still need unceasing interactions with others to obtain increasingly clearer and more comprehensive pictures of God's all-determining, all-encompassing truth, and so learn to love him and others more.

For Sachedina, the universal *fitra*, coupled with the notion of the heart (*qalb*), provides the Islamic basis for affirming God's universal gifting of moral and intellectual goodness and excellence to every human being. While the heart can become veiled, sick, and corrupt, bending people away from the righteousness and rationality of the *fitra*, its presence still ensures every person retains the rational and moral capacity to discern and practice what is right and just. The heart can be restored and returned to faith and a right understanding through the process of dialogue with others as they provide moral and intellectual challenge, as well as accountability and insight. And this dialogical challenge includes insight from the Qur'an and other possible sources of divine inspiration as well. In Sachedina's words,

> God . . . has endowed human beings with the necessary cognition and volition to further their comprehension of the purpose for which they were created . . . . It is ingrained in the soul . . . [and] involves spiritual and moral development; something that is challenging in the light of basic human weakness indicated by the Qur'an (70:19–20).
>
> This weakness reveals a basic tension that must be resolved by further acts of guidance by God. It is at this point that God sends the prophets and "Books" (revealed messages), to show human beings how to change their character and bring it in conformity with the divine plan for human conduct (2:2, 5).[39]

Added to concepts of the *fitra* and heart is Sachedina's insight into the libertarian nature of genuine religious belief. It can only be real if not coerced but freely and personally chosen. The only way to persuade people to embrace truth freely is to interact continually and voluntarily with one another. People must be open to revision and change, including the possibility of religious conversion. As the Qur'an teaches, there must be "no compulsion in religion," and since God sent prophets to other non-Islamic peoples and places in time, truth can be found in them as well. Thus, Sachedina affirms a *Muslim* need to open up public space in society for interreligious interaction and encounter with a view to embracing at least some of the perspectives and insights of others who also possess the God-given *fitra*, who have been given prophetic truths for their respective times and places, and who must be given freedom to enable their beliefs to be passionately sincere. Consequently, the *fitra*, the prophets of old, and the idea of genuine religious belief become the foundation for societal space to pursue interfaith dialogue together with the hope of realizing more libertarian, just, peaceful, and moral human communities that benefit from the gifts, insights, talents, and practices of all.

This recognition of God's image in humanity and the resulting gifts and abilities, despite the corrupting power of sin and the finitude of human beings, is considered by many Christian theologians to be an important facet of God's common grace. As John Calvin notes, using non-Christian writers as a particular example of a more general truth,

---

39. Sachedina, "Creation of a Just Social Order," 103.

> Whenever we come upon these matters in secular writers, let that admirable light of truth shining in them teach us that the mind of man, though fallen and perverted from its wholeness, is nevertheless clothed and ornamented with God's excellent gifts. If we regard the Spirit of God as the sole fountain of truth, we shall neither reject the truth itself, nor despise it *wherever it shall appear*, unless we wish to dishonor the Spirit of God. For by holding the gifts of the Spirit in slight esteem, we condemn and reproach the Spirit himself. What then? Shall we deny that the truth shone upon the ancient jurists who established civic order and discipline with such great equity? Shall we say that the philosophers were blind in their fine observation and artful description of nature . . . ? Shall we say that they are insane who developed medicine, devoting their labor to our benefit? What shall we say of all the mathematical sciences? Shall we consider them the ravings of madmen? No, we cannot read the writings of the ancients on these subjects without great admiration. We marvel at them because we are compelled to recognize how preeminent they are. But shall we count anything praiseworthy or noble without recognizing at the same time that it comes from God? *Let us be ashamed of such ingratitude*, into which not even the pagan poets fell, for they confessed that the gods had invented philosophy, laws and all useful arts. Those men whom Scripture calls "natural men" were, indeed, sharp and penetrating in their investigation of inferior things. Let us, accordingly, learn by their example how many gifts the Lord left to human nature even after it was despoiled of its true good.[40]

To benefit accordingly from such divine blessings in humanity, we must risk encountering and then, to some degree, embracing otherness expressed in people of different cultures and religious traditions. Otherwise, we not only miss their rich gifts for ourselves and future generations, we also fail to appreciate and give thanks to *God* since they are expressions of his goodness and grace to all. Such interactions have the potential to produce more open, just, and peaceful human societies, especially when these gifts, values, truths, and abilities are invited to be expressed and embraced in the public arenas of societal politics and legislation. This affirmation of a need for religious truth claims and

---

40. Calvin, *Institutes*, 273–75 (bk. 2, ch. 2, sec. 15); emphasis added. Calvin is not really dealing here with the question of revelation per se. He is focusing on the *imago Dei* and its impact upon humanity as a whole. For his views on divine revelation see bk. 1, chs. 3–8, 14.

practices to be publicly recognized leads us to a fourth area of dialogical concern, namely freedom of religious practice and expression.

The Need for Religious Freedom and Expression in Just and Peaceful Societies

Sachedina's concern for societies where religion is publicly influential without being externally coercive has already been noted, but it warrants brief reiteration. It should also be coupled with Pannenberg's similar affirmation that religion must be both public and private. We will only examine the subject briefly since it will be revisited in more depth later.

First, Sachedina reminds us that religiously ruled societies are not necessarily free societies. Imposing religion upon the masses by external governmental and legislative enforcement does not usually lead to more just, peaceful, and moral communities. Often the lack of accountability, challenge, and open dialogue with members of society produces increasingly detached ruling elites out of touch with the people they are meant to protect, provide for, empower, and serve. Consequently, these governments are increasingly forced to resort to controlling and manipulative measures to retain power no longer legitimately granted them by the governed. As Sachedina argues, this is not only ill-advised politics; for Muslims, this is also condemned by the Qur'an. It explicitly states God *ordains* plurality to create intra- and interreligious competition to outperform one another in acts of justice and righteousness.[41] There must be no compulsion in religion, for compulsory religious belief and practice is only superficial and hypocritical. Thus, Islam must allow religious freedom and open interreligious exchange as part of God's plan for better and more humane communities. The *fitra* reminds us that every human being is part of the world community, created by God for goodness and rationality, regardless of cultural or religious affiliation. This divinely constituted *fitra* provides everyone with the limited ability to understand and obey what is right.[42]

---

41. See Q. 5:48.

42. Although the Christian doctrine of depravity tempers this optimism toward humanity's goodness, Christians affirm that even in its corrupted and deceived state, moral goodness and rational understanding expressed through human conscience can

Contemporary Muslim and Christian Responses to Religious Plurality

Pannenberg also notes society's need for religious input and influence based upon his concept of truth being inherently public. Religious truth claims cannot and should not be walled off from public arenas of politics and social policy. But beyond this, if people—especially religiously devoted people—are prevented from openly contributing to the norms and ideals of society, vital aspects of God's revelation are missed. Because God reveals himself in all of history, and because the comprehensive truth and meaning of any particular moment can only be discerned in light of all events, past, present, and future, the wider the scope of input a community receives, the more likely it is to be correct about its understanding of God and his creation, and the more probable that its ethical norms and practices are just and moral. There must be a pursuit of increasingly comprehensive and coherent systems of thought and practice drawing from the rational insights and ethical practices of all human societies and religions, if God's all-encompassing and eschatological truth and righteousness are to be properly instantiated in the provisional here and now.[43]

Therefore, there must be a refusal by religious practitioners to accept secularist demands that religious belief remain solely private.[44]

---

be discerned, especially since God's grace is continually given to all human beings.

43. One of the big concerns with what Pannenberg calls a "syncretistic" process is that of *evaluative discernment*. For Sachedina, the standard of discernment is clearly the divinely authoritative texts of the Muslim faith, especially the Qur'an. Since the absolute authority of this text is almost universally accepted by Muslims, apart from his use of well-known juridical sources and interpreters, he has little need to argue for alternative evaluative sources. For Pannenberg, in contrast, since the rise of the historical-critical method in biblical interpretation and a growing awareness of the interpretive and hermeneutical problems created by the historical distance (G. E. Lessing's "ugly wide ditch") between the scriptural authors and our modern era, the source of discernment can no longer be a simple appeal to the unquestioned authority of the divinely inspired Christian Scriptures or ecclesial tradition. In "Crisis of the Scripture Principle" Pannenberg argues that the bases of evaluation must be widened to include what he calls "universal history" (p. 12) rather than just the specialized history of the biblical revelation. Thus, other arenas of human knowledge, including science, anthropology, sociology, history, philosophy, etc., must also be considered as they stand in relation to the Christian concept of God. As an evangelical, I remain staunchly committed to the divine authority of the Scriptures as being the primary standard of discernment, but I also recognize the limitations of my own understanding and application of those biblical truths. Thus, I have a deep appreciation for the program Pannenberg is attempting to carry out, even if I find myself cautiously concerned and in many places in direct disagreement with some of its points and implications.

44. Some of the problems with such an attitude were already laid out in chapter 5

Problems and Possibilities of Religious Plurality Revisited

Because religious peoples comprise the majority of contemporary societies, especially in Asia, the Middle East, Africa, and the Americas, this has implications for those claiming to provide genuinely democratic states. If secularists in these societies continue attempting to exclude religious ideals and practices in all public arenas, this can only lead to the tyranny of the few over the many. But even in political contexts where religious traditions officially comprise only a minority of the general populace (as in Communist China, for example), the systematic and intentional exclusion of religious influence upon such societies also leads to political tyranny and the eventual and ultimate impoverishment of its peoples.

Successful and long-lasting societies are built upon shared language, goals, ideals, practices, and values. But beyond this, history shows they only succeed when such features are informed and empowered by common ethical and ideological commitments. This does not deny the presence of variable and even radically different beliefs and practices among its peoples, but it does affirm that there are certain concrete moral and practical aspects in societies that have flourished over time. These values and practices are, to greater and lesser degrees, embedded within world religions that have similarly prospered and grown through time. To ignore them is to impoverish and limit ourselves from time-proven, rich deposits of priceless communal resources.

Thus, contemporary societies must find specific and concrete ways to allow religions to impact and influence public governance and policy openly so that everyone gives input into the process and allays the tendency of leaders to abuse and hold tightly onto power. Only by insuring comprehensive and widespread input can societies benefit from the enduring values, ideals, goals, and practices of religious traditions. In short, including these in public policy making is the most desirable way to achieve truly good, just, and peaceful societies.

This all stands and falls on an aspect of interfaith dialogue that is too often ignored or even disparaged by some of the more pluralistic visions of how religious others should interact. If resources within the various world religions are to be properly ascertained and applied, they must be allowed to remain as they actually are without prior revision or misrepresentation.

---

and need not be revisited here.

Letting Religious Claims and Practices Remain Unrevised

Concerning this need to let religious claims and practices be honestly expressed and exchanged, Sachedina states, "An essential prerequisite in commencing dialogue, to be sure, is toleration, not acceptance, of what we consider to be the morally or religiously wrong position of the other. . . . This cognitive leap is a difficult one, especially when the cultural other happens to be a religious other. . . . The only way to bridge this cognitive gap is to allow the sources and people we are studying to speak for themselves."[45] Later he argues all genuine dialogue must draw from the sacred and authoritative resources at its disposal, because these resources are the most pregnant with possibilities for interreligious exchange. Thus, "Any serious dialogue between peoples of different religious traditions has to be anchored in their normative teachings, for it is, finally, revelatory guidance that governs the possibilities for an interreligious relationship between communities with different doctrinal traditions."[46]

Consequently, the need to hear and explore religions (and cultures) as they really are is linked to the need to mine the actual resources these world religions and cultures provide, rather than some unrecognizably distorted version of those original claims and practices.[47] Otherwise, the

---

45. Sachedina, *Roots*, 12.

46. Ibid., 41.

47. Granted, postmodernism's reminder that no one can see with complete objectivity, and that to some degree the perspectives we receive from others will be revised according to the limitations of our own conceptual categories and plausibility structures, is well taken. But I would challenge the (self-refuting) assumption that often follows from this recognition—that the product of such understanding is therefore wholly relative and thus untrue, or at least impossible to know whether or not it is true. Our grasp of truth is certainly limited, but not therefore untrue. It is true as far as we can currently understand and see it, granting us what has been called by Alasdair MacIntyre "warranted assertibility." In addition, the plausibility structures and categories with and through which we are able to see and discern truth are not unalterable. They can be challenged, modified, and even radically revised in the light of new experiences and information utilized in conjunction with our reflections and appropriations of those resources. However, as postmodernism also reminds us, this process is more than a personal discipline. It must also be a communal affair where others around us help us better see, know, and practice truth in a community of the faithful. Against the relativist, and for the notion of truth and warranted assertibility, MacIntyre (*Whose Justice? Which Rationality?*, 363–64) says: "Warranted assertibility always has application only at some particular time and place in respect of standards

actual resources within religions and the potential benefits they might provide for other traditions and societies could be missed. Therefore, Pannenberg and Sachedina's theologies of religions are praiseworthy not only in their refusal to remove religious truth claims and practices from their historical contexts, but also their insistence that such claims and practices should be allowed to stand and speak as they really are.

As Pannenberg insists, contesting for competing religious claims and living them out well makes God's comprehensive and coherent truth more evident. Similarly for Sachedina, letting religious peoples speak and act freely allows them to express accurately the God-given *fitra* and practice the divine virtues of forgiveness and mercy toward others without pretense or deception.

Given these basic resources for Christian-Muslim dialogue, we can now examine some of the essential elements required for the creation of just, free, and plural societies. The creation of such communities is only possible in an atmosphere of continuous grassroots communication between its members. It can also be promoted and strengthened by societal leadership. Because Islam emphasizes political and legislative aspects of religious adherence in human societies, Sachedina is particularly concerned with the formation of cooperative, democratically plural, free, and just human communities. These kinds of societies are impossible to maintain without a governing system that encourages and enables the exercise of genuine religious freedom. Thus, we will first focus on potential problems and solutions concerning this challenging subject.

---

then prevailing at some particular stage in the development of a tradition of enquiry. . . . The concept of truth, however, is timeless. To claim that some thesis is true is not only to claim for all possible times and places that it cannot be shown to fail to correspond to reality . . . but also that the mind which expresses its thought in that thesis is in fact adequate to its object. The implications of this claim made in this way from within tradition are precisely what enable us to show how the relativist challenge is misconceived." Incidentally, as valuable as MacIntyre's perspectives are in responding to the relativist challenge, there are problems with some aspects of his thesis. For a critical and insightful analysis of MacIntyre's views (and those who agree with and follow him), see Smith, *Virtue Ethics and Moral Knowledge*.

Political, Legislative, Religious, Cultural, Social, and Moral Aspects of Communal Formation: Elements, Examples, and Challenges to Success

This chapter is primarily concerned with Christian and Muslim dialogue. Therefore, the complex and intricate aspects of contemporary society formation cannot be examined in any comprehensive way. Nevertheless, I would be lax if at least some of the political, legislative, and social aspects of Sachedina and Pannenberg's theologies of religions were left unexplored, especially since they are central concerns for Sachedina.[48] Thus, the democratic aspects of his vision, along with their potentially pluralistic implications, benefits, and applications, will be addressed. Primary to Sachedina's vision for democratically plural societies is the deliberate promotion and practice of interreligious *dialogue*. He notes the need this way:

> In a world in which religious differences historically have been manipulated to burn bridges between communities, recognition and understanding of religious differences require us to enter into knowledgeable dialogue with one another, even in the face of major disagreements. A morally and spiritually earnest search for common undertakings within our particular religious traditions can lead the way for society as a whole. Religious pluralism can function as a working paradigm for a democratic, social pluralism in which people of diverse religious backgrounds are willing to form a community of global citizens.[49]

Thus, Sachedina argues that interreligious cooperative efforts and interactions provide a concrete working model for human societies in general.

The Politics of Freedom:
Fitra, *Qalb*, and a Genuinely Libertarian Faith

The exemplary pluralist model Sachedina envisions is especially concerned about the politics of religious *freedom*. A pluralistically free

---

48. After all, the title of his landmark book includes the words "Democratic Pluralism."

49. Sachedina, *Roots*, 35.

Problems and Possibilities of Religious Plurality Revisited

society must include the voices not only of Christians and Muslims, but of all human communities and traditions that constitute its members. However, such freedom must begin with religious examples of successful interfaith plurality. It should also include a way to hear perspectives from those outside the bounds of one's own community since this prevents the stagnation and short-sightedness that often comes from protectionistic stances of power-hungry regimes as well as (unfortunately) religious leaders.

The failure of many Islamically-controlled societies to provide opportunities for minorities and others outside the society to live freely and give input into the governance of the society, makes Sachedina work particularly hard to create communal space for the lifestyles and voices of religious and ideological others. The God-given *fitra* provides the resources for this societal space by affirming its universal presence in every human being, no matter how immoral and ignorant that person may be. This does not deny this *fitra* (like the conscience as part of God's image in Christian theology) cannot be corrupted, obscured, and underutilized. Indeed it can. For Sachedina, "the heart (*qalb*, plural *qulüb*) in Koranic usage is the 'seat of consciousness, thoughts, volitions and feelings.' Hence, the heart is the physical locus of the fitra, that inherent capacity that is affected by the choice made in the matter of faith." [50] It can therefore become "veiled" and sick, preventing the person from rightly seeing and assessing a given ethical situation or choice. Sachedina puts it this way: "When a person rejects faith, the heart becomes veiled and is deprived of its ability to understand the moral situation. The heart thus functions as a faculty for distinguishing truth from falsehood, good from evil, the beneficial from the harmful."[51]

For Sachedina, the universal *fitra* provides the critical basis for permitting human beings to be heard in the public square of any given society. Since all people have the God-given ability to reason and morally discern right from wrong, opening up society to the perspectives of religious (and even non-religious) outsiders makes available potential resources that can help the society gain deeper insight into the truth and see a demonstration of moral goodness that might otherwise be

---

50. Ibid., 91.
51. Ibid.

missed or misunderstood.[52] Also inherent in the *fitra* is the idea of human freedom. Thus, human beings must be allowed and encouraged to exercise their God-given capacity to be creative and religiously free.

Sachedina notes that religious freedom is a direct corollary of genuine religious belief and practice. Without freedom of religion, genuine religious practice is slowly smothered and curtailed. In fact, as Abdolkarim Soroush points out, to quench religious freedom is to strangle genuine religiosity. Thus, "It is in this sense that a religious society, based upon free faith, dynamic understanding, and individual presence before God, cannot be but democratic. Thus, fearful and forced compliance with religious law should not be taken as the touchstone of a religious society."[53] Consequently, if religions are to be genuinely practiced within a society and be beneficial to it, governing authorities must make adequate legislative and structural space for religious freedom. Sachedina gives Islam a distinctly Qur'anic and anthropological basis for that kind of social freedom. For Christians, that freedom has been similarly grounded in the doctrine of being created in God's image with free will, moral conscience, and natural creativity. God has made us free and given us the ability to make ethically sound moral choices for which we are held accountable. This freedom has implications for both societies in general and intrareligious practices in particular. Beginning with a cursory discussion of religious freedom and the role of the state in granting and encouraging it, both topics will be considered in turn.

Inter-Institutional Freedom: Religion and State

Successful states must grant religious freedom (alongside other civic freedoms), but this requires leaders to listen to and allow perspectives and lifestyles they would not necessarily agree with or promote themselves.[54] This governmental stance is no small thing since free societies

---

52. Christians can similarly affirm that even if we are not related to one another by a regenerative second birth (having been "born again"), we are certainly related to one another by our first birth as creations and "offspring" of God (Acts 17:28), bearing the universal stamp of his moral and rational image.

53. Soroush, *Reason, Freedom, and Democracy*, 143. Similarly, Ramachandra (*Faiths in Conflict?*, 157) says that in America, "It was not democracy that paved the way for freedom of worship, but freedom of worship that made democracy possible."

54. To grant this kind of freedom is to rule out in advance the possibility that such

always risk exposing the community to the insidious persuasions and machinations of evil people and false ideologies. But beyond this, as Pannenberg points out, religions freely practiced (especially the proleptic and eschatologically oriented Christian religion) serve as constant (and often irritating) reminders of the inherently provisional, temporal, and limited nature of any given governing regime. Governments open to religious freedoms must be wise and humble enough to welcome such ongoing input and reminders for the long-term health and prosperity of the entire society it governs. Refusal to risk (perhaps in the name of "protecting" and "helping" societal members) is to close society off from benefits and resources potentially available to it through religions.

In addition, religious practitioners constitute a major resource for positive expressions of religious values that promote social welfare, cohesion, moral rectitude, and personal freedom, coupled with a sense of ethical responsibility and sensitivity. Too often communities have depended upon governing leaders and infrastructure for help and guidance to the neglect of their own personal creativity, responsibility, and accountability before fellow members of society. Religious people freely practicing the moral obligations of their faith tradition are more likely to be pillars for the betterment of society as a whole than those who ignore, deny, or distort religious values and resources. As Sachedina puts it, "Human beings are subject to weakness, temptation, arrogance, narrow-mindedness, and, self-interest. . . . In this struggle, religion is the fount of inspiration. It inculcates ethical responsibility and personal accountability for one's actions. Furthermore, it generates incentives to correct one's social misconduct by emphasizing consequences of moral choices. The religious belief in the hereafter prompts human beings to identify actively with the cause of justice and work for it."[55]

Because of this human tendency to give in to "weakness, temptation, arrogance, narrow-mindedness, and, self-interest," governing authorities must also have discernment to regulate and monitor hu-

---

governments would officially uphold one particular faith tradition to the persecution, exclusion, and elimination of all others. This does not mean that those in authority will not be members of a particular faith tradition or that such governors will not allow their religious faith to influence their policy-making. However, on Sachedina's view, the public nature of religious faith in Islam does not automatically rule out a Muslim regime from openly allowing the religious practices and proclamations of non-Muslims. The same can be said for other religions as well.

55. Sachedina, *Roots*, 129.

man freedoms appropriately since they sometimes result in disruption of overall peace and safety. Thus, freedom-granting states walk the fine line between domineering overregulation and naïve libertarianism that does not adequately recognize or understand the dangerous and dissipative tendencies of the unbridled human spirit.[56] The state has the additional responsibility of determining where to draw the line on certain religious practices it deems socially dangerous and morally reprehensible, as well as how to punish individuals and groups who cross the boundaries of moral and social decency. These decisions also have aspects of public and private, as well as practical and theological import, making them even more difficult to resolve. Thus, governments must often legislatively regulate certain public activities, regardless of their ideological/theological/religious bases. Good governments realize that the short- and long-term social impacts of private and public actions must be carefully evaluated over time.

Deciding which activities are public and which are private, and which are harmful (long and short-term) to the society as a whole and to what degree, is one of the most difficult tasks any political system faces.[57] It also must decide what punishments are fitting for which crimes. This all requires exceptional insight and wisdom. It could even be said it requires *divine* wisdom and insight. In addition, beliefs and

---

56. In an ideal situation, this should be a synergistic process where religions provide governments with compelling visions and warnings concerning the moral foibles and perils inherent in humanity, and then governments take active measures to guard against such negative inclinations within itself as well as others. In the US, for example, it was the *theological* doctrine of human depravity that led to a *political* system of government that was supposed to have "checks and balances" to prevent any one branch or person from having too much power. Whether or not it actually worked (or works now) that way is debatable, but the decision to share, check, and balance political power was explicitly a *religiously* informed one. It was informed by several other concerns and considerations as well, but the point here is that religion played an indispensable role in the process of deciding the ideal political structure of human government. This example suggests an accurate picture of human nature is one vital element for the long-term success of a society. Conversely, the advocacy of deficient or incomplete views of human nature inevitably leads to impoverished, isolated, and disjointed communities that do not function optimally. Thus, religiously-informed anthropological visions should be taken seriously by governing institutions since those institutions are themselves comprised of human beings.

57. The distinction between public and private is notoriously ambiguous. Can anything really be done privately that has no impact whatsoever on the public arena? Still, some behaviors and practices are undoubtedly more publicly influential than others.

Problems and Possibilities of Religious Plurality Revisited

belief systems (religious and otherwise) influence long-term societal values, practices, and attitudes. Thus, some religious beliefs considered fallacious could, nevertheless, be not obviously or immediately socially harmful, and yet, over time, they may slowly and subtly undermine values and motivations required for the long-term health and prosperity of a community. If, for example, a society finds certain desirable moral practices are more likely to be upheld by those adhering to Islamic doctrines, it is tempting to make incentives—perhaps even compelling ones—for members to embrace the Muslim faith. In addition, when practices deemed immoral by the legal and moral codes of a society are intimately linked with religious ones, tensions between religious freedom and governmental coercion inevitably arise. Who, then, decides what is permissible and what is not? Can some religious communities be granted permission to fulfill certain religious practices that are withheld from the remainder of society? Is it even possible or desirable to create this kind of tribalistic moral and religious isolation?[58] How responsible is a government to monitor such beliefs, and how can it do so without significant bias?[59] In short, relationships between religious beliefs and practices are often extremely complex. Religions can have very

---

58. For example, in the US, Native Americans have lobbied for permission to smoke the illegal hallucinogenic drug peyote in their religious ceremonies since it has been an integral part of them for generations. What is more disturbing, however, is when the state sees religious injunctions, like preventing practicing homosexuals from being church leaders, for example, as a threat to the integrity and peaceable function of the state and its citizens. In these cases, it can be argued the state must give truly overwhelming evidence in favor of their compelling interest. Even then, room should be made for religious protest and, if at all possible, religious exemption.

59. Along these lines, good governments should generally not be in the business of forcing its people to believe certain religious or ideological doctrines and creeds that are specific to a single faith tradition or philosophical camp. But again, there are tensions here because legislative and social values and practices do not come from nowhere. They often find their most powerful rationales in expressly religious *beliefs* and *belief systems*. Thus, governments are often put into the difficult position of trying to determine which of these to promote and discourage in subtle and not-so-subtle ways. One obvious example might be belief in God. Atheism could easily be seen as a long-term barrier to just and moral human societies since atheists are not motivated by fear of or concern for the afterlife and a subsequent moral judgment. Many atheists would respond that no such concern is even remotely relevant to living a moral life on earth. Morality can be based in such things as human self-interest (ethical egoism), deep emotional reactions (emotivism), a calculus of cost and benefit analysis to find out which ends justify which means (utilitarianism), and natural law (idealism), without any reference at all to religious or theological bases.

similar practices, but carry them out for vastly different reasons. Thus, governments must attempt to make these vital distinctions between activities and beliefs. I would argue such distinctions are often impossible to determine in advance. As Pannenberg explains, for certain issues, it is only through time and interreligious contestation that certain beliefs and their long-term social, moral, and religious ramifications can ultimately be discerned.

Added to these challenges is the question about which moral norms are more cultural and which are more religious. Can such a differentiation be profitably made, and if so, how? For various reasons, certain societies are bothered by certain public practices and truth claims, whereas other societies are not.[60] This raises the additional knotty issue of what things in religious belief and practices have become tied to culture and what things are genuinely and cross-culturally and trans-temporally right and wrong, true and false. In this regard, dialogue opens up avenues for greater understanding, not only of the other, but also of the self. Often practices and taboos are developed over time that have become largely detached from their original contexts and so have little significance and meaning for today. In dialogue, these "contextless" and more cultural and time-bound aspects of religions can be challenged and exposed for what they really are.[61]

Consequently, Sachedina's project to provide historical context to Muslim laws and sacred writings is extremely pertinent. Only by exposing and explaining these contexts can an accurate picture of trans-temporal and cross-cultural norms and beliefs be accurately (re)understood and (re)applied in different settings. Similarly, Pannenberg's notion of revelation as history and his understanding of how any particular event

60. In parts of Asia, for example, it is inappropriate for women to reveal bare shoulders in public. Some (Americans, for example) might be tempted to laugh at this cultural norm, but it is a real offense and concern for certain Asians nevertheless.

61. The classic and ridiculously mundane example is the story of the woman who for many years purchases a pot roast, cuts off two inches, throws it away, and then roasts the rest. When asked why by her husband, she inquires of her mother who also did the same. When her mother is also not sure why she did this, the mother asks her mother (the first woman's grandmother). The grandmother replies she always cut off two inches because her oven and roasting pan were not large enough to accommodate a normal-sized roast. Religious taboos and practices are usually far more complex and historically extended than something this inane, but the point is the same. Dialogue forces religious adherents to explore the history and reasons behind what they think and do, especially in the areas of core disagreement.

can only be fully discerned in view of history as a whole provides helpful insights into the need for dialogue to expand understanding and knowledge of all human history. After all, what is truth if it is not in some way historical? Our grasp of theological truth about God does not just "hang in mid-air" unaffected by the context within which it is instantiated, understood, lived out, and proclaimed. To be sure, truths are in one sense trans-temporal, but this does not simultaneously make them *ahistorical*. Otherwise, they could not be truly trans-*temporal* and therefore *in time*. Similarly, what are moral norms if they are not embodied in some concrete way? Ethical principles unapplied in concrete forms are often too vague and abstract to help cement societies together. A general principle might be quickly agreed upon, but its application often is not. The more removed principles are from their concrete contexts, the less likely they are to be controversial, but the less likely they are to be properly understood and applied.

Consequently, the real difficulty with coming up with a truly practical and workable set of ethical norms is that those norms—like justice, mercy, goodness, etc.—cannot be left to vague, transcendent, and disembodied descriptions. They must be expressed in tangible forms and examples. Herein lies a critical set of questions: will our justice be egalitarian or hierarchical? Will our goodness (what is *goodness*?) be Qur'anic, biblical, or both—and in what sense? And if goodness will be "biblical," will that ethic be informed through the lens of the New Testament or the Old—or something of both? Whose theological and ethical vision of these two Testaments will be utilized? What aspects of dispensation legitimately come into play when talking about theocratic Israel, the New Testament church beneath the boot of Rome, or Arabic Islam in the age immediately following the death of Muhammad? Who will arbitrate between Qur'anic and biblical clashes, and on what bases will that judgment be carried out? What kind of power brokerage will such a process ultimately entail?

Far from academic, these questions are intensely practical and pragmatic, but are nevertheless extensively informed by theoretical, theological, historical, sociological, and cultural aspects of any given religious and philosophical perspective. To use a single practical example, feminine modesty is a strong Islamic value.[62] However, the concept

---

62. Feminine modesty is also a strong Christian value (e.g., 1 Pet 3:3–4). This may be surprising to some given the shocking immodesty and pornography that flows so

of modesty means very little without a concrete expression of what is considered modest or immodest. Thus, if we say modesty is virtuous, when can we say modesty has been violated? And how far should a government go to promote modesty among its citizens? Does the line get drawn at public nudity, as in most societies? Or should a society provide legitimate but highly regulated venues for public nudity?[63] Should see-through clothing be allowed? What about strapless shirts or short shorts? Dresses above the knee? Body-length burquas where only the eyes show from behind a darkened veil? Again, what is the standard of government here and how do religious values and virtues aid in the determination of such standards? Should any of this be enforced by the government, or should it be a matter of personal and corporate piety enforced more informally or somewhat privately by religious and/or familial standards set down within non-governmental institutions—or perhaps something of both? These are issues that strike at the core of what it means to be moral and how both faith traditions and governments can and should provide resources for legislative and punitive social structures that encourage morality and reasonably suppress immorality.

One more concern governments must address when a society is religiously plural are areas of tension between religious sects, traditions, and the special interests of government and society. These tensions can be interreligious, as well as between religious ideals and the political needs of the community.[64]

---

freely out of the supposedly "Christian" West. But the oversimplified perception that Western societies are "Christian" is misleading in this regard since they are currently far are more secularized than they are Christianized. To be sure, Christianity has had an enormous impact on Western civilization, but many other overtly non- and anti-Christian influences have also had significant influences upon Western acting and thinking. Concerning female modesty (or the lack of it), Westerners have been far more influenced by secular hedonism and materialism than by Christian ideals of modesty, chastity, and purity, both in and outside of marriage.

63. In modern Europe, for example, public nudity is permitted at certain beaches, but not in the society at large. Historically, in Ancient Rome, the public baths were places of permitted nudity as well.

64. One obvious example of a tension between the government and religion is religious pacifism as it relates to military service. In its responsibility to provide international safety for its citizens, voluntary (or even mandatory) military service is often a direct corollary to this need. And yet, religious beliefs can often be the strongest barriers to active military involvement. It has already noted how some religious beliefs

Problems and Possibilities of Religious Plurality Revisited

Interreligiously, the practices and beliefs of one religion can become the source of tensions with one or more other religions. Islamic *halal* regulations concerning proper handling and preparation of food, and the prohibition against consuming pork, potentially conflict with Christian attitudes. Similarly, eating beef in Muslim communities can be troublesome to Hindus, who have overtly religious reasons for not eating it. Some Buddhists eschew all meat-eating, leading to additional interreligious challenges. Beyond dietary issues, there are also serious moral conflicts that must be sorted through. If, for example, a religion advocates using women sexually in some of its rituals, it would be called to moral account by Abrahamic faith traditions. Nevertheless, some Hindu sects (for example) do not see the sexual use of young women in some of their religious rites as exploitation at all. In an important sense, they would claim such practices are moral exemplifications of divine *worship* for those involved.[65]

Certain religious truth claims and practices can also be problematic for the peace, unity, and security of diverse religious societies. The Muslim (or Christian) claim that all religious others are condemned to an eternity in hell apart from God can easily become a source of social antagonism.[66]

This all highlights the difficulty of governing well if leaders decide in advance that all explicitly religious input into the legislative and punitive process of societal formation, regulation, and continuation will be excluded or ignored. It also provides a powerful reminder and motivation for all governments to pursue ongoing input from its religious members. Not only this, they must also open themselves to perspectives

---

are coupled with certain ideologies in order to promote revolutionary (and military) agendas, but that is not our main concern here.

65. I am not intentionally being provocative here. The sexual aspects of some forms of tantric Shakti Hindu worship are well documented and often *religiously* justified and authorized. Of course, there is a huge debate within Hinduism itself about such practices, and most Hindus would not condone such erotic expressions of so-called "worship." Still, such things have gone on and tragically still do go on in the name of religion. Thus, evaluative criteria must be supplied to determine which religious expressions can be legislatively allowed, even encouraged, and which must be regulated, discouraged, and even outlawed altogether.

66. In Singapore, for example, there is an anti-proselytizing law toward Muslims. Because of the touchy nature of the conversion of Muslims to a religion besides Islam, Singapore has decided the best way to maintain societal peace is to outlaw any attempt to convince a Muslim to forsake his or her religion and join a different faith tradition.

from those outside their communal borders for mutual enrichment in order to keep from becoming too ingrown and impecunious.

Thus, in summation, societal laws are definitely needed to guide and direct as well as prevent both fools and evil people from harming themselves and fellow society members. They provide structure for social goods and services as well as motivation to do what is right and avoid what is wrong. Regarding democracy and religious freedom, there are dangers in claiming democracy is the solution to religious coercion and societal impoverishment. Democracy alone cannot be the solution since democracy can lead to a tyranny of the majority. Sachedinian democracy is not a simple unregulated democracy. Rather, it is a pluralistic democracy that is explicitly *religious* in nature and therefore regulated by moral principles, practices and ideals that are sacred and secular in nature.[67] However, it does not follow that such moral visions as they are applied must simultaneously be accompanied by religious (or secular) coercion.[68] Coercion is enforced at the level of the moral life of the societal member—but only insofar as this moral life is of public and social concern. Again, the tension here lies in the nature of any given moral action. Determining the "publicity" of some private actions can be exceedingly difficult for a society and its leaders to ascertain, especially when those private actions do not have any immediate obvious ramifications for either communal harm or benefit.[69]

67. History shows that secular coercion is sometimes no less disturbing or dangerous in its scope than religious coercion. It is the aspect of coercion that seeks to dominate, oppress, and subjugate the other to a certain vision of the "good society" that is troublesome here, no matter what kind of impetus lies behind such compulsion. Thus, some communist states (for example), in their unceasingly ideological drive to eliminate all religion, class, and distinction (i.e., the *otherness*), have produced some of the most wickedly coercive and oppressive societies the world has ever known.

68. I suspect all such visions are never exclusively or purely sacred or secular. There is an inescapable intermingling of cultural norms, practices, and beliefs that are at play in any long-standing and dynamic human society. Many Muslims and Christians would even challenge the notion that a strict separation between the secular and sacred is even possible given the fact that we all live in God's world, and he continually consecrates the common (what some would call the secular) aspects of human existence. Thus, while there are those who wish to secularize the sacred, it would seem that many in Islam and Christianity would prefer to pursue the opposite course of "consecrating the secular."

69. One example might be the private but excessive consumption of alcohol. At what point does the freedom to become intoxicated in the privacy of one's own home spill over into certain activities that might endanger the well-being of others and the

Problems and Possibilities of Religious Plurality Revisited

One solution to these challenges is to create societies where interfaith dialogue is continually encouraged, formally and informally, with governing authorities, other powerful segments of society, and in the daily lives of the general population. However, dialogue alone is not enough. Concrete laws and their attendant punitive measures must be enacted for society to survive long-term. To ignore completely the wealth of past expressions of Muslim *Sharī'ah*, as well as Christian and Jewish social law is to lose rich resources history has bequeathed to us in the present.[70] Still, none of the tensions over just governance, legislation, moral practice, and religious belief are easily resolved. Broad-based ongoing dialogues must be encouraged to assuage the dangerous tendencies all governments (and majority groups) struggle with. This raises additional questions without easy answers, namely, what structures will be provided to give an influential voice to the marginal and minimal segments of society? What criteria will be used to sift and judge alternative ethical visions? Someone or something will inform these decisions. The only real question is, will they be informed by a variety of religious people or not?

---

community as a whole? Some societies, both historically and currently, have sought to solve the social ramifications by completely banning the consumption of alcohol in public or private. Others have tried to minimize the public impact by regulating some of the more social activities of an individual when they are intoxicated—like driving a car, for example. Another example is tobacco smoking. For many years it was not well known that exposure to "second-hand" tobacco smoke is so harmful to non-smokers. Thus, some activities and moral choices do not immediately show themselves to be harmful to a community until many years later. Such was the case of China's social programming through its "one child" and "forced abortions" policies. No one could have predicted how devastating such a requirement would be for Chinese society in the long-run. Because of the deep-rooted patriarchal structure of familial welfare, the ratio of males to females is now dangerously out of balance, forcing China to create special incentives to encourage its families to have more girls. I would suggest this was also the case with "no-fault" divorce laws developed in the 1970s in the US. These laws were intended to make divorce fairer, cheaper, and less "messy," but the social fallout from such laws ended up creating far more damage to the family and society as a whole than was ever anticipated at the outset.

70. Friedmann (*Tolerance and Coercion*, 19–27) notes that there is a long and contentious debate among Muslims about the value and significance of Christian and Jewish law. Sachedina appears to be from the camp that supports its ongoing legitimacy based upon its divine origin, although he is clear that variations from Muslim *Sharī'ah* are based upon the situated nature of the revelation to those particular communities. In this sense, he sees Islamic law as divine in a more universal sense, but not without ignoring its historical particularity.

Ultimately, plurality cannot pander to or please everyone. We can never tolerate any and all. We can only ask the more important question: who and what shall we tolerate, and where do the limits of our tolerance lie? Evil is not an abstract threat, but a living and concrete reality manifest daily in the actions of those seeking to take advantage of others who are peaceful and good. Thus, evil is parasitic, thriving on the right behavior of others. Tolerance must have limits, and the indiscriminate embrace of others is *not* the best policy, especially when embracing others involves supporting and promoting what is evil. In fact, exclusion and prevention of evil is moral rectitude! Consequently, right governance serves a critical role in actively restraining evil persons and encouraging and rewarding moral goodness, not merely through persuasion and information, but also through forceful restraint and prevention.[71]

As important as the role government plays in promoting social freedom in general and religious freedom in particular, nowhere is the expression of religious freedom more important than within and between religious traditions themselves. Sachedina in particular believes that interfaith dialogue and relations can and should provide the broader community with a concrete and living example of the kind of interpersonal human freedom all should enjoy in religiously plural, democratic, and just societies. Attention will therefore be given to this subject as well.

Religious Freedom within and between Faith Traditions

Providing societal room for religious freedom cannot merely be a state responsibility. It is also a function of religions themselves. They must allow some degree of personal and sectarian freedom concerning belief and practice if their members are to be genuinely faithful followers. In Christianity, for example, there is an enormous variety of denomina-

---

71. I should add here liberation theology's important reminder that institutions, and not merely individuals, can also be oppressively evil. Institutions refusing input and reform are far more likely to become evil than those that regard the input and challenge of as many members of society as possible. In this way, interfaith dialogue serves as an additional safeguard against the propensity of governments and other institutions to use power oppressively and wrongly. For the classic presentation of this warning, see Gutierrez, *Theology of Liberation*.

tions exhibiting an incredible array of cultural and communal expressions.[72] However, as with the state, this kind of religious freedom of expression and practice still remains a matter of internal debate concerning extent and degree. There are certain core beliefs and practices that must be maintained if such religions are to remain distinct from each other as well as true to their own internal resources. This is why for Christians, rejection of the central importance and divine identity of Jesus is not only considered blasphemous, but also a clear and unacceptable departure from a basic tenet of that faith. Such a person or group could forsake all religion(s), embrace a different religion, or even create his or her own cultic form of religion and call it "Christian" or something else, but all claims to the contrary, he or she would no longer be a part of a *genuinely Christian* religion.[73]

---

72. This diversity was not just a product of the Reformation period. Prior to that time, there were Copt, Assyrian (Nestorian), Celtic, Catholic, Waldensian, and Orthodox Christians (to only name a few) all practicing their faith in very different and yet still distinctly *Christian* ways. In addition, there were and are many sects and forms of Christian faith and practice within these various broader expressions. My point here is that diversity of expression is not always negative. Although diversity does sometimes arise out of negative and unfortunate circumstances and events in history, this kind of spiritual variance is an inevitable aspect of religious (and social) freedom. Islam is similarly diverse, and so has been described by some (like Malaysian Ng Kam Weng, for example) as "Islams," suggesting that it also has a rich history of granting religious freedom.

73. This kind of rejection is why many have questioned whether it is still appropriate to categorize John Hick's theology of religions as truly *Christian*. While the lines between heretics and the faithful can sometimes get very fuzzy, Hick's philosophical and theological journey has taken him so far away from the biblical, historical, and traditional tenets of the Christian faith that I, for one, am inclined to agree that he can no longer legitimately be called "Christian" in any meaningful sense of the term. This is not a soteriological judgment on him. God only knows where Hick stands with respect to eternity. However, it is an *associative* judgment that affirms that there are necessary limits of belief and practice that help define religious traditions and other general systems of thought and practice. In the New Testament, 1 John, for example, provides a number of criteria for determining whether or not a person can legitimately be considered a Christian. These are the test of confession of sin (1 John 1:8-10), the test of obedience to God and Christ (1 John 2:3-6; 5:3), the test of love for fellow believers (1 John 2:9-11; 3:11-16; 4:7-12, 20-21), the test of enduring fellowship (1 John 2:18-19), the test of an orthodox confession concerning Christ (1 John 2:21-23; 4:1-3, 15), the test of a holy lifestyle (1 John 3:9-10, 24; 5:18), the test of active generosity toward others (1 John 3:17-18), the test of an inner witness (1 John 3:19-21, 24; 4:13), the test of faith (1 John 3:23; 5:5, 10), the test of hearing (1 John 4:5-6), and the test of victory over the ungodly world system (1 John 5:4-5).

This question of determining who stands inside and outside a religion raises the knotty issue of what constitutes social and religious *identity*. Religious distinctiveness is difficult to address because it is often closely associated with expressions of that tradition in a particular time and place. Religions and ideologies often attempt to make certain temporal and/or cultural expressions the ideal and timeless ones, "freezing" them into what is advocated to be their most perfect forms. But this ignores the situated and incarnated aspects of a tradition. And, as Pannenberg explains, this also closes the tradition off to the dynamic power of God's future unfolding revelation which brings greater clarity, meaning, and truth into the various and ambiguous events and ideologies of the past and present.

Thus, one of the benchmarks of a healthy and resourceful faith tradition is its ability to *translate* itself successfully into other cultural and social contexts, both presently and historically. Through this process, religions creatively change, adapt, and mold to the shifting times while continuing to influence, impact, and shape the times and cultures they infiltrate and are part of. At the same time, they retain, maintain, reinterpret, and reapply certain central identities and standards that warrant some sort of sanction when these core beliefs and practices have been unacceptably altered, ignored, or forsaken. Of course, what these core beliefs and practices are often becomes a matter of vigorous and ongoing intrareligious (and even interreligious) debate, but history has provided faith traditions with fairly central dogmas and duties that demand the adherence of virtually all of its followers. How apostates and heretics are dealt with may widely vary, especially over time, but every religion has ways of identifying and dealing with religious unfaithfulness among its members. Thus, religious freedom is necessary for the spiritual health of any faith tradition, but it also creates tensions since freedom cannot be completely unregulated. Freedom has a price; the price of tension at the borders of belief and practice. But religions refusing to grant significant freedom to their members also run the more serious risk of becoming stagnant and closed off to God's unfolding eschatological truth.

If a society is to be genuinely free in its diversity, *intra*religious freedom must also be coupled with a large degree of space for *inter*religious freedom. As Pannenberg notes, failure to interact across the boundaries of religious traditions and other kinds of ideological perspectives shuts

Problems and Possibilities of Religious Plurality Revisited

a tradition off not only from resources of truth and goodness present within other viewpoints, but also from the opportunity to see particular events of history in light of an ever-expanding set of alternative understandings. The cross-pollination of ideas and practices also challenges traditions to contend publicly for their views. This may strengthen, modify, or defeat the tradition, but regardless, God's truth is hopefully clarified for all participants. Similarly, for Sachedina, the *fitra* opens up room for religious freedom not only in societal politics, but also intrareligiously. This supports an Islamic celebration of diverse confessions and practices in the Muslim tradition, providing impetus for inter-faith and inter-ideological interaction to discover divine aspects present in all religions and peoples of the world. The refusal to hear and take seriously other views is the refusal to be open to ways God has revealed and is revealing himself through those others.[74]

Given this motivation for inter- and intrareligious freedom, as well as providing real societal room for religious input and exchange, how does political nationalism help and hinder the need to create more pluralistic, democratically free, and ethically better societies?

Nationalism and Religious Loyalties in Society

One governmental challenge is the creation of greater social cohesion. This requires the creation of an overarching social vision that somehow *transcends* its cultural, racial, and religious particularities, while still attempting to *include and celebrate* them as well.[75] For many reasons,

---

74. I am not dealing here with the question of criteria for discerning between divine truth and goodness versus false and demonic claims and practices. Those criteria are laid out by each of the traditions respectively and themselves become a matter of elucidation and debate. The important point here is to state the need that all traditions have to interact and (respectfully) contend with one another for the truth of their perspectives to remain healthy and open to God's unfolding future for all.

75. The Singaporean government, for example, uses the binding forces of a common language (English), nationalism/patriotism, social harmony, and personal affluence in an attempt to convince all Singaporeans to get along and work with one another to create a cohesive multicultural and multireligious society. In addition, when making major social policy changes, the government actively seeks input from all major religions (Christianity, Islam, Hinduism, and Buddhism). For example, the 2006 debate over bringing casino gambling to Singapore intentionally included significant input from all of these religions. Incidentally, while all of them expressed serious reservations, in the end the government decided to approve the construction and

this is exceedingly difficult to achieve. In an attempt to succeed in this endeavor, some forms of secularism have attempted to solve the problem by relegating religious confession and practice to the realm of the private, while offering its own ideological vision of society, church, and state.[76] By keeping religions as far out of public policy making as possible, these governments claim to alleviate the problems of imposing a particular religion's policies and practices upon the society. The fallacy of this approach is that secular governments must still provide moral and ideological justification, even if they do not overtly admit it. As Pannenberg observes, these claims tend to take on an almost divine and absolute status, especially when governments are trying to substantiate their power, legislative decisions, and other policies in society at large. Often, secularist claims take on arbitrational powers that try to ignore, scorn, and refute certain religious claims to absolute truth and goodness that threaten its own ideologies.[77]

Given this secularizing tendency in the West, it is not surprising that the process of "pluralizing" a society is often equated by Muslims with "Westernizing" and "de-Islamicizing" it. This may not be far from the truth if there is no way for Muslims to separate realms of public governance from the religious confessions and practices of Islam. This is why Sachedina's program is so critically important for Muslims (and others) to understand and apply in their contemporary settings. He offers a future where Muslim faith is practiced publicly while a plu-

---

legalization of casinos on the basis of what it saw as the long-term financial benefits. At the same time, the government began the groundwork for creating and supporting religiously based programs to help those who become entrapped in the social tragedy of gambling addiction.

76. Another secular way to provide social cohesion is to attempt to eliminate all otherness coercively, be it religious, cultural, racial, or some combination thereof.

77. One obvious example of this would be in the arena of atheistic evolution in American education. Any attempts to bring religious perspectives on creation into public American classrooms have largely been met with a cry for the need to separate church (religion) and state and the claim that religious faith and true science are somehow inherently incompatible and mutually exclusive. Evolution per se is not the problem here, but a distinctly secular and atheistic view of it. The decision to make American scientific education overtly atheistic is an ideological one that balks at the idea that it might be challenged by other possible views. This kind of secular absolutism and exclusivism is just as morally reprehensible as the religious fundamentalist who would seek to impose his or her brand of religion upon all others without opportunity for challenge, dissent, or discussion.

rality of religious, and even non-religious, others may simultaneously act freely within the boundaries of certain overarching moral and legislative principles. And yet, while these governmental responsibilities are distinguished from religious ones in crucial ways, neither are they unaccountable to or detached from them. What those legislative principles and punitive measures will be for the entire society remains controversial, but the idea of an unsurpassable distinction between state and religion(s) is a critical starting point for everyone who longs for a pluralistic society where freedom of religious faith and practice is the great and ongoing opportunity of every community and individual.

Ultimately, freely multicultural and *multireligious* societies succeed by walking the fine line between encouraging religious diversity and mutual acceptance through ongoing dialogue while still regulating certain aspects of religious practice that have historically upset the delicate balance of peace, harmony, and unity. Nevertheless, significant tensions remain because states still require loyalty and allegiance. When religious conflicts arise with other religions and/or the state, the state almost always preserves the social order, even if that order needs moral and legal revision.

One more important observation should be reemphasized. Sachedina's insight concerning the libertarian nature of authentic religious belief reminds us that only the most thoughtful and genuine religious adherents will be most amenable to religious freedom, for only they know what real religious commitment and belief entail—freedom. In short, genuine religious faith can only be personally voluntary. Those using coercive political ends and enforced religious conformity to create monolithic communities of their own vision and design are the real charlatans and abusers of religion. Granted, some who are zealous for the truth and holiness of God seek to impose their religious vision upon all. However, I maintain such zealots (perhaps unwittingly) fail to grasp the true nature of religious commitment and ignore the Qur'an's call for "no compulsion in religion." To coerce religious commitment is in the same breath to abolish it. Thus, religious freedom also supports and upholds plurality in the wider social order.

The invitation for religions to be freely lived out without undue opposition and oppression in society also includes the opportunity to interact significantly with one another, state leaders, and policy makers. It also includes opportunities for religions to promote and practice their faith in missional and evangelistic ways. While certain limits may be placed upon the methods and extent of this type of interaction, all freely religious societies must provide opportunities for genuine and recognized religious conversion. This exceptionally contentious religious freedom raises the difficult subject of apostasy.

The Problem of Apostasy[78]

If a society is to be religiously dialoguing, diverse, and free, one inevitable risk and result is conversion to other faiths. Some will also reject any and all religion, or perhaps alter time-honored traditions of belief and practice within their own faith tradition. Such issues have produced long and checkered histories for both Islam and Christianity. Thus, dealing with apostasy involves several controversial questions about Christian and Muslim mission, evangelism, and definitions of religious heresy, blasphemy, and apostasy. Sanctions for those deemed unacceptable, as well as what core beliefs and practices societies should demand of its members legislatively and socially, must also be considered. Each of these on its own constitutes an excellent subject for future interfaith dialogues. However, if some of these are not adequately resolved through interreligious discussion and concretized into practical social policies, there is little hope for realizing genuinely free and religiously diverse societies.

Before going further, basic terms must be clarified. Historically, heresy, blasphemy, and apostasy are related but distinguishable, especially in Christian theology. Heresy in Christianity is applied to claims and/or practices that are considered Christian by their proponents but have been sufficiently altered to be outside the bounds of orthodoxy and orthopraxy.[79] Heretics still wish to be considered Christians, but

---

78. There are, of course, a huge number of other controversial subjects that could be explored. I am singling out apostasy here because it is still considered by most Muslims to be closely tied to matters of law and the power of the state. Issues of heresy and blasphemy are closely related, but not strictly the same. Thus, as they become relevant to the discussion, they will be addressed and distinguished as well, but will not be examined in any significant way.

79. This word is transliterated from the Greek word *hareisis*, meaning "choice" or "faction," and is used by early Christians (like Irenaeus) in a negative way to describe sects or factions that do not conform to generally accepted Christian standards.

Problems and Possibilities of Religious Plurality Revisited

no longer hold to certain central aspects considered necessary to remain Christian. In contrast, apostates are those who once claimed to be Christians but have now openly "fallen away" from Christianity and no longer see themselves within the faith.[80] They can be either those who convert to another religion or those who forsake religion in general. In Christian history, the semantic range for these two words has increasingly overlapped, although the distinction is still upheld in treatments of the subject. Concerning blasphemy, this charge is reserved for a relatively limited number of infractions considered especially offensive and grievous to God and the religious community.[81]

With important caveats, there are major parallels in Islamic thought concerning these three words. They are used similarly, where "heresy" denotes when a Muslim changes some basic Islamic belief or practice while still considering him- or herself a Muslim.[82] "Apostasy" still means a forsaking or falling away from (Islam in this case), but due to different political climates and general attitudes of Muslim leaders, the significance of this falling away is treated differently than it is in most contemporary Christian communities. Similarly, what constitutes "blasphemy" (also called *vilification*) and how it is handled is considerably different from Christianity.[83]

---

80. This term is also transliterated from the Greek word *apŏstasia*, meaning to "forsake" or "fall away from" (the truth). Biblically, it is used in Acts 21:21 and 2 Thess 2:3 to describe a forsaking of or falling away from accepted teachings of divine truth. It was applied by Christians to the Roman Emperor Julian in the late fourth century when he forsook Christianity and reverted to the paganism of ancient Rome.

81. This word is transliterated from the Greek word *blasphēmia*, meaning "to vilify, curse, or slander." In the New Testament it was particularly directed toward speaking falsely or slanderously about or toward God. Although the meaning of the phrase is extensively debated by Christians, the New Testament singles out "blasphemy of the Holy Spirit" as the only unforgivable type of blasphemy (sin). According to certain passages in the New Testament, the religious leaders accused Jesus of blasphemy because although he was a human being, he made himself out to be God (e.g., John 10:33).

82. For example, many Sunni Muslims consider Shi'ite Muslims to be heretics—and vice versa.

83. While many things are considered blasphemous by Muslims, according to Friedmann (*Tolerance and Coercion*, 152) early and medieval Islam reserved a special charge of "aggravated" blasphemy for those who insulted or questioned the divine veracity and authority of the sacred Qur'an, and/or especially for those who insulted or questioned the status of Muhammad as the definitive and final divine spokesperson (i.e., the Prophet). As in Christianity, the charge of blasphemy is not reserved for

Because apostasy has great import for forming religiously free and plural societies, I find Sachedina's treatment in *Roots* disappointing. Recall that Sachedina claims confusion has arisen over Islam's understanding of apostasy based upon the Arabic word *irtdād*, translated "apostasy" in English. The word generally means "'rejection' or 'turning away from,' [and] was historically applied to the battles that were fought against those Muslims who had refused to pay taxes to the Islamic political authority after the prophet's death."[84] Thus, apostasy was not so much about religious orthodoxy as it was about radical and revolutionary subversion of established Islamic order from within or without. In Sachedina's view, while the Qur'an advocates religious freedom and plurality, following Muhammad's death, early historical factors forced Muslim leaders to adopt stricter penalties against this kind of apostasy to create a more cohesive and distinct Muslim community.[85] Because this apostasy threatened Islamic stability, unity, and identity, and was not merely a religious offense against a righteous and holy God, it was viewed as politically treasonous and met with harsh social penalties including death.[86] According to Sachedina, herein lies the crucial difference between current Islamic and Christian views of apostasy. Christians see apostasy as almost completely religious—the abandoning of one faith for another and little more, whereas Muslims consider apostasy to be a threat to social stability and unity. Thus, it is

---

members of the faith tradition alone, but extends to anyone who commits this kind of heinous infraction.

84. Sachedina, *Roots*, 99–100.

85. Friedmann (*Tolerance and Coercion*, 124) makes the similar assertion that "The idea that conversion to Islam ought to be irreversible developed as a result of the desire to protect the integrity of the early Muslim community." He goes on to argue that "Muslim tradition makes a sustained effort to demonstrate that the Qur'ānic view according to which apostasy is punishable only in the hereafter began to change while the Prophet was still alive." Shortly after he says, "the Bedouin insurrection against the nascent Muslim state after the Prophet's death was the background for this development" (p. 126).

86. The penalty of death was by no means an uncontested universal judgment in early Islam. According to Friedmann (*Tolerance and Coercion*, 121–59) in certain special cases, especially those involving women and slaves, only imprisonment and/or beating was meted out (versus death) to those who were considered apostates. In addition, many were granted the opportunity to repent and return to Islam in order to escape their prescribed penalties. Still, Friedmann admits that "Most classical jurists agree that the execution of the unrepentant apostate is the proper punishment for his transgression" (p. 127).

not merely forsaking God—something he alone can and will handle in the afterlife—it is also forsaking the *community*. Because early Muslims were guarded by political structures rather than just ecclesial ones (as in Christianity), it was the government who dealt with and punished apostates. And because conversion (or reversion) to other religions threatened the fledgling Islamic community's strength, it was publicly and politically deterred.[87]

Here it is helpful to supplement Sachedina's work in *Roots* with another piece addressing the subject where he claims,

> The question of apostasy is particularly important for understanding the discrepancy between the Qur'anic emphasis on religious liberty . . . and the intolerant, sometimes even harsh, attitude of Muslim jurists concerning the treatment of apostates. . . . [W]ith the exception of apostasy, no legal penalties are provided for offenses against religion as such; they will be dealt with in the hereafter. This exception in regard to apostasy stems from the inability of classical jurists to distinguish the admittedly complex relationship between a moral and a religious action.[88]

Thus, although the Qur'an advocates religious freedom and religious plurality, the intricate relationship religious belief has with matters of state in religiously ruled societies led early Muslim jurists to downplay or even ignore these Qur'anic affirmations to secure what they thought would be the long-term health and success of Muslims states. By enforcing a policy of monolithic religion, it was believed Islam had a better chance to survive, defend itself, and expand its influence.

Presumably, since no parallel situations exist today, Muslim governments no longer need to react harshly to religious conversions and apostasies. Thus, Sachedina argues the commonly administered death penalty for Islamic apostasy should be abolished since it "is in direct conflict with the Qur'anic spirit of religious liberty."[89] In addition, he encouragingly notes, "recent rulings in the matter of apostasy are refreshingly against [the] death penalty because the penalty is derived from the traditions rather than the Qur'an, where one's rejection of Islamic faith after having accepted it is regarded as a sin against God,

---

87. Sachedina, *Roots*, 100.
88. Sachedina, "Freedom of Conscience," 78.
89. Ibid., 83.

and hence, beyond the jurisdiction of Muslim political authority."[90] Consequently, apostates will ultimately be dealt with by God in the afterlife, taking the punishment outside the realm of the temporal and making it an issue for him alone.[91]

In this context, Sachedina concludes his analysis of apostasy with this observation: "The Muslim civil authority has the ultimate responsibility for using its discretionary power to assess the level of discord created by a public declaration of an apostasy and to lay down the appropriate measures to deal with it."[92] He further clarifies this by stating that while the Qur'an does give authority to governments to maintain communal stability and unity by putting down rebellious groups and individuals, even by means of the appropriate use of force, "At no point does the Koran endorse the community's use of political power to compromise freedom of conscience, which is an inalienable right through the very creation of the *fitra* in humankind. The state would forfeit its claim to be Islamic if it were to coerce people in the matter of the God-human relationship. Consequently, the case of apostasy in sacred law must be reinterpreted to allow for pluralism to emerge as a permanent feature of political life."[93]

In addition, this use of power is legitimate only if the government can compellingly show "that any decision to use compulsion in matters impinging on a person's faith is in no way aimed at changing that person's belief, but simply at enforcing basic moral and civic requirements."[94]

What is disappointing in Sachedina's treatment of apostasy here is that although he makes a strong case for the Qur'anic advocacy of religious freedom and God-ordained plurality, he still concludes his thoughts by largely delegating the resolution of the issue to Muslims

90. Sachedina, FRC, 3.

91. This position is based on verses like Q. 2:217, but isn't quite the whole story of Sachedina's position. He still leaves room for governmental punishment of what it deems to be *seditious* acts of apostasy that go beyond mere religious rejection. Along these lines, Friedmann (*Tolerance and Coercion*, 137 n. 102) classifies Sachedina as someone who advocates the position that "apostasy has two aspects. It is a religious transgression to be punished by God in the hereafter; it is also a political crime, likely to be followed by rebellion. Only this latter aspect of apostasy is punished here and now."

92. Sachedina, *Roots*, 101.

93. Ibid., 127.

94. Sachedina, "Freedom of Conscience," 85.

leaders and governments. And while he suggests these governments are moving toward less harsh punishments for apostasy (and that these punishments should not be used to coerce religious reorientation), I am left feeling troubled about the future of religious freedom in Muslim contexts where traditionalist views are so firmly entrenched.[95] In many of these situations, a great deal of doublespeak concerning religious freedom and the problem of apostasy is still evident. For example, concerning apostasy and religious conversion, Muslim Ahmad Yousif claims that non-Muslims living under Islamic rule are "free to do missionary activities and propagate their faith. . . . The non-believer enjoys the right to convince the Muslim of his/her views . . . just like the Muslim enjoins the right to propagate Islam . . ."[96] Nevertheless, earlier in the same article Yousif shares the following unidirectional limitation on religious freedom in Muslim societies: "the *Shari'ah* does not permit a Muslim to deny or denounce his/her religion (apostize) once he/she has accepted Islam . . ."[97] Apparently, the non-believer is allowed to share his/her faith, but conversion away from Islam is not a non-punishable option for the Muslim. Similarly, Yousif claims non-Muslims are free to live out their faith as a minority in a Muslim state as long as they "consider the feelings of Muslims and respect the sanctity of Islam" so that their actions do not "provoke [Islamic] anger and thereby lead to disorder and sedition."[98] He adds that, "if non-Muslims engage in practices which are forbidden in Islam" they must do so

---

95. I note this concern based not on some vague sense of unease, but rather on my personal knowledge of two court cases in 2007. In one, two Christians were charged (using a relatively new law) with insulting their national heritage based upon the fact that they were proclaiming their Christian faith to some fellow nationals who happened to be Muslims. Their evangelistic actions were cited as *political* sedition because such evangelism overtly suggested that Islam was not the true religion. State lawyers argued that to be a member of the nation was to be a Muslim. In a second case, several Christians were (inadvertently) caught making a home video that explained *to other Christians* why they believed that the Bible was superior to the Qur'an. In the process of filming, the Bible was held up higher than the Qur'an, an Islamic offense of blasphemous vilification. They were subsequently tried and convicted by the government of insulting the Qur'an and each given jail terms of *several years*.

96. Yousif, "Minorities and Religion," 36. Of course, according to Yousif, this evangelistic activity must be done morally and without resorting to "bribery or coercion, or any other means other than of an intellectual or spiritual nature . . ." (p. 37).

97. Ibid., 36.

98. Ibid., 37.

privately and not "in a way that may constitute a challenge to Islamic beliefs and practices."[99] Ultimately, since "it is the duty of the Islamic state to preserve the *deen* (religion) and build a God-conscious society ... groups that make a mockery of the supremacy of God have limited place within this system."[100] One is left with the distinct impression that it is the supremacy of the *Muslim* understanding of God in view here, and that "freedom" in this context is rather restricted and in many ways directly dependent upon the (positive and negative) reactions of Muslims to non-Muslim practices and beliefs in society.

I do not think this reflects Sachedina's contemporary Islamic vision for social harmony and religious plurality. However, in this kind of traditionalist environment, leaving decisions of how to handle apostasy to Muslim governments is not only unnecessary, it is ill-advised. Instead, advocating interreligious dialogue to help decide how to create unity and stability in multi-religious societies is a more fruitful avenue. Input from different faith traditions provides a more inclusive and less threatening basis for determining which core social/religious values (rather than particular and tradition-specific creedal affections) would create lasting cohesion and unity in culturally and religiously diverse communities. Given the history of Islamic governance, can people from other faiths comfortably integrate themselves into such societies without serious concerns over the ways in which such governments will respond to apostasy? Without concrete governmental assurances that real opportunities and safeguards are in place, I seriously doubt it. Thus, Sachedina's treatment of apostasy in *Roots* is at best incomplete. He misses a golden opportunity to utilize his Qur'anic notion of the *fitra* to suggest an alternative way of dealing with Islamic apostasy in particular and religious apostasy in general. This incompleteness is especially disappointing since Sachedina had already offered such an alternative in an earlier work.[101]

99. Ibid.

100. Ibid., 40. Unless the *Sharī'ah* can be openly questioned and modified in some significant way, it appears that the religious freedom suggested here is more akin to claiming a Muslim is religiously free so long as he/she remains a Muslim, and non-Muslims are free so long as they stay quietly submissive and religiously marginalized and isolated.

101. This piece by Sachedina is a collaborative effort with Little and Kelsay, entitled "Human Rights and the World's Religions." On p. 235 they make the concluding argument that, "Given the indisputable evidence for ideas of religious liberty in the Qur'ān

Problems and Possibilities of Religious Plurality Revisited

In view of these issues, questions arise over how religious freedom and plurality can become increasingly genuine features of society. For example, what constitutes apostasy, and what is the appropriate response to it? Who should enforce such responses—the religion, the state, or in some way both? Can we adequately distinguish between religious apostasy and social rebellion? What criteria can be used to judge basic differences between the two? Should seditious apostasy (if there is such a thing) require the death penalty? Why or why not? Should it only mean exclusion from the religious community? Should it just be ignored? What opportunities should be given for apostates to repent and return to the fold? Should we and can we let God be the final judge of apostates as both the Qur'an and the Bible suggest? Do we believe God is big enough to make himself known in the midst of human sin and error and to defend himself adequately in the midst of the conflicts and obfuscations these kinds of problems produce? And yet, what place does human judgment and sanction have in the process? To what extent are human beings agents of God's truth and justice upon earth? And even if human agency is involved, what manner of human agency is most appropriate—not merely based on some separate humanistic ideal of human interaction, but based upon resources within the faith tradition? In short (using Islam as an example), is it truly *Islamic* to threaten,

---

... one can imagine a doctrine which emphasizes the moral aspects of universal guidance [through the God-given *fitra* or conscience], and which views the existence of such knowledge as the possibility for good public order.... In this way, the 'soundness or sickness' of the conscience could be viewed in *moral* terms—i.e., the 'sound' conscience would be one which acknowledges and adheres to certain basic moral obligations ... and the 'sick' conscience would still be one which fails to do so. Certainly, the 'sick' conscience would still be subject to the power of the state. But such power would be exercised vis-à-vis basic moral beliefs, whereas religious faith would be a matter beyond the state's control, with disagreement to be viewed in terms of an error which cannot be corrected by coercive force. That is, while it is not necessary to become ... 'indifferent' in religious matters, an Islamic state would emphasize that true faith is a gift of God, the outcome of God's work in the heart and thus beyond the reach of the power of the sword." By arguing thus, they suggest that apostasy is a *religious* issue to be dealt with non-coercively and ultimately by God, whereas the government is concerned to enforce issues of moral import. In their own words, this view seems to "exhibit greater respect for the Qur'ānic proclamation of religious liberty ... ; at the same time it allows for another element which is equally important to the Qur'ānic witness: the concern for a just public order. What we are suggesting is that 'religion' and 'morality' may be distinguished in Islam at least vis-à-vis state authority." While this is an argument for Islamic governments in particular to consider, I would suggest the additional element of interreligious dialogue should also be added to the process.

harm, imprison, or even kill those who do not agree with Muslim doctrine or reject it for another faith tradition, or are such practices merely outmoded and irrelevant holdovers from previous historical eras?

None of these questions are easily answered, but for that very reason plural societies should not leave them in the hands of any one faith tradition, organization, or government alone. The answers are inherently communal and inter- and intratraditional, and should be significantly informed by those directly affected by them. They should also be influenced by divinely inspired resources within religious traditions, and not as much in bureaucratic legal codes freighted with historical judgments that have often become extraneous to contemporary contexts. Granted, religious resources are also historically conditioned, but they often reflect transcendent values and principles that constantly inform and reform many of the legal codes developed in and through time. Such codes, while often based upon these trans-temporal religious ideals, are still highly conditioned by the contexts in which and for which they were codified, so much so that they can obscure or distort these principles when new settings and situations arise. As Sachedina observes, "the public order, based on the Shariʿa, as well as state acts and the rulings and legal opinions of the jurists on matters arrived at through independent judgement of human reason, was subject to adaptation and refinement to meet changing conditions and developing exigencies in the community."[102] Thus, absolutizing them and ignoring their contextual nature not only makes them *irrelevant* to contemporary communities, it is also potentially makes them *dangerous* because they can so easily be misapplied and abused under different circumstances. In short, laws are made in time, by and for particular people who live under their jurisdiction. If contextual aspects are ignored or denied in later generations, the informing principles lying behind them are often hidden, unappreciated, and misapplied.[103]

---

102. Sachedina, "Creation of a Just Social Order," 109.

103. In the case of apostasy, the historical context precipitating the (perceived) "need" for religious conformity in the (Muslim) state was left behind long ago, but, unfortunately, the prescribed laws and their punishments were largely retained—so much so that they obscured the more important and divinely authoritative Qur'anic call to promote religious tolerance and diversity. I am singling out Islam since conversion from Islam to some other faith still represents a major problem for many Muslims who believe it must be punished very harshly by the state. Nevertheless, historically, Christianity is by no means innocent in this regard. The point here is that although

Problems and Possibilities of Religious Plurality Revisited

Are there other more constructive options to pursue that are more consistent with the sacred resources of our respective faith traditions? Can we openly question some current ethical teachings and legal codifications of Christianity and Islam, especially when prompted by particular historical situations and perceived needs? Again, history shows preventing open expressions of doubt, disagreement, and new perspectives on the meaning and significance of ancient sacred texts not only suppresses the libertarian nature of religious faith, it also leads to intellectual stagnation and impoverishment. Refusing to hear new and sometimes even radically different voices in our midst forces us and all subsequent generations to rely solely upon the insights of our own limited voices (and preserved past voices), rather than contemporary insights God may be offering to us in the present through an ever-widening circle of others. However, history also shows freedom often comes at the price of complete safety and control. It can lead to widespread apostasy and social degradation when left unchecked and unregulated. Thus, risk is inherent in the process of religious change, intellectual discovery, challenge, and acquisition of new insights. Still, social and religious decay is a long-term consequence of attempting to coerce and control everyone rather than granting them significant freedom. But this is only true if religions are given significant opportunities to influence state policies. Without their input, states becomes cut off from the bases and resources they need to create compelling and plural visions for healthy, ethical, and peaceful societies.

Currently, one of Islam's greatest challenges is to figure out how questions surrounding nationalism, identity, and religious apostasy and blasphemy can best be resolved in pluralistic contexts. But this cannot be adequately accomplished through internal conversations alone. They

---

they once did, most Christians no longer see apostasy as a governmental affair and are content to deal with the risk and handle it internally as an inevitable corollary of human religious freedom. Many Muslims, on the other hand, are still struggling through the process of discerning how apostasy should be handled religiously, socially, and legislatively/punitively. In this kind of climate, the need for sound exegesis of the Qur'anic and *hadithic* texts that gives thoughtful and due attention to the historical and temporal aspects of these writings, as well as their timeless principles, is crucial, for it points the way forward to an Islam that is both faithful to its divine revelations and successfully integrated into the modern pluralistic milieu. It is precisely this kind of exegetical work that Sachedina and many others like him provide for the Islamic world of today and tomorrow. We can only hope their visions shine ever brighter in the hearts and minds of Muslims everywhere.

must actively elicit significant input from others who have wrestled and are continuing to wrestle with these difficult issues. As well, Muslim leaders must more clearly determine who has the ultimate authority to enforce specific penalties in each of these distinguishable realms.[104]

Conclusion

In conclusion, interfaith dialogue is not a cure-all answer to the knotty questions surrounding apostasy, conversion, blasphemy, heresy, mission, evangelism, and their appropriate relationship to religions and governments. However, it points us toward relationship, understanding, mutual sharing, and friendship, where we can hear and honor the voices of minorities and the marginalized alongside those of the majority. Of course, not every view can be given equal validity or weight, but the various perspectives can at least all be given some consideration. How else can we work out intractable differences, and yet benefit from one another, agree to disagree, and continue to live side by side in freedom and peace? In the process, serious disagreements are inevitable, but inappropriate responses to them are not.

In this light, one of the most enduringly contentious issues between Christians and Muslims lies in the arena of theology proper. From the beginning of their interreligious interactions, Christian and Muslim perspectives on God have deviated in significant and seemingly irresolvable ways. Much time, thought, and effort have been given to this subject without producing much resolution. In light of Pannenberg's argument that the most fruitful subjects of interreligious dialogue of-

104. Christianity, for example, practices aspects of internal sanction in the arenas of aberrant belief and practice that have been called "excommunication" and "church discipline." Scriptural passages used to support this practice include Matt 18:15–17; 1 Cor 5:1–13; 2 Thess 3:6; and 1 Tim 1:18–20. However, in recent times they have generally not requested help from state authorities to carry out this ecclesiastical process. In some unusual cases they may seek such governmental aid in situations where, for example, an official restraining order against some individual or group is requested. Concerning apostasy, little or nothing is done outside of certain social and familial discouragements and encouragements that try to persuade the apostate to return freely to the fold of the faithful. In short, they are trying to persuade the world and the members of the community that Christianity is true by "competing with one another in doing good deeds." But legally and governmentally, virtually *nothing* is done since secular governments are unconcerned about the realignment of people from one faith to another, as so long as no major threats to social harmony and order arise.

ten lie in the hotly contested areas between the faiths—especially those concerning God's nature, this topic remains one of the most critical to pursue dialogically. Thus, in the following chapter we will briefly examine the issue of God's nature from a distinctly Christian point of view.

7

Applying Principles of Interfaith Dialogue: Father, Son, and Holy Spirit—A Trinitarian Look at Potential Problems and Possibilities

While most recognize there are significant affinities between Christian and Muslim views of God, a vigorous debate over whether Christians and Muslims worship the same God continues. For example, in Rome on May 9, 1985, at a symposium address to Muslims on "Holiness in Christianity and Islam," Pope John Paul II claimed, "[Y]our God and ours is one and the same . . ."[1] Yet Catholic theologian Jacques Dupuis says this: "It is clear that the God of Islam . . . cannot . . . be the God of the Christians since he unveils the error which belief in the Trinity and the incarnation—without which there is no Christianity—necessarily constitutes for every Muslim."[2] Pannenberg falls somewhere in between, claiming, "This is a question to be decided by God, not us."[3]

Because of its complexity, many theologians do not give an unqualified yes or no to this question.[4] But if one claims that at least in

---

1. Cited in Jukko, *Christian-Muslim Encounters*, 95.
2. Cited in ibid., 98.
3. Pannenberg, "Religious Pluralism," 103.
4. For a concise but nuanced exploration of this issue, see Woodberry, "Do Christians and Muslims Worship the Same God?" He answers the title's question like this: "Christians, Muslims and Jews as monotheists refer to the same Being when they refer to God—the Creator God of Abraham, Ishmael, Isaac and Jacob. But in signifi-

some sense Christians and Muslims *are not* worshiping the same God, then what critical differences have given rise to this debate? We could, at this point, concern ourselves with things like the etymology of the terms "Allah" and "God," but for focus, important theological meanings ascribed to God and his nature will primarily be pursued.[5] In particular, the Christian idea of God as *triune* will be explored to demonstrate one possible avenue of interfaith interaction between Christians and Muslims that I believe holds great promise.

Again, it may seem surprising to argue that the idea of the Trinity could be a resource for future Christian-Muslim dialogue, especially given Islam's insistence upon God's indivisible oneness (*tawhīd*). Nevertheless, along with Pannenberg, I think it is within the seams of fundamental differences where we find not only the most interesting topics for conversations and contestations, but also the most promising ones for real interfaith dialogical progress. Not only this, our theological views of God and his creation significantly mold our moral, social, and anthropological visions. The way we see ourselves, others, and our world as a whole are all indelibly and inescapably shaped by and grounded in our understanding of what God is like and how and why he reveals himself in and throughout human history.[6] Thus, our concept of God is essential for correctly assessing ourselves, others, and the world we inhabit. Not only this, we must follow God's self-revelation wherever it leads, even when it does not cohere with our preconceived notions of who he is.

---

cant ways they do not have the same understanding about him, even though they also agree in significant ways."

5. For a look at the etymological question see Geisler and Saleeb, *Answering Islam*, 13–16. Historically, Muslims took the more general and categorical Arabic term for God, "Allah," and made it into God's proper name for institutional Islam. This theological co-opting of linguistic terms is common to all religious faiths, especially as they are explained and translated into a particular cultural and semantic frame of reference. One well-known Christian example of this is John's identification of the complex Greek term *logos* with Jesus of Nazareth.

6. In Ps 135:15–18 we are called to forsake idol worship because those who worship deaf, dumb, and blind idols ultimately become like them. Thus, we tend to become like the things we think about, worship, and adore.

The Contemporary Muslim Concept of God: Tawhīd and Transcendence[7]

Primary to contemporary Islamic theology is the emphatic declaration God is *one*. He is completely undivided, and there is no plurality whatsoever in him since he has no partners or equals. This is the Islamic doctrine of *tawhīd*. Ascribing to God any multiplicity at all is considered to be the grave and idolatrous sin of *shirk*. Given the historical context (of Arabic polytheism) from which Islam arose, it is not surprising God's oneness would be so strongly emphasized.[8] A second distinctive of Islamic theology is that God is wholly transcendent from creation and has absolute lordship over it (the doctrine of *tanzīh*). He is ineffable and cannot be known by us for who he really is in his inner being.[9] As the late Isma'il al-Fariqi said, "in Islam God only reveals his will, not himself."[10] Similarly, Michael Nazir-Ali states, "Islām not only believes in the hiddenness of God [because of his transcendence], but, more seriously, in the impossibility of ever knowing him. Believers can only know his will which he has revealed to them."[11] Thus, the best we can have is a revelation of God's *will*, but this does not reveal his essence or true internal nature. Even the famous ninety-nine names of God in Islam do not reveal his being apart from his indivisible oneness.[12] As

---

7. The following section is not intended to provide a comprehensive view of God in Islamic theology. For the sake of focus, only the most pertinent theological aspects will be delved into here. In addition, little will be said with respect to Sachedina's theological views since he does not directly address this issue in his writings. However, the basic contemporary views of God in Muslim thought lie behind much of what he writes and so form an important backdrop to his theology of religions.

8. For a helpful look at the important historical settings within which Islam arose see Riddell and Cottrell, *Islam in Context*, esp. 13–31.

9. In fact, Christians would admit that as finite human beings we cannot know God fully in His inner being, but we can know about Him truly. Even the more apophatic branches of Christianity (like orthodoxy, for example) that tend to emphasize God's otherness and transcendence still believe God can be known, even if only by the *via negativa*, or "way of negation." Somewhat ironically, it is this same Christian denomination that emphasizes our mystical union and intimacy with God in salvation leading to the "deification" or *theosis*, or becoming more like God in Christ) of humanity. For a concise and helpful summary of this concept, see Kärkkäinen, *One with God*, 17–36.

10. Cited in Woodberry, "Do Christians and Muslims Worship the Same God?," 36.

11. Nazir-Ali, *Frontiers*, 20.

12. For a list of the ninety-nine names of Allah, see Geisler and Saleeb, *Answering*

Muzammil H. Siddiqi argues, "In Islamic theology it is affirmed that attributes do not exist *apart* from the being attributed. Hence, even in prayer one is not allowed to address the attributes (*sifat*) but the attributed being (*mawsuf*)."[13]

Despite the apparent consensus in contemporary Islam concerning this emphasis on God's absolute unity and transcendence, these doctrines have a long history of debate and development in Muslim thought, and are by no means noncontroversial. For example, there are competing themes in Islamic theology concerning the immanence of God. In one Qur'an passage God is said to be closer to us than the jugular vein (Q. 50:16), and yet, apart from the more mystical Sūfī movement within Islam, this aspect of God's immanence is neglected by the majority of Muslim scholars.[14] Thus, "Muslims ... tend to speak of God's presence in terms of 'presence with' rather than 'presence in.'"[15] God is with us, but only as a radically transcendent Being. There is an unsurpassable gap between humanity and the divine that cannot be bridged, making something as intimate as divine incarnation unthinkable.

In addition, the concept of *tawhīd* and God's attributes are by no means without controversy in Islam's history. In a fascinating historical survey of the way God's attributes were understood by Muslim scholars, Joseph Cumming observes that by the fifth/eleventh century[16] the teachings of Abū al-Hasan 'Alī ibn Ismā'īl Al-Ash'arī "gradually overcame rival doctrines like Mu'tazilism until . . . Ash'arite doctrine became recognized as the official orthodoxy of Sunni Islam."[17] Eventually,

---

Islam, 22–25.

13. Siddiqi, "Muslim Response," 213.

14. For a concise look at some of this "immanence of God" debate, see Tennent, *Religious Roundtable*, 148–51.

15. Nazir-Ali, *Frontiers*, 21.

16. By using dual date designations like this in his paper, Cumming recognizes the fact that the beginning of the Islamic calendar is based on the life events of Muhammad versus the life of Jesus. Because I am specifically referring to Cumming's work, I have retained this dual designation here.

17. Cumming, *Possible Christian Parallels*, 1. This has special significance in light of Sachedina's decision (in *Roots*, 89) to embrace explicitly a Mu'tazilite view of human nature and freedom against an Ash'arite one. There he claims in Ash'arite thought the *fitra* was what "compels a person to affirm the unity of God (*al-tawhīd*). Such an interpretation rules out the notion that human beings can freely affirm religious faith. . . . On the other hand . . . the Mu'tazilite theory of individual autonomy . . . interprets fitra as '*khilqa*,' that is, 'natural disposition,' in the sense that God has created

Mu'tazilite doctrines emphasizing human reason and freedom were even labeled *heretical*. For Mu'tazilites,

> God does not have knowledge, power, word, etc., except in a strictly verbal sense. In this view, the Qur'ān's references to God's knowledge, power, word, etc. were nothing more than circumlocutions for God the Knowing One, the Powerful One, the Speaking One. For if these *sifāt* [attributes] were realities other than God's essence... and if they were eternal, then there would have to be multiple eternal beings, which would be polytheism. The problem with this theory was that it seemed to most people to be exegetically unfaithful to the Qur'ān, and it seemed to contain logical inconsistencies.[18]

In contrast, Ash'arites taught that essential attributes of God (meaning those that he possesses without reference to creating or impacting anything outside of himself) "are not merely ways of speaking; they are realities/things ... [and] have existed eternally."[19] In addition, "The Qur'ān describes God's knowledge and word as having some kind of agency in creation. That is, God creates *by* them."[20]

According to Cumming, the potential parallels between Christian understandings of God as unified but possessing distinct and distinguishable attributes in the Trinity, and this differentiated Ash'arite conception of God's attributes were so obvious to some that they even saw them as nearly synonymous.[21] Nevertheless, Cumming points out that there are crucial differences as well. First, the "list of seven *sifāt*

---

in humans a capacity to affirm freely God's unity and submit to God's will." In short, the centrally important notion of *fitra* in Sachedina's view of human nature hinges upon the affirmation of an Islamic view that has a highly debated history. We shall see in a moment how this debate might be significant with respect to Christian-Muslim dialogue concerning the unity and (triune) nature of God.

18. Cumming, *Possible Christian Parallels*, 20. The term "*sifāt*" here is intentionally left un-translated by Cumming because of what he sees as the potential confusions related to the meaning of the English term ("attributes") that is usually used as a translational equivalent. For the sake of simplicity, I will utilize attributes since it still seems to provide the clearest and simplest English meaning for our current purposes.

19. Ibid., 35.

20. Ibid.

21. Cumming (ibid., 36–44) cites several historical and contemporary examples of both Muslims and Christians who have noticed this important similarity between Ash'arite concepts of God's attributes and essence alongside the notion of God's triunity.

of essence which eternally subsist in God's essence . . . is not necessarily a closed list, whereas Christians insist on speaking of three and only three subsistences in God."[22] Second, "al-Ash'arī explicitly rejected equating God's life with God's spirit on the grounds that life is an 'accident' (*'arad*) in created beings and a *sifa* in God, but spirit is a substance (*jism*) which can have life subsisting in it but which cannot *be* life."[23] Third, "al-Ash'arī explicitly rejects the idea that God's word could become incarnate or have *hulūl* ('taking up residence', or 'descent') in any particular place (*mahall*), since God's *sifāt* do not have location or space, but only subsistence in God's essence."[24] Fourth, al-Ash'arī insists that any conception of God having a "son" or "offspring" is absolutely unacceptable.[25] Thus, there are significant differences between Ash'arite theology and Christian concepts of the Trinity. However, Cummings hopefully concludes, "apart from these [potentially bridgeable] differences there is a huge amount of common ground between Muslims and Christians on the fundamental issues at stake in the *sifāt* and in the Trinity—far more common ground than is generally supposed by either Muslims or Christians."[26]

I have given special attention to this historical survey to make an important point concerning the doctrines of *tawhīd* and the Trinity. As insistent as most Muslims are upon the absolute unity of God, historical exploration of the debates surrounding God's attributes suggests

---

22. Ibid., 45.

23. Ibid., 47. Cumming goes on to note, however, that this difference "seems to be more of a difference in definition of the term 'spirit' rather than an unbridgeable difference."

24. Ibid. As serious as this difference sounds, Cumming muses, "one wonders whether al-Ash'arī does not, after all, imply elsewhere that God's word *does* have *hulūl* in the Qur'ān" since al-Ash'arī holds the view that the Qur'an is eternal and uncreated, creating an interesting conundrum over the exact relationship between the physical book of the Qur'an and the eternal word of God.

25. Ibid., 48. This rejection is more likely based upon a serious misunderstanding of what Christians really mean when they apply the title "Son" to Jesus. And, in a related fashion, Cumming says this misconception is not surprising since "al-Ash'arī . . . rejects all use of metaphor (*majāz*) in describing God." Such a move has serious theological problems that force al-Ash'arī to claim that when the Qur'an talks about God's hands and sitting on a throne (for example), these are literal truths, although it is impossible to understand *how* this can be the case. It must simply be affirmed on the basis of faith alone.

26. Ibid., 50.

that ascribing distinction and differentiation in God is not inherently anti-Islamic or anti-Qur'anic. In short, the doctrine of *tawhīd* could potentially serve a different and more useful function than a polemic against Christian concepts of the Trinity. Passages in the Qur'an rejecting the idea that God has "partners" (Q. 16:86 and 30:40), or saying Jesus ('*Īsā*) could never be God's (literal) "son" (Q. 9:30–31), or that Christians should not say God is "three" (e.g., Q. 4:171–72),[27] should all be reexamined in view of other viable theological possibilities.[28]

Still, this is nothing more than a starting point for Muslims to consider the fact that the doctrine of *tawhīd* itself has a history and that there are potential resources in historical Muslim theology that provide ways to see God as essentially unified and still able to be internally differentiated—at least from our finite perspective. However, this notion of differentiation says nothing about how we know God is not monotarian, binitarian—or even septitarian—for example. What drives Christians to affirm no less and no more than three persons in the Godhead? As Muzammil Siddiqi puts it when speaking about John Hick's attempt to categorize the ninety-nine beautiful names of God into a trinitarian framework, "why should one force these attributes into three columns, and not four or five or two?"[29]

The answer is found in Pannenberg's insistence that what drives trinitarian theology is not some philosophical concept about how God's unity can be differentiated regarding his attributes—although this may move us in the right direction. Neither is it an arbitrary framework of "threeness" imposed upon our notion of God and his creation.[30] Rather,

27. The Arabic term in this verse is "three," but two recent translations of the Qur'an into English (Khalifa and Ali) use the word "Trinity." Such translational moves suggest in my mind some of the bias many Muslims display toward specifically Christian concepts about God. The number "three" has somehow been transformed into referring specifically to the Christian doctrine of the Trinity without comment or justification.

28. For example, if by "partners" the Qur'an means potential and perceived rivals to the majesty and sovereignty of the one and only true God, then Christianity agrees with this requirement without reservation.

29. Siddiqi, "Muslim Response," 212.

30. This is one criticism that has been leveled against Panikkar's so-called "trinitarian" cosmotheandric pluralism. For example, after surveying Panikkar's extensive and difficult writings, Ramachandra (*Recovery of Mission*, 99) critically comments that Panikkar's "'christic principle' and 'trinity' are very loosely related to the historical event of Jesus Christ. The latter simply becomes a launching pad, as it were, to project into universal orbit a trinitarian way of speaking about reality." In this sense, Panikkar

this is how God has revealed (and is revealing) himself to humanity in history—especially in the concrete historical life, death, and resurrection of Jesus of Nazareth. Thus, a Christian understanding of God is *necessarily* trinitarian on the basis of his historical self-revelation.[31] Consequently, Christians are *compelled* to embrace God's triunity whether they wish to or not.[32] This basic affirmation brings us to the distinctly Christian concept of God.

The (Pannenbergian) Christian Concept of a Triune God[33]

God as Three in One: Economy and Immanence

The unique way Pannenberg presents the doctrine of God in volume one of his *Systemic Theology* has already been noted. He *precedes* his

---

can be accused of arbitrarily assigning trinitarian structures to creation that are not based in anything other than an imposition of an *ideology of threeness* and not an historically trinitarian Christian theology.

31. This historical drive to describe the one true God as triune is one of the reasons why Muslims have actively sought out resources to discredit the reliability of the New Testament to create an image of a Christ that is prophetic and holy, but certainly not divine. Unfortunately, many of those discrediting resources have been produced and celebrated by scholars and laymen within the Christian community of faith. For a look at some Christian resources that speak thoughtfully and positively to the question of the biblical and history reliability of the Christian faith, see Bruce, *Canon of Scripture*; Comfort, ed., *Origin of the Bible*; and Bloesch, *Theology of Word & Spirit*.

32. It is no secret that many Christians would probably prefer *not* to have to explain the doctrine of the Trinity. In a sense, we are *forced* to do so because this is the way God makes himself known. I am reminded of C. S. Lewis' words in *Mere Christianity*, 46–48, "It is no good asking for a simple religion. After all, real things are not simple. . . . Reality, in fact, is usually something you could not have guessed. That is one of the reasons I believe in Christianity. It is a religion you could not have guessed. If it offered us just the kind of universe we had always expected, I should feel we were making it up. But in fact, it is not the sort of thing anyone would have made up. It has just that queer twist about it that real things have. So let us leave behind all these [children's] philosophies—these over-simple answers. The problem is not simple and the answer is not going to be simple either." This is not some sort of ad hoc appeal to "mystery." Rather, it taps into an intuitive sense in everyone that suggests reality is not always divisible into neat little packages that can be easily categorized and fully understood by finite human minds.

33. Given the limited scope of our concern, even a cursory survey of the various (contemporary and historical) ways Christianity understands and has understood the triune nature of God is impossible to provide here. For an excellent look at contempo-

discussion of God's unity with a thorough exploration of God's "threeness." This discussion is preceded by an examination of the concepts surrounding the inherently historical nature of divine revelation and the Bible's relationship to it. Thus, "To find a basis for the doctrine of the Trinity we must begin with the way in which Father, Son, and Spirit come on the scene and relate to one another in the event of revelation . . . based on the biblical witness . . ."[34] We must examine the activity of God revealed in history to discover his true nature. Thus, God reveals himself not merely functionally ("economically,"), but also ontologically ("immanently").[35]

Consequently, the concrete historical life of Jesus is particularly important for Christian theology's trinitarian turn, since his life and message, finally confirmed by his resurrection, reveals a distinctly trinitarian God. Jesus is the new eschatological man[36] as well as the clearest window into a trinitarian view of God.[37]

But beyond this, the resurrection becomes the proleptic irruption or inbreaking of God's eschatological kingdom into the present. Thus, Christians have a foretaste of humanity's consummated eschatological life in God. This aspect is also distinctive to Pannenberg's view of the

---

rary views, see Kärkkäinen, *Trinity*. Since our interest has been centered on Sachedina and Pannenberg, and because the Trinity is a major focus in Pannenberg's theological enterprise, this section will emphasize his trinitarian concepts of God as a starting point for Christian-Muslim dialogue concerning God's true nature.

34. *ST* 1:299.

35. Here Pannenberg uses Karl Rahner's well-known "rule" concerning the economic and immanent Trinity, namely that the economic Trinity is the immanent Trinity and vice versa. For Pannenberg, this "rule" reminds us that we must "constantly link the trinity in the eternal essence of God to his historical revelation, since revelation cannot be viewed as extraneous to his deity" (*ST* 1:328). What this does for Pannenberg is open the way to explain God's relationship to creation as both transcendent (God the Father) and immanent (Jesus and the Spirit). He is affected by history because the other two members of the Trinity are affected by it, yet as Father he remains distinct from and sovereign over creation and history.

36. That is to say, he is the new Adam (cf. Rom 5:12–21) and the prototype for a new humanity.

37. The reason for a *trinitarian* formulation (versus a binitarian or monotarian one) is found not only in Jesus' active filial submission to God the Father, but also through his life in the Spirit. The Spirit plays a significant and differentiated role in Jesus' birth, baptism, ministry, and resurrection, and imparts Jesus' sonship to Christian believers, enabling them to have intimate fellowship with God. In addition, Jesus is involved in sending and imparting the Spirit, so there is a mutually dependent relationship of reciprocity, rather than one of subordination.

immanent and economic relation in the Trinity, one not emphasized by other theologians. For Pannenberg, the ultimate unity between these two comes not in the present, but in the eschaton when the whole series of God's economic workings will finally confirm his immanent nature. This is significant since it moves ultimate confirmation of such claims into the future. And yet, Christ's proleptic resurrection brings that power of the future into present focus, especially for believers. How then, does God reveal himself in time as triune?

Using insights from Athanasius and Hegel's concept of "self-differentiation" to describe the interdependence of trinitarian divine life, Pannenberg argues that by giving oneself to the other, identity is given both to the self and the other. Thus, Jesus is not the Son apart from the Father, nor is the Father the Father apart from the Son, while the Spirit provides the infinite bond of unifying love within the intertrinitarian life of the Godhead.

The Father loves and sustains his creation through the Son, who provides the ontological basis and "space" for a free and independent creation through his self-differentiation from the Father. At the same time, the Son's dependence upon the Father is the basis for creation's dependence upon God—a dependence mediated by the Spirit who renews and gives life to all creation.[38] The Spirit also provides the basis for the immanence of God in creation while he simultaneously ecstatically lifts human beings outside of and beyond themselves toward an eschatological unity with God and one another.

Eschatologically, the Father gives the Son the kingdom, and the Son hands the kingdom back to the Father in the eschaton—making this aspect of God's kingdom essentially trinitarian. In addition, the Spirit mediates the intertrinitarian communal life, glorifying the Son and the Father together, differentiating himself from both, but also providing the eternal bond between them—the "essence," if you will, of divine communal unity and life. This is why the Bible says God is "love" and God is "spirit." They are aspects of God's infinity standing in opposition to the finite, but also encompassing it since the infinite must encompass everything—even the finite. To embrace such existence requires the Spirit to be the bond of love between the Father and the Son, but also

---

38. This same Son, through his incarnation in Jesus of Nazareth, provides a concrete historical example of what it means to live in filial submission to and dependence upon God the Father and the Holy Spirit.

to possess his own center of action. Therefore, God's essence is both love and spirit. Also linked to God's deity is the concept of dominion. If God does not rule the universe, he cannot really be God. Ultimately, his rule will only be completely manifest in the eschaton. Meanwhile, he is proleptically present through the ministry of the risen Christ and the ecstatic work of the Holy Spirit, who draws all people outside of themselves and toward a unified fellowship with God and each other.

To summarize, "If the trinitarian relations among the Father, Son, and Spirit have the form of mutual self-distinction, they must be understood not merely as different modes of being of the one divine subject but as living realizations of separate centers of consciousness."[39] Thus, Pannenberg rejects a single divine center of consciousness. The three persons self-differentiate uniquely because they are real "separate centers of consciousness."[40] Therefore, God is only God as he is seen in all three persons *together* reciprocally relating to one another in mutual love and fellowship, and these "relations between the persons are constitutive not merely for their distinctions, but also for their deity."[41] What Pannenberg is saying is that the relations do not merely distinguish them from each other, but actually constitute the nature of deity itself in an interpenetrating reciprocity of eternal mutual give and take.

This provides Pannenberg with a new way of conceiving divine essence that is no longer abstract, but inherently relational and concretely demonstrated in time. Thus, "The unity of the essence may be found only in their concrete relations."[42] Since we covered much of Pannenberg's understanding of God's intertrinitarian relations in previous chapters, only a quick summary is provided here. What is more interesting, especially in view of the doctrine of *tawhīd*, is the way Pannenberg develops and describes the absolute oneness and unity of God, a task to which we now turn.

---

39. *ST* 1:319.

40. Because of the qualitative gap between human thought and action, we can only speak metaphorically about God in such ways, but there is still truth to be discerned within the metaphor.

41. *ST* 1:323.

42. *ST* 1:335.

God as One in Three: Essential Unity in Relational Diversity

Reviewing the biblical and historical materials, Pannenberg observes that although the New Testament describes the interactions of Father, Son, and Holy Spirit, it does "not clarify the interrelations of the three."[43] Thus, "If it is clear that there are both distinctions and relations among Father, Son, and Spirit, the question is all the more pressing how to harmonize these with the monotheistic character of the biblical belief in God and the tradition of philosophical theology."[44] In short, if God has revealed himself to be three *and* one, how can he intelligibly be both simultaneously?[45]

For Pannenberg, just as the triunity of God is manifest in the intertrinitarian relations, so too is the essential unity. Thus, "The trinitarian persons . . . are simply manifestations and forms—eternal forms—of the one divine essence."[46] Identity is granted in the Godhead through self-differentiation *and* mutual dependence. The triune persons eternally depend upon each other for their distinctive identity, and this is demonstrated through interrelational *love*. Therefore, God is love and this love flows out from their intertrinitarian relations. It is not love of self, but love of the other as the Father loves the Son, the Son loves the Father, the Spirit loves the Son, and so on. Again, it is reciprocal and mutually giving and empowering for the loved one and the lover, not based on one-sided dependence, but rather *interdependence*. To say God is Spirit is to say "The Spirit is the power of love that lets the other be. This power can thus give existence to creaturely life because it is already at work in the reciprocity of the trinitarian life of God . . ."[47]

---

43. *ST* 1:269.

44. *ST* 1:273.

45. The primary charge Muslims ascribe to the Christian doctrine of the Trinity is that it is contradictory and unintelligible. How can three be one and vice versa? This Islamic accusation is not without warrant, of course. Pannenberg claims traditional and historical attempts to ground God's unity in abstract concepts like mind, rational soul, supreme reason, or unlimited will ultimately produced a plethora of intractable problems and bifurcations in the essence of God. Since this kind of historical review takes us away from our current focus, see, Kärkkäinen, *Trinity*, 19–64, for a succinct look at some of these historical attempts in Christian theology to provide such bases for unity in the triune God.

46. *ST* 1:383.

47. *ST* 1:427.

Succinctly summarizing his understanding of divine unity in the Trinity, Pannenberg says,

> The divine persons, then, are concretions of the divine reality as Spirit. They are individual aspects of the dynamic field of the eternal Godhead. This means they do not exist for themselves but in ec-static relation to the overarching field of deity which manifests itself in each of them in their interrelations. . . . [E]ach personality is mediated by the relations to the other two persons. The Son has a share in the eternal deity, and is the Son, only with reference to the Father; the Father has his identity as the Father, and is (Father) God, only with reference to the Son; the Father and Son have their unity, and therefore their divine essence, only through their relation to the Spirit; and the Spirit is a distinct hypostasis only by his relation to the distinction and fellowship of the Father and the Son in their differentiation. For the Spirit has full personal independence, not as proceeding from the Father, as radiating from his divine essence, but only in his distinction from the Father and the Son in their differentiation.[48]

Thus, "divine love constitutes the concrete unity of the divine life in the distinction of its personal manifestations and relations. The personal distinctions . . . cannot be derived from an abstract concept of love. We may know them only in the historical revelation of God in Jesus Christ."[49]

How, then, can we show God is truly unified and not a loose collection of eternal attributes/essences? Infinite love encompasses all, but maintains transcendence in the Godhead through the eternal self-differentiation of the three persons of the triune God. Still, this kind of divine love is ultimately eschatological and eternal in nature. Thus,

> Only with the consummation of the world in the kingdom of God does God's love reach its goal and the doctrine of God reach its conclusion. Only then do we fully know God as the true Infinite who is not merely opposed by the world of the finite, and thus himself finite. To this extent, Christian dogmatics in every part is the doctrine of God. Even the question of God's reality, of his existence in view of his debatability in the world . . .

---

48. *ST* 1:430.
49. *ST* 1:432.

can find an answer only in the event of the eschatological world renewal if God is viewed as love and therefore as true Infinite.[50]

To summarize, the notion that God is love is not grounded in a single unitary subject, but in the intertrinitarian relations of the Godhead. And this love is the essence of God's unity. It overflows from the Trinity into creation as God expresses this love through his unfolding purposes and plans for humanity. Thus, Pannenberg makes love a correlate of infinity, grounding the oneness of God in the harmonious and constitutive fellowship of the three persons of the Godhead. These relations are inherently *reciprocal* and therefore the deity of all three divine persons depends *mutually* upon the activities and relations of the others. Thus, Jesus and the Spirit are not dependent upon the Father for their divinity any more or less than the Father depends upon them for his.

Explanatory Power and Some Theological Implications of the Doctrine of God[51]

When considering the Islamic/*tawhīdian* and Christian/trinitarian understandings of God, several practical implications result. And while it is impossible to cover these comprehensively, some observations are warranted, beginning with unity and differentiation in God.

Unity and Differentiation in God

Joseph Cumming's work regarding Mu'tazilite and Ash'arite understandings of God's attributes has already been briefly examined, but even within the Qur'an and *hadith* there are references to the Spirit (*rūh*) and especially Jesus (*'Īsā*) that suggest avenues for future dialogue about divine differentiation and triunity. Jesus, for example, is considered one of the five (or possibly six if Adam is included) *ulu'l-'Azm*, or prophets of

---

50. *ST* 1:447–48.

51. Whole books have been written on the topics that are included in the subsequent section. Thus, what follows is exceptionally cursory and only intended to raise awareness of just a few of the ways trinitarian theology (versus strict transcendent monist theology) can impact and be applied to one's view of God, humanity, and the world.

special rank.[52] Besides "prophet," Jesus is given other remarkable titles in the Qur'an, including "Messiah" (*Al-Masīh*, used eleven times),[53] the word (*kalima*) of God,[54] and an apostle or messenger (*rasūl*) of God.[55] Jesus is also closely linked in the Qur'an with the work of God's Spirit (*rūh*),[56] and in one passage he is called a spirit (*rūh*) from God.[57] From the *hadith*, or prophetic tradition, a letter Muhammad supposedly sent to Negus of Abyssinia says, "I bear witness that Jesus son of Mary is the spirit of God and his word which he cast to Mary the virgin." Thus, some Muslim writers have called Jesus "the Spirit" or "Spirit of God."[58]

For each of these titles, contemporary Muslims are clear: given God's unitary nature (*tawhīd*), such ascriptions cannot and *must* not refer to any sort of divine essence in Jesus. They refer to his status as an honored prophet, righteous man, and important spokesman for God, but nothing more. Thus, while Jesus is "The Messiah . . . , the son of Mary, . . . a messenger of God, and His word . . . and a revelation [or spirit—Arabic, *rūh*] from Him, . . . you shall not say, 'Three!' God is only one God. Be He glorified; He is much too glorious to have a son" (Q. 4:171). More remarkably, according to the Qur'an, God asks Jesus about the matter point blank in Q. 5:116 and following: "And when God said: 'Jesus, son of Mary, did you tell mankind: Take me and my mother as two gods beside God?' Jesus said: 'Glory be to you! It cannot be that

---

52. Geisler and Saleeb, *Answering Islam*, 54.

53. As Parrinder (*Jesus*, 34–35) notes, there is another term used of Jesus three times in the Qur'an that is closely related to Messiah, namely "servant" (*'abd*). It seems to be related to the humanity of Jesus as well as his submission to God's will. For a full list of the eleven times Jesus is called Messiah in the Qur'an, see ibid., 30.

54. Q. 4:171.

55. Q. 4:156–57. There are several other titles ascribed to Jesus that will not be pursued here. For a list of them see Parrinder, *Jesus*, 51–54.

56. For example, Q. 2:87.

57. Q. 4:171. Interestingly, Khalifa translates this phrase as "*revelation* from God" rather than "*spirit* from God." Unfortunately, he fails to clarify or give reasons why he made this translational choice.

58. Parrinder, *Jesus*, 50. Concerning these titles, special care must be given to the *Muslim* meaning ascribed to them. As Geisler and Saleeb (*Answering Islam*, 61) wisely warn, "Many Christian writers have tried to read too much into these passages in their attempts to prove certain biblical doctrines from the text of the Qur'an." Thus, Christians still need to let Islamic theology *speak for itself* and not automatically pour specifically Christian understandings into the things that are said in the Qur'an (and the *hadith*).

Applying Principles of Interfaith Dialogue

I would say that which is not mine by right. Had I said it, You would have known it. You know what is in my soul, but I know not what is in Yours.'"[59]

Although more could be said about Jesus and God's Spirit in the Qur'an, the primary point is that Islamic rejection of any possible plurality in God may be misplaced—even based on their own sacred writings. A detailed study of the Qur'an and the *hadith* should be undertaken to discover ways they talk about Jesus and God's Spirit to show how these parallel with and differ from Christian theology.[60]

In addition, the way Muslims understand the term "Son" in reference to Jesus needs significant clarification. Most Christians know the idea of Jesus being God's Son is potentially confusing. The most common way to clarify this confusion is to argue that Christians refer to Jesus as God's Son *metaphorically*. Thus, Christians do not understand the divine sonship of Jesus in the ways Islam accuses it of. For example, the word "son" in Arabic is potentially misleading. When Christians speak of "Father" and "Son" in the Godhead, they are not using terms of procreation and progeny. What the Qur'an condemns first and foremost is this: that God the Father literally procreated with a semi-divine Mary, producing a divine offspring, Jesus, who therefore was "God's son." This is emphatically *not* what Christians claim about Jesus' sonship. Rather, Christians understand the concepts of Father and Son in the Trinity as metaphorical in a very important sense. As Tennent states, "In Christianity, the terms *father* and *son* refer to a spiritual, not a physical, relationship. The ideal father is related to his son through love, tenderness, and communion, and it is these relational qualities that the words convey."[61]

---

59. This translation is quoted in Khalidi, *Muslim Jesus*, 13. Notice the accusation includes the call to worship *Mary* (and not only Jesus) as a God.

60. There are many works on the subject of Jesus in the Qur'an and the *hadith*, but far fewer on the subject of God's Spirit in Islam and possible parallels with Christian (and Jewish) theology.

61. Tennent, *Religious Roundtable*, 157. Perhaps some of this confusion arose due to certain linguistic misappropriations early on in the history of Islam. There are two important words for "son" in Arabic. The first, *walad*, means a son (or more generally, a child) who is the product of the physical union between a man and a woman. It very well may be that in early Islamic theology this semantically limited term was wrongly, perhaps unwittingly, applied to the concept of Jesus' divine sonship. There is a second term in Arabic, *ibn*, which is used to denote a literal son as well, but it can also be

Beyond specifically trinitarian questions of God's nature as Father, Son, and Holy Spirit, much has been made of God's ninety-nine beautiful names. As much as Muslims try to deny any hint of essential divine attribution in these names, I am not convinced these denials can be maintained without emasculating their theological beauty and significance. How do Muslims even know at the start that God is utterly transcendent and one? Without a coherent concept of revelation and the relationship of the transmitter to the receiver(s), more theological problems are created than solved. For example, if God revealed himself to Muhammad, did he not reveal something of himself in his inner being? Was not some divine differentiation made known in the sacred writings of Islam? Was God not personally involved in breaking through the barriers of transcendence to be somehow immanent to humanity? Islamic discomfort with divine incarnation seems to be a direct result of their refusal to entertain the idea that God not only created this universe to be other than himself, but that he also created it in order to be intimately involved with it. In Christianity, because God is creation's source and sustainer, his gracious entrance into it "is no alien thing,"[62] even if aspects remain profoundly mysterious for our limited comprehension.

Thus, the contemporary Islamic notion of *tawhīd* is probably more of a polemic against polytheism and Christianity's concept of God than a requirement of the Qur'an. Nor is the way the doctrine of God's oneness as it is currently taught in most Muslim circles consistent with how the Qur'an speaks about and depicts God's character. This represents an irresponsibility on the part of Muslim scholars and teachers, and a failure of Christians to understand and explain the Trinity clearly. Consequently, Muslims are consistently taught a caricature of the Trinity

---

used *metaphorically*. For example, Muslims often describe a traveler as a "son of the road," or *ibnussabil*. Obviously, there is no literal or genealogical connection here. It is a metaphorical way of communicating a certain type of relationship between the person and the road. In a similar way, no matter how the relationship is metaphorically described by various Christian theologians, the Father-Son relationship in the triune Godhead is illustrative of the unique and intimate relationship they continually enjoy with each other and with the Holy Spirit. Furthermore, Tennent (*Religious Roundtable*, 157) and Geisler and Saleeb (*Answering Islam*, 243) both note that the semantic range for "father" and "son" in Arabic is narrower than many other languages (including English) that tend to use these terms in more freely metaphorical ways.

62. *ST* 2:386.

Applying Principles of Interfaith Dialogue

that hardly resembles the Christian understanding, and this requires more dialogue concerning God's nature in Islam and Christianity. At minimum, Muslims should stop accusing Christianity of tritheism and recognize that when the Qur'an speaks about the Trinity, much of what it rejects is *not* a Christian understanding of God's triunity.[63]

With reference to unity and differentiation in God, Sachedina's desire to create social and political space for religious belief and practice by means of supporting arguments from the Qur'an itself is heartening. This movement away from theological and ethical monism toward a vision of religious plurality in unity is an encouraging development, for it not only opens up ways for Muslims (and others) to examine the doctrine of God in ways that have been obscured and neglected in Islamic theology for too long, it also challenges Christians to explain more thoughtfully their trinitarian understandings of God. In fact, for Sachedina, one of the bases for providing sacred space for the other is the recognition that God ordains and delights in otherness and praxiological competition. Thus, God's oneness does not require the corollary presupposition that human societies must also reflect monolithic oneness by eliminating all difference. Creational examples of diversity and unity molded together to form an integrated system of exchange and reception abound.

Similarly, Christians must be challenged by the Islamic emphasis upon God's absolute (but not necessarily undifferentiated) unity. Some recent social trinitarian doctrines do border on tritheism.[64] Although

---

63. I am not suggesting the Qur'an is pro-trinitarian in its theology. However, I am saying it often rejects concepts that may have been ascribed to Christian teachings on the Trinity (like the worship of Mary, for example), but were actually *distortions and misunderstandings* of that doctrine. To be sure, to find full support for the idea of a triune God, Muslims have to (re)examine New Testament sources of divine revelation, although there are hints of this doctrine to be found in the Old Testament witness as well. For a look at some of these Old Testament trinitarian soundings, see Kärkkäinen, *Trinity*, 3–7.

64. Perhaps the most notable example of this borderline tritheistic treatment of the triune God is found in Moltmann, who is consistently subjected to this criticism—and not without reason. For a look at his views of the Trinity, see especially his *Trinity and the Kingdom*. Concerns about the issue of *perichoresis* (interpenetration) and unity in God are perhaps the most frequently raised with respect to Moltmann's trinitarianism—so much so that according to Kärkkäinen (*Trinity*, 117) "The most that can be said about the unity of the Triune God in Moltmann's theology is that he has not successfully satisfied even the most moderate critics."

far from being tritheistic, Pannenberg's relational essentialism in God has been seen by some as such.[65] In our attempts to describe God's trinitarian relations, the commitment to monotheism must not be abandoned for some incoherent notion that borders on affirming there are three Gods and yet somehow only one God—a charge Muslims sometimes raise against Christianity.

Muslims must also reconsider the historical materials driving Christians to trinitarian formulations of God's divine nature, especially landmark events like Jesus' resurrection. If not a mythical event, then its miraculous nature screams for an adequate explanation. If we have access to history, we must deal with all of it, not just certain faith traditions' selective interpretations of it. We also need to recognize ways various faiths have historically interacted with and impacted one another. How has this influenced their beliefs and practices—for better and for worse? How did reactions from these encounters obscure rather than reveal truth, as in the polemical responses of Islam to Christianity (and vise versa), for example? If the doctrine of God's oneness is pressed into a philosophical abstraction, the idea of God being at work in human history becomes equally abstract and disconnected from everyday existence. Instead, "the [Christian] doctrine of the Trinity is in fact concrete monotheism in contrast to notions of an abstract transcendence of the one God . . . that leave no place for plurality."[66]

Ultimately, the Trinity opens up ways for explaining many things concerning creation, human nature, and the nature of social communities that Muslim theology remains hard-pressed to understand and account for. In addition, if God really is triune, I would suggest other religious conceptions of God are, to some extent, inherently impoverished since they deny, ignore, and/or miss(interpret) God's ongoing triune work in time. This loss is not merely a present deficit, but includes impending warning and eschatological judgment. If Jesus is to judge the nations, then denying his divine power and wisdom to accomplish

---

65. For example, Blocher ("Immanence and Transcendence," 107) explicitly claims, "The trend toward 'social' views of the Trinity looks dangerously unaware of the gravity of tritheism: assigning to the Three a generic or corporate unity equals tritheism, it *is* tritheism!" This is not a claim directed against Pannenberg in particular, but rather toward all who would suggest a relational essence in God versus a more abstract and monistic one. The legitimacy of categorizing *all* social views of the Trinity as tritheistic remains debatable, of course.

66. *ST* 1:335–36.

this is tantamount to missing a critical aspect of God's character and plan.

I am not suggesting other religions are completely impoverished in their knowledge and understanding of God, who reveals himself in all creation, of course. In fact, it is possible some religious persons (especially within Abrahamic faiths like Muslims and Jews—with their emphasis on the power and justice of God) have more deeply developed conceptions of God than some Christians. This is especially likely since Christians often do not adequately understand or appreciate the doctrine of the Trinity, and consequently have superficially nominal conceptions of God's character and purposes. Ultimately, Pannenberg notes, God's self-revelation is not unequivocal. Some ambiguity remains since all of the provisional parts are not yet known in the context of the completed and comprehensive whole. Christians have proleptic access to the whole of history through the resurrected Christ and the ecstatic work of the Holy Spirit who brings the eschatological future into the provisional present. Yet, finitude and sin ensure Christians are still sometimes shortsighted and confused about the meaning of events today and yesterday. Along the way, the realization we might be in error drives us to dialogue and explore. Living under sin's curse in a world that has not yet reached history's culmination means that when it is pursued with humility and grace, honest interfaith dialogue is one pathway to understanding more clearly the fullness of God as he makes himself known through time. However, to say we know only a little about God's infinite purposes and character is not to say we know nothing. That would deny God's gracious and revelatory nature. Christians do know about God and are able to approach, however provisionally, a real understanding of his person and plans as they embrace the fullness of revelation given through Jesus Christ.

God and the Nature of Creation[67]

It was earlier suggested that if God is triune, his creation should reflect diversity in unity in several ways, some of which bear mentioning here.

---

67. I am not speaking here about natural theology, but a theology of nature that examines how creation reflects and reveals the glory and majesty of its triune Maker.

First, the Trinity provides a resource for understanding the dynamism and energies within creation. If God's essence is dynamically relational, the various energies and force fields found in creation are to be expected and are *natural*, so to speak. They flow from the powerfully free creativity of God's own being.[68] Thus, static and changeless theological conceptions of God based in Greek philosophical notions of being never found a comfortable home in biblical depictions of a dynamically relational and integrally involved God who cares for, interacts with, and responds to his creation.[69]

A second area where trinitarian theology aids us concerns the philosophical problem of the one and the many in creation. Why is the universe a fine-tuned unified whole that simultaneously displays an astounding array of creativity and diversity? Why is there so much difference in creation, and yet at the same time, an unmistakable underlying unity and interdependence? Even cursory glances at the magnificently diverse nature of creation and humanity's stark otherness from God, exemplifies his love of *otherness and difference*. It is built into the fabric of the universe. It appears God puts it there not only for us to marvel at and enjoy, but to learn from and appreciate as a revelation of his comprehensive wisdom and magnificence. Only a monistic God would create worlds where everything exhibited the same shape, size, texture, taste, smell, color, composition, and consistency. And yet, amazingly, this astonishing diversity is not unbounded, disconnected, atomistic, or incomprehensible.[70] For all of its multiplicity, it still displays an inte-

---

68. This concept of divine dynamism is one reason why Pannenberg can link and compare the activity of the Holy Spirit to the contemporary scientific concept of "force field." The Spirit is not the force field itself, but is manifest in a way that is similar to force field operations. For a look at this idea, see *ST* 2:82ff.

69. In a related vein, Gunton ("Relation and Relativity") notes that although personal human freedom flows directly from God's being, the principles of indeterminacy and contingency in non-personal creation may also flow from God's being as a creative force in nature. He puts it this way on p. 105: "The world is such that inherent contingencies within its structure mean that minor alterations of initial conditions rule out the possibility of certain prediction. There is chaos but stability . . . , contingence but reliability. . . . The universe is not only contingent—free in its own way; but contingency operates so as to be creative."

70. Of course, this unity is not perfectly discernible, nor is it unambiguous, especially in light of the effects of the fall upon creation. Perfect harmony and unity were disrupted and obscured as a result. Pannenberg (*ST* 2:171) notes that evil comes from "the refusal to accept one's own finitude, and in the related illusion of being like God

Applying Principles of Interfaith Dialogue

grated rationality and unity that enables (for example) scientific investigation. In Gunton's words, "Science could not come to be until it came to be believed that the structure of material reality . . . was intelligible in its contingent relations."[71] Without an understanding of a God who is unequivocally one and yet also three (plural), what explanatory sense can be made of a world and a universe such as ours? Contemporary Islam faces this same challenge, but without the same resources of unified otherness in God so evidently present in trinitarian theology.

In addition, how can we speak of independence and freedom in creation[72] while affirming creation's finitude, limitations, and utter dependence upon God? In Pannenberg's trinitarian formulation, Jesus' self-distinction from the Father "forms a starting point for the otherness and independence of creaturely existence,"[73] and generates the multiplicity of creatures who are themselves distinct from one another. The Spirit simultaneously provides "the link and movement that connects the creatures to one another and to God."[74] He successfully unifies the immanence of God in creation with the transcendence of God in his being. Eschatologically, he also enables God's future to enter into the provisional present as "the possibility field of the future," "a kind of inkling of eternity" that protects all creatures, who are subject to entropy from "the tendency to disintegrate that follows from their independence."[75] Consequently, eschatology is intimately related to creation because only in the eschaton will creaturely existence finally reach its goal of full fellowship with and participation in the life of God.

(Gen. 3:5)." Thus, independence rather than ontological limitation (finitude) becomes the real basis for the possibility of evil. By attempting to remove themselves from God's life-giving presence (that is, by trying to be *independent*), human beings subject themselves (and according to biblical theology, the rest of creation as well) to entropy, evil, suffering, and death. Thus, the human tendency to move away from unity and integration and toward unbridled absolute independence is a result of sin and creates disunity, disharmony, and dissimilation in the self, others, and creation in general.

71. Gunton, "Theology of Nature," 99.

72. Gunton (ibid., 102) describes this creational independence as having its own "intrinsic rationality," and goes on to argue that this kind of independence is actually a reflection of God's independent nature. In this way, "the world reveals its maker not because it is continuous with God, but because it is distinct, different even."

73. *ST* 2:22.

74. *ST* 2:84.

75. *ST* 2:102.

Meanwhile, the whole Trinity is always present and at work in creation's continued sustenance and unfolding direction. This is true even when those within creation are unaware or even in open rebellion against this creative, sustaining, and sovereign activity of God.

In conclusion, I do not think Islam has thought deeply enough about this problem of the many and the one. How is it that we find ourselves in a uni-verse? Why is there so much variation and difference and yet interdependence and mutual relation in creation and with one another? In addition, how can creaturely freedom and independence be reconciled with utter dependence and finitude? Islam's doctrines of *tawhīd* and transcendence must be better able to account for this observed creational reality. In contrast, God's relationality, far from jeopardizing his unity, helps us make better sense of ourselves and creation. We sense an interrelation between us and the rest of creation, but we also are keenly aware of our independent differences from the other. We reflect God's image not only morally, but also ontologically. And this creational imprint is stamped upon all that proceeds from God who is the ground and ongoing source of all existence. In short, "The world reveals the hand that made it in the remarkable combination of unity and diversity, of relationality and particularity . . . , marks that can be recognized by their analogy to the unity and diversity of the triune God."[76] Only the trinitarian God adequately supplies the ontological space for variety and freedom in creation as well as a sensible basis for its dependence and unity. Further, because human beings are made in God's image, our constitutional nature may be the best place to see trinitarian structures in creation. Thus, it is to this subject we now turn.

God and the Nature of Humanity and Society

While human beings are made in God's likeness and image, there is still an impassable gap between the infinite and unlimited Lord and Creator of all and humanity. And yet, God's transcendence from us as Creator does not prevent his immanent care for us. Nor does it hinder his ability to enter, through Christ's incarnation, into our finitude and weakness, since his infinity and omnipotence encompass all creaturely frailty and finitude.

---

76. Gunton, "Theology of Nature," 103.

Primary to the way human beings reflect God's nature is the issue of relationality. For Pannenberg, love is the essence of God (1 John 4:8). That love is grounded in the intertrinitarian relations between Father, Son, and Holy Spirit since genuine love is not possible apart from some sense of personal otherness. Without this, love could not be present within God until after creation appears. And yet, love itself forms the motivation for the trinitarian God to actualize creatureliness, since it spills out into all creation from the intertrinitarian life through the sovereign Lordship of the Father, the self-differentiation of the Son, and the unifying, life-giving action of the Spirit. Love, by its very nature, is freely given and freely received. This intertrinitarian relation was especially revealed in the concrete life of Jesus and his relation to the Father and the Spirit. Thus, "If the incarnate Son's life is to be understood in terms of His free relation to the Father, it would seem to follow that there is in the divine eternity a freedom corresponding to it . . . , [something that] can only be called freedom in the relations of eternal Father, Son and Spirit."[77]

This divine love and freedom also manifests itself in human life and society since human beings are created in God's image. The ability to love freely is a manifestation of God's own relational nature. As well, this aspect of relation is constitutive of personhood. Without love, we are not merely undefined, we are also unable to exist as complete persons. Humanity's social and communal nature is essential to identity, health, and growth. We must be in society as both a "self" and as an "other" before other selves. Otherness, then, is integral to personhood, especially concerning other persons.[78] In these interrelations, the values of embrace, distinction, tolerance, understanding, peace, love, and

---

77. Gunton, "Relation and Relativity," 99.

78. This is precisely why in Gen 2:1–25 Adam's relations to the created order through the tending of the garden and the naming of the animals was not a sufficient condition for truly human relationship. He was still "alone" and his solitude was "not good." Eve becomes the fulfillment of an otherness that uniquely meets the need for human relation to another human being and to God. In addition, it is no coincidence that Eve's humanness still reflects difference in that she was a *woman* rather than a carbon copy of the man, Adam. The two become unified and "one" (Gen 2:24) in a complementary fashion that could not be expressed through a strict equality of identity. Thus, from the beginning of human creation we see the same complementary unity in difference reflected in the creativity of a triune God, who says in Gen 1:26, "Let *us* create human beings in *our* image."

fellowship are all expressed to create communities that harmoniously reflect dynamic freedom and uniqueness integrated with an awareness of mutual dependence and inherent interconnectedness.

From human history, a consistent social temptation is to create peace by eliminating otherness through exile, coercion, or destruction, or by walling off people into self-contained separate societies or tribes. Against this, the Trinity suggests a model for harmonious and peaceful plurality that lovingly exists through the free embrace of the creative and significant other, an embrace that gives ontological definition to both the self and the other *simultaneously and necessarily*. And this gift of identity comes not merely from relationship with other human beings, but foundationally through our creational relationship with a loving personal God alongside our basic need for intimate relationship with the One who exists in eternal dynamic relationship. It can be argued this existential longing for intimate relationship is the universal ecstatic work of the Spirit drawing humanity beyond itself and into unifying fellowship with God and others. Thus, human religiosity becomes the concrete expression of the interpersonal human search for intimate fellowship with the triune God.

Due to this need and longing for intimacy with a personal God, it is no accident that a sustained mystical Sūfī movement arose within Islam. I believe this movement is an inevitable existential response to Islam's tendency to depersonalize God by overemphasizing his transcendence and otherness. Sufism transforms the doctrine of *tawhīd* into a radical life goal where God's absolute transcendent oneness is understood as encompassing unity with human creatures and all creation.[79] This unity overcomes in a limited way the infinite qualitative distinction between God, creation, and humanity. Without a deeper and more developed concept of immanent relationality between God and humanity, Islam cannot provide a satisfactory explanation for the unquenchable longing for an experiential encounter with the living God.

---

79. For a brief exploration of the potentially trinitarian nature of mystical Sūfī experiences, see Poupin, "Trinitarian Experience in Sufism?" Poupin reminds us there is such an experience, but "it is only a possible *experience* of a trinitarian type. . . . [It] is not a way of conceiving what could be a close experience of the economical aspect of the trinitarian life, manifested most precisely in the cross" (p. 86–87). Thus, we should be careful not to add Christian meaning to Sūfī mystical thought and practice that they themselves would not affirm.

Disillusionment with a distant God is inevitable given that we are made in the triune God's image. Christianity's concept of God better explains the human longing for personal connection with the divine and one another. The infinitely relational Father God loves us, and grants us limited independence through the Son's self-differentiation. God also draws all people proleptically and ecstatically by the Spirit's power away from unhealthy independence and toward an interdependent, unified, and universal fellowship with him and one another.

This relational understanding of God and humanity has ramifications not only for the sociability of human societies. It also explains the human need for variety and otherness in interpersonal relationships. Such relationships provide a healthy sense of identity as well as opportunities to love and influence others freely for the good. As individuals, we are integrated selves, and yet, we are not identical or indistinguishable from others upon whom we depend and are interdependent with. Thus, to be genuinely human, we *need* ongoing interaction with and connection to God and others. This has obvious implications for interfaith dialogue, our concluding topic.

God and the Nature of Interfaith Dialogue[80]

If God is triune and essentially relational, with clear roles and distinctions in the Godhead, it is not that surprising human existence is characterized by structured social relationships.[81] These relationships provide identity and opportunities to love and be loved—by God and others. Consequently, no person can exist for, by, or within him- or herself. But even more so, the trinitarian nature and economy of God

---

80. As a brief but important caveat, some mention needs to be made here concerning the idea of using the categorical and more generic concept of God. According to Pannenberg, as Christians we have to talk about God as he reveals himself to us through salvation history (what God says to us about himself), but we also need to refer to and retain the wider idea of God (of which the Christian God is a type). Only in this way can we avoid "subjectivizing" the God of Christianity and making it irrelevant to the world around us. By connecting Christianity's God with the more general category of God discussed in philosophy, we are able to connect the generic concept of God with the particular God of Christianity in a more universal way and expand the boundaries of our concerns and interests.

81. Pannenberg makes this connection explicitly in *Anthropology in Theological Perspective*, 531–32.

lays the groundwork in dialogue for pursing particular aspects of God's revelation in time and space (especially through Jesus) alongside more universal aspects of God's sustaining and wooing work in all of creation (especially through the Spirit). Dialogue is the discovery of God's universality as well as the particularities of other human selves. Otherness is inherent to the process. We discuss to understand God, ourselves, others, and creation as a whole so that we can better see commonality as well as difference. And while dissimilarity between the self and others can sometimes lead to violence, it need not do so. Thus, recognizing differences "is not the equivalent of promoting discord. It is a way of taking other people seriously."[82] In addition, acknowledging distinction is not a license to "subsume but *submit* to the Other insofar as we must be willing to put our beliefs to critical tests. We must remember that our theological formulations are always provisional."[83]

This provisionality is especially true with God since he is utterly inexhaustible in his being. Thus, his infinity lends itself supremely to constant and unending exploration—at least until the eschaton. But even then, an infinite God is deeper than finite creatures can ever plumb the depths of. Thus, we will likely spend eternity in perfect fellowship with God, exploring the inexhaustible richness of his infinite being. Therefore, dialogue about God is based directly upon his infinite nature over and against our unsurpassable finitude.

One final aspect of God's trinitarian nature relating to interfaith dialogue bears mentioning, namely Jesus' incarnation, and the particular way divine revelation is given in space and time. I am speaking here of the concept of *translation* developed by Andrew Walls in his book *The Missionary Movement in Christian History*. The ways successful religious traditions grow and change, and yet remain identifiable through the process of cultural expression and translation over time, have already been described. Critically necessary to this process are the resources available within these traditions. Sacred authoritative texts and the writings and lifestyles of certain individuals within those traditions become sources of translatable material. Through the long process of translation, these traditional truth claims become reenlivened and reconsidered again and again. First and foremost, God translates not

---

82. DiNoia, *Diversity of Religions*, 169.
83. Vanhoozer, "Does the Trinity Belong?," 68.

only his truth, but himself into concrete historical moments, especially through the ministry of Jesus. Walls identifies this process as divine translation. In Jesus, divinity is "translated" into humanity and the word of God or *logos* becomes flesh and blood (John 1:14). In the ongoing process of translating the gospel into the vernaculars of all peoples and cultures, the truth of God is once again revealed to those who have not yet considered or become aware of it. Thus, translation is also revelatory, bringing the truth of God to the multifaceted world of others.[84]

One of the beautiful aspects of translation is that it incorporates the complex and intricately woven facets of God's self-disclosure to the world. Translation involves languages—those from which the message comes as well as those into which the translation is encoded. It also involves concrete instances of time. Through God's disclosure, the word is sent forth, deciphered, and applied, and so the power of the word at home in the world is incarnated, not mythically or poetically so much as literally and concretely. Thus, history becomes *his* story and it realizes the character and purposes of God in the world through time. All three persons of the triune God were actively involved in the particularity of Christ's incarnation, but they continue to work in the particularities of transformed history as it flows away from that alpha *and* omega point. Thus, the life, death, resurrection, and ascension of Christ mark particular moments in time, but they also mark points of embarkation that draw us toward God's eschatological culmination. It does not end with the cross—nor does it start there. But everything after the cross necessarily flows away from it through the ongoing architecture of God the Father, alongside the mediating work of Jesus Christ the living Word, and the translating and enlivening activity of the Holy Spirit, speaking and realizing that living Word into new and changing moments of human history. It is this activity of translating the living Word of God spoken forth by the Holy Spirit into the particular settings of human culture and existence that gives dialogue its perpetual livelihood. Incarnating this Word requires the never-ending task of translation into new tongues, new situations, and new moments in time, giving life to the process of dialogue. Thus, dialogue is not merely the simple restating of old truths (although it includes this), it is also the activity of reinterpreting, reenvisioning, reenlivening, recapitulating, and rein-

---

84. For a closer look at Walls' thesis, see *Missionary Movement*, esp. 26–42.

carnating the ever-expanding and all-encompassing truth of the living, revealing, and triune God.[85]

Summary and Conclusion

We have covered much ground in this chapter, examining the Muslim and Christian concepts of God's nature and how they influence our notions of creation, humanity, society, and interreligious dialogue itself.

---

85. In light of the Islamic emphasis upon the otherness of God, it is not surprising Muslims take a very negative stance toward the idea of divine immanence and incarnation. It is also understandable why Islam officially states God's word revealed in the Qur'an is only perfectly such when it remains in the original Arabic in which it was given by God. For Muslims, translations are only *interpretations*, but cannot be *responsible reproductions* of the word of God in other tongues. In addition, the concept of divine otherness is increasingly reinforced as the distance between the period of Qur'anic composition and the contemporary era grows ever greater. Thus, while this decision to discourage Qur'anic translation might not be directly related to the Muslim concept of an utterly transcendent God, it certain is reinforced by that theological understanding. In contrast, I would argue that this decision to keep its sacred texts almost solely in the original language seriously impoverishes Islam's ability to responsibly, adequately, and accurately instantiate itself within cultures and languages and peoples who are very distant from the original people, language, and culture of the Qur'an. Not only this, it prevents them from being more open to new possibilities of divine understanding that invariably arise through the translational process of indigenization and contextualization. God is still at work in the world revealing himself to all humanity, especially through the missional work of his people in the world. The translation of God's revelation in history calls our attention to see more clearly the contiguous ways God is making himself known now, even as he has already made himself know then. To use Ramachandra's words in *Faiths in Conflict?*, 132, we find in Christianity an "endless translatability" of the gospel because it is grounded in an infinite God who has, in time, intentionally incarnated and translated himself into the languages and cultures of human beings. Inevitably, *some* theological translation *must* take place for a religion to spread beyond the borders of its own language, time, and culture. Islam, through its strong sense of mission, has accomplished this, of course, but primarily through a process of oral and praxiological transmission and translation, with all of its attendant and unavoidable difficulties, dangers, and even strengths. Left behind in this process has been the painstaking textual translation of its traditional resources. Its many commentaries and other writings have also served a similar translational purpose. So much more could be said here, but the idea is offered in a cursory way as a potential avenue for further discussion between Christians and Muslims with respect to their notions of God, divine disclosure, the unending temporal process of cultural and linguistic change through time, and how it impacts and alters the beliefs and practices of the various faith traditions as well as the cultures and peoples into which these faith traditions are ultimately translated.

Applying Principles of Interfaith Dialogue

Clearly, there is infinitely more ground yet to be traversed. This seems to be the nature of any honest and ongoing pursuit of truth, goodness, and interfaith relations. It reflects the daunting nature of pursing increasingly comprehensive and coherent conceptions of God and his creation. Given this inherent incompleteness, what specific and practical ways can Christian-Muslim dialogue be pursued today, and what other crucial topics are yet to be explored? It is to these concerns we now turn to conclude this study in chapter 8.

8

Hope against Hope: Potential Progress in the Face of (Seemingly) Intransigent Ideologies

Looking back over the past decades of interfaith dialogue, there is much to celebrate and much to be concerned about. As Charles Kimball puts it, "There is no magic wand to wave or single formula to follow. . . . After half a century of thoughtful interfaith dialogue programs, it is frustrating to realize how much remains to be done at the most basic level."[1] And yet, progress is often made through time, little by little, conversation by conversation. Occasionally groundbreaking paradigm shifts occur, but more frequently development is gradual and almost imperceptible.

I begin this chapter by summarizing the significance and value of Christian-Muslim dialogue in view of Sachedinian and Pannenbergian resources. I then give recommendations for the future of such dialogue, before concluding with suggested subjects for further investigation and interaction.

---

1. Kimball, "More Hopeful Future," 379.

Looking to the Future by Means of the Past and Present: The Significance, Value, and Meaning of Christian-Muslim Dialogue

In genuine dialogue, little can be determined in advance. The more that is decided beforehand, the more artificial, monolithic, and uninteresting dialogues tend to become. Thus, beyond the commitment to talk honestly and openly about one's religious convictions in a respectful and nonviolent manner, little can be preprogrammed. This is exactly Pannenberg's point concerning true dialogue's open-ended and genuinely historical nature. It has no definitive predetermined agenda or outcome. In the contested seams of dialogue—places pluralists might least expect truth to emerge—the most important concepts of right and wrong, truth and falsehood arise. This provides a powerful impetus to stop avoiding disagreements, and spend more time exploring them to find divine truth and goodness.[2] It also requires viewpoints to be creatively and clearly articulated and defended, leading to health and growth for faiths possessing the internal resources that enable them to make increasingly good sense of the world in which we live. However, this explanatory power can only be employed if *all* traditional resources are thoroughly examined together through candid ongoing dialogue.

Sachedina shows that the Qur'anic concept of a God-given universal *fitra* supports the possibility of the presence of divine truth and goodness in those who may not institutionally be Muslims, but who nevertheless reflect God's image through the right exercise of their rationality and morality. The Qur'an also teaches that God ordains plurality and there is no compulsion in religion. Thus, God has a purpose for religious others who possess divine gifts for the building of democratically free, ethical, and plural societies. Consequently, interfaith dialogue is not only part of the Muslim calling to witness, it is also foundational for such communities. Dialogue, far from being a pluralist concern *of* the modern era, is a timelessly *Qur'anic* concern *for* the modern era. This gives dialogue an urgent and even deontological tone since it becomes a matter of fuller obedience to God and a deeper appreciation for his purposes for humankind. Since God has sovereignly designed human religiosity to be without compulsion and ordained that we should compete with and outdo one another in good works,

---

2. Common areas are not lost in this process, but neither are they (over)emphasized to the neglect of contested areas.

dialogue augments the Islamic call to live free moral lives by encouraging that communal and personal example to be defended and lived out openly before all other human societies and faith traditions. In this way, Islamic interfaith dialogue is not only missional, it is *Qur'anic*.

For Christians, dialogue is also part of witnessing to others. From a Pannenbergian viewpoint it matters because until the eschaton, divine revelation is constantly unfolding within the concrete events of space-time history. Only through an ever-increasing knowledge of history in its entirety can we see with greater clarity and comprehensiveness the truth about God and his world. Without this kind of pursuit, our understanding and knowledge of all things divine will be limited by neglect rather than merely by the deterring influences of human finitude and sin. Dialogue, then, is more than witness; it is also an opportunity to mature in our understanding of God and his creation. Without it, Christians might become increasingly ingrown and irrelevant to the purposes and plans God has for creation.

Because revelation is historical, as Christians retell the ancient stories and truths of sacred Scripture we reinstantiate and re-reveal the things of God to each new generation. It is not merely a verbal or orthodox revelation, but also a praxiological one where we demonstrate the character and purposes of God in the body-life of the church in the world. The divine Spirit works in the body to illuminate truth, elucidate meaning, and instantiate goodness wherever and whenever we are. In this sense, Sachedina's historically sensitive reappropriation of Islamic resources for the contemporary context has the potential to reactualize the truths and standards of God present in Islam.

Biblically, all people are created in God's image[3] and can rightly be called his "offspring."[4] Pannenberg notes incurable religiosity is a universal feature of human existence and reveals aspects of God's truth in the existential and transcendental process of searching for it. He grounds this religiosity in a formulation of the image of God that is distinctly *trinitarian*. Thus, the Father, through his love for the Son, who is the mediator of creaturely independence, loves his creation and longs for it to be drawn into fellowship with himself. The Son in turn provides the undeniable sense of otherness and independence in humanity through

3. Gen 1:26–27.
4. Acts 17:28.

his self-differentiation from the Father. And the Spirit, who provides the bond of unity in the Godhead, supplies the universal ecstatic longing in people to be drawn outside of themselves toward relational unity with God and others. In Pannenberg, this constitutional triune relation is not dependent upon one's explicit or implicit religious affiliation. It is true of all and opens up the possibility of discovering insights into God that others—Christians included—might not yet know or be fully aware. Thus, the triune image of God in humanity supports the need for interfaith dialogue as a means of revealing and discovering divine truth.

Beyond this trinitarian framework for interfaith interactions, other resources Christians draw from to support interfaith relations include the fact that the church, by its very nature as the proleptically eschatological people of God, provides the world with a living testimony to the truth and ultimate plans of God. In that sense, it cannot help but be a living witness to the world around it.

As was noted in chapter 2, witness and mission are controversial subjects for Christian-Muslim dialogue. Thus, it must be reiterated that denying Christians (and Muslims) the opportunity to see dialogue as one aspect of witness is to obscure the universal scope of their claims, hindering them from obeying and fulfilling a direct commissional aspect of their faith tradition(s). Nevertheless, dialogue and witness are not strictly equivalent. Because witness primarily involves the declaration of truth claims through word and deed with a view to bringing about conversion and reorientation of another person's life, its purposes are more limited in scope, even if they are universally directed. Dialogue adds elements of listening, learning, receiving from, and cooperating with the other. Thus it is more comprehensive in its scope than witness, although it certainly (and, I would argue, *inevitably, invariably, and inescapably*) includes witness.[5]

One challenge every society faces is how to encourage citizens from different cultural, religious, familial, social, economic, intellectual, and ideological backgrounds to work together toward desirable com-

---

5. Some would argue that witness also includes these aforementioned elements and so is not so very different from dialogue, but dialogue tends to emphasize understanding, appreciation and need for religious others—even when discussing critical points of disagreement. Still, in practice it is difficult to create a strict line of separation between the two. I am not sure that the attempts to do so in order to avoid the problems with witness have been very successful or helpful for the overall process of advancing interreligious dialogue.

mon goals. People who disagree on a host of other issues and practices will come together in a pluralistic society to support causes and ends deemed important enough to lay aside differences. Francis Schaeffer used the term "cobelligerents" to describe alliances between individuals and groups who may fundamentally disagree with one another on certain core issues and truth claims (and so would not normally work together), but are nevertheless able to agree upon and work together in certain ethical arenas of common concern and viewpoint.[6] How, then, can Christians and Muslims come together practically and effectively as cobelligerents in contemporary societies? Sachedina's Qur'anic vision of friendly interfaith "competitions" to outdo one another in good deeds provides a promising impetus for Christians and Muslims to overcome mutual suspicions and hostilities. And *dialogue* is a critical part of that goal. We cannot and will not cooperate with one another if we continue to isolate ourselves and vilify one another using false caricatures and clichéd overgeneralizations about the other.

Ultimately, these resources help move us toward greater appreciation for and understanding of one another. As Sperber reminds us concerning some of the standoffs between Christians and Muslims, perhaps "real rapprochement is not to be expected. In such a situation it already means a lot if the one can see the other as he/she sees him/herself from the exchange on the spiritual level."[7] The hope is that at least Christians and Muslims will live respectfully alongside each other without seeking to subjugate or even kill one another—even if we continue to criticize and disagree with each another. But this goal is more than mere survival or a bare minimalist tolerance. Survival without religious liberty is not enough, and neither is a tolerance that allows the presence of religious others but does not support the freedom and flourishing of those others. The goal for which we must strive is a tolerance that pursues an embrace of understanding and cooperation with the other

---

6. To use one of Schaeffer's favorite examples, abortion was one issue where Christians could work together with people of other religions and ideologies, so long as they all agreed that abortion was morally reprehensible and must be discouraged. Other examples of this kind of cobelligerent cooperation in diverse and pluralistic communities include working for proper medical care, development of basic infrastructure, protection through policing and military services, and promotion of commerce (to name only a few), all of which contribute to the betterment of human life, social peace, and overall prosperity.

7. Sperber, *Christians and Muslims*, 99.

in the ongoing concerns of human life—even when we disagree. But in such an embrace, there must always remain genuine space for the presence and identity of the other. Thus, embrace is not consuming or subjugating the other, but acknowledging and affirming the other. It is an embrace that recognizes one another's differences, diversities, limitations, and contributions as we struggle together to live in submission to the Almighty Creator and sovereign Lord. In Volf's words, "for embrace [of the religious other] to take place, more is needed. We need to make space for them in our own identity and in our social world (though how that space will be made remains open for negotiations). We need to let them reshape our identity so as to become part of who we are, yet without in any way threatening or obliterating us but rather helping to establish the rich texture of our identity."[8] Thus, we not only receive, we also offer the enriching potential of goodness and truth to others. And we should have this conviction without apology or shame. As we interact, we both change the other and are changed by the other in a dialectical journey of exchange, incorporation, reorientation, and reinvigoration of the practices and truth claims we hold dear. There is, of course, risk in this process, a risk that may result in the loss or gain of membership, depending on how things go in the contestation over time. But without such risk and opportunity, traditions become stagnant, closed off from the future of new possibilities, and increasingly impoverished in their outlook.

Having shared some of the significance and value of future of Christian-Muslim dialogue, I will now provide some very modest and basic recommendations for expanding and enriching this interfaith conversation.

Some Modest Recommendations for Future Christian-Muslim Dialogues

The process of interfaith dialogue is daunting and never fully complete, at least until the eschatological intervention of God. Nevertheless, real progress can result, and one of the most important dialogical tasks before Muslims and Christians is the production of more thoughtful

---

8. Volf, "Living with the 'Other,'" 17. This article echoes the main themes of his earlier work, *Exclusion and Embrace*.

and widely differentiated theologies of religions, especially from those outside Western contexts. This is not to say projects in the West no longer matter. On the contrary, they also provide important resources for the discussion. However, since few non-Western theologies of religions have been produced, it is my hope that such projects will become increasingly common. This need is especially acute in Islam, although thankfully projects like Sachedina's are becoming more widely known and accepted. We have a beginning, but the undertaking is far from finished. The ultimate goal is a theology of religions that is increasingly all-encompassing in scope while at the same time realizing that it is highly unlikely that any one person, group, or religion will be able to produce a singularly comprehensive theology of religions. Thus, we must consign ourselves to pursue the production of a variety of specialized *theologies* of religions that are universally directed and not sheltered from or ignorant of alternative and broader views. As Netland notes, "Developing a comprehensive theology of religions is an enormous task that will demand collaborative work from specialists in various disciplines."[9]

These theologies provide legitimacy to and impetus for more people to avail themselves to the process of interreligious dialogue and cooperative social ventures. When people see the bases for such endeavors are grounded in their own sacred resources, and as they see their theological, missiological, and social import, they are more likely to prioritize such activities.

In a closely related vein, the *kinds* of theologies of religions need to be more oriented toward encouraging faith traditions to speak and act as they really are, rather than trying to press them into some external pluralistic or inclusivistic mold. In this way, religions can promote and contend for the things that are most precious and important to them—their unique and distinguishing distinctives. Again, from a Pannenbergian perspective, the places where there is contestation and difference are often the loci for the most fruitful, interesting, and progressive dialogues. Thus, more exclusivistic theologies of religions need to be produced and applied in dialogue so that religions will not be afraid to discuss spiritedly and thoroughly contested claims about God, creation, humanity, society—everything imaginable!

Beyond this, opportunities for formal and informal interfaith dialogue need to be more intentionally pursued and supported by both

---

9. Netland, *Encountering*, 313.

faith traditions. It is one thing to affirm the need for such conversations, but quite another to provide the time and logistical support to actualize such exchanges.[10] This often requires a properly supported "point person" in an organization or church to ensure opportunities are regularly created and utilized. Churches, denominations, organizations, and mosques all need to initiate programs that encourage the acceleration of interfaith conversations as well as day-to-day interactions of Christians and Muslims with one another in their places of work, play, rest, and worship. This will improve the art as well as the science of interfaith dialogue. The more we discuss matters of faith, politics, education, law, etc., the better we can become at listening, understanding, articulating, defending, and incorporating the viewpoints of our own faith and others, and the more likely our claims about God and his world will be increasingly comprehensive, coherent, and therefore *true*.

Although currently there is a lot of talk about interreligious dialogue, a related but frequently less-mentioned need is for increasing levels of *intra*religious dialogue. As Sachedina emphasizes, one of the most important aspects of genuine religious belief is freedom of worship. Because some of the worst conflicts and most violent persecutions in history have been intrareligious, it behooves all to reexamine our commitments to interact and discuss matters of faith and practice with those who are different from us and yet still stand within our own faith traditions. For example, evangelicals need to dialogue more with non-evangelical Christians to be challenged by and gain from the insights of these others—and vice versa. In this way, we could all be enriched and challenged in our mutual desire to honor Jesus Christ and be genuinely dialogical with other religious adherents. This kind of unity in diversity provides a model for the outside world to know that we are Christians by the way in which we genuinely love one another.[11]

---

10. For a practical guide to successful interfaith dialogues between Muslims and evangelicals in North America, see McDowell and Zaka, *At the Table*, 220–37.

11. I am not suggesting some sort of emotional, non-doctrinal unity that has no basis in truth. Heresy is alive and well in the churches of the twenty-first century, including those within evangelicalism. However, the tendency to narrow the limits of orthodoxy and orthopraxy are well documented in Christianity. It seems to me that while we can disagree with one another about numerous things, if we affirm the essentials of the Christian faith (that are themselves a matter of intrareligious debate) then there is tremendous room for freedom and variety.

Although a sensitive subject, Muslims and Christians must allow witness and mission to be part of dialogue. These are inevitable elements of dialogue anyway, so pretending we can dialogue without actually bearing witness to and arguing for the truth is not only unnecessary, it is potentially disingenuous. We have already noted that many pluralists and inclusivists have insisted Christians and Muslims affirm the other faith is salvifically sufficient for its members. But this begs a crucial question. As Sachedina observes, part of the joy of religious plurality stems from the Qur'anic command to compete with one another by doing good works. This is inescapably missional and evangelistic, but not necessarily derogatory, violent, or exclusionary. Our witness is not coercive or manipulative. It is open, honest, and persuasive in a way that welcomes as well as challenges the other, and does not always agree with or affirm everything about the other.

Beyond this is a need to recognize our finitude and sinfulness alongside a corresponding need for humility, grace, and forgiveness. This is especially important for those from more exclusivistic perspectives since these tend to be more easily exploited by exclusionary ideologies. We stand within the tension of holding to the truth of our faith while still giving humble recognition that we may have missed aspects of God's comprehensive truth in the world. As Pannenberg reminds us, truth is only fully known when everything is seen from beginning to end. Until the eschaton, our comprehension of comprehensive truth is *provisional*, even if our current limited grasp of it is very likely to be reliable and accurate, so far as we can see. We hold our views with conviction, but not without a willingness to explore alternative ways to explain and comprehend what we have experienced and grasped for ourselves. This is a stance I call "confident humility."

One area that has received little attention until recently is that of education. The so-called problem of plurality" will not go away anytime soon, and the faster we thoughtfully respond to it, the more robust our theology and witness in the world will become. We cannot ignore the challenges, but also opportunities, that plurality affords both Christians and Muslims. One way we can respond is by encouraging a more religiously plural education. Through education, we not only promote understanding, but help reduce stigmas we have toward those who are "strange" and "different" from us. This is not to say such an education must be somehow egalitarian, where all religious faiths are described in some sort of rough parity by some unbiased and neutral outside party (that is likely impossible to provide anyway). Rather, it is an education that is provided by religious insiders who can accurately and passionately explain and live out their respective faith traditions. How exactly this will work is less clear at this point and requires a great deal more thought and consideration, but providing religious caricatures of alternative faiths is not only damaging to the future of interfaith dialogue, it dishonors and distorts the truth.

One final aspect of interfaith dialogue that is often neglected is the historical one. Frequently, adherents of various faith traditions are largely ignorant of their own religious histories, not to mention the histories of other world religions. If Pannenberg is right about our need to seek comprehensiveness in our pursuit of religious truth, then surely a limited knowledge of the contemporary is wholly insufficient in its scope. We need to expand our knowledge of the past so we can better understand what God is doing in the present and see emerging patterns that help us discern the course of the future. As well, we need to debate the reliability and meaning of certain historical texts, accounts, and events, especially those that are faith-defining.

Overall, Christians and Muslims are moving in the right direction in dialogue, but such efforts need to be accelerated and multiplied to provide communities with the resources they need to be ethical, free, peaceful, and plural. This will not be easy. It requires a long-term view and a cooperatively creative mentality, but it will be worth the efforts invested.

Having given these recommendations for future Christian-Muslims dialogue, we will conclude by sharing specific subjects needing more intentional discussion and review.

Areas for Further Interaction

A comprehensive list for further Christian-Muslim dialogical research would be enormous and potentially unending. Thus, what follows is only a selective inventory of what I consider to be some of the most significant and potentially fruitful topics for future interaction, argumentation, and cooperation. It is offered as a subject of dialogue and debate on its own, and little comment will be made on each potential topic.

Contemporary Muslim and Christian Responses to Religious Plurality

To begin, much remains to be outlined and pursued with regard to *the nature of God*, especially areas of parallel thought between Christians and Muslims that have been polemically obscured by a Muslim desire to avoid any identification with Christian ideas about God and Jesus Christ. In addition, there is a need for Christians to provide greater clarification and strengthening of trinitarian terminology, formulations, and analogical supports. This would include looking at concepts surrounding the terms "Father," "Son," and "Spirit" (among many others) as they are applied to God. We must provide better and clearer analogies for communicating the intelligibility, meaning, and significance of God as triune. Christologically, Christians need to continue to share persuasively the biblically reliable depiction of the particularities of the historical life and message of Jesus with Muslims and others without apology or shame. With regard to the Trinity's pneumatological aspects, much more needs to be done in terms of connecting the Holy Spirit with the universal work of God in creation, redemption, and renewal. The Spirit's trinitarian role in other religions still needs much clarification and elaboration.[12] This is especially important concerning Judaism and Islam, since they often mention God's Spirit in their sacred writings and traditional resources. In addition, the trinitarian doctrine of God holds great promise for significant interaction with respect to a number of important aspects of human life and existence, an arena that has only recently begun to be explored and considered. And Christians need to continue to press Muslims to explain their concepts of God and how they might be seen as more viable and coherent.

Because the origin and reliability of sacred scripture in Islam and Christianity is questioned by both religions, an examination of their respective claims to divine derivation, authority, and historical reliability must continue to be discussed and pursued with all its attendant challenges. In a related fashion, the phenomenon of translation needs to be considered more carefully, especially since Islam has spoken against translating the Qur'an into any language other than the original Arabic. Also, it would be good to examine the question of how radical ideologies are able to utilize sacred resources to promote ungodly agendas. This is a hermeneutical question that would need to investigate which

---

12. As was noted earlier in this work, some of this has already been done by Clark Pinnock, Amos Yong, and Veli-Matti Kärkkäinen, but so much more has yet to be considered and explored.

passages in particular lend themselves to violent misinterpretations and misappropriations and how they can be better understood and applied (using appropriate historical-critical tools) in the contemporary context. It is also a contextual question that would need to explore the interactive ways in which religious faiths have effectively (or ineffectively) integrated and utilized cultural and ideological resources at various times and places in history.[13]

Something that has received little attention here but is an important subject for further discussion concerns the salvific status of Christianity and Islam. Both have significantly developed soteriologies and eschatologies suggesting that those who are not believers are condemned to unending damnation. Since the eternal destinies of all people are at stake, this must not be passed over lightly or assumed, as many pluralists have done, that it is no longer an important question to be examined. In fact, it incorporates issues of revelation, anthropology, harmartiology, theology proper, and a myriad of other subjects that stand at the very heart of matters of truth and religious contestation. Thus, the inclusion of more conservative adherents of both Islam and Christianity will inevitably drive discussions toward this issue and force dialogue partners to (re)consider the ceaselessly relevant and critical question, "What must I do to be saved?"[14]

Along these lines, if one affirms that God reveals himself through history not only in Christianity but also other religions, much more needs to be done by Christians to answer questions surrounding the recognition, discernment, and significance of these outside revelatory resources.[15] How can we differentiate the cultural, anthropological, and even demonic when dialoging with other faith traditions? In addition, how can we look more closely at history and see more clearly how it reveals important truths about God, his creation, and ourselves as human beings?

We have already noted the controversy surrounding mission, conversion, witness, and apostasy, especially in more conservative branches of Islam. Much work remains in this area to ensure religious freedom

---

13. This is where studies like Tanner's *Theories of Culture* are so important and useful.

14. Acts 16:30.

15. This is where McDermott's work on revelatory types could be very fruitful to pursue and develop.

for all is genuinely granted and that the state will permit a religious plurality that is not static or illusory, but dynamic and real. Careful criteria must be provided and enacted through the process of dialogue to help determine if and when the state should step into a religious dispute. It should be a policy that, as much as possible, reduces ambiguity and loopholes that might allow unjust governments and overly zealous adherents of a given faith tradition to penalize religious apostates inappropriately and ruthlessly.

Along these lines, the presence and treatment of *dhimmī* (religious minorities in Muslim contexts) must be revisited and resolved so that liberty is given and plurality is celebrated, rather than isolating them into carefully delineated societal enclaves. In the meantime, problems surrounding majority and minority status in general need to be examined and addressed by Christians and Muslims alike. When there are problems with "protected minorities" in Muslim-majority contexts, questions must be asked about how many of the problems are related to the more general issue of how minority groups often feel and are treated, whether or not they find themselves in a Muslim context. That is to say, how much of the problem is inherent to the problems of minority status and how much is related to the nature of Islam? Why does Islam seem to struggle with this issue, but largely only from the perspective of the oppressed minority? Or is this oppression observed by outsiders as well? Why do some Muslims seem to have trouble seeing the potentially, if not actually, oppressive policies enforced upon minority groups within Muslim-governed societies? And when Muslims find themselves as minorities in non-Islamic contexts, especially in the West, much discussion should be given to the questions surrounding identity crises, social integration, secularization, and nationalism as it relates to Islamic faith and practice in these kinds of contexts.[16]

This raises the subject of contemporary society. What should its laws, ethical norms, and punitive structures be? How should these be determined and enforced? How can such societies avoid religious disestablishment and secularization? How can religions provide states with the accountability they need to discourage them from the tendency to grab and hold onto power illegitimately? And how do we keep states from using religion to recruit societal members to advance pseudo-religious radicalist political/ideological agendas? How do we

16. This is what makes books like Ramadan's *Western Muslims* so important.

set up structures in society that encourage the participation of all in the legislative and social process of societal formation, organization, and continuation? How can we fairly and justly arbitrate between seemingly incommensurable truth claims and moral virtues? Is it even possible to do so impartially? And if not, what safeguards might be put in place to discourage abuses?[17]

Similarly, concerns over the treatment of women and Muslim family law need careful examination to see how much of these rulings are based in timeless principles laid out in the Qur'an and how much are time-bound cultural expressions needing thoughtful revision and reapplication for contemporary contexts.

Politically, issues surrounding the struggles in Israel and Palestine continue to be important alongside the added challenges of recent international policies in places like Iraq and Afghanistan. Because Islam and Christianity possess many resources for the practice of interreligious, intercommunal, and international peace, they must provide constant input for these difficult sociopolitical situations. Beyond conceptual resources, Christian-Muslim dialogues provide a concrete exemplary model of interreligious peace that can be translated into viable expressions of intracultural, intercultural, and international peace.

These more pragmatic and distinctly non-theoretical political problems remind us how important Christian-Muslim dialogue is for social ethics and other global crises. The moral wisdom and ethical norms present within both of these traditions should not be ignored as governments and transnational organizations attempt to find and apply solutions to ecological, social, and technological problems that could potentially destroy all life on planet earth.

Ultimately, adequate answers to questions like these are impossible to find and apply without an ongoing commitment to interfaith dialogue, since it is within the faith traditions of our world where we find many of the necessary resources to envision and enact human communities that reflect values of peace, morality, justice, freedom, and

---

17. One very promising model for dealing with very difficult and practical issues such as these comes from Ng's *The Quest for Covenant Community*. Here Ng explores the overlapping Islamic and Christian concept of covenant as a way to forge a pluralist democracy in the Muslim-majority context of Malaysia, but the idea has significant potential to be applied fruitfully in other similar cultural, societal, and political contexts as well.

diversity in a harmonious and unified blend of beliefs and practices that honor people as made in God's image and glorify God as the sovereign Lord of all.

Final Summary and Conclusions

In Pannenberg and Sachedina we find rich resources for interfaith dialogue that promote a passion for God's truth and seek to produce increasingly free, just, and unified societies where religions are centrally important to their ongoing governance and success. However, both Pannenberg and Sachedina's projects, while seeking to be universal in nature and scope, remain inherently limited and provisional. They are best understood as proposals, working hypotheses for others to examine and test to see if they provide the best way to offer our world the resources that it needs to form religiously and ideologically pluralistic, diverse, and free societies that are still moral, peaceful, and just. They are not perhaps the only ways to accomplish this goal, and the goal itself must remain a subject of vigorous debate and interaction.

Despite potential limitations, Sachedina's appreciation of and sensitivity to the historical context of the Qur'an enables him to reexamine several key Islamic doctrines to help Muslims see their ancient faith in new and more relevant ways in the contemporary world. By emphasizing the pluralistic message of the Qur'an, he encourages a more open and accepting stance toward all religions concerned with social justice and ethical living. In addition, he opens up public space for religious others through his development of the Qur'anic concept of the God-given *fitra* present in every human being. Finally, he provides new insight into the inherently free nature of religious belief, enabling Muslims to realize the need for more religious liberty across the spectrum of society.

In Pannenberg's trinitarian theology grounded in the historical life and ministry of Jesus, we find a solid basis for the unity and diversity we see in creation, as well as several critical new avenues for Christian-Muslim dialogue. His notion of prolepsis enables him to maintain a genuine openness to the future and yet retain an aspect of completed totality and finality in the work of the Spirit and Jesus Christ. In addition, secular history is no longer "walled off" from salvation history as if God was only operative in one realm of reality. If God really is the "all-determining reality," then history in its entirety, *every single event*, must be pregnant with divine purpose and meaning. Therefore, Pannenberg encourages the pursuit of a comprehensive, coherent project that brings all events and ideas of known human history and knowledge into dialogue and dialectical encounter with the Christian tradition. In the process, Christianity is transformed by a broader understanding of what the triune God has done and is doing in his world, but it also brings a specifically *Christian* interpretation and understanding to these historical events.

Such claims cannot be fully vindicated in the present, of course, and they always remain open in principle to confirmation, modification, and even refutation until the eschaton of God has finally come in all its fullness and splendor. The ambiguity of finite and sin-tainted human life stands between the beginning and end of all time, and leaves us longing in faith for the fulfillment of God's glorious kingdom, when all will be brought into a perfect communion and everything will ultimately vindicate the sovereign glory of the one true and living God. In the meantime, we are all consigned to "eagerly wait for a Savior, the Lord Jesus Christ; who will transform the body of our humble state into conformity with the body of His glory, by the exertion of the power that He has even to subject all things to Himself."[18] And while we wait in humble anticipation, we must accept that, "For now we see in a mirror dimly, but then face to face; now [we] know in part, but then [we] shall know fully just as [we] also have been fully known."[19]

---

18. Phil 3:20–21.

19. 1 Cor 13:12.

Bibliography

Abou El Fadl, Khaled. "The Place of Tolerance in Islam." In *The Place of Tolerance in Islam*, edited by Joshua Cohen and Ian Lague, 3–23. Boston: Beacon, 2002.
———. "Reply." In *The Place of Tolerance in Islam*, edited by Joshua Cohen and Ian Lague, 93–111. Boston: Beacon, 2002.
Adeney, Bernard T. *Strange Virtues: Ethics in a Multicultural World*. Downers Grove, IL: InterVarsity 1995.
Ahmed, Akbar, et al. "Open Letter to Pope Benedict XVI." *Islamicamagazine.com* 18 (2006) 25. Online: http://islamicamagazine.com/?p=634.
Akhtar, Shabbir. *A Faith for All Seasons Seasons: Islam and the Challenge of the Modern World*. Chicago: Ivan R. Dee, 1991.
Ali, Tariq. "Theological Distractions." In *The Place of Tolerance in Islam*, edited by Joshua Cohen and Ian Lague, 37–41. Boston: Beacon, 2002.
Ali, Abdullah Yusuf, translator. *The Qur'an: Translation*. 10th ed. Elmhurst, NY: Tahrike Tarsile Qur'an, 2003.
Anderson, Norman. *Islam in the Modern World: A Christian Perspective*. Leicester, UK: Apollos, 1990.
Aslan, Adnan. "Islam and Religious Pluralism." *The Islamic Quarterly* 40.3 (1996) 172–87.
———. *Religious Pluralism in Christian and Islamic Philosophy: The Thought of John Hick and Seyyed Hossein Nasr*. London: Routledge/Curzon, 1998.
Aydin, Mahmut. "Religious Pluralism: A Challenge for Muslims—A Theological Evaluation." *Journal of Ecumenical Studies* 38.2 (Summer 2001) 330–52.
———. "Religious Pluralism as an Opportunity for Living Together in Diversity." In *Muslim and Christian Reflections on Peace: Divine and Human Dimensions*, edited by J. Dudley Woodberry et al., 89–101. Lanham, MD: University Press of America, 2005.
Ayoub, Mahmoud. "Christian-Muslim Dialogue: Goals and Obstacles." *The Muslim World* 94.3 (July 2004) 313–19.
Bacevich, Andrew J. "Encountering Islam." *First Things* 122 (April 2002) 54–57.
Balci, Israfil. "An Islamic Approach Toward International Peace." In *Muslim and Christian Reflections on Peace: Divine and Human Dimensions*, edited by J. Dudley Woodberry et al., 116–22. Lanham, MD: University Press of America, 2005.
Basinger, David, and Randall Basinger, editors. *Predestination and Free Will: Four Views of Divine Sovereignty and Human Freedom*. Downers Grove, IL: InterVarsity, 1985.

Bibliography

Bediako, Kwame. *Christianity in Africa: The Renewal of a Non-Western Religion.* Maryknoll, NY: Orbis, 1995.

Benedict XVI. Regensburg Address. "Faith, Reason and the University Memories and Reflections." Delivered September 12, 2006, at the University of Regensburg. Official English translation online: http://www.vatican.va/holy_father/benedict _xvi/speeches/2006/september/documents/hf_ben-xvi_spe_20060912 _university-regensburg_en.html.

Bennett, Clinton. *Muslims and Modernity: An Introduction to the Issues and Debates.* London: Continuum, 2005.

Bilgrami, Akeel. "The Importance of Democracy." In *The Place of Tolerance in Islam*, edited by Joshua Cohen and Ian Lague, 61–66. Boston: Beacon, 2002.

Blocher, Henri. "Immanence and Transcendence in Trinitarian Theology." In *The Trinity in a Pluralistic Age: Theological Essays on Culture and Religion*, edited by Kevin J. Vanhoozer, 104–23. Grand Rapids: Eerdmans, 1997.

Bloesch, Donald G. *A Theology of Word & Spirit: Authority & Method in Theology.* Downers Grove, IL: InterVarsity, 1992.

Borelli, John. "Christian-Muslim Relations in the United States: Reflections for the Future after Two Decades of Experience." *Muslim World* 94.3 (July 2004) 321–33.

Braaten, Carl E., and Philip Clayton, editors. *The Theology of Wolfhart Pannenberg: Twelve American Critiques with an Autobiographical Essay and Response.* Minneapolis: Augsburg, 1988.

Brown, Stuart. *Meeting in Faith: Twenty Years of Christian-Muslim Conversations Sponsored by the World Council of Churches.* Geneva: WCC Publications, 1989.

Bruce, F. F. *The Canon of Scripture.* Downers Grove, IL: InterVarsity, 1988.

Brunner, Emil, and Karl Barth. *Natural Theology: Comprising "Nature and Grace" by Emil Brunner and the reply "No!" by Karl Barth.* Translated by Peter Fraenkel. London: G. Bles, Centenary, 1946.

Burford, Grace. "If the Buddha Is So Great, Why Are These People Christians?" In *Buddhists Talk about Jesus—Christians Talk about the Buddha*, edited by Rita Gross and Terry Muck, 131–37. New York: Continuum, 2000.

Cairns, Earle Edwin. *Christianity through the Centuries: A History of the Christian Church.* 3rd ed. Grand Rapids: Zondervan, 1996.

Calvin, John. *Institutes of the Christian Religion.* Vol. 1. Edited by John T. McNeill. Translated by Ford Lewis Battles. Philadelphia: Westminster, 1960.

Carson, D. A. *The Gagging of God: Christianity Confronts Pluralism.* Grand Rapids: Zondervan, 1996.

Comfort, Philip Wesley, editor. *The Origin of the Bible.* Wheaton, IL: Tyndale, 1992.

Cumming, Joseph. "Did Jesus Die on the Cross? Reflections in Muslim Commentaries." In *Muslim and Christian Reflections on Peace: Divine and Human Dimensions*, edited by J. Dudley Woodberry et al., 32–50. Lanham, MD: University Press of America, 2005.

———. "*Sifāt al-Dhāt* in Al-Ashʿarī's Doctrine of God and Possible Christian Parallels." Unpublished paper, 2001.

D'Costa, Gavin, editor. *Christian Uniqueness Reconsidered: The Myth of a Pluralistic Theology of Religions.* Maryknoll, NY: Orbis, 1990.

———. *The Meeting of Religions and the Trinity.* Maryknoll, NY: Orbis, 2000.

DiNoia, Joseph A. *The Diversity of Religions: A Christian Perspective.* Washington, DC: Catholic University of America Press, 1992.

Bibliography

Dupuis, Jacques. *Toward a Christian Theology of Religious Pluralism*. Maryknoll, NY: Orbis, 1997.

Dyrness, William A. *The Earth Is God's: A Theology of American Culture*. Maryknoll, NY: Orbis, 1997.

Erickson, Millard J. *How Shall They Be Saved? The Destiny of Those Who Do Not Hear of Jesus*. Grand Rapids: Baker, 1996.

———. *Postmodernizing the Faith: Evangelical Responses to the Challenge of Postmodernism*. Grand Rapids: Baker Academic, 1998.

Farquhar, John Nicol. *The Crown of Hinduism*. London: Oxford University Press, 1913.

Flannery, Austin P., editor. *Documents of Vatican II*. Grand Rapids: Eerdmans, 1975.

Friedmann, Yohanan. *Tolerance and Coercion in Islam: Interfaith Relations in the Muslim Tradition*. New York: Cambridge University Press, 2003.

Geisler, Norman L., and Abdul Saleeb. *Answering Islam: The Crescent in Light of the Cross*. Grand Rapids: Baker, 1993.

Goddard, Hugh. *A History of Christian-Muslim Relations*. Chicago: New Amsterdam, 2000.

Grenz, Stanley J. "Commitment and Dialogue: Pannenberg on Christianity and the Religions." *Journal of Ecumenical Studies* 26.1 (1989) 196–234.

———. *Reason for Hope: The Systematic Theology of Wolfhart Pannenberg*. Oxford: Oxford University Press, 1990.

Groothuis, Douglas. *Truth Decay: Defending Christianity against the Challenges of Postmodernism*. Downers Grove, IL: InterVarsity, 2000.

Gündüz, Sinasi. "Hegemonic Power Versus *tawhīd*: A Decisive Concept of Islam on Interfaith Relations." In *Muslim and Christian Reflections on Peace: Divine and Human Dimensions*, edited by J. Dudley Woodberry et al., 123–34. Lanham, MD: University Press of America, 2005.

Gunton, Colin E. "Relation and Relativity: The Trinity and the Created World." In *Trinitarian Theology Today: Essays on Divine Being and Act*, edited by Christoph Schwöbel, 92–112. Edinburgh: T. & T. Clark, 1995.

———. "The Trinity, Natural Theology, and a Theology of Nature." In *The Trinity in a Pluralistic Age: Theological Essays on Culture and Religion*, edited by Kevin J. Vanhoozer, 88–103. Grand Rapids: Eerdmans, 1997.

Gutierrez, Gustavo. *A Theology of Liberation: History, Politics and Salvation*. Marykoll, NY: Orbis, 1988.

Haddad, Yvonne, and Wadi Zaidan Haddad, editors. *Christian-Muslim Encounters*. Gainesville, FL: University Press of Florida, 1995.

Heim, S. Mark. *The Depth of Riches: A Trinitarian Theology of Religious Ends*. Grand Rapids: Eerdmans, 2001.

———. *Salvations: Truth and Difference in Religions*. Maryknoll, NY: Orbis, 1995.

Held, David, et al. *Global Transformations: Politics, Economics and Culture*. Stanford, CA: Stanford University Press, 1999.

Hermansen, Marcia. "How to Put the Genie Back in the Bottle? 'Identity' Islam and Muslim Youth Cultures in America." In *Progressive Muslims: On Justice, Gender, and Pluralism*, edited by Omid Safi, 306–19. Oxford: Oneworld, 2003.

Hick, John. *A Christian Theology of Religions: The Rainbow of Faiths*. Louisville: Westminster, 1995.

———. *God and the Universe of Faiths: Essays in the Philosophy of Religion*. London: Macmillan, 1973.

Bibliography

———. *God Has Many Names*. Philadelphia: Westminster, 1982.

———. *The Metaphor of God Incarnate: Christology in a Pluralistic Age*. Louisville: Westminster John Knox, 1993.

———, editor. *The Myth of God Incarnate*. Louisville: Westminster John Knox, 1977.

———. *Truth and Dialogue in World Religions: Conflicting Truth Claims*. Philadelphia: Westminster, 1974.

Hocking, William Ernest, editor. *Rethinking Missions: A Layman's Inquiry after One Hundred Years*. New York: Harper, 1932.

House, H. Wayne, and Thomas D. Ice. *Dominion Theology: Blessing or Curse?* Portland: Multnomah, 1988.

Hussain, Amir. "Muslims, Pluralism, and Interfaith Dialogue." In *Progressive Muslims: On Justice, Gender, and Pluralism*, edited by Omid Safi, 251–69. Oxford: Oneworld, 2003.

Jan, Abid Ullah. "The Limits of Tolerance." In *The Place of Tolerance in Islam*, edited by Joshua Cohen and Ian Lague, 42–50. Boston: Beacon, 2002.

Jensen, Robert. "Jesus in the Trinity: Wolfhart Pannenberg's Christology and Doctrine of the Trinity." In *The Theology of Wolfhart Pannenberg: Twelve American Critiques with an Autobiographical Essay and Response*, edited by Carl E. Braaten and Philip Clayton, 188–206. Minneapolis: Augsburg, 1988.

Johnston, David L. "*Maqāsid Al-Sharī'a*: Epistemology and Hermeneutics of Muslim Theologies of Human Rights." *Die Welt des Islams* 47.2 (2007) 149–87.

Jukko, Risto. *Trinitarian Theology in Christian-Muslim Encounters*. Helsinki: Luther-Agricola-Society, 2001.

Kärkkäinen, Veli-Matti. *An Introduction to the Theology of Religions: Biblical, Historical & Contemporary Perspectives*. Downers Grove, IL: InterVarsity, 2003.

———. *One with God: Salvation as Deification and Justification*. Collegeville, MN: Liturgical, 2004.

———. *Toward a Pneumatological Theology: Pentecostal and Ecumenical Perspectives on Ecclesiology, Soteriology, and Theology of Mission*. Edited by Amos Yong. New York: University Press of America, 2002.

———. *Trinity and Religious Pluralism: The Doctrine of the Trinity in Christian Theology of Religions*. Burlington, VT: Ashgate, 2004.

———. *The Trinity: Global Perspectives*. Louisville: Westminster John Knox, 2007.

Khalidi, Tarif. *The Muslim Jesus: Sayings and Stories in Islamic Literature*. Cambridge, MA: Harvard University Press, 2001.

Khalifa, Rashad, translator. *Quran: The Final Testament*. 2nd rev. ed. Fremont, CA: Universal Unity, 2000.

Kimball, Charles. "Toward a More Hopeful Future: Obstacles and Opportunities in Christian-Muslim Relations." *Muslim World* 94.3 (July 2004) 377–85.

Knitter, Paul F. *Introducing Theologies of Religions*. Maryknoll, NY: Orbis, 2002.

———. *One Earth, Many Religions: Multifaith Dialogue and Global Responsibility*. Maryknoll, NY: Orbis, 1995.

———. "Toward a Liberation Theology of Religions." In *The Myth of Christian Uniqueness: Toward a Pluralistic Theology of Religions*, edited by John Hick and Paul F. Knitter, 178–218. Maryknoll, NY: Orbis, 1987.

Kraemer, Hendrik. *The Christian Message in a Non-Christian World*. New York: Harper, 1938.

Bibliography

Kurzman, Charles. "Liberal Islam and Its Islamic Context." In *Liberal Islam: A Sourcebook*, edited by Charles Kurzman, 3-26. New York: Oxford University Press, 1998.
Lawrence, Bruce. *Defenders of God: The Fundamentalist Revolt against the Modern Age*. New York: Harper & Row, 1989.
Lehrer, Keith. *Theory of Knowledge*. Boulder, CO: Westview, 1990.
Lewis, C. S. *Mere Christianity*. New York: Macmillan, 1960.
———. *Reflections on the Psalms*. New York: Harcourt Brace, 1958.
Lindbeck, George A. *The Nature of Doctrine: Religion and Theology in a Postliberal Age*. Philadelphia: Westminster, 1984.
Little, David. "The Western Tradition." In *Human Rights and the Conflict of Cultures: Western and Islamic Perspectives on Religious Liberty*, by David Little et al., 13-32. Columbia, SC: University of South Carolina Press, 1988.
———, et al. "Human Rights and the World's Religions: Christianity, Islam, and Religious Liberty." In *Religious Diversity and Human Rights*, edited by Irene Bloom et al., 213-39. New York: Columbia University Press, 1996.
MacFarland, Ian A. *The Divine Image: Envisioning the Invisible God*. Minneapolis: Fortress, 2005.
MacIntyre, Alasdair. *Three Rival Versions of Moral Enquiry*. Notre Dame, IN: University of Notre Dame Press, 1990.
———. *Whose Justice? Which Rationality?* Notre Dame, IN: University of Notre Dame Press, 1988.
McDermott, Gerald R. *Can Evangelicals Learn from World Religions? Jesus, Revelation & Religious Traditions*. Downers Grove, IL: InterVarsity, 2000.
———. *God's Rivals: Why Has God Allowed Different Religions? Insights from the Bible and the Early Church*. Downers Grove, IL: InterVarsity, 2007.
McDowell, Bruce A., and Anees Zaka. *Muslims and Christians at the Table: Promoting Biblical Understanding among North American Muslims*. Phillipsburg, NJ: P&R, 1999.
Meacham, Jon. "A Pope's Holy War." Newsweek, September 15, 2006. Online: http://www.msnbc.msn.com/id/14866559/site/newsweek/.
Moaddel, Mansoor, and Kamran Talattof, editors. *Contemporary Debates in Islam: An Anthology of Modernist and Fundamentalist Thought*. New York: St. Martin's, 2000.
Mohammed, Ovey N. *Muslim-Christian Relations: Past, Present, Future*. Maryknoll, NY: Orbis, 1999.
Moltmann, Jürgen. "Is 'Pluralistic Theology' Useful for the Dialogue of World Religions?" Translated by Marianne M. Martin. In *Christian Uniqueness Reconsidered: The Myth of a Pluralistic Theology of Religions*, edited by Gavin D'Costa, 149-56. Maryknoll, NY: Orbis, 1990.
———. *The Trinity and the Kingdom: The Doctrine of God*. Translated by Margaret Kohl. San Francisco: Harper & Row, 1981.
Moosa, Ebrahim. "Abdulaziz Sachedina, *The Islamic Roots of Democratic Pluralism*." *Journal of Religion* 85.1 (January 2005) 172-74.
Moucarry, Chawkat. *The Prophet & the Messiah: An Arab Christian's Perspective on Islam and Christianity*. Downers Grove, IL: InterVarsity, 2001.
Murphy, Nancey. *Anglo-American Postmodernity: Philosophical Perspectives on Science, Religion, and Ethics*. Boulder, CO: Westview, 1997.

Bibliography

Nasr, Seeyed Hossein. "Comments on a Few Theological Issues in the Islamic-Christian Dialogue." In *Christian-Muslim Encounters*, edited by Yvonne Hadd ad and Wadi Zaidan Haddad, 457–67. Gainesville: University Press of Florida, 1995.

Nazir-Ali, Michael. *Frontiers in Muslim-Christian Encounter*. Oxford: Regnum, 1987.

Netland, Harold. *Dissonant Voices: Religious Pluralism and the Question of Truth*. Grand Rapids: Eerdmans, 1991.

———. *Encountering Religious Pluralism: The Challenge to Christian Faith and Mission*. Downers Grove, IL: InterVarsity, 2001.

Ng, Kam Weng. *The Quest for Covenant Community and Pluralist Democracy in an Islamic Context*. Edited by Mark L. Y. Chan. The Centre for the Study of Christianity in Asia Annual Lectures 2006. Singapore: Trinity Theological College Publications, 2008.

Noor, Farish. "What Is the Victory of Islam? Towards a Different Understanding of the *Ummah* and Political Success in the Contemporary World." In *Progressive Muslims: On Justice, Gender, and Pluralism*, edited by Omid Safi, 320–32. Oxford: Oneworld, 2003.

Okholm, Dennis L., and Timothy R. Phillips, editors. *Four Views on Salvation in a Pluralistic World*. Grand Rapids: Zondervan, 1996.

Pannenberg, Wolfhart. "A Response to My American Friends." In *The Theology of Wolfhart Pannenberg: Twelve American Critiques with an Autobiographical Essay and Response*, edited by Carl E. Braaten and Philip Clayton, 313–36. Minneapolis: Augsburg, 1988.

———. *Anthropology in Theological Perspective*. Translated by Matthew J. O'Connell. Edinburgh: T. & T. Clark, 1985.

———. "The Crisis of the Scripture Principle." In *Basic Questions in Theology*, translated by George H. Kehm, vol. 1, 1–14. Philadelphia: Fortress, 1970.

———. "God's Presence in History: How My Mind Has Changed." *The Christian Century*, March 11, 1981, 260–63.

———. *Jesus—God and Man*. 2nd ed. Translated by Lewis L. Wilkins and Duane A. Priebe. Philadelphia: Westminster, 1977.

———. "Redemptive Event and History." In *Basic Questions in Theology*, translated by George H. Kehm, vol. 1, 15–80. Philadelphia: Fortress, 1970.

———. "Religious Pluralism and Conflicting Truth Claims: The Problem of a Theology of World Religions." In *Christian Uniqueness Reconsidered: The Myth of a Pluralistic Theology of Religions*, edited by Gavin D'Costa, 96–106. Maryknoll, NY: Orbis, 1990.

———. *Revelation as History*. Translated by David Granskou. London: Macmillan, 1967.

———. *Systematic Theology*. 3 vols. Translated by Geoffrey Bromiley. Grand Rapids: Eerdmans, 1991.

———. *Theology and the Philosophy of Science*. Translated by Francis McDonagh. Philadelhpia: Westminster, 1976.

———. *Toward a Theology of Nature*. Edited by Ted Peters. Louisville: Westminster John Knox Press, 1993.

———. "Toward a Theology of the History of Religions." In *Basic Questions in Theology*, translated by George H. Kehm, vol. 2, 65–118. Philadelphia: Fortress, 1971.

———. "What Is Truth?" In *Basic Questions in Theology*, translated by George H. Kehm, vol. 2, 1–27. Philadelphia: Fortress, 1971.

Bibliography

Parrinder, Geoffrey. *Jesus in the Qur'ān*. London: Faber and Faber, 1965.
Pinnock, Clark. *A Wideness in God's Mercy: The Finality of Jesus Christ in a World of Religions*. Grand Rapids: Zondervan, 1992.
———. *Flame of Love: A Theology of the Holy Spirit*. Downers Grove, IL: InterVarsity, 1996.
Placher, William C. "Revealed to Reason: Theology as 'Normal Science.'" *The Christian Century*, February 19, 1992, 192–95.
Plantinga, Richard J., editor. *Christianity and Plurality: Classical and Contemporary Readings*. Oxford: Blackwell, 1999.
Poupin, Roland. "Is There a Trinitarian Experience in Sufism?" In *The Trinity in a Pluralistic Age: Theological Essays on Culture and Religion*, edited by Kevin J. Vanhoozer, 72–87. Grand Rapids: Eerdmans, 1997.
Qutb, Sayyid. "War, Peace, and Islamic Jihad." In *Contemporary Debates in Islam: An Anthology of Modernist and Fundamentalist Thought*, edited by Mansoor Moaddel and Kamran Talatoff, 223–46. New York: St. Martin's, 2000.
Race, Alan. *Christians and Religious Pluralism: Patterns in the Christian Theology of Religions*. London: SCM, 1983.
Rahner, Karl. "Christianity and the non-Christian Religions." In *Theological Investigations*, vol. 5, 115–34. New York: Crossroad, 1966.
———. "Jesus Christ in the Non-Christian Religions." In *Theological Investigations*, vol. 17, 39–50. New York: Crossroad, 1981.
———. "On the Importance of the Non-Christian Religions for Salvation." In *Theological Investigations*, vol. 18, 288–95. London: Darton, Longman & Todd, 1983.
Ramachandra, Vinoth. *Faiths in Conflict? Christian Integrity in a Multicultural World*. Leicester, UK: InterVarsity, 1999.
———. *The Recovery of Mission: Beyond the Pluralist Paradigm*. Carlisle, UK: Paternoster, 1996.
Ramadan, Tariq. *Western Muslims and the Future of Islam*. New York: Oxford University Press, 2004.
Rescher, Nicholas. *The Coherence Theory of Truth*. Oxford: Clarendon, 1973.
———. *Pluralism: Against the Demand for Consensus*. Oxford: Clarendon, 1993.
Richardson, Don. *Eternity in Their Hearts: Startling Evidence of Belief in the One True God in Hundreds of Cultures Throughout the World*. Rev. ed. Ventura, CA: Regal, 1984.
———. *Lords of the Earth*. Ventura, CA: Regal, 1977.
———. *Peace Child*. Ventura, CA: Regal, 1974.
———. *Secrets of the Koran: Revealing Insights into Islam's Holy Book*. Ventura, CA: Regal, 2003.
Riddell, Peter G., and Peter Cottrell. *Islam in Context: Past, Present, and Future*. Grand Rapids: Baker, 2003.
Rizvi, Mashhood. "Intolerable Injustices." In *The Place of Tolerance in Islam*, edited by Joshua Cohen and Ian Lague, 67–71. Boston: Beacon, 2002.
Rushdoony, Rousas John. *The Institutes of Biblical Law*. Phillipsburg, NJ: Presbyterian and Reformed, 1973.
———. *Law and Society*. Vallecito, CA: Ross House, 1982.
Sachedina, Abdulaziz A. "A Crisis of Interpretation." *Washington Post*, On Faith, July 27, 2007. Online: http://www.newsweek.washingtonpost.com/onfaith/abdulaziz_a_sachedina/2007/07/a_crisi_of_interpretation.html.

Bibliography

———. "Activist Shi'ism in Iran, Iraq, and Lebanon." In *Fundamentalisms Observed*, edited by Martin E. Marty and R. Scott Appleby, 403–56. Chicago: University of Chicago Press, 1991.

———. "The Creation of a Just Social Order in Islam." In *The Search for Faith and Justice in the Twentieth Century*, edited by Gene G. James, 97–115. New York: Paragon House, 1987.

———. "Freedom of Conscience and Religion in the Qur'an." In *Human Rights and the Conflict of Cultures: Western and Islamic Perspectives on Religious Liberty*, by David Little et al., 53–90. Columbia, SC: University of South Carolina Press, 1988.

———. "Freedom of Religion and Conscience: The Foundation of World Order." Unpublished lecture obtained directly from the author, May 2005.

———. *The Islamic Roots of Democratic Pluralism*. New York: Oxford University Press, 2001.

———. "Islamic Theology of Christian-Muslim Relations." *Islam and Christian-Muslim Relations* 8.1 (March 1997) 27–38.

———. "Justifications for Violence in Islam." In *War and Its Discontents: Pacifism and Quietism in the Abrahamic Traditions*, edited by J. Patout Burns, 122–66. Washington, DC: Georgetown University Press, 1996.

———. "Pluralism's 'Live and Let Live' Undermined by Attitudes of Superiority." *Washington Post*, On Faith, November 29, 2006. Online: http://newsweek.washingtonpost.com/onfaith/abdulaziz_a_sachedina/2006/11/.

———. *The Role of Islam in the Public Square: Guidance or Governance?* Amsterdam: Amsterdam University Press, 2006.

———. "Universal and Particular Discourse in the Islamic Tradition: A Muslim Response." *Church and Society* 83 (September-October 1992) 34–37.

Safi, Omid. "Introduction: *The Times They Are A-Changin*'—A Muslim Quest for Justice, Gender Equality, and Pluralism." In *Progressive Muslims: On Justice, Gender, and Pluralism*, edited by Omid Safi, 1–29. Oxford: Oneworld, 2003.

Sahih al-Bukhari: Arabic-English. Translated by Muhammad Muhsin Khan. 9 vols. Beruit: Dar Al Arabia, 1985.

Schaeffer, Francis. *Escape from Reason*. Downers Grove, IL: InterVarsity, 1968.

Schleiermacher, Friedrich. *On Religion: Speeches to Its Cultured Despisers*. Translated by John Oman. Louisville: Westminster John Knox, 1994.

Shihab, Alwi. "Christian-Muslim Relations into the Twenty-First Century." *Islam and Christian-Muslim Relations* 15.1 (January 2004) 65–77.

Shults, F. LeRon. *The Postfoundationalist Task of Theology: Wolfhart Pannenberg and the New Theological Rationality*. Grand Rapids: Eerdmans, 1999.

Siddiqi, Muzammil H. "A Muslim Response to John Hick: Trinity and Incarnation in the Light of Religious Pluralism." In *Three Faiths—One God: A Jewish, Christian, Muslim Encounter*, edited by John Hick and Edmund S. Meltzer, 211–13. New York: State University of New York Press, 1989.

Smith, R. Scott. *Virtue Ethics and Moral Knowledge: Philosophy of Language After MacIntyre and Hauerwas*. Burlington, VT: Ashgate, 2003.

Smith, Wilfred Cantwell. *The Faiths of Other Men*. New York: Harper, 1972.

———. *The Meaning and End of Religion*. Minneapolis: Fortress, 1991.

Soroush, Abdolkarim. *Reason, Freedom, and Democracy in Islam: Essential Writings of Abdolkarim Soroush*. Translated and edited by Mahmoud Sadri and Ahmad Sadri. Oxford: Oxford University Press, 2000.

Sperber, Jutta. *Christians and Muslims: The Dialogue Activities of the World Council of Churches and Their Theological Foundation.* New York: de Gruyter, 2000.
Sullivan, Francis A. *Salvation Outside the Church?* New York: Paulist, 1992.
Takim, Liyakatali. "From Conversion to Conversation: Interfaith Dialogue in Post 9–11 America." *Muslim World* 94.3 (July 2004) 343–55.
Tanner, Kathryn. *Theories of Culture.* Minneapolis: Fortress, 1997.
Tennent, Timothy C. *Christianity at the Religious Roundtable: Evangelicalism in Conversation with Hinduism, Buddhism, and Islam.* Grand Rapids: Baker, 2002.
———. "Was Socrates a Christian before Christ? A Study of Justin Martyr's Use of Logos Spermatikos." In *Christianity at the Religious Roundtable: Evangelicalism in Conversation with Hinduism, Buddhism, and Islam,* 199–210. Grand Rapids: Baker, 2002.
Vanhoozer, Kevin J. "Does the Trinity Belong in a Theology of Religions?" In *The Trinity in a Pluralistic Age: Theological Essays on Culture and Religion,* edited by Kevin J. Vanhoozer, 41–71. Grand Rapids: Eerdmans, 1997.
Vasquez, Manuel A., and Marie Friedmann Marquardt. *Globalizing the Sacred: Religion across the Americas.* New Brunswick, NJ: Rutgers University Press, 2003.
Volf, Miroslav. *Exclusion and Embrace: A Theological Exploration of Identity, Otherness, and Reconciliation.* Nashville: Abingdon, 1996.
———. "Living with the 'Other.'" In *Muslim and Christian Reflections on Peace: Divine and Human Dimensions,* edited by J. Dudley Woodberry et al., 3–22. Lanham, MD: University Press of America, 2005.
Walls, Andrew F. *The Missionary Movement in Christian History: Studies in the Transmission of Faith.* Maryknoll, NY: Orbis, 1996.
Winkler, Lewis. "Contested Views of Christ in Christianity and Islam: A Pannenbergian Program." *Theology News and Notes* 52.1 (Winter 2005) 13–15, 23.
———. "Tradition on Its Way to the End: Truth and the Rational Enterprise in Alasdair MacIntrye and Wolfhart Pannenberg." Unpublished article, 2003.
Woodberry, J. Dudley. "Can We Dialogue with Islam? What 38 Muslim Scholars Said to the Pope in a Little-Known Open Letter." *Christianity Today* 51.2 (February 2007) 108–9.
———. "Do Christians and Muslims Worship the Same God?" *The Christian Century,* May 18, 2004, 36–37.
———. "Toward a Common Ground in Understanding the Human Condition." In *Muslim and Christian Reflections on Peace: Divine and Human Dimensions,* edited by J. Dudley Woodberry et al., 23–31. Lanham, MD: University Press of America, 2005.
Yilmaz, Mehmet Nuri. "The Context for Reflection." In *Muslim and Christian Reflections on Peace: Divine and Human Dimensions,* edited by J. Dudley Woodberry et al., xi–xii. Lanham, MD: University Press of America, 2005.
Yong, Amos. *Beyond the Impasse: Toward a Pneumatological Theology of Religions.* Grand Rapids: Baker, 2003.
———. *Discerning the Spirit(s) A Pentecostal-Charismatic Contribution to Christian Theology of Religions.* Sheffield: Sheffield Academic, 2000.
Yousif, Ahmad. "Islam, Minorities and Religious Challenge to Modern Theory of Pluralism." *Journal of Muslim Minority Affairs* 1.20 (2000) 29–41.
Zizioulas, John. *Being as Communion: Studies in Personhood and Communion.* Crestwood, NY: St. Vladimir's Seminary Press, 1985.

Index

abortion, 249n69, 302n6
Abou El Fadl, Khaled, 31, 34, 35
abrogation, 132, 133–34, 163
absolute truth. *See* exclusivism
Acceptance, 19–20
Adeney, Bernard, 12, 224
Ad Gentes, 51
Akhtar, Shabbir, 38–39
Al-Ash'arī, Abū al-Hasan 'Alī ibn Ismā'īl, 271
alcohol, consumption of, 248–49n69
al-Fariqi, Isma'il, 270
Ali, Tariq, 34, 172
anonymous Christian, 23, 53
anthropological views, examination of, 197–98
Anthropology in Theological Perspective (Pannenberg), 105
apostasy, 146–48, 165–66, 200, 256–66
    differing Islamic and Christian views of, 258–59
    handling of, questions related to, 263–64
    Islam's approach to, 258–62
    seditious acts of, 260n91
Ash'arites, 144n94, 271, 272
Aslan, Adnan, 39, 67–68
Aydin, Mahmut, 39, 41
Ayoub, Mahmoud, 215–16

Bacevich, Andrew, 161–62
Balci, Israfil, 65
Barth, Karl, 21, 89

behavior, as best indicator of relation toward the future of God, 113
Benedict XVI, 55–56
Bilgrami, Akeel, 34
bin Laden, Osama, 34
blasphemy, 257
Buddhism, 122–23
Burford, Grace, 37n85

Calvin, John, 231–32
Can Evangelicals Learn from World Religions? (McDermott), 58
centrist typology, as approach to theology of religions, 20–30
children, religious education for, 80–81
Christ. *See also* Jesus
    as foundation for truth's unity, 99
    presence of, in other religions, 24
Christian fundamentalism, 215
Christianity
    challenged by Islamic emphasis on God's absolute unity, 285–86
    developing ideas about relationship with other religions, 45–47
    diversity of expression in, 251n72
    endless translatability of, 296n85
    first-century, religious pluralism surrounding, 14
    influence of, on Islam, 15
    moving to more pluralistic territory, 19–20
    outgrowing the denominational age, 178

Christianity (*continued*)
    public practice of, 16
    seen as highest form of religion, 45, 103–4, 109
    superior explanatory power of, 90
    tests for, 251n73
    truth of, in the present, 98
    understanding of father/son relationship in the Trinity, 283
Christianity at the Religious Roundtable (Tennent), 62–64
Christian mission, Muslim suspicion of, 74, 79
Christian-Muslim dialogue
    calls for, following Benedict XVI's Regensburg speech, 56–57
    conflicts and barriers in, 70–81
    evangelical perspective on, 56
    Islamic pursuit of, 66–70
    mutual understanding as goal of, 66
    rising interest in, 42
    themes of commonality in, 82–85
    WCC fostering, 48–49
Christian-Muslim Encounters, 66–67
Christian and Muslim Reflections on Peace, 64–65
Christian-Muslim relations
    early days of, 43
    significance of, 43–44
Christian reconstructionists, 16n7
Christians
    claiming supremacy, 171
    distinguishing between state and religion, 77
    provisionally participating in the future, 98
    witnessing of, 30
christocentric exclusivism. *See* ecclesiocentrism
christocentrism, 23–25, 75
Christology, 118n131
church
    avoiding confusion with state, 180
    called to perform an inclusive mission to the world's peoples, 114
    providing testimony to God's plan, 301
    relativizing role of, 179
    as sign of the future fellowship of humanity, 114
church discipline, 266n104
church-state distinction, 193–94
church-state linkage, as Abrahamic approach, 142
cobelligerents, 302
coercion, secular, 248n67
coherence
    as prior condition underlying theological revelation, 92
    related to truth of one's faith tradition, 181
coherentism, 91
Commission on World Mission and Evangelism (CWME), 47, 48
commonalities
    focus on, in interreligious dialogue, 63
    themes of, in Christian-Muslim dialogue, 82–85
common goals, working toward, in a pluralistic society, 301–2
competitions, interfaith, 302
compulsion, 144, 154, 197, 233
conscience, 137n56, 145n98
contemporary society, 310–11
contextualization, 157–58n155
contingency, 288n69
cooperation, interfaith, as goal, 302–3
correspondence, truth related to, 92–94
corruption, 163
Cragg, Kenneth, 57n52
creation
    diversity in, 288–89
    nature of, and God, 287–90
Crown of Hinduism (Farquhar), 46n10
culture, relationship of, with religion, 2–3
Cumming, Joseph, 271–73, 281

D'Costa, Gavin, 53, 118, 206–7n91
death penalty, for Islamic apostates, 259–60

Index

degree Christology, 26
deity
   truth claims about, 111–12
   unity of, 105
democracy
   dynamism in, 199n66
   religious freedom and, 248
depravity, 233n42, 242n56
Depth of Riches, The (Heim), 28
DFI (WCC sub-unit on dialogue), 48, 49
dhimmī, 71, 77n145, 140, 146, 310. *See also* minorities
dialogue
   eschatological nature of, 212
   as opportunity for Christians to mature in understanding of God, 300
   separate from witness, 301
   as timeless Qur'anic concern, 299–300
discernment, evaluative, 234n43
disestablishment, 15–16, 83, 198–99
diversity
   of expression, 251n72
   in humans, ordained by God, 186–87
divine immanence, Muslims' negative stance toward, 296n85
divine revelation, 143. *See also* revelation
   contextual nature of, 163
   expression of, 135–36
divine truths, 58
dominion theologians, 16n7
Dupuis, Jacques, 11, 53, 268
dynamism, divine, 288n68

Ecclesiam Suam ("His Church") (Paul VI), 50
ecclesiocentrism, 21–23, 75
eco-human justice, 27–28
economic systems, in Muslim-majority contexts, 166
education
   religiously plural, encouragement of, 306–7
   significance of, 85

Edwards, Jonathan, 58–59
Encountering Religious Pluralism (Netland), 22
enculturation, 4
engagement, mutual, 9–10
enlightenment, 122–23
Erickson, Millard, 21, 22, 225
eschatocentrism, 21, 28–30
eschatological transformation, uniting all humanity under God, 101–2
eschatology, 188–89, 309
esperanto religion, 158n157
Eternity in Their Hearts (Richardson), 59n61
ethical challenges, approaches to, 27–28
ethical imperatives, shared in all religions, 158
ethical norms, 164
   cultural vs. religious, 244–45
   expressing in tangible forms, 245–46
ethical social life, pursuit of, 179
ethical themes
   as barriers to Christian-Muslim dialogue, 79–81
   common ground for, in Christian-Muslim dialogue, 84–85
ethicocentrism, 21, 27–28
ethics
   as basis for acceptance into God's eschatological fellowship, 185–86
   place of, in theology of religions, 187–88
   providing basis for ideal and public social order, 137
Euangelii Nuntiandi (Paul VI), 54
evangelical Christians
   in interreligious conversations, 224–25
   involvement of, in interfaith dialogue, 57–66
evangelism, 54
evolution, atheistic approach to, 254n77
exclusivism
   aggressive forms of, 220–21
   blamed for problems in interreligious relations, 215

Index

exclusivism (*continued*)
    Christian approach to, 17–18, 75
    in every religion, 172–73
    Muslim approach to, 35–37
    negative effects of, 129
    practitioners of, using religion to justify imperialistic impulses, 172
    used for unrighteous ends, 221–22n19
excommunication, 266n104

faith principle, 61
filioque clause, 118, 204–5n81
finitude, recognizing, 306
fitra, 8–9, 131–35, 197
    corruption of, 239
    empowering a return to God, 149
    granting moral freedom, 143
    heart related to, 144–45
    human freedom inherent in, 240
    opening room for religious freedom, 253
    providing backdrop for pluralistic ethic, 141, 142–43
Flame of Love (Pinnock), 61
forgiveness, 149, 151, 200–201, 225–26, 306
"Freedom of Religion and Conscience," (Sachedina), 151
freedoms, governmental monitoring of, 241–44
Friedman, Yohanan, 169
Fulfillment, 18–19
future, openness to, 185

Gaudium et Spes, 51, 52
globalization, 1–2
God
    attributes of, as controversy in Islam's history, 271–74
    basic nature of, 190–91
    categorical concept of, 293n80
    Christians enjoying full revelation of, 29
    commonly held views of, for Pannenberg and Sachedina, 177–82
    contemporary Muslim concept of, 270–75
    continuously revealed in history, 201–2
    deity of, manifest at end of time and history, 113–14
    differentiation in, 281–87
    disillusionment with, 293
    gifts of, to the human race, 228–33
    hiddenness of, 270–71
    history as self-revelation of, 96–97, 184–85, 201–2, 234
    immanence of, 271
    indescribable nature of, 25–26
    intimacy with, longing for, 292
    kingdom of, 27, 114
    limited conception of, 287
    as Lord of all history, 89–90
    as love, grounded in Godhead's intertrinitarian relations, 281
    love of, including those outside the Christian church, 115–16
    Muslims and Christians worshiping the same, 268–69
    nature of, as barrier to Christian-Muslim dialogue, 72–73
    and the nature of creation, 287–90
    and the nature of humanity and society, 290–93
    and the nature of interfaith dialogue, 293–96
    ninety-nine names of, 270, 274, 284
    non-Christians experiencing, but less fully, 29
    noumenal, 25
    Old Testament concept of, 108–9
    ordaining human diversity, 186–87
    revealed in history of interreligious interaction, 191
    revealing himself to those outside chosen Israel, 58
    as source of all good, 229
    sovereignty and lordship of, 201
    as Trinity, 202–6. *See also* Trinity

triune vs. indivisibly one, 190–91
unity in, 279–87
variety of perspectives on, 113
work of, seeing in all religions, 61
worship of, common ground on, 82–83
Goddard, Hugh, 215
gods, local names for, 108–9n95
good works, 164
Gotthard, Bill, 3n8
governance, in Muslim-majority contexts, 166–67
government
monitoring freedoms, 241–44
role of, in dealing with apostasy, 259–62
secular, providing moral and ideological justification, 254
secularization of, 83–84
grace, 231–32
based on Christ alone, 19
centered within Jesus Christ, 24
given to non-Christian religious peoples, 24–25
need for, 306
Grenz, Stanley J., 96, 119, 182, 206
Gündüz, Sinasi, 35, 37, 168, 222–23

Haddad, Wadi, 15
Haddad, Yvonne, 15
heart (*qalb*), 132, 137n56, 144
becoming veiled and sick, 239
problems of, 167–68
Heim, S. Mark, 21, 28–30, 217, 219
heresy, 256–57
Hermansen, Marcia, 4–5
Hick, John, 12, 17, 25–26, 68, 129–30, 251n73, 274
historical argumentation, 96
history
as disclosure of Godself, 184–85
end result of, 100
God continuously revealed in, 96–97, 184–85, 201–2, 234
importance of, 96
truth and, 94–97

History of Christian-Muslim Relations, A (Goddard), 43n2
human community, 132
human freedom, Mu'zilite/Ash'arite debate over, 168
humanitarian aid, 79n151
humanity
God's image in, 231–32
nature of, and God, 290–93
religiously inclusive visions for, 187
humankind, as one community, 130–31
humanness, 197
meaning of, as barrier to Christian-Muslim dialogue, 74
human rights, 80–81
humans, caught up in a religious quest, 186
human sacrifice, 59
human society, spaces between sacred and secular arenas of, 179–80
human thought, radical historicness on, 95
humility, 226–28, 306
Hussain, Amir, 68–69

immigration, 2, 4
incarnation, 26, 296n85
inclusiveness, political effect of, 130
inclusivism
Christian approach to, 17
eschatological, 193
as important dialogical starting point, 223
leading to exclusivism, 172–73, 219–20
Muslim approach to, 38–40
subsuming religious others in a subcategory of the inclusivist religion, 218
inclusivist view of salvation, 121
indeterminacy, 288n69
institutions, as evil, 250n71
interfaith dialogue. *See* interreligious dialogue
inter-institutional freedom, 240–41
International Missionary Council, 46, 47

Index

interreligious competition, 140–41
interreligious dialogue
    barriers to, 214–23
    encouraging, 249
    God and the nature of, 293–96
    growing in importance for
        Christians, 45
    historical aspect of, 307
    humility in, 226–28
    importance to, of competing claims, 190–91
    increasing intentional pursuit of, 304–5
    intended to bring fuller understanding of Christ's gospel, 61–62
    motivation for, 122–23
    Muslim need for, 231
    necessity of, 7, 202, 207, 230–31
    Pannenberg's openness to exchange in, 120
    preconditions for, 216n7, 225
    primary rules for, 69
    purpose of, 195–96
    requiring affirmation of religious pluralism, 151–52
    Sachedina's promotion of, 238
    as source of progress, 212
    suggestions for, 308–12
    used to create stability in multireligious societies, 262
interreligious interaction, ongoing, assumed, 180
interreligious tension
    government addressing, 246–47
    as source of social antagonism, 247–48
intolerance, Islamic, 31
intrareligious dialogue, increasing levels of, 305
intrareligious freedom, 250–52
Islam. *See also* Muslims
    affirming religious plurality, based on the Qur'an, 161
    anti-Westernism in, 139
    arrogance and jealousy as elements of, 149–50
    born in context of religious pluralism, 15
    challenges for, as publicly expressed religion, 165
    Christian influence on, 15
    contemporary concept of God, 270–75
    creating space for private expression of faith, 131–32
    current challenges for, 2–5
    demonstrating propensity for violence, 149
    distinction in, between religious adherence and governmental rule of law, 127
    distinguishing between apostasy, blasphemy, and heresy, 257–58
    emphasizing responsible political leadership, 150
    exploited by radical ideologies, 148
    failing to respond to the modern nation-state, 139
    as faith in the public realm, 178
    fundamentalism rising in, 139
    fundamentalists marginalizing the truth, 138
    governance in, functional secularity of, 161
    governing systems of, as exclusivistic and divisive, 127
    growing interest of, in interreligious dialogue, 68–70
    involvement in political systems, results of, 141
    John Paul II's openness toward, 55, 56
    locked in the past, 138–39
    multiplicity within, 32
    negative stance of, toward divine immanence and incarnation, 296n85
    other religions related to, through submission to God, 38–39
    overemphasizing vengeance, 149
    political vision of, 136–37
    presenting special challenge to Christianity, 73

as public religion, 131
public practice of, 16
pursuing Christian-Muslim
  dialogue, 66–70
radicalist visions of, leaders' refusal
  to reject, 222
rebellion in, communal aspect of,
  155
reciprocal relation within, between
  religion and politics, 35
reflecting God's truth, McDermott's
  view of, 60
required to allow religious freedom,
  233
resources in, for developing
  pluralistic societies, 128
restorative justice in, 155–56
self-criticism within, 32
silent majority in, 222
as sole source for critique of
  secularist society, 170–71
as superficial and unoriginal
  religion, 46–47
superiority in, toward non-Muslims,
  146
theology of, related to law and
  human rights, 169–70n182
Vatican II's statement on, 52
viewing non-Muslims as equals in
  creation, 150–51
virtue of humility in, affecting
  classical Muslim jurists, 158
islamic, vs. Islamic, 9
Islamic law, 3–4, 164–65
*Islamic Roots of Democratic Pluralism,
  The* (Sachedina), 8, 126, 129,
  140, 151, 157, 167, 258, 262

Jan, Abid Ullah, 31
Jensen, Robert, 116–17
Jesus. *See also* Christ
  common ground on, 83
  expansive particularity of, 22–23
  as holy man, 26
  incarnation of, 294–95
  Islamic conceptions of, 64, 281–82
  resurrection of, 98, 192, 204, 286
  Sonship of, revealed in incarnation,
    204
  varying conceptions of, 72–73
jihād, 200
  contemporary, peaceful
    understanding of, 153–54
  improper understanding of, 156
  justification for, 36, 154
  political interpretation of, 154–55
John Paul II, 44, 52n31, 54–55, 268

Kärkkäinen, Veli-Matti, 11–12, 122, 203,
  206, 207, 208
  on Hick's theocentric view, 25–26
  on Pannenberg's *Systematic
    Theology*, 88
  on Pinnock, 60
  on *Redemptoris Missio*, 54
Khodr, Georges, 57n52
Kimball, Charles, 43, 298
Knitter, Paul, 18–20, 21, 23, 27, 216–17
Kraemer, Hendrik, 21, 46–47, 57

Lessing, G. E., 45n6
Lewis, C. S., 220–21, 275n32
liberation theology, 27, 250n71
life dialogue, 44
Lombardi, Frederico, 56
Lords of the Earth (Richardson), 59n61
Lumen Gentium, 51

MacIntyre, Alasdair, 225, 228n36,
  236–37n47
marriage, interfaith, 80–81
McDermott, Gerald R., 58–60
mercy, 200–201, 225–26
Middle East conflict, 71, 76
militancy, religious communities
  moving toward, 5–6
military service, 246n64
millet system, 146
minorities. *See also dhimmī*
  rights of, 80, 81
  treatment of, in Islam, 140–41, 154
mission, allowing, as part of dialogue,
  306

Index

Missionary Movement in Christian History, The (Walls), 294–95
Moaddel, Mansoor, 36
modernity, 22
modesty
 feminine, 245–46
 principle of, 3
Mohammed, Ovey, 49
Moltmann, Jürgen, 176, 216–17, 285n64
Moosa, Ebrahim, 167
moral impoverishment, resulting from disestablishment, 198–99
moral virtue, pursuit of, in Islam, 140
motives, ulterior, in Christian-Muslim dialogue, 71–72
Mu'tazilites, 144n94'tazilites, 271–72
multireligious societies, tensions within, 255
Muslim Aid, 79n151
Muslim family law, 311
Muslims. *See also* Islam
 claiming Islam as the best community, 158–59
 demanding full soteriological legitimacy, 75, 79
 equating pluralizing with Westernizing, 254–55
 facing challenges in cross-cultural assimilation and adjustment, 4–5
 intolerance of, linked to Western culture, 31
 proselytizing of, 247n66
 viewing West as anti-Islamic, 4
 views of, on Christians' salvation, 75
Muslims and Christians at the Table, 65–66
mutual trust, in Christian-Muslim dialogue, 71
Mutuality, 19
Mystici Corpus (Pius XII), 50n25

Nasr, Seeyed Hossein, 66–68
nationalism, religious loyalties and, 253–56
nature, primordial (noble), 131–32
Nazir-Ali, Michael, 270

Netland, Harold, 14, 17–18, 21, 22, 53, 219–20, 304
Nielsen, Jørgen, 4
no-fault divorce laws, 249n
Noor, Farish, 32, 174
Nostra Aetate, 51–52

one-child policy (China), 249n
other, interaction with, 224–26

pacifism, religious, 246n64
Pancasila form of government, 167n175
Pannenberg, Wolfhart, 6–8
 audience for, 180–81
 on the christological method, 90
 committee to reciprocity in theological method, 105
 critiques regarding his approach to theology of religions, 121–24
 developing a theology of religions, 103–19
 doing theology from above and below, 90
 eschatocentric inclusivism of, 219
 eschatological vision of, 100–102
 ground principles in thought of, 88
 on humility, 227–28
 importance to, of the idea of God and reality, 89–91
 on interfaith dialogue as pursuit of truth, 122–23
 lacking interaction with postmodern concerns, 121–22
 offering general theological model, 176–77
 offering insight into the state's provisional role, 210–11
 offering trinitarian theology of religions, 116–21
 presenting the concept of a Triune God, 275–81
 reciprocity in theology of, 90
 rejecting the *filioque* clause, 118
 scope of his writings, 176
 selective use of Christian scripture, 121
 strengths of his approach to theology of religions, 120–21

Index

systematic theology of, 88–102
tending toward notion of
    universalist salvation, 121
theology of religions, resources for,
    201–9
on truth and anticipation/prolepsis,
    98–100
on truth as coherence, 91–94
on truth and the future, 100–102
on truth and history, 94–97
understanding Christianity in
    context of other religions, 103
views of God, in common with
    Sachedina, 177–82
wanting to see Christianity as option
    among other religions and
    sciences, 106–7
writings of, 87–88
Partial Replacement, 18
particularism, 18. *See also*
    ecclesiocentrism
Paul VI, 50, 54
peace, promoting, 65
Peace Child (Richardson), 59n61
personhood, 291–92
Pinnock, Clark, 60–62
Pius XII, 50n25
Placher, William, 176
pluralism. *See* religious pluralism
plurality
    inherent in relational and trinitarian
        God, 28
    making space for, in modern society,
        179
pneumatological theology, 61
pneumatology, 118n131
political themes
    as barriers to Christian-Muslim
        dialogue, 76–78
    common ground for, in Christian-
        Muslim dialogue, 83–84
Postfoundationalist Task of Theology, The
    (Shults), 88–89
postmodernism, 121–22, 236n47
power, human tendency to abuse, 168
praxiological themes
    as barriers to Christian-Muslim
        dialogue, 79–81
    common ground for, in Christian-
        Muslim dialogue, 84–85
prayer, interfaith, 80
Progressive Muslims (Safi), 33
prolepsis, eschatological emphasis on,
    208
pseudopluralisms, 220n16

Quest for Covenant Community, The
    (Ng), 311n17
Qur'an
    addressing forgiveness toward
        humankind, 149–60
    affirming a religiously diverse
        society, 9
    claiming that all humans are part of
        one community, 132
    concerned with created just and
        moral societies for all, 146
    condemning religious control of
        societies where the governed
        don't grant it, 233
    conscience addressed in, 131–32
    fitra not dependent upon, 8–9
    forbidding religious compulsion
        and oppression of minorities,
        154–55
    giving authority to governments to
        put down rebellion, 156
    hostility verses in, 134
    justifying violence to restore justice,
        156–57
    keeping in original language,
        296n85
    nature and authority of, 73
    pluralistic vision of, 68, 136–38, 162
    requiring a just approach to
        religious diversity and interfaith
        existence, 152
    as resource for reconciliation and
        social justice, 149
    Sachedina's method of interpreting,
        128–29
    teaching salvific legitimacy of other
        monotheistic religions, 132–34

Index

Qutb, Sayyid, 36

Race, Alan, 17
Rahner, Karl, 23–24, 53
Ramachandra, Vinoth, 21, 22–23
Ramadam, Tariq, 3, 5, 69–70
rebellion, communal aspect of, needed for legitimation, 155
redemptive analogies, 59n61
Redemptoris Missio (John Paul II), 54–55
relationality, 291–93
relativism, increasing influence of, 197
religion
    becoming detached from the concept of God, 104
    claims and practices of, allowing to remain unrevised, 236–37
    coerced, breeding hypocrisy, 159
    common source and destiny of, 25
    as contested interaction of truth claims about God and creation, 230
    disestablishment of, 198
    essence of, 104
    goal of, one interpretation of, 218n13
    as human interpretation of reality, 25
    needing to remain public, 234–35
    Pannenberg's concept of, 103–7
    phenomenology of, 104
    in public societies, 233
    recognizing variations within each, 64
    relationship of, with culture, 2–3
    as search for best explanation of reality in light of religious concept of God, 107–8
    subjectivity in, 107
    theology of. *See* theology of religion
    translating, into other cultural and social contexts, 252
    unfolding history of, 7
religions
    all included in triune God, 29
    beliefs and practices of, complex relationships between, 243–44
    checkered histories of political power plays, 141
    conflict among, 108
    as contenders for truths, 202
    God resolving differences between, 189
    inclusivistic view of, 28–30
    needed in social life, in postmodern and secular age, 199
    reality-centric approach to, 26
    secular anthropologies of, 105–6
    some expressing more moral character than others, 229
    theology of. *See* theology of religions
    understanding, as embedded in space and time, 105
religiosity, incurable, 300
religious belief
    libertarian nature of, 231, 255
    voluntary nature of, 255
religious differences, God required for mediation of, 152
religious disestablishment, 170
religious error, revelation from God in midst of, 59
religious freedom
    across religious traditions, 252–53
    democracy and, 248
    as direct corollary of religious belief and practice, 240
    within faith traditions, 250–52
    in just and peaceful societies, 233–35
    in Muslim-majority contexts, 166
    for Muslims, 196–97
    making space for, in modern society, 179
    promotion of, 238
    risk inherent in, 265
religious identity, determining, 252
religious loyalty, nationalism and, 253–56
religious minorities, tension among, 146
religious other, growing from relationship with, 173

Index

religious pluralism, 2, 12, 17, 151–52
   becoming a dictatorial religious ideology, 216
   becoming exclusivist, 220
   cosmotheandric, 274n30
   extreme, 129–30
   as important dialogical starting point, 223
   Muslim approach to, 40–41
   Muslims living in context of, 4–5
   needed for interfaith dialogue, 151–52
   shortcomings of, 215–17
   touted as solution to interfaith quarrels, 215
Religious Pluralism in Christian and Islamic Philosophy (Aslan), 67–68
religious plurality, 12–13
   arranging Christian responses to, 17–20
   Christian approach to, 20–30
   effects on, 129–30
   goal of, 135
   Muslim response to, 30–41
   roots of, 14
religious tolerance, 78
religious traditions, retaining core of common principles, 136
religious truth claims
   arguing for, 107
   making public, 120
   taking at face value, 120
   testing of, 109–10, 111
religious values
   effects of, upon society, 241
   presence of, in democratic secular society, 141
representation, as issue in Christian-Muslim dialogue, 70–71
restorative justice, in Islam, 155–56
resurrection
   apocalyptic hope of, 98–99
   Muslim denials of, 171n186
Rethinking Missions (Hocking), 46n10
retribution, 149, 200–201
retributive justice, 157

revelation. *See also* divine revelation
   differences in, among religions, 183–84
   divine and demonic aspects of, distinguishing between, 123
   historically situated, 181
   historical nature of, 182–85, 200, 211
   non-salvific, 59–60
   other sources of, 228–29n37
   preparatory, 59n61
   rejection of, 145n99
   supplementary nature of, 143
   understanding, as area for future progress, 309–10
   unfolding, 252
revenge, 200–201
Richardson, Don, 59n61
Rizvi, Mashhood, 34–35
Roman Catholic Church, 44, 50–57

Sachedina, Abdulaziz, 8–9
   on apostasy in Islam, 146–48
   audience for, 181
   on Benedict XVI's Regensburg comment, 55–56
   calling for universal plurality, 166–67
   on challenges in seeing democratically plural Islam, 126
   countering self-righteous exclusivism, 130–31
   criticism again, 161–62
   distinguishing between religious commitment and moral accountability, 143–44
   emphasizing historical nature of revelation, 200
   emphasizing Islamic revelatory resources, 176
   emphasizing libertarian nature of religious belief, 210
   emphasizing religion's role in establishing public ethical norms, 163
   ethicocentric inclusivism of, 218

Index

Sachedina, Abdulaziz (*continued*)
  failure of, to explore alternative interpretations in the Qur'an, 169
  on growing secularization, 5
  on humility, 226–27
  insight of, into libertarian nature of religious belief, 231
  on interfaith dialogue, 151–53
  on Islam's inability to deal with contemporary life, 157–58
  on Islam's fundamental problem, 171–72
  on Islam's political vision, 136–37
  on matters influencing religious plurality, 129–30
  offering public practice of Islam alongside plurality of religious others, 254–55
  purpose of his writings, 175
  rejecting exclusivistic religious ideologies, 127
  on rejection of faith, 239–40
  on religious sensibility among all people, 127
  on secularist approaches to plurality, 127
  on social responsibility, 128
  textual interpretation of, 128–29
  theology of religions of, 183–84, 196–201
  tracing history of religious and political relationships in Islam, 142
  views of God, in common with Pannenberg, 177–82
  vision of, for contemporary Islam, 160
sacred writings, nature and authority of, as barrier to Christian-Muslim dialogue, 73
Safi, Omid, 10, 33
salvation, 191–93
  based on Christ alone, 19
  centered around ministry of the church, 21–22
  exclusive, 37. *See also* exclusivism
  inclusivistic concept of, 54–55
  interreligious comparisons difficult for, 218n12
  Islam's inclusivist approach to, 39–40
  Jesus Christ as norm and standard of, 24
  universalist, 121
Schaeffer, Francis, 226–27n33, 302
Schleiermacher, Friedrich, 11n25, 45n6
scripture, religions' claims about, as area for future progress, 308–9
Secrets of the Koran (Richardson), 59n61
secularism
  attempting to privatize religion, 198
  becoming tyrannical, 198
  Islam's critique of, 170–71
  relegating religion to the private realm, 254
secularization, 5–6, 15–16, 83–84
self-differentiation, 205n82, 277–78
Sharī'ah, 3–4, 83–84, 85
  appropriate application of, 76–78
  inflexibility of, 142
Shults, F. LeRon, 88–89, 96
Siddiqi, Muzammil H., 271, 274
sin, 168
sinfulness, recognizing, 306
Singapore, as multireligious society, 253–54n75
Sistani, Ali, 9n22
Smith, Wilfred Cantwell, 2, 39, 57n52
social engagement, 151
social justice, 84
societal laws, necessity of, 248
society
  communal nature of, importance of, 137
  nature of, and God, 290–93
sociopolitical considerations, influencing Muslim thinking on religious pluralism, 34–35
Soroush, Abdolkarim, 197, 240
soteriology, 191–93
  as area for future progress, 309
  as barrier to Christian-Muslim dialogue, 75

Index

Sperber, Jutta, 72–77, 80–86, 302
Spirit
    drawing everything toward eschatological future in God, 206
    ministry of, in creation, 205–7
    providing basis for unity in the Godhead, 204–5
    self-communicating to all humanity, 23–24
    thematic use of, in Christian theologies of religion, 118–19
state
    avoiding confusion with church, 180
    provisional nature of, 179
submission, at root of Islam, 38
Sūfī, mystical thinking in, 292n79
supersession, 108, 132–34
syncretism, Christian concern about, 80
syncretistic process, 108
systematics, goal of, 94
systematic theology, 203
Systematic Theology (Pannenberg), 7

Takim, Liyakatali, 222
Talatoff, Kamran, 36
tawhīd, 37, 72–73, 190, 270, 271–72, 274, 284–85
Taylor, John B., 82
Tennent, Timothy C., 62–64
theocentrism, 25–26, 75
theological themes
    as barriers to Christian-Muslim dialogue, 72–76
    commonality of, in Christian-Muslim dialogue, 82–83
theology, truth of, dependent on its presentation, 91–92
theology of religion, 7, 11
theology of religions, 11–12
    comprehensive approach to, 304
    eschatological aspects of, 188–89
    inclusive approaches to, 187–88
    Muslim approach to, 33
    Pannenberg's approach to, 110–16, 120–24, 201–9
    Sachedina's, 183–84
    trinitarian, 116–21
theonomists, 16n7
tobacco, 249n
tolerance, 9–10
    limiting, 250
    Qur'anic notions of, 34
Total Replacement, 18
translation, 294–96, 308–9
trinitarian belief, development of, 117–18
trinitarian doctrine, as area for future study, 308
trinitarian theology, 58–59, 62
Trinity
    based on historical self-revelation, 274–75
    as basis for Christian-Muslim exchange, 211, 212
    Christian and Muslim understandings of, 283–84
    importance of, to Pannenberg's theology of religions, 202–6
    as manifestation of God's essential unity, 279–81
    Pannenberg's approach to, 275–81
    possible parallels of, to Ash'arite conceptions of God, 272–73
    providing a resource for understanding creation, 288–90
    Rahner's "rule" relating to, 276n35
    as resource for future Christian-Muslim dialogue, 269
    self-differentiation used to describe, 277–78
    suggesting a model for peaceful plurality, 292
tritheism, 285–86
Troeltsch, Ernst, 45n6
true religion, expressed by means of submission and surrender, 136
truth
    anticipation/prolepsis and, 98–100
    as coherence, 91–94
    comprehensive search for, 184
    as external correspondence, 92–94
    and the future, 100–102
    historical nature of, 182

truth (*continued*)
    history and, 94–97
    importance of, for Christianity's relation to other religions, 93
    interfaith dialogue as quest for, 122–23
    process of, 95–96
    public contestation of, 186–87
    public nature of, 94, 234
    as unified whole, 182
truth claims. *See also* religious truth claims
    absolute, 97
    contradictory, arbitrating between, 219

understanding, interfaith, as goal, 302–3
United Methodist Committee on Relief (UMCOR), 79n151
unity
    absolute, Islam's emphasis on, 285–86
    seeking, through an expanding view of God, reality, and truth, 95

Vanhoozer, Kevin J., 207n

Vatican II, 50–53
"Venice Statement," 54
violence
    attributing, to exclusivism, 171–72
    resulting from disestablishment, 198
Volf, Miroslav, 217, 303

Walls, Andrew, 294–95
Western Muslims (Ramadan), 69–70
Whose Justice? Which Rationality? (MacIntyre), 162–63n170
witness
    allowing, as part of dialogue, 306
    separate from dialogue, 301
women, treatment of, 311
World Council of Churches, 6, 44, 47–50
world religions
    equality of, 40
    status of, centered around ministry of the Christian church, 21–22
worship, interfaith, 80

Yilmaz, Mehmet Nuri, 65
Yong, Amos, 60n66
Yousif, Ahmad, 261–62